ハヤテのごとく! 21
Hayate the combat butler

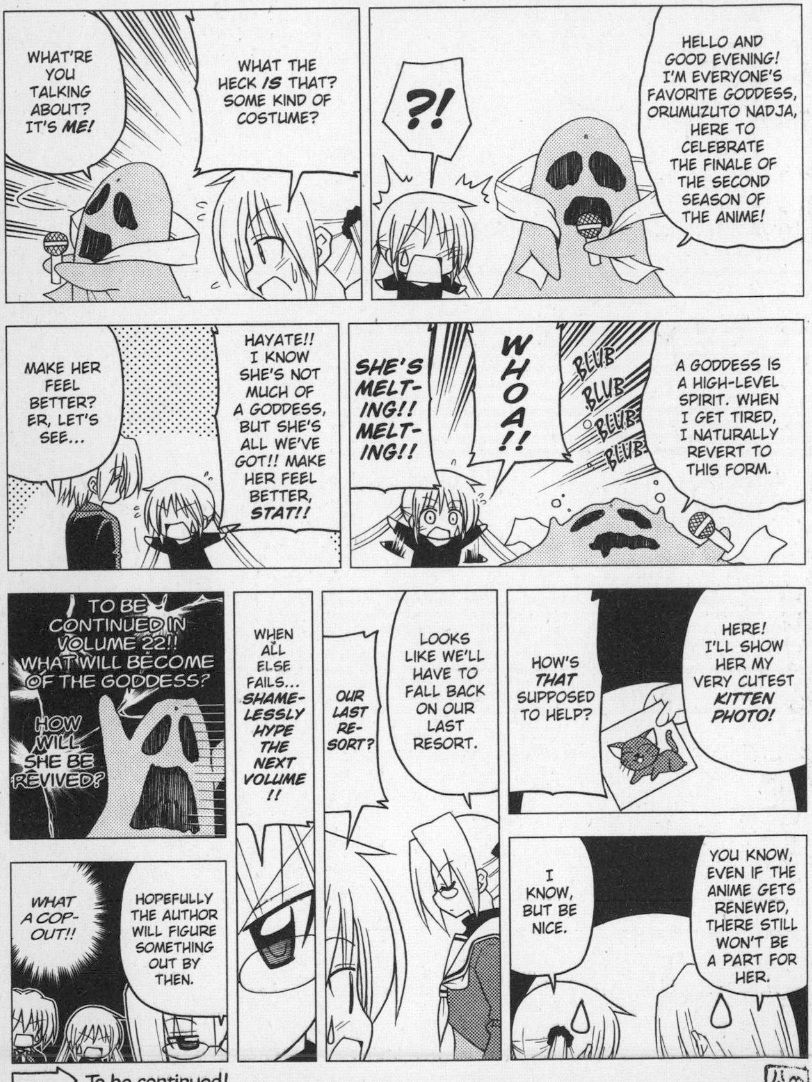
HELLO AND GOOD EVENING! I'M EVERYONE'S FAVORITE GODDESS, ORUMUZUTO NADJA, HERE TO CELEBRATE THE FINALE OF THE SECOND SEASON OF THE ANIME!
?!
WHAT THE HECK IS THAT? SOME KIND OF COSTUME?
WHAT'RE YOU TALKING ABOUT? IT'S ME!
A GODDESS IS A HIGH-LEVEL SPIRIT. WHEN I GET TIRED, I NATURALLY REVERT TO THIS FORM.
BLUB BLUB BLUB BLUB
WHOA!!
SHE'S MELTING!! MELTING!!
HAYATE!! I KNOW SHE'S NOT MUCH OF A GODDESS, BUT SHE'S ALL WE'VE GOT!! MAKE HER FEEL BETTER, STAT!!
MAKE HER FEEL BETTER? ER, LET'S SEE...
HERE! I'LL SHOW HER MY VERY CUTEST KITTEN PHOTO!
HOW'S THAT SUPPOSED TO HELP?
YOU KNOW, EVEN IF THE ANIME GETS RENEWED, THERE STILL WON'T BE A PART FOR HER.
I KNOW, BUT BE NICE.
LOOKS LIKE WE'LL HAVE TO FALL BACK ON OUR LAST RESORT.
OUR LAST RESORT?
WHEN ALL ELSE FAILS... SHAMELESSLY HYPE THE NEXT VOLUME!!
TO BE CONTINUED IN VOLUME 22!! WHAT WILL BECOME OF THE GODDESS?
HOW WILL SHE BE REVIVED?
HOPEFULLY THE AUTHOR WILL FIGURE SOMETHING OUT BY THEN.
WHAT A COP-OUT!!

→ To be continued!

HAYATE THE COMBAT BUTLER
VOL. 21
Shonen Sunday Edition

STORY AND ART BY
KENJIRO HATA

© 2005 Kenjiro HATA/Shogakukan
All rights reserved.
Original Japanese edition "HAYATE NO GOTOKU!" published by SHOGAKUKAN Inc.

English Adaptation/Mark Giambruno
Translation/Yuki Yoshioka, Cindy H. Yamauchi
Touch-up Art & Lettering/Hudson Yards
Design/Yukiko Whitley
Editor/Shaenon K. Garrity

Printed in Canada

Published by VIZ Media, LLC
P.O. Box 77010
San Francisco, CA 94107

10 9 8 7 6 5 4 3 2 1
First printing, February 2013

Hayate the Combat Butler

the Combat Butler

21

KENJIRO HATA

*The sparklers spell out "Table of Contents."

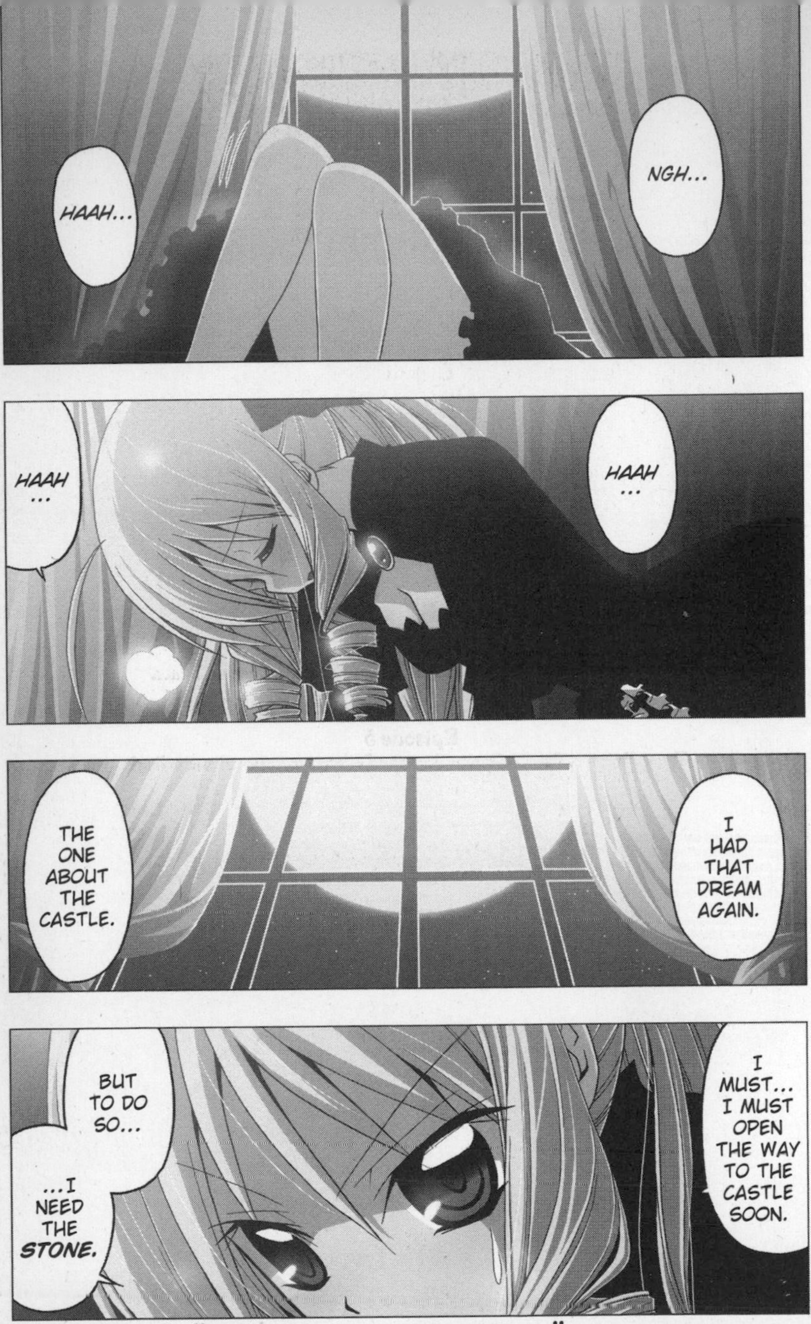
NGH...
HAAH...
HAAH ...
HAAH ...
I HAD THAT DREAM AGAIN.
THE ONE ABOUT THE CASTLE.
I MUST... I MUST OPEN THE WAY TO THE CASTLE SOON.
BUT TO DO SO...
...I NEED THE STONE.

Episode 1: "The Stone of Bonding"

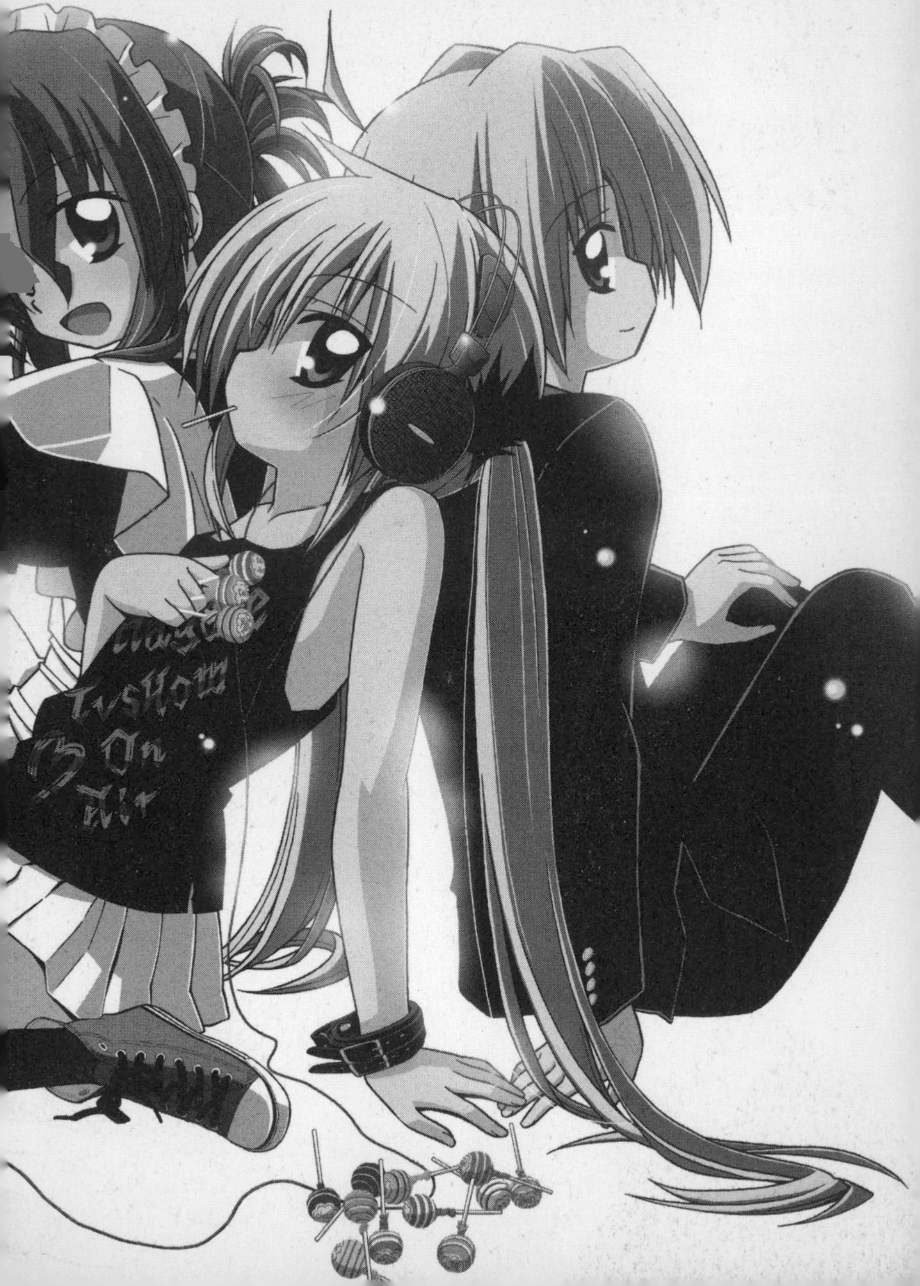

Episode 1: "The Stone of Bonding"

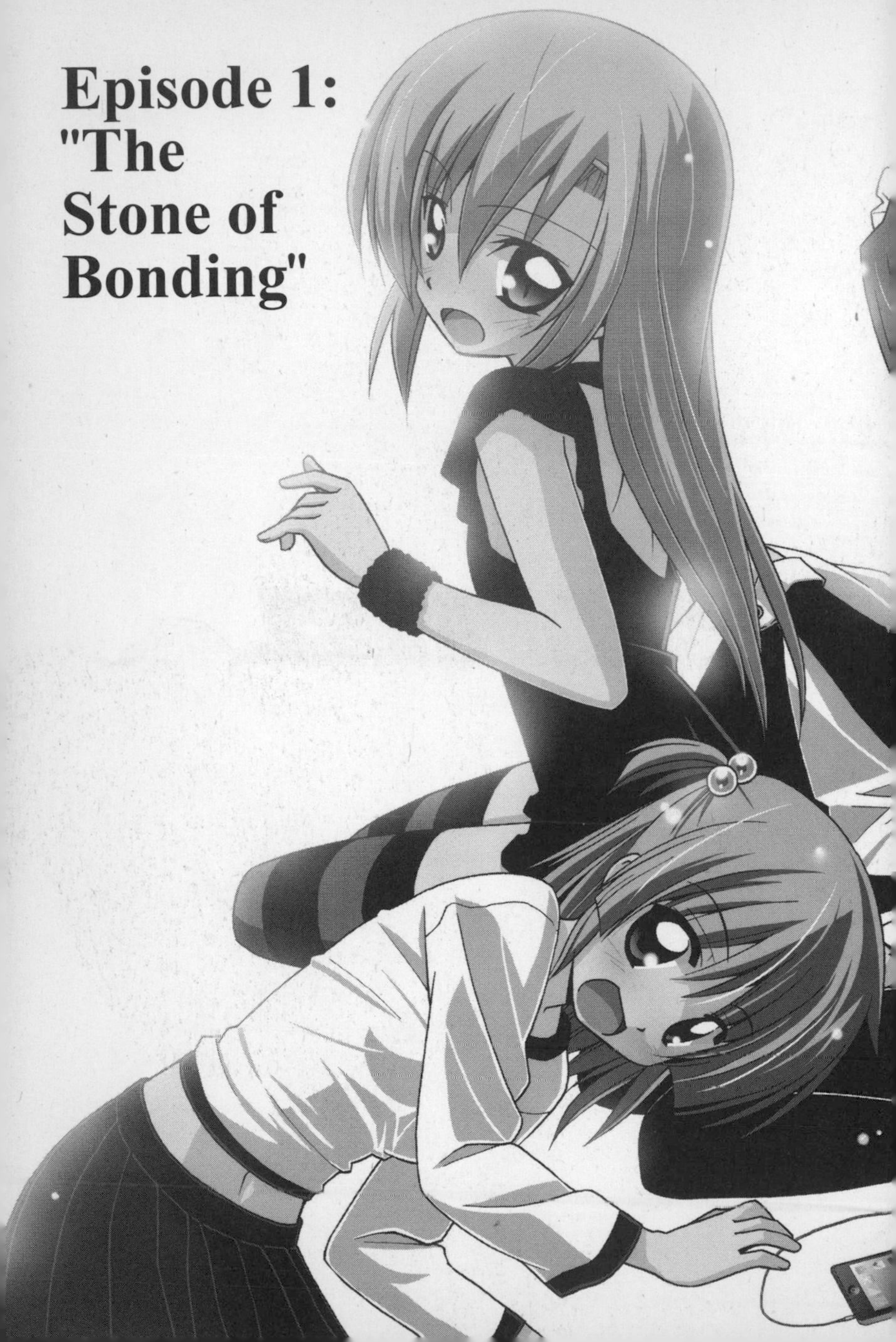

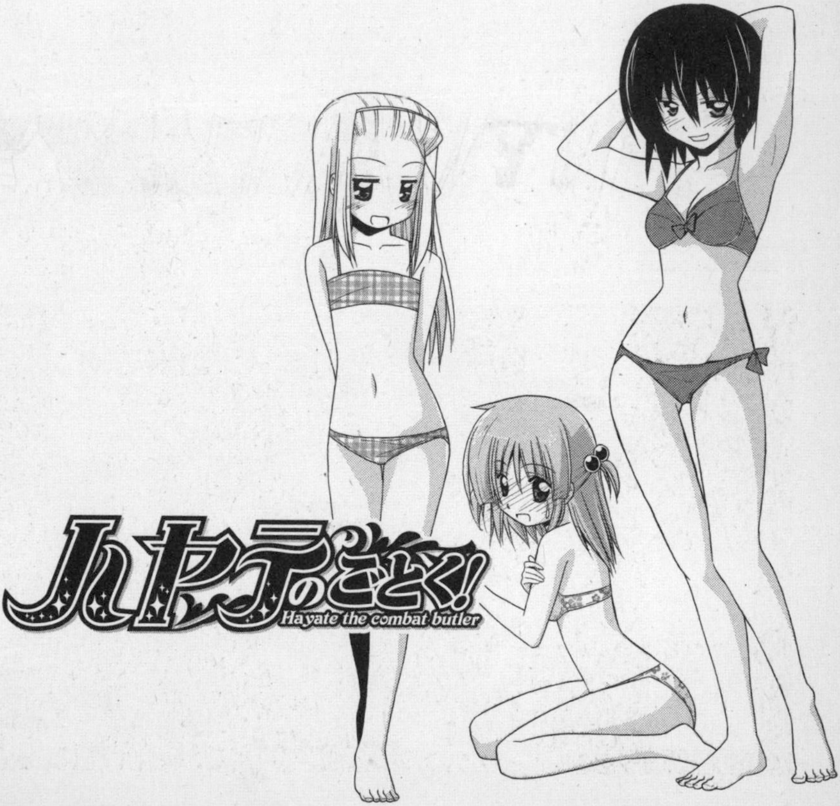
ハヤテのごとく!
Hayate the combat butler

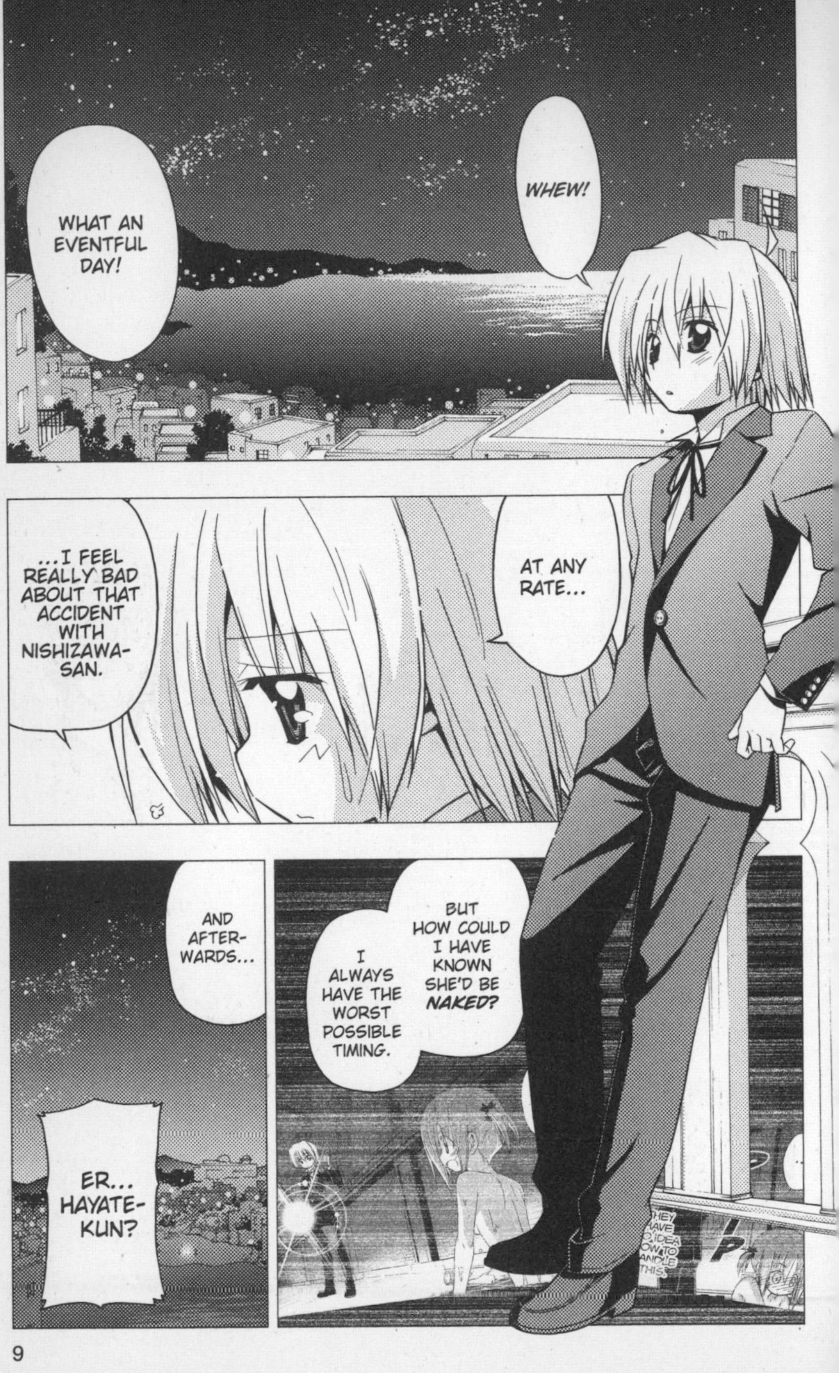
WHEW!
WHAT AN EVENTFUL DAY!
AT ANY RATE...
...I FEEL REALLY BAD ABOUT THAT ACCIDENT WITH NISHIZAWA-SAN.
BUT HOW COULD I HAVE KNOWN SHE'D BE *NAKED?*
I ALWAYS HAVE THE WORST POSSIBLE TIMING.
AND AFTER-WARDS...
ER... HAYATE-KUN?

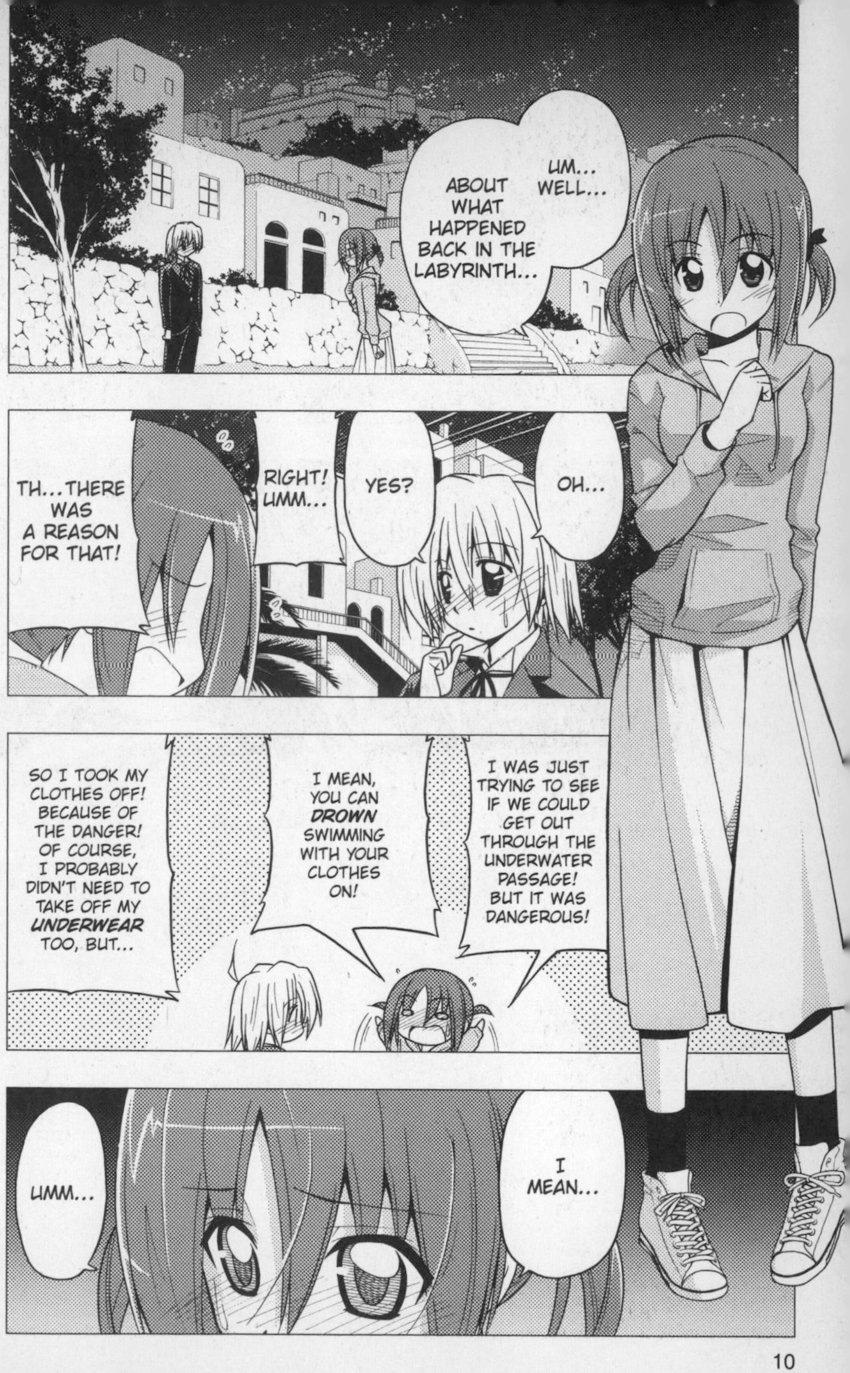
UM... WELL... ABOUT WHAT HAPPENED BACK IN THE LABYRINTH...
OH...
YES?
RIGHT! UMM...
TH...THERE WAS A REASON FOR THAT!
I WAS JUST TRYING TO SEE IF WE COULD GET OUT THROUGH THE UNDERWATER PASSAGE! BUT IT WAS DANGEROUS!
I MEAN, YOU CAN DROWN SWIMMING WITH YOUR CLOTHES ON!
SO I TOOK MY CLOTHES OFF! BECAUSE OF THE DANGER! OF COURSE, I PROBABLY DIDN'T NEED TO TAKE OFF MY UNDERWEAR TOO, BUT...
I MEAN...
UMM...

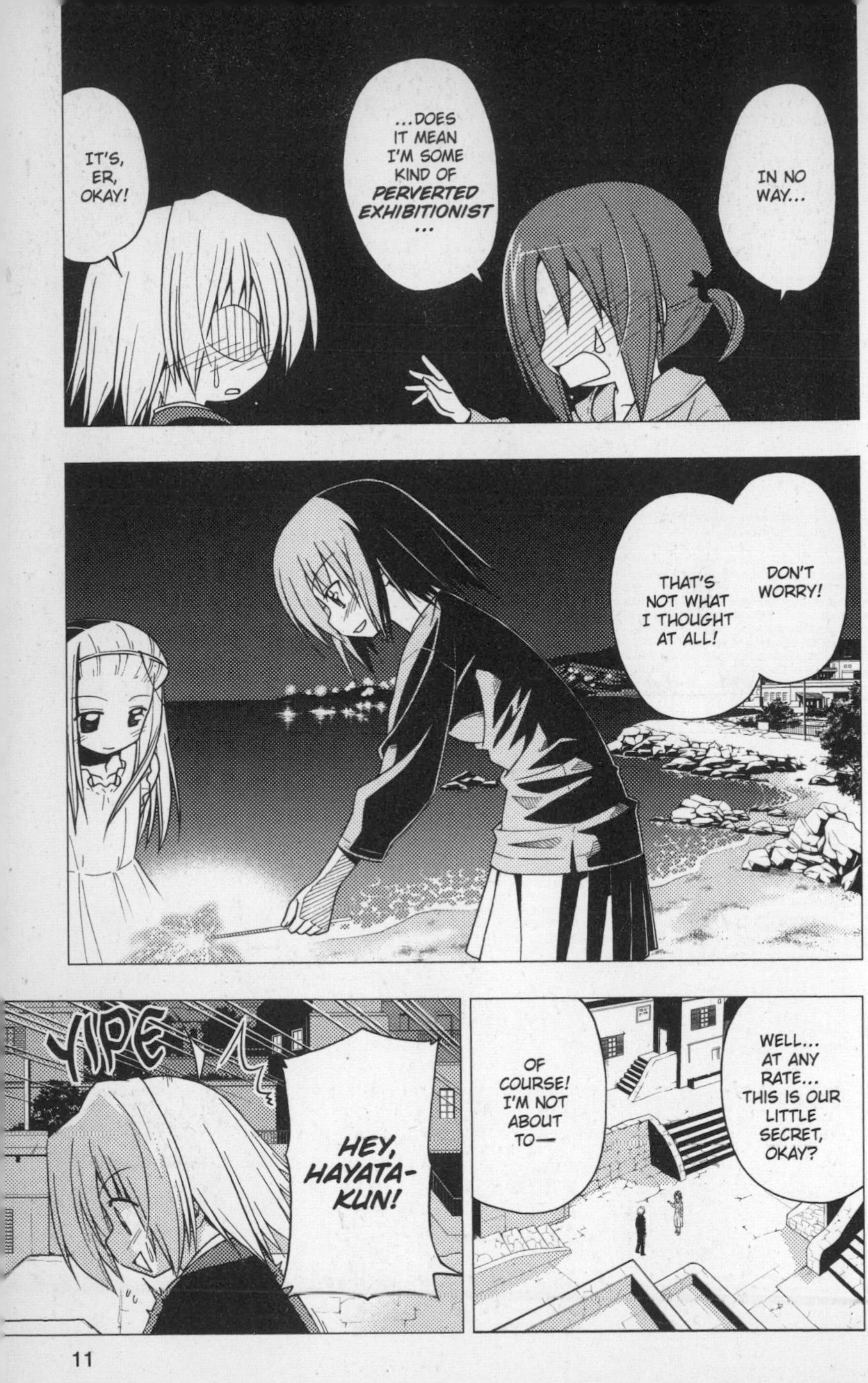
IN NO WAY...
...DOES IT MEAN I'M SOME KIND OF PERVERTED EXHIBITIONIST...
IT'S, ER, OKAY!
DON'T WORRY!
THAT'S NOT WHAT I THOUGHT AT ALL!
WELL... AT ANY RATE... THIS IS OUR LITTLE SECRET, OKAY?
OF COURSE! I'M NOT ABOUT TO—
HEY, HAYATA-KUN!
YIPE

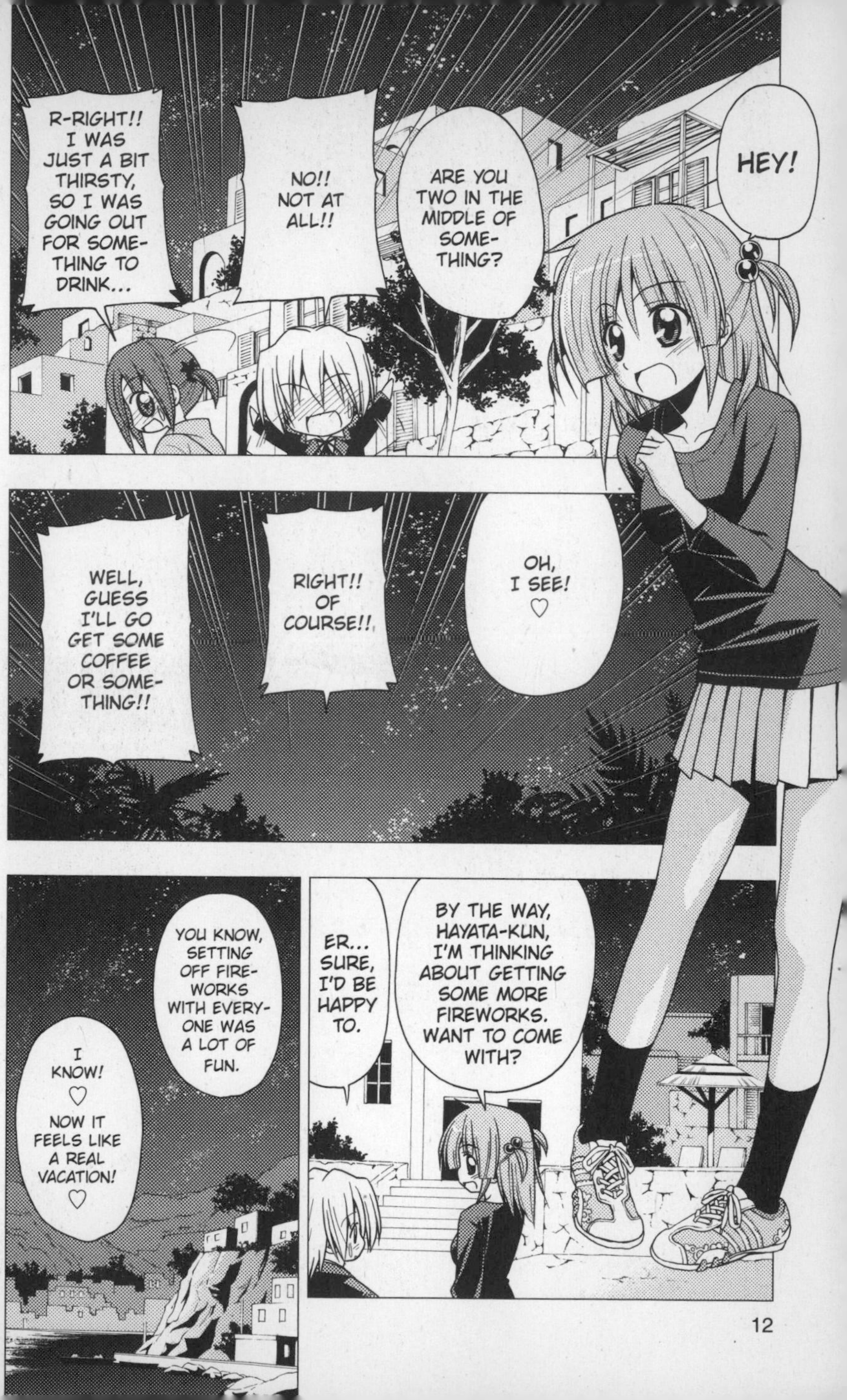
HEY!
ARE YOU TWO IN THE MIDDLE OF SOME-THING?
NO!! NOT AT ALL!!
R-RIGHT!! I WAS JUST A BIT THIRSTY, SO I WAS GOING OUT FOR SOME-THING TO DRINK...
OH, I SEE! ♡
RIGHT!! OF COURSE!!
WELL, GUESS I'LL GO GET SOME COFFEE OR SOME-THING!!
BY THE WAY, HAYATA-KUN, I'M THINKING ABOUT GETTING SOME MORE FIREWORKS. WANT TO COME WITH?
ER... SURE, I'D BE HAPPY TO.
YOU KNOW, SETTING OFF FIRE-WORKS WITH EVERY-ONE WAS A LOT OF FUN.
I KNOW! ♡ NOW IT FEELS LIKE A REAL VACATION! ♡

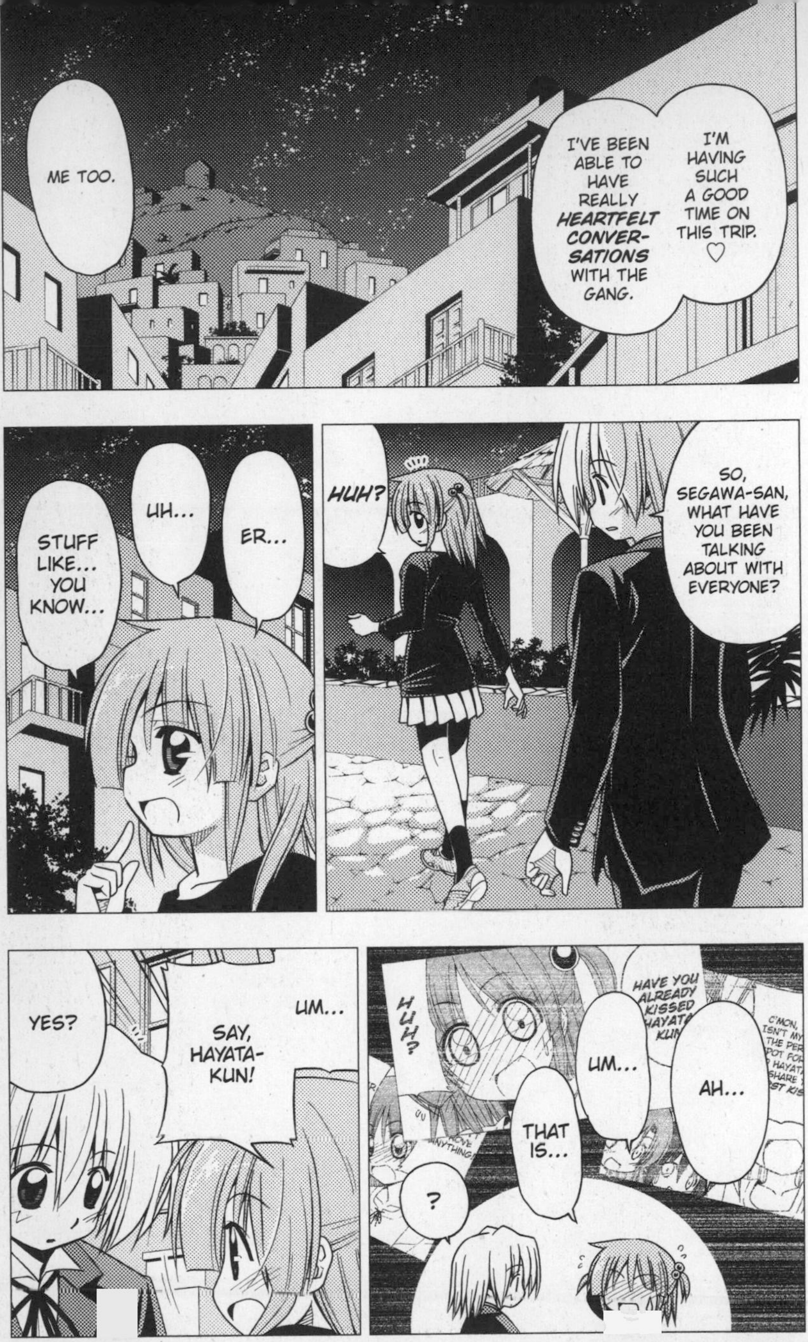
I'M HAVING SUCH A GOOD TIME ON THIS TRIP. ♡
I'VE BEEN ABLE TO HAVE REALLY *HEARTFELT CONVERSATIONS* WITH THE GANG.
ME TOO.
SO, SEGAWA-SAN, WHAT HAVE YOU BEEN TALKING ABOUT WITH EVERYONE?
HUH?
ER...
UH...
STUFF LIKE... YOU KNOW...
AH...
HAVE YOU ALREADY KISSED HAYATA-KUN
UM...
HUH?
THAT IS...
?
UM...
SAY, HAYATA-KUN!
YES?

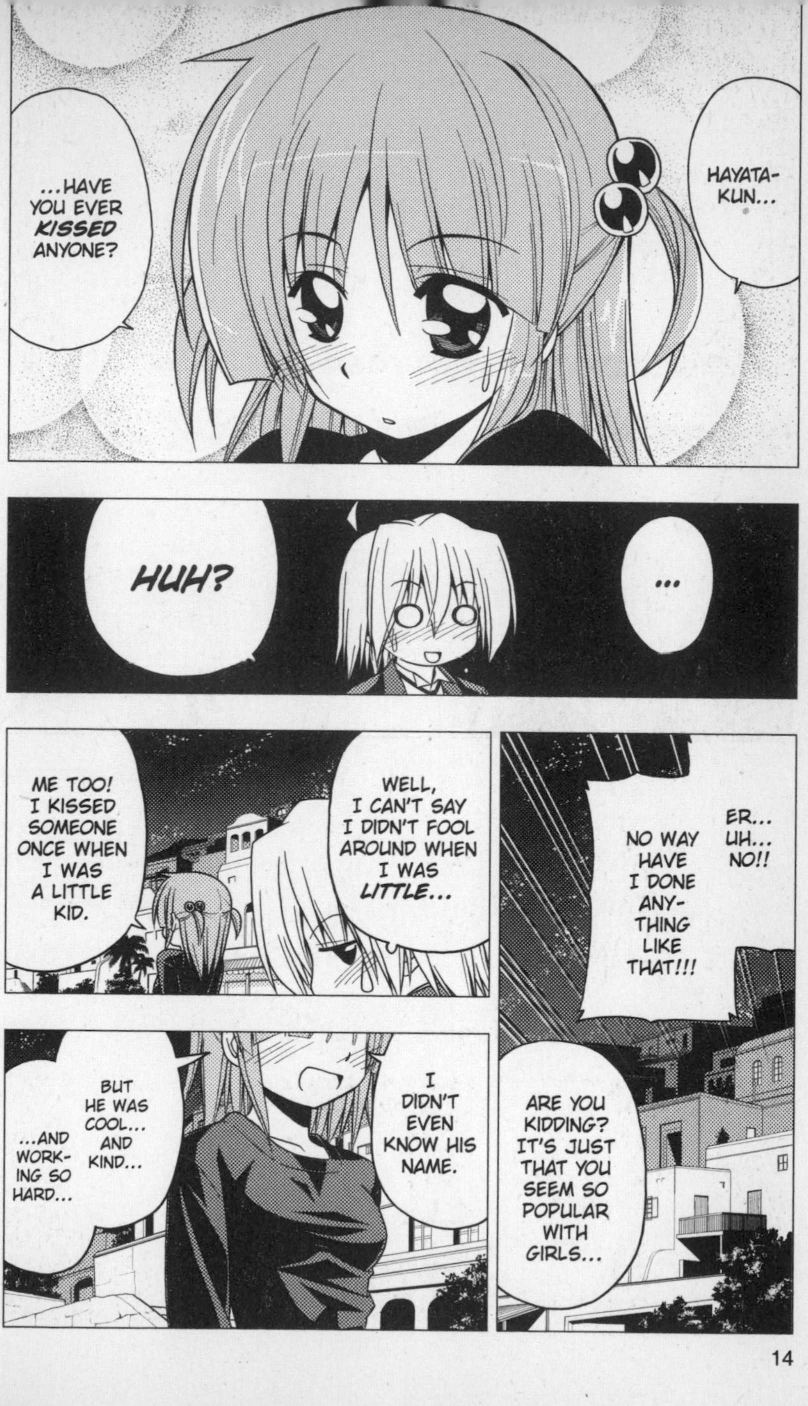
HAYATA-KUN...
...HAVE YOU EVER KISSED ANYONE?
...
HUH?
ER... UH... NO!!
NO WAY HAVE I DONE ANYTHING LIKE THAT!!!
ARE YOU KIDDING? IT'S JUST THAT YOU SEEM SO POPULAR WITH GIRLS...
WELL, I CAN'T SAY I DIDN'T FOOL AROUND WHEN I WAS LITTLE...
ME TOO! I KISSED SOMEONE ONCE WHEN I WAS A LITTLE KID.
I DIDN'T EVEN KNOW HIS NAME.
BUT HE WAS COOL... AND KIND...
...AND WORKING SO HARD...

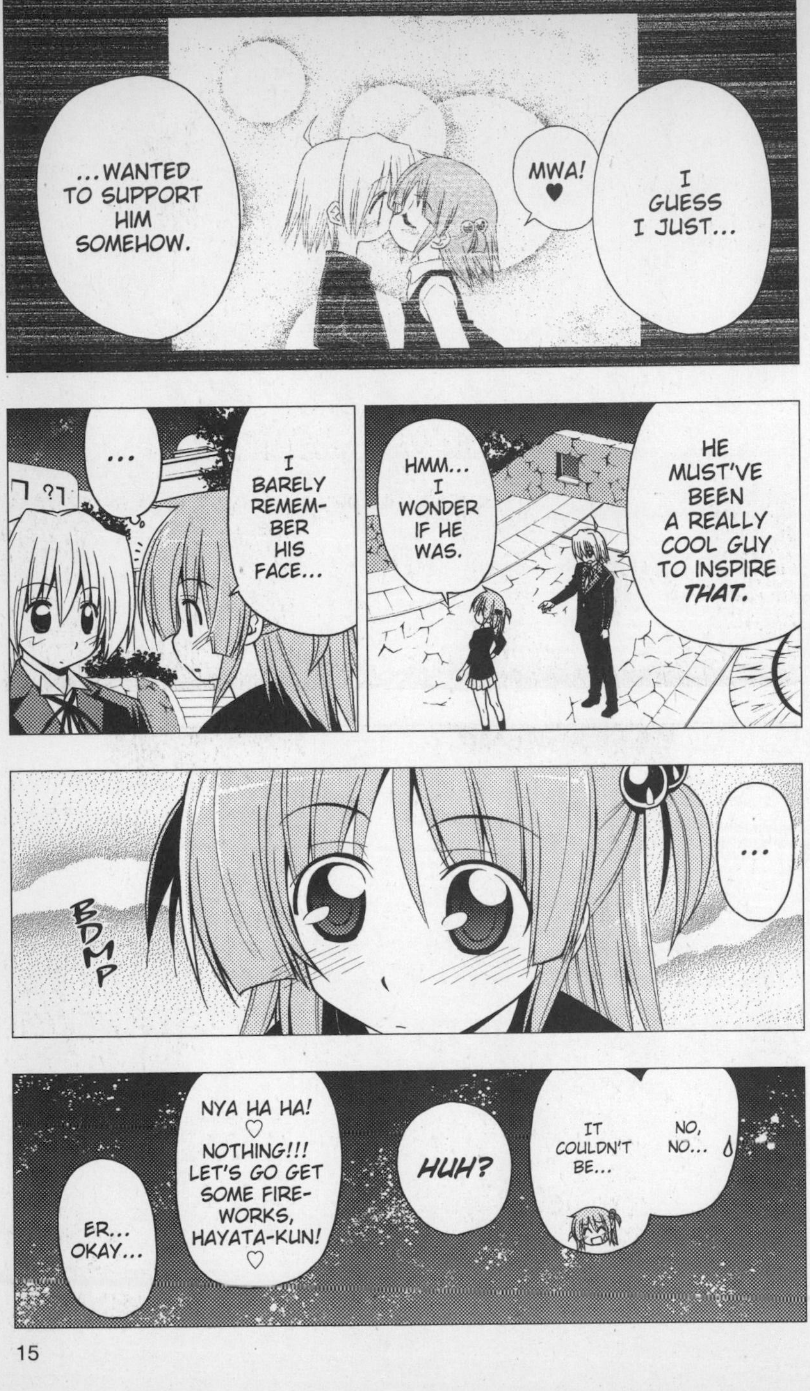
I GUESS I JUST...
MWA! ♥
...WANTED TO SUPPORT HIM SOMEHOW.
HE MUST'VE BEEN A REALLY COOL GUY TO INSPIRE *THAT.*
HMM... I WONDER IF HE WAS.
I BARELY REMEM-BER HIS FACE...
...
...
BDMP
NO, NO...
IT COULDN'T BE...
HUH?
NYA HA HA! ♡ NOTHING!!! LET'S GO GET SOME FIRE-WORKS, HAYATA-KUN! ♡
ER... OKAY...

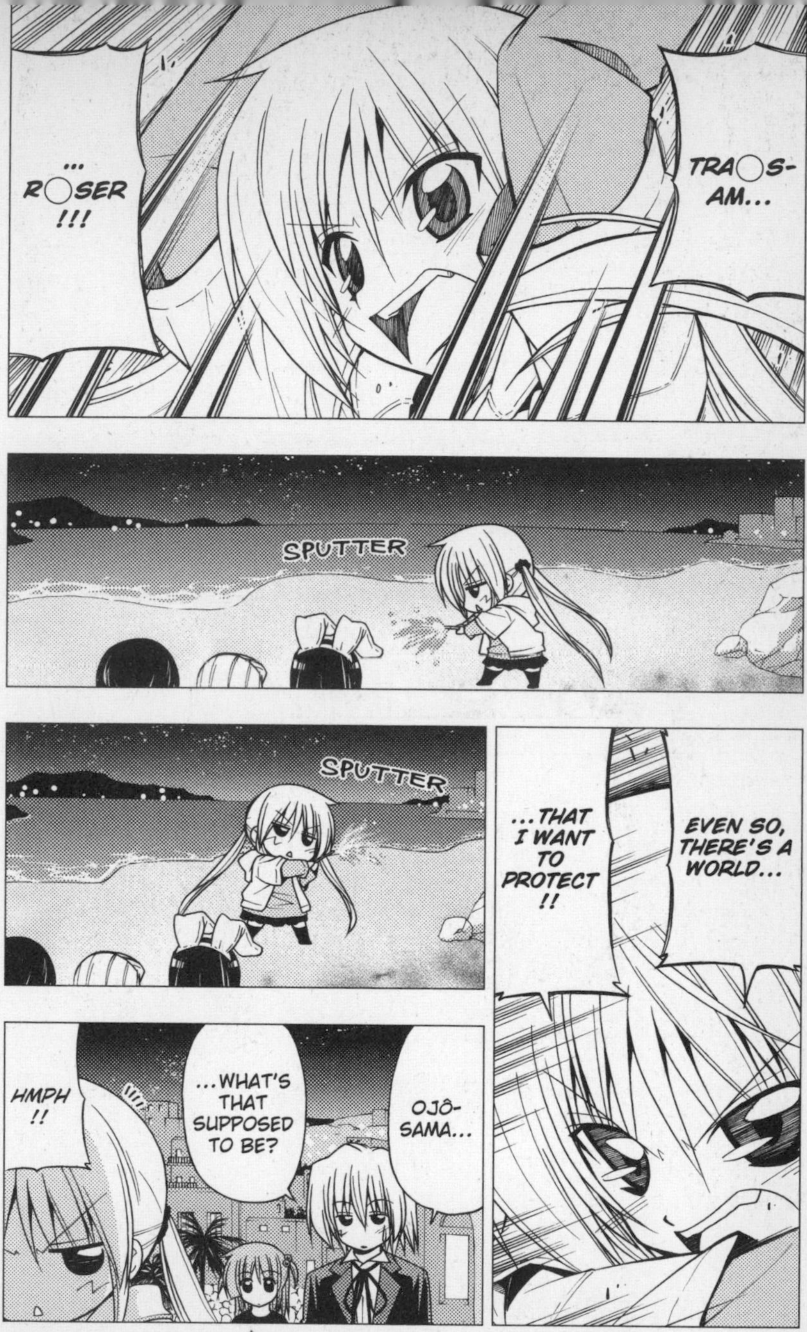
TRA◯S-AM...
... R◯SER !!!
SPUTTER
SPUTTER
EVEN SO, THERE'S A WORLD...
...THAT I WANT TO PROTECT !!
OJÔ-SAMA...
...WHAT'S THAT SUPPOSED TO BE?
HMPH !!

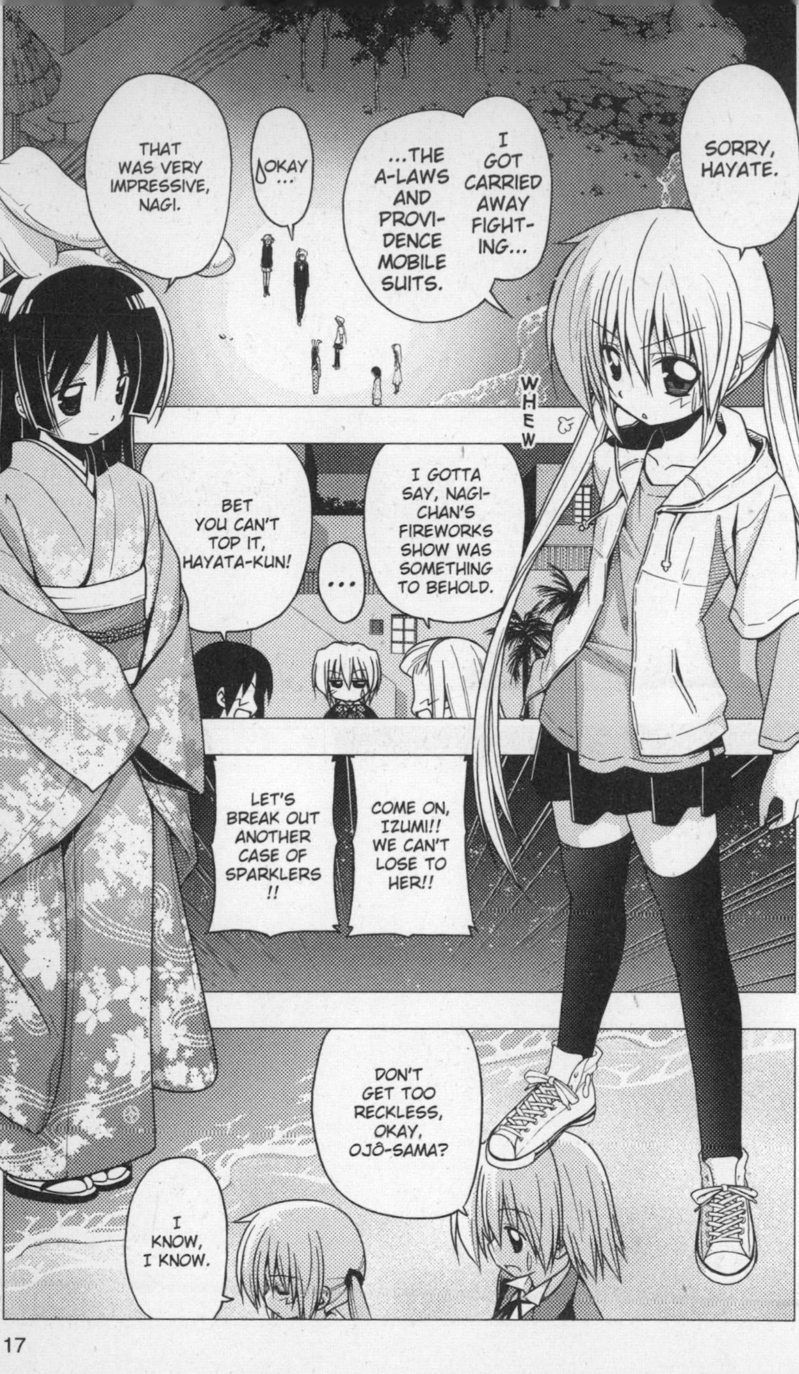
SORRY, HAYATE.
I GOT CARRIED AWAY FIGHT-ING...
...THE A-LAWS AND PROVI-DENCE MOBILE SUITS.
OKAY...
THAT WAS VERY IMPRESSIVE, NAGI.
WHEW
I GOTTA SAY, NAGI-CHAN'S FIREWORKS SHOW WAS SOMETHING TO BEHOLD.
...
BET YOU CAN'T TOP IT, HAYATA-KUN!
COME ON, IZUMI!! WE CAN'T LOSE TO HER!!
LET'S BREAK OUT ANOTHER CASE OF SPARKLERS !!
DON'T GET TOO RECKLESS, OKAY, OJÔ-SAMA?
I KNOW, I KNOW.

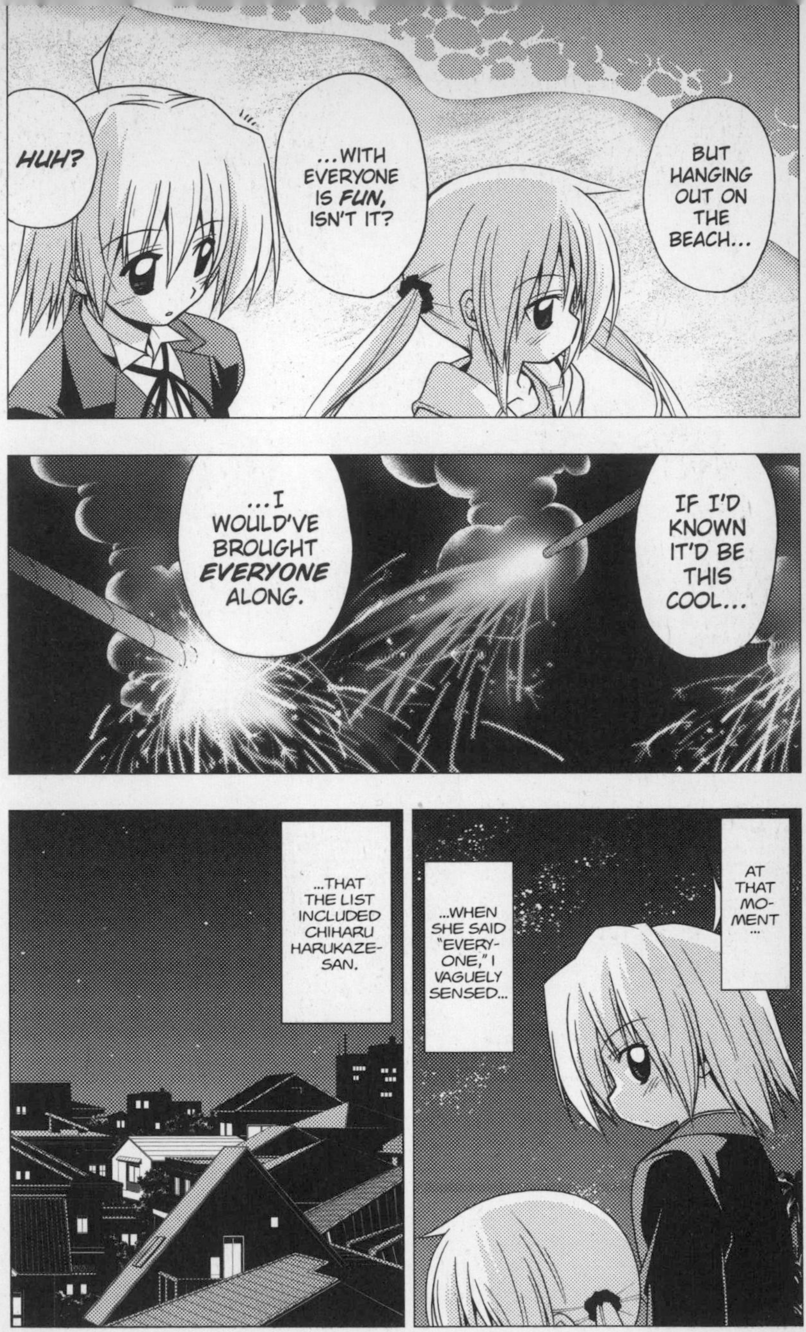
BUT HANGING OUT ON THE BEACH...
...WITH EVERYONE IS FUN, ISN'T IT?
HUH?
IF I'D KNOWN IT'D BE THIS COOL...
...I WOULD'VE BROUGHT EVERYONE ALONG.
AT THAT MOMENT...
...WHEN SHE SAID "EVERYONE," I VAGUELY SENSED...
...THAT THE LIST INCLUDED CHIHARU HARUKAZE-SAN.

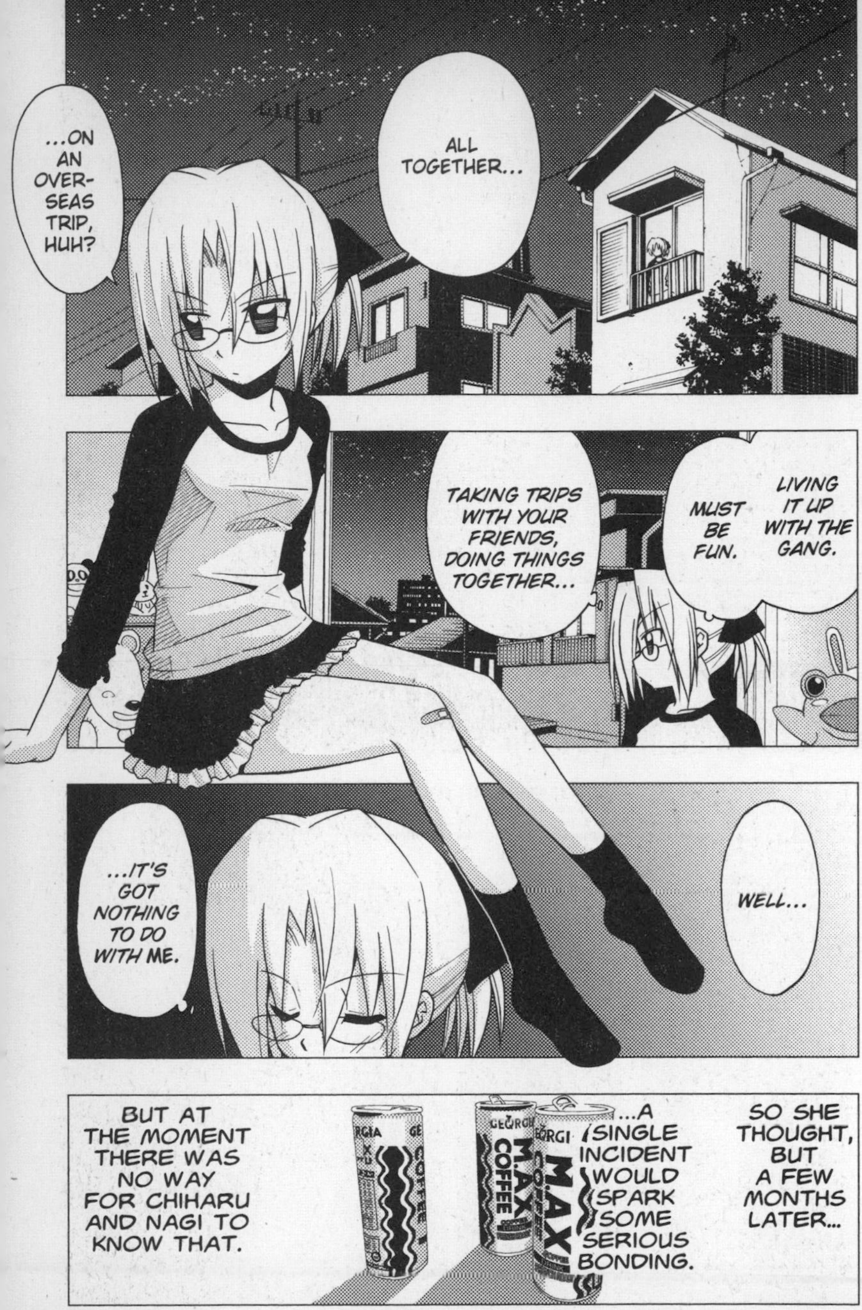
ALL TOGETHER...
...ON AN OVERSEAS TRIP, HUH?
LIVING IT UP WITH THE GANG.
MUST BE FUN.
TAKING TRIPS WITH YOUR FRIENDS, DOING THINGS TOGETHER...
WELL...
...IT'S GOT NOTHING TO DO WITH ME.
SO SHE THOUGHT, BUT A FEW MONTHS LATER...
...A SINGLE INCIDENT WOULD SPARK SOME SERIOUS BONDING.
M.A.X COFFEE
BUT AT THE MOMENT THERE WAS NO WAY FOR CHIHARU AND NAGI TO KNOW THAT.

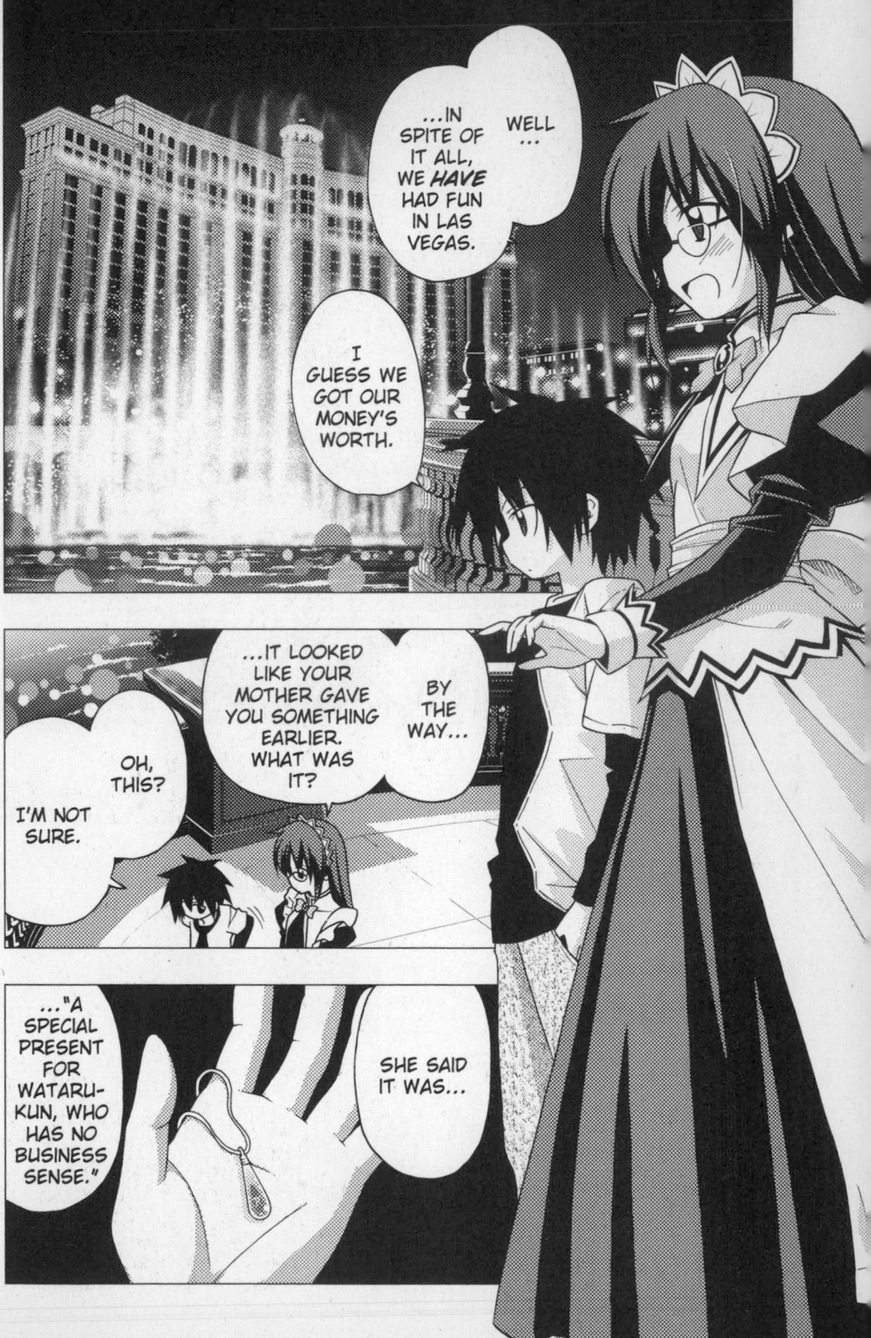
WELL ...
...IN SPITE OF IT ALL, WE *HAVE* HAD FUN IN LAS VEGAS.
I GUESS WE GOT OUR MONEY'S WORTH.
BY THE WAY...
...IT LOOKED LIKE YOUR MOTHER GAVE YOU SOMETHING EARLIER. WHAT WAS IT?
OH, THIS?
I'M NOT SURE.
SHE SAID IT WAS...
..."A SPECIAL PRESENT FOR WATARU-KUN, WHO HAS NO BUSINESS SENSE."

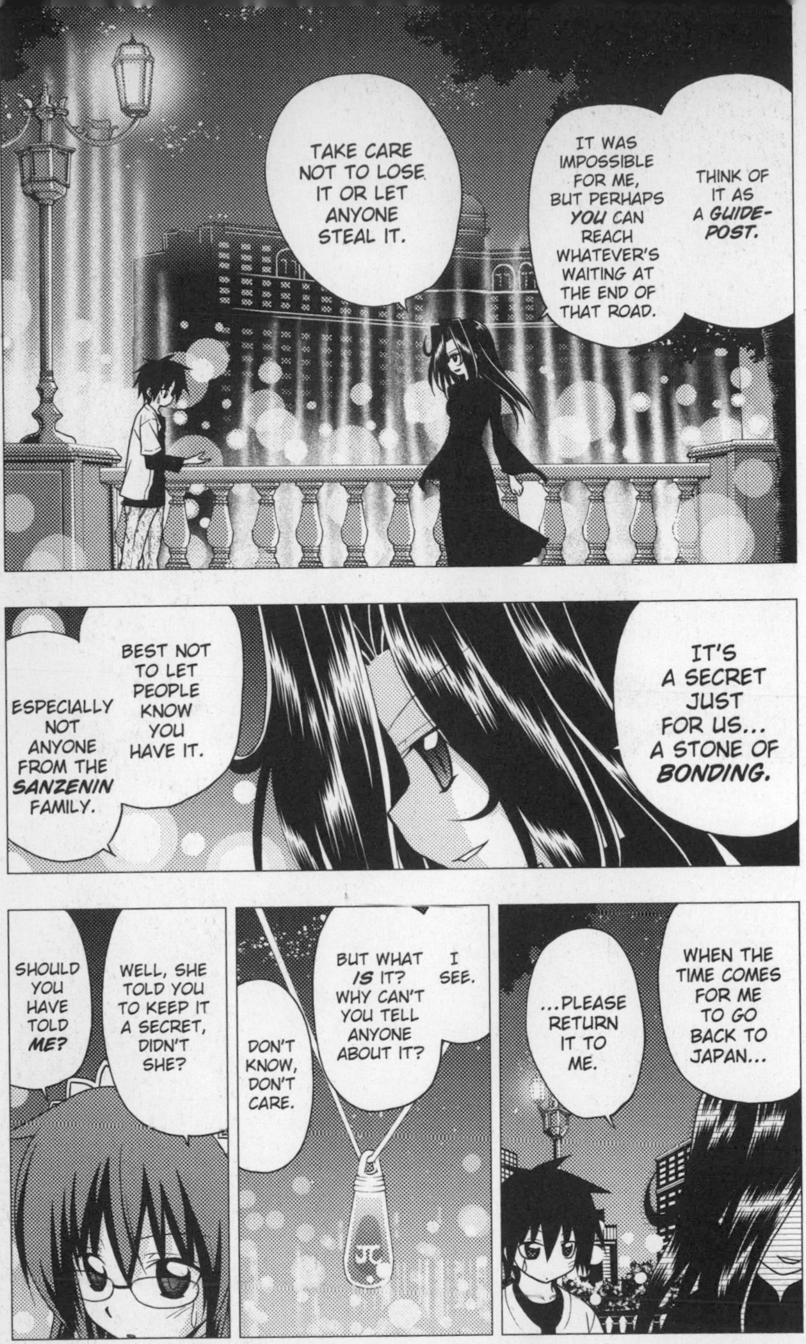
THINK OF IT AS A GUIDE-POST.
IT WAS IMPOSSIBLE FOR ME, BUT PERHAPS YOU CAN REACH WHATEVER'S WAITING AT THE END OF THAT ROAD.
TAKE CARE NOT TO LOSE IT OR LET ANYONE STEAL IT.
IT'S A SECRET JUST FOR US... A STONE OF BONDING.
BEST NOT TO LET PEOPLE KNOW YOU HAVE IT.
ESPECIALLY NOT ANYONE FROM THE SANZENIN FAMILY.
WHEN THE TIME COMES FOR ME TO GO BACK TO JAPAN...
...PLEASE RETURN IT TO ME.
I SEE.
BUT WHAT IS IT? WHY CAN'T YOU TELL ANYONE ABOUT IT?
DON'T KNOW, DON'T CARE.
WELL, SHE TOLD YOU TO KEEP IT A SECRET, DIDN'T SHE?
SHOULD YOU HAVE TOLD ME?

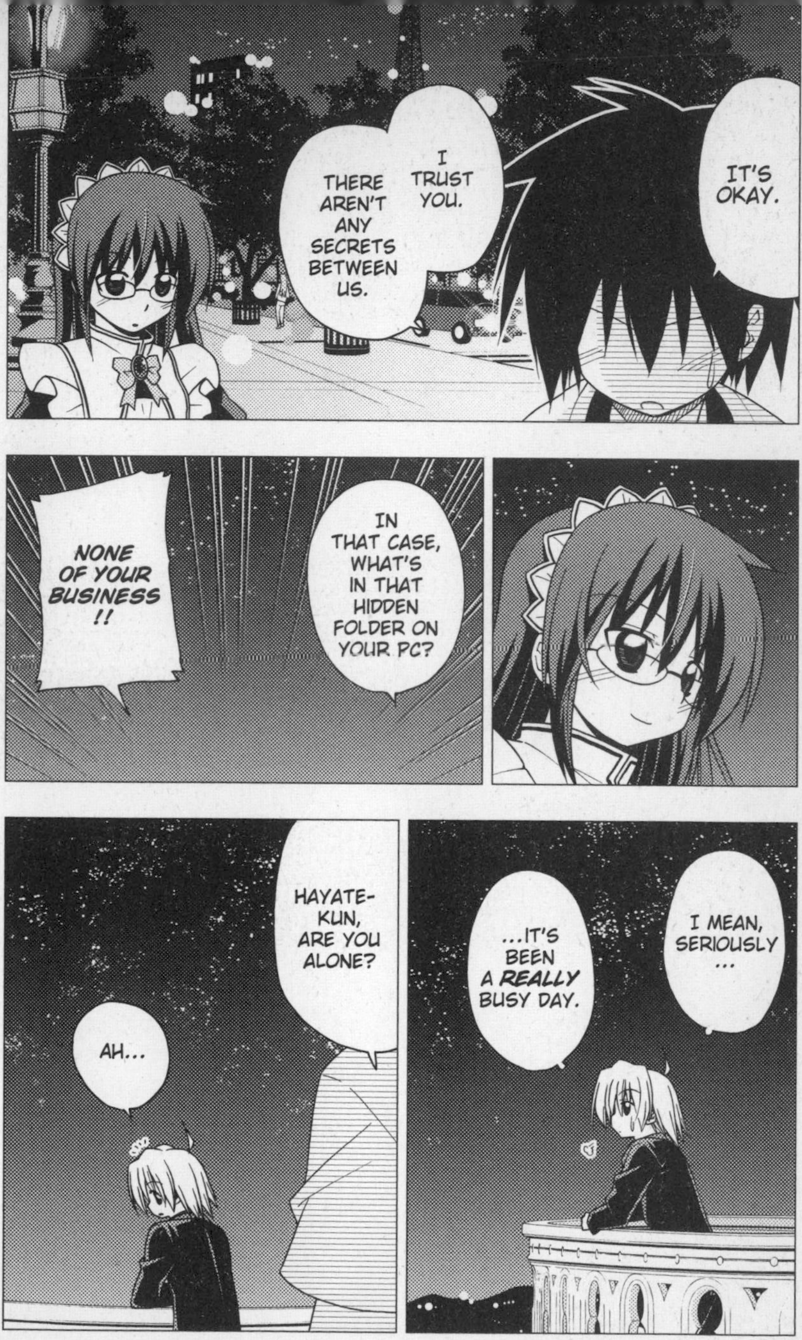
IT'S OKAY.
I TRUST YOU.
THERE AREN'T ANY SECRETS BETWEEN US.
IN THAT CASE, WHAT'S IN THAT HIDDEN FOLDER ON YOUR PC?
NONE OF YOUR BUSINESS !!
I MEAN, SERIOUSLY ...
...IT'S BEEN A REALLY BUSY DAY.
HAYATE-KUN, ARE YOU ALONE?
AH...

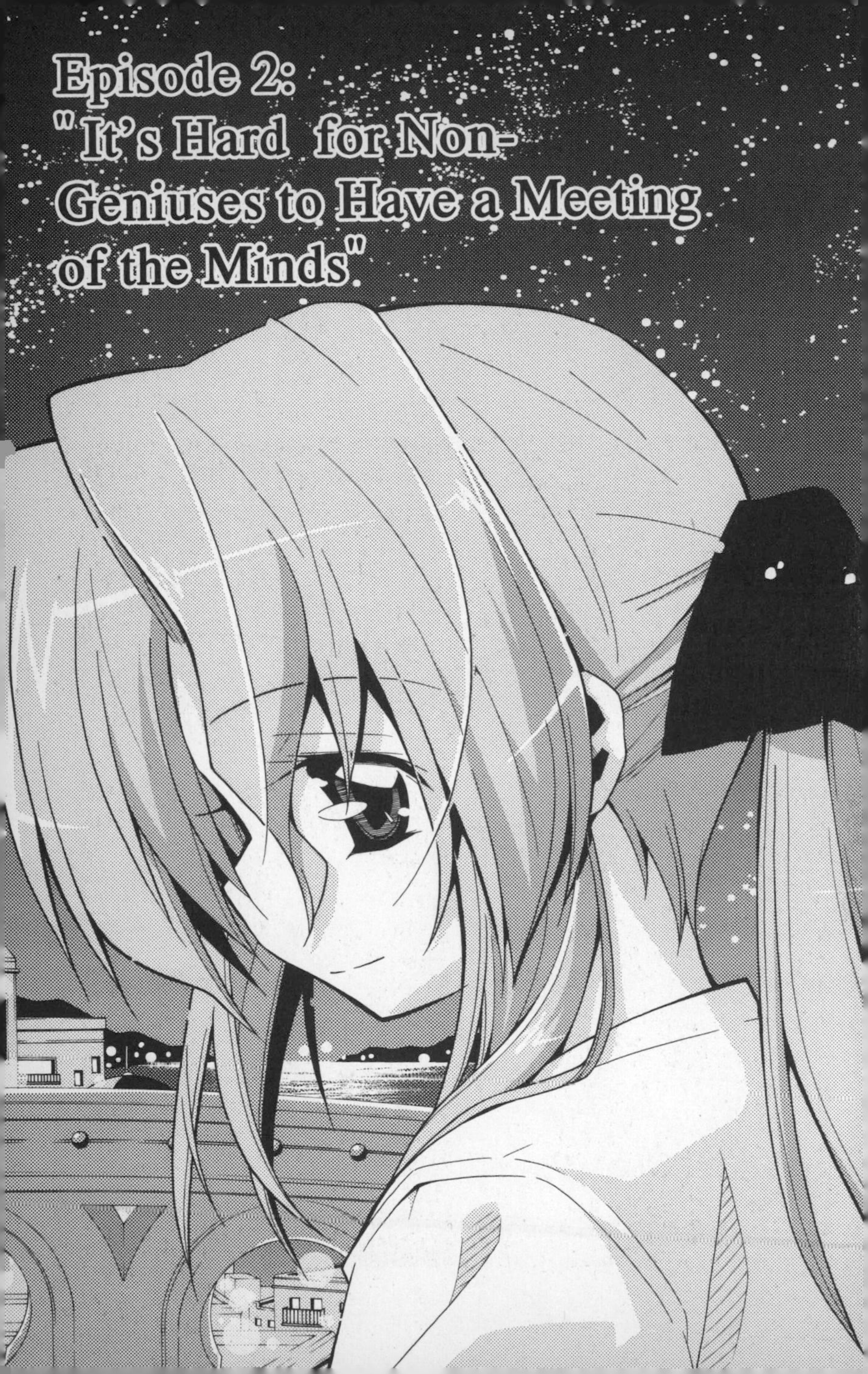
Episode 2:
"It's Hard for Non-Geniuses to Have a Meeting of the Minds"

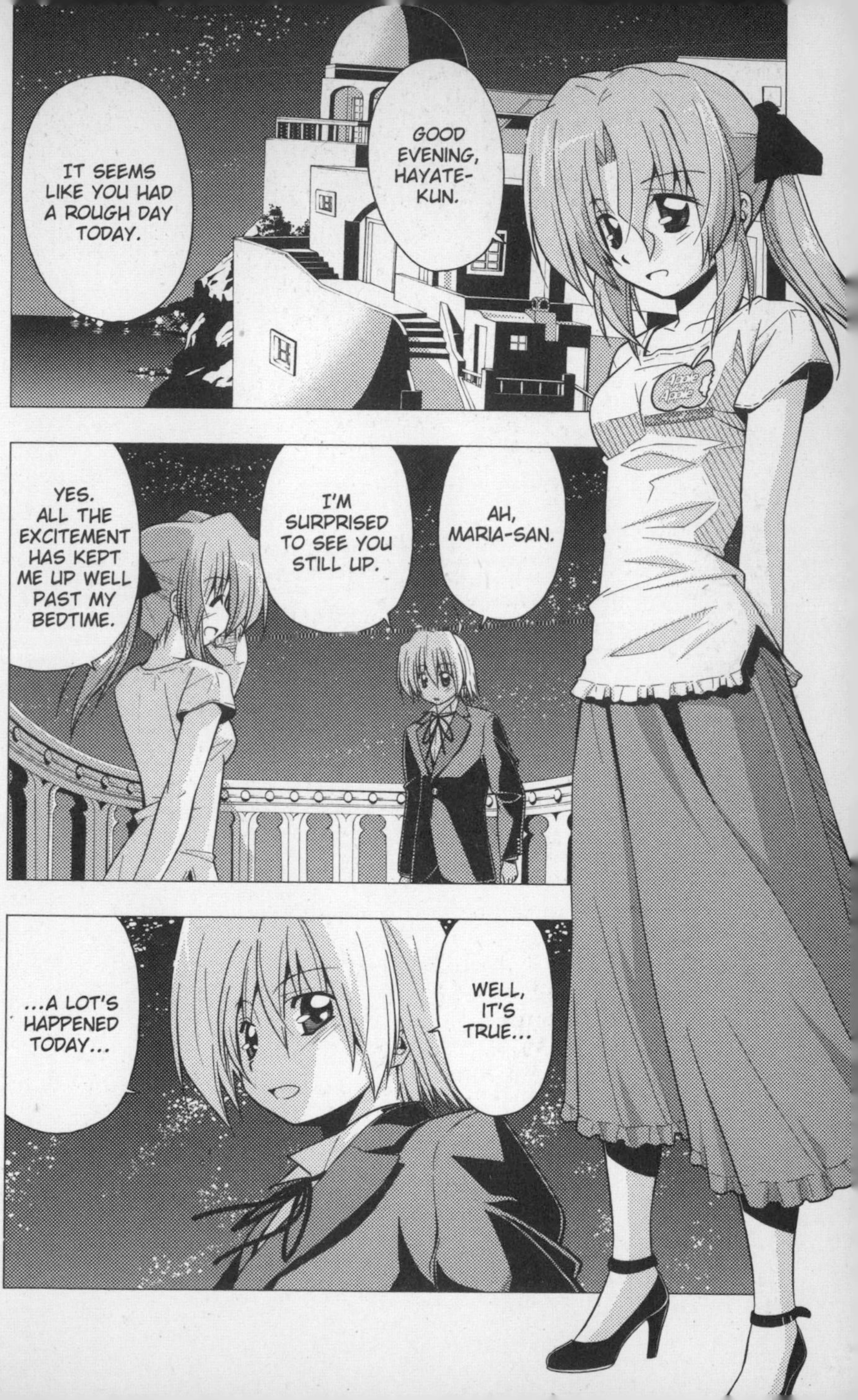
GOOD EVENING, HAYATE-KUN.
IT SEEMS LIKE YOU HAD A ROUGH DAY TODAY.
AH, MARIA-SAN.
I'M SURPRISED TO SEE YOU STILL UP.
YES. ALL THE EXCITEMENT HAS KEPT ME UP WELL PAST MY BEDTIME.
WELL, IT'S TRUE...
...A LOT'S HAPPENED TODAY...

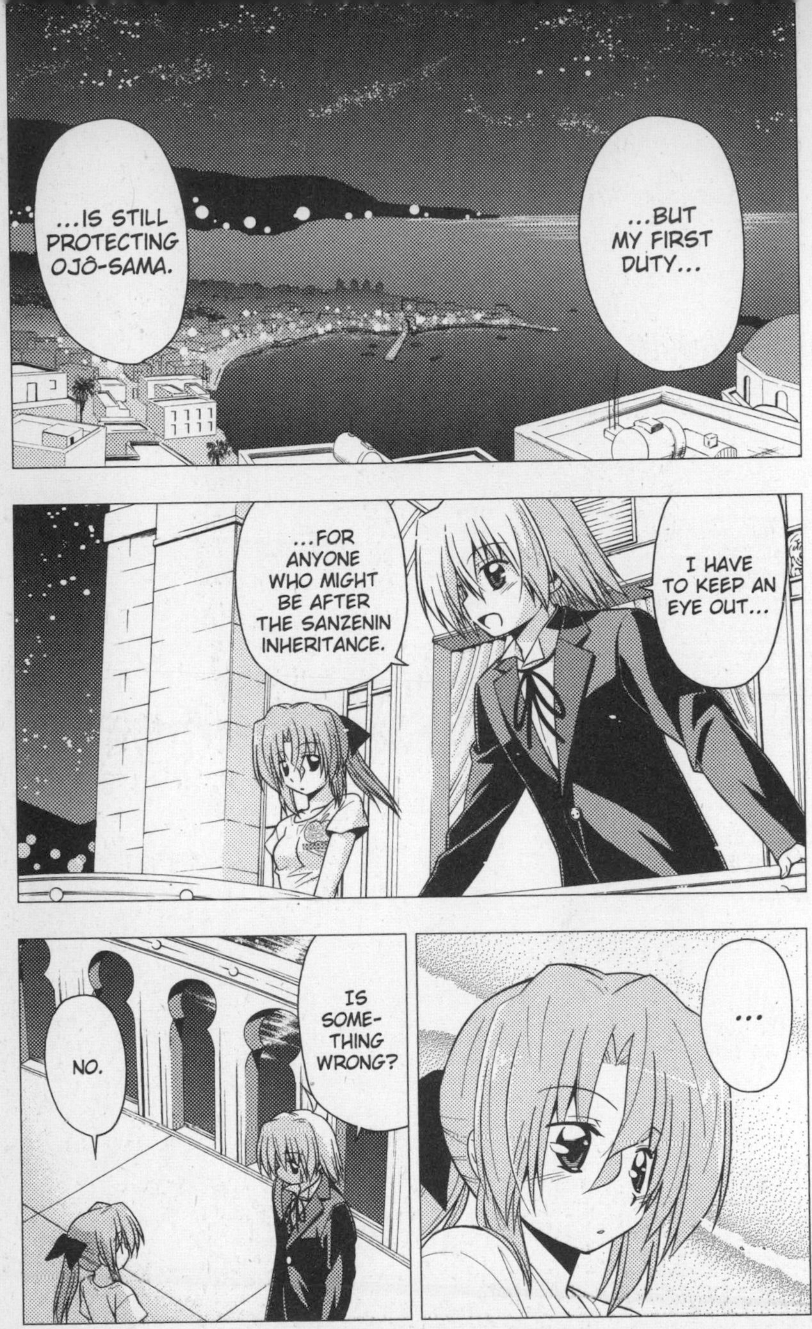
...BUT MY FIRST DUTY...
...IS STILL PROTECTING OJÔ-SAMA.
I HAVE TO KEEP AN EYE OUT...
...FOR ANYONE WHO MIGHT BE AFTER THE SANZENIN INHERITANCE.
...
IS SOME-THING WRONG?
NO.

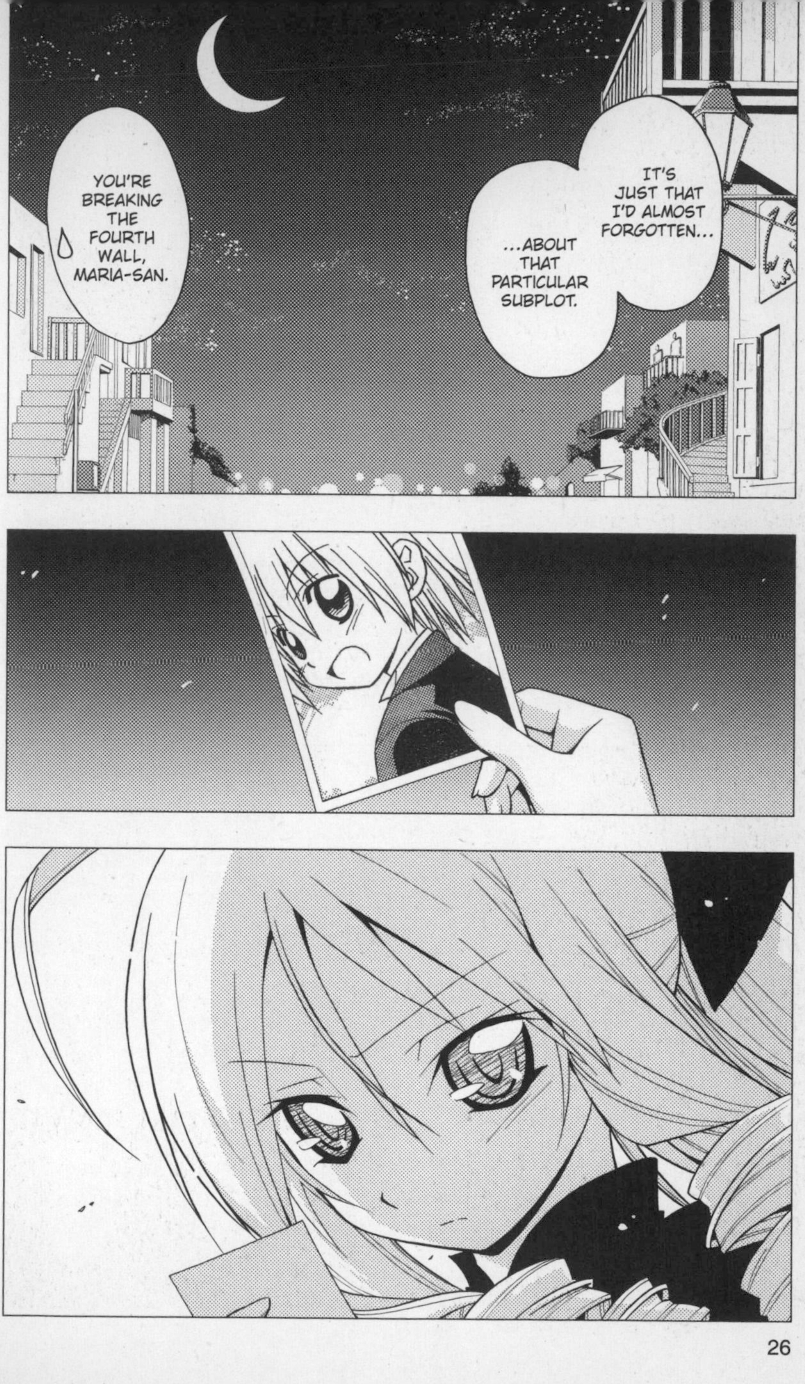
IT'S JUST THAT I'D ALMOST FORGOTTEN...
...ABOUT THAT PARTICULAR SUBPLOT.
YOU'RE BREAKING THE FOURTH WALL, MARIA-SAN.

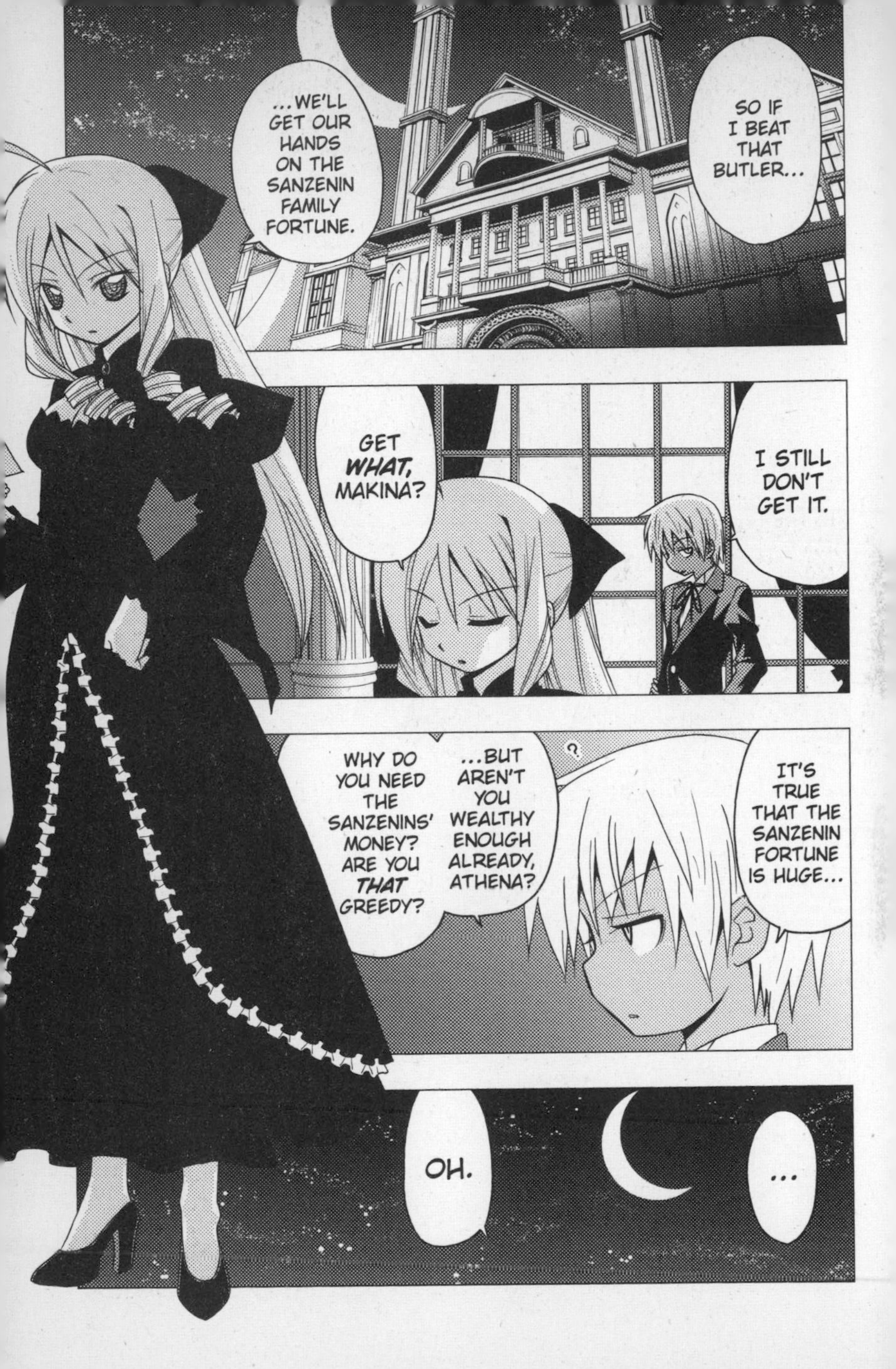
SO IF I BEAT THAT BUTLER...
...WE'LL GET OUR HANDS ON THE SANZENIN FAMILY FORTUNE.
I STILL DON'T GET IT.
GET *WHAT,* MAKINA?
IT'S TRUE THAT THE SANZENIN FORTUNE IS HUGE...
...BUT AREN'T YOU WEALTHY ENOUGH ALREADY, ATHENA?
WHY DO YOU NEED THE SANZENINS' MONEY? ARE YOU *THAT* GREEDY?
...
OH.

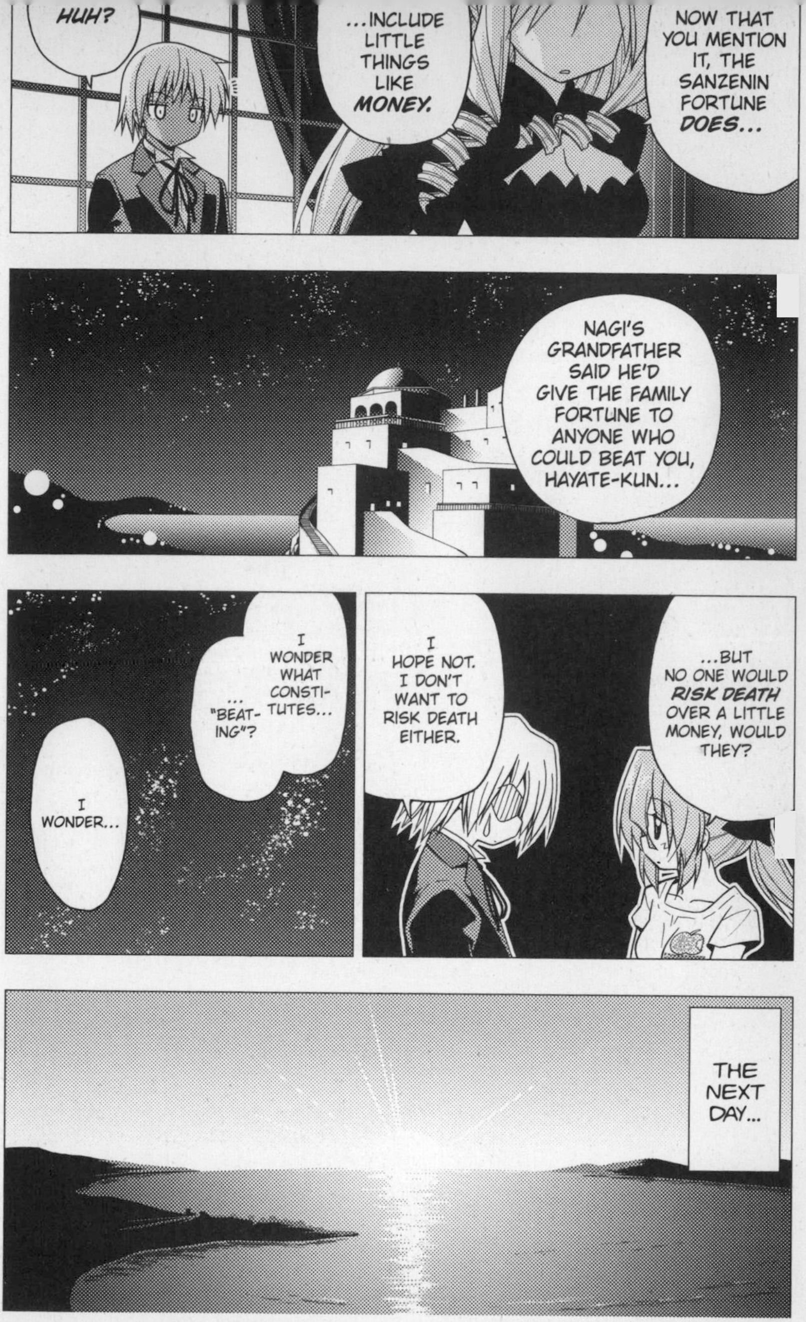
NOW THAT YOU MENTION IT, THE SANZENIN FORTUNE **DOES...**
...INCLUDE LITTLE THINGS LIKE **MONEY.**
HUH?
NAGI'S GRANDFATHER SAID HE'D GIVE THE FAMILY FORTUNE TO ANYONE WHO COULD BEAT YOU, HAYATE-KUN...
...BUT NO ONE WOULD **RISK DEATH** OVER A LITTLE MONEY, WOULD THEY?
I HOPE NOT. I DON'T WANT TO RISK DEATH EITHER.
I WONDER WHAT CONSTITUTES... ..."BEATING"?
I WONDER...
THE NEXT DAY...

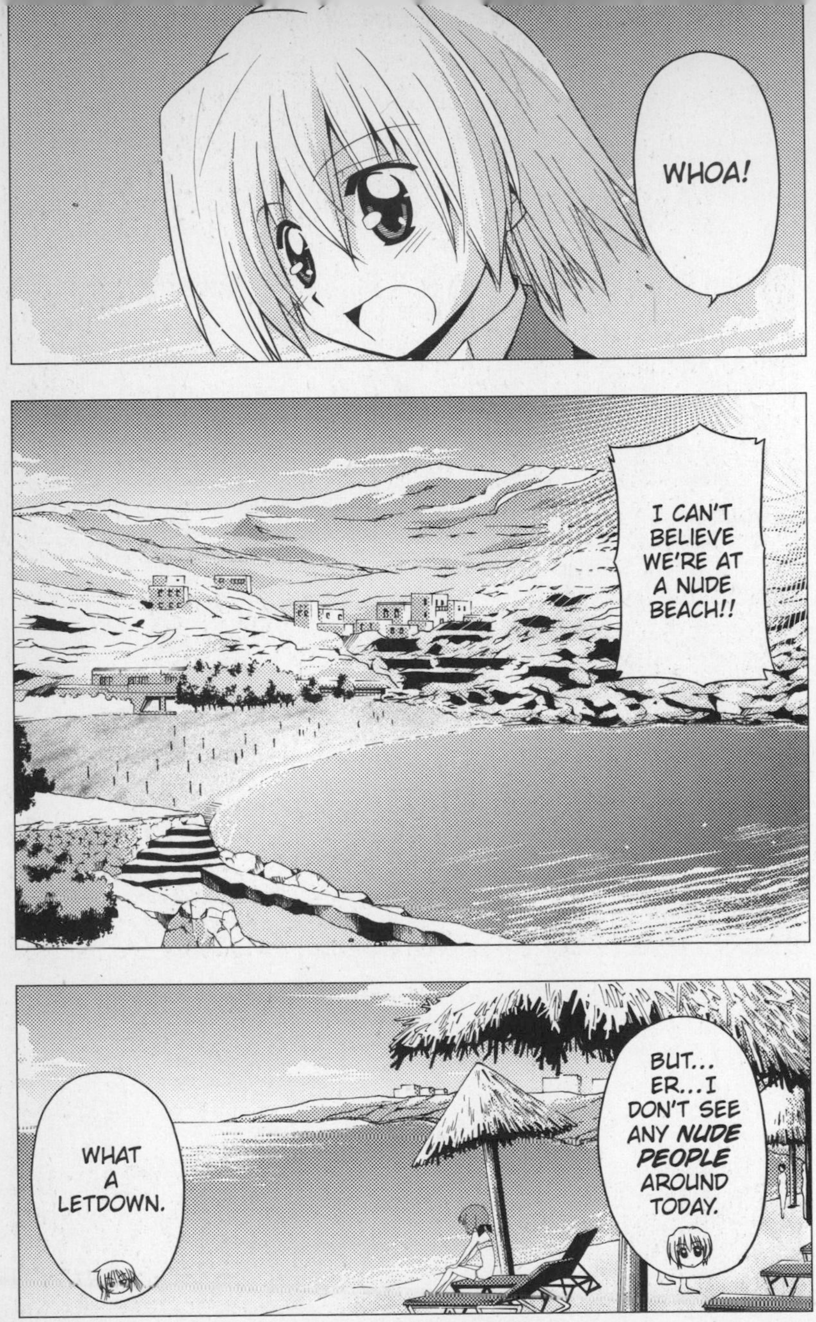
WHOA!
I CAN'T BELIEVE WE'RE AT A NUDE BEACH!!
BUT... ER...I DON'T SEE ANY *NUDE PEOPLE* AROUND TODAY.
WHAT A LETDOWN.

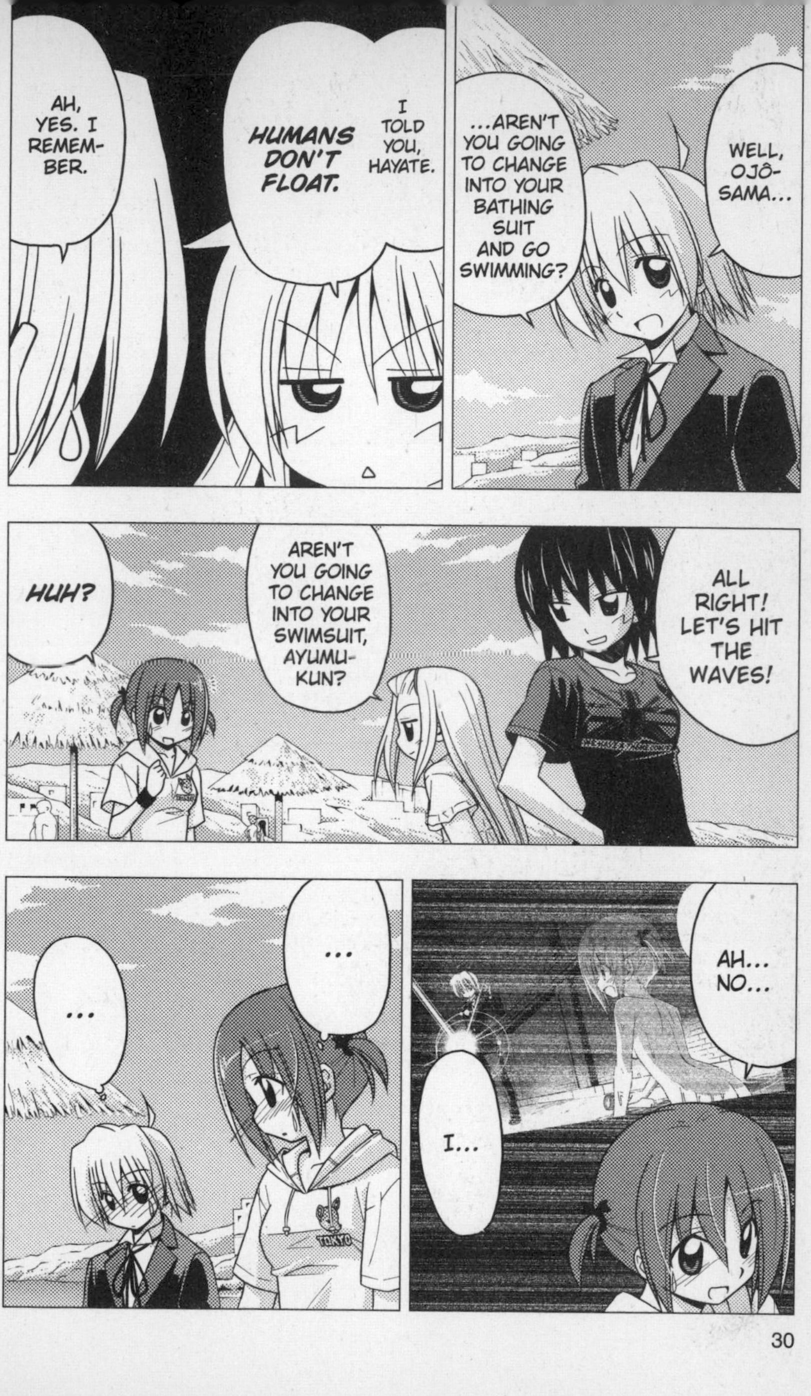
WELL, OJÔ-SAMA...
...AREN'T YOU GOING TO CHANGE INTO YOUR BATHING SUIT AND GO SWIMMING?
I TOLD YOU, HAYATE.
HUMANS DON'T FLOAT.
AH, YES. I REMEMBER.
ALL RIGHT! LET'S HIT THE WAVES!
AREN'T YOU GOING TO CHANGE INTO YOUR SWIMSUIT, AYUMU-KUN?
HUH?
AH... NO...
I...
...
...

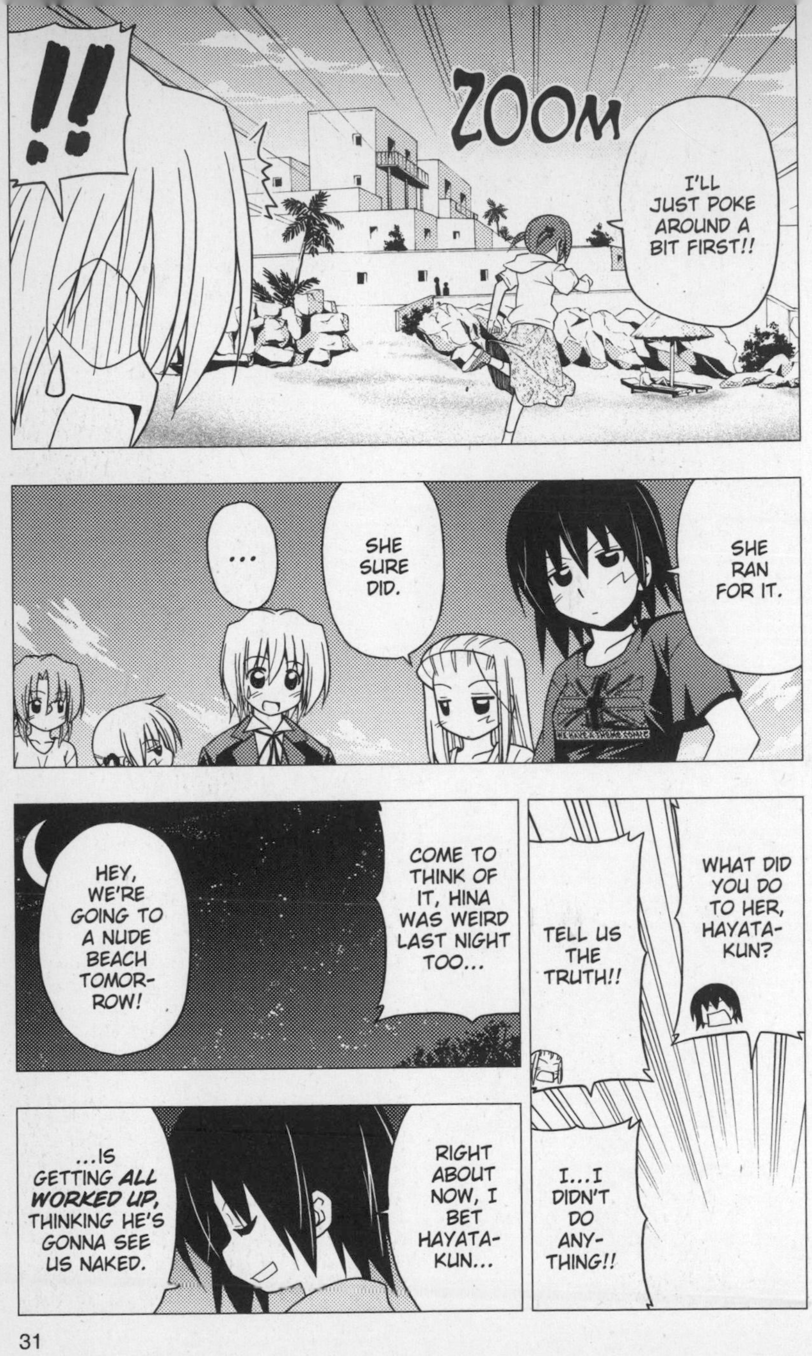
I'LL JUST POKE AROUND A BIT FIRST!!
ZOOM
!!
SHE RAN FOR IT.
SHE SURE DID.
...
WHAT DID YOU DO TO HER, HAYATA-KUN?
TELL US THE TRUTH!!
I...I DIDN'T DO ANYTHING!!
COME TO THINK OF IT, HINA WAS WEIRD LAST NIGHT TOO...
HEY, WE'RE GOING TO A NUDE BEACH TOMORROW!
RIGHT ABOUT NOW, I BET HAYATA-KUN...
...IS GETTING *ALL WORKED UP*, THINKING HE'S GONNA SEE US NAKED.

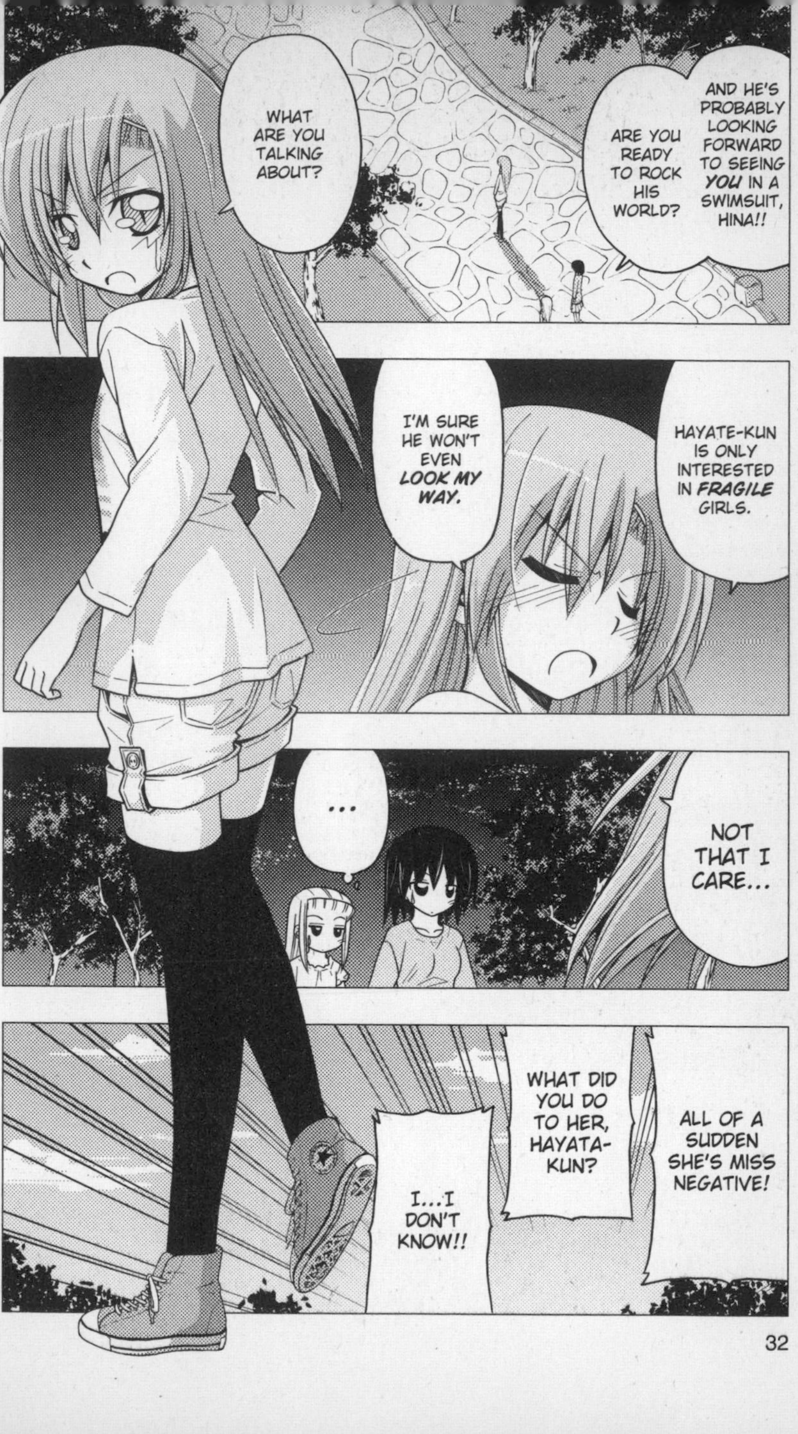
AND HE'S PROBABLY LOOKING FORWARD TO SEEING *YOU* IN A SWIMSUIT, HINA!!
ARE YOU READY TO ROCK HIS WORLD?
WHAT ARE YOU TALKING ABOUT?
HAYATE-KUN IS ONLY INTERESTED IN *FRAGILE* GIRLS.
I'M SURE HE WON'T EVEN *LOOK MY WAY.*
NOT THAT I CARE...
...
ALL OF A SUDDEN SHE'S MISS NEGATIVE!
WHAT DID YOU DO TO HER, HAYATA-KUN?
I...I DON'T KNOW!!

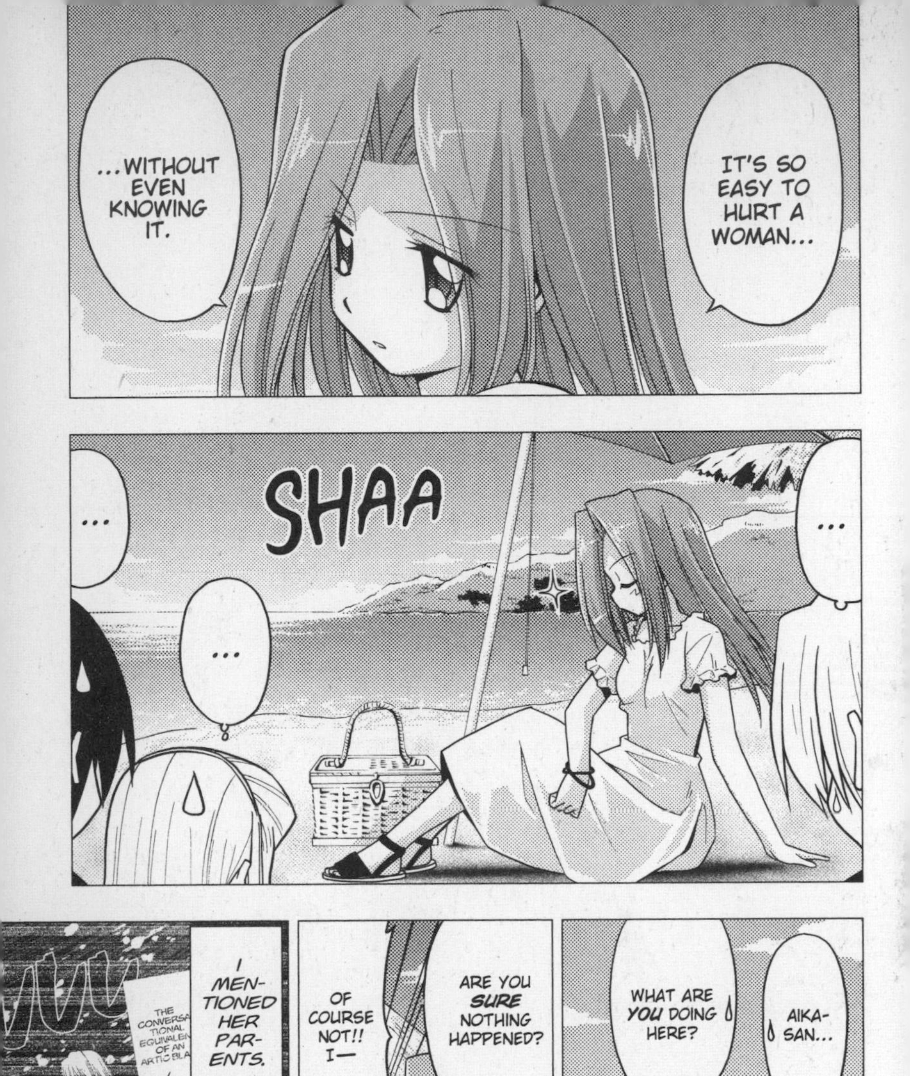
IT'S SO EASY TO HURT A WOMAN...
...WITHOUT EVEN KNOWING IT.
...
SHAA
...
...
AIKA-SAN...
WHAT ARE *YOU* DOING HERE?
WELL, EVERYONE SEEMED TO BE HAVING FUN.
ARE YOU *SURE* NOTHING HAPPENED?
OF COURSE NOT!! I—
I MEN-TIONED HER PAR-ENTS.
THE CONVERSA-TIONAL EQUIVALEN OF AN ARTIC BLA
I DIDN'T MEAN TO BE INSENSI-TIVE...

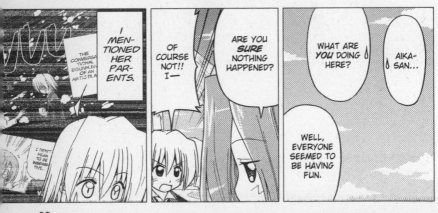

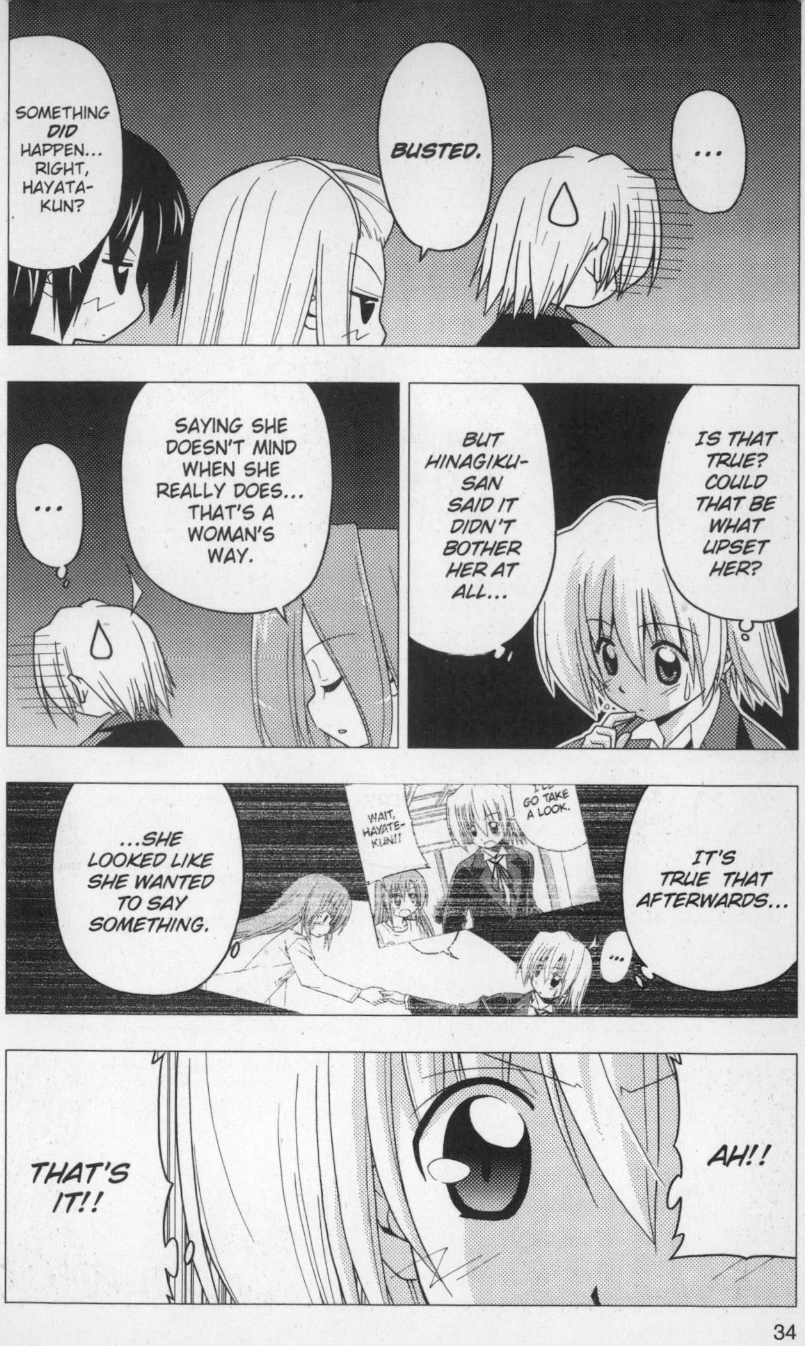
...
BUSTED.
SOMETHING DID HAPPEN... RIGHT, HAYATA-KUN?
IS THAT TRUE? COULD THAT BE WHAT UPSET HER?
BUT HINAGIKU-SAN SAID IT DIDN'T BOTHER HER AT ALL...
SAYING SHE DOESN'T MIND WHEN SHE REALLY DOES... THAT'S A WOMAN'S WAY.
...
IT'S TRUE THAT AFTERWARDS...
GO TAKE A LOOK.
WAIT, HAYATE-KUN!!
...
...SHE LOOKED LIKE SHE WANTED TO SAY SOMETHING.
AH!!
THAT'S IT!!

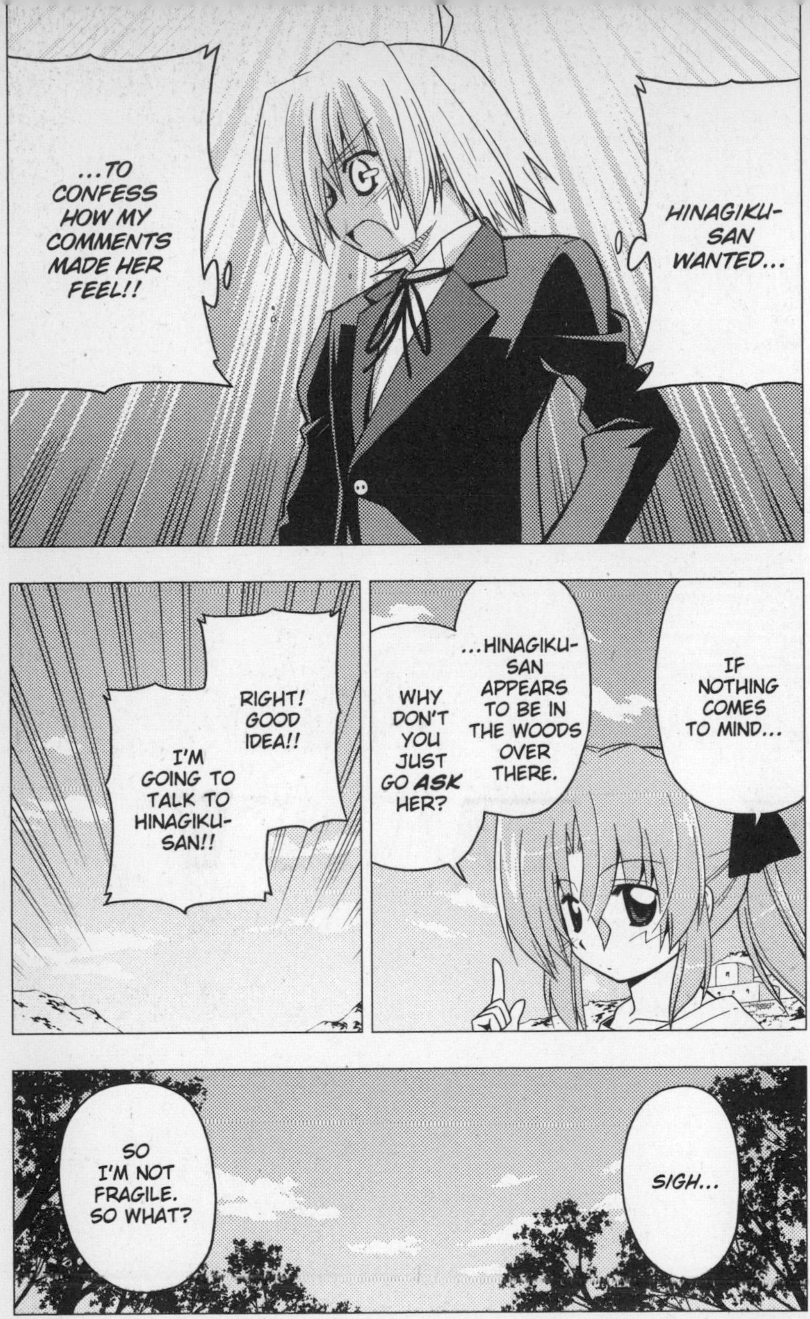
HINAGIKU-SAN WANTED...
...TO CONFESS HOW MY COMMENTS MADE HER FEEL!!
IF NOTHING COMES TO MIND...
...HINAGIKU-SAN APPEARS TO BE IN THE WOODS OVER THERE.
WHY DON'T YOU JUST GO ASK HER?
RIGHT! GOOD IDEA!!
I'M GOING TO TALK TO HINAGIKU-SAN!!
SIGH...
SO I'M NOT FRAGILE. SO WHAT?

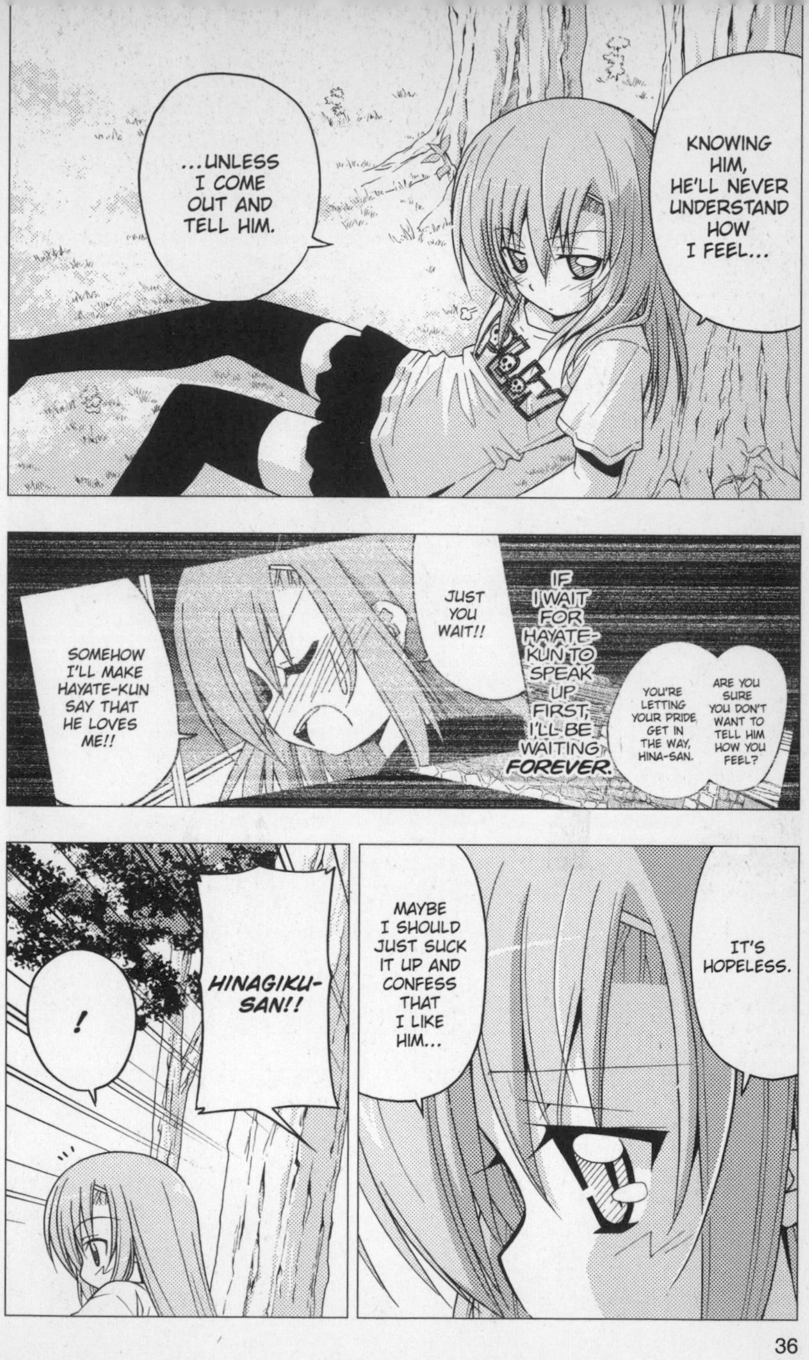
KNOWING HIM, HE'LL NEVER UNDERSTAND HOW I FEEL...
...UNLESS I COME OUT AND TELL HIM.
ARE YOU SURE YOU DON'T WANT TO TELL HIM HOW YOU FEEL?
YOU'RE LETTING YOUR PRIDE GET IN THE WAY, HINA-SAN.
IF I WAIT FOR HAYATE-KUN TO SPEAK UP FIRST, I'LL BE WAITING FOREVER.
JUST YOU WAIT!!
SOMEHOW I'LL MAKE HAYATE-KUN SAY THAT HE LOVES ME!!
IT'S HOPELESS.
MAYBE I SHOULD JUST SUCK IT UP AND CONFESS THAT I LIKE HIM...
HINAGIKU-SAN!!
!

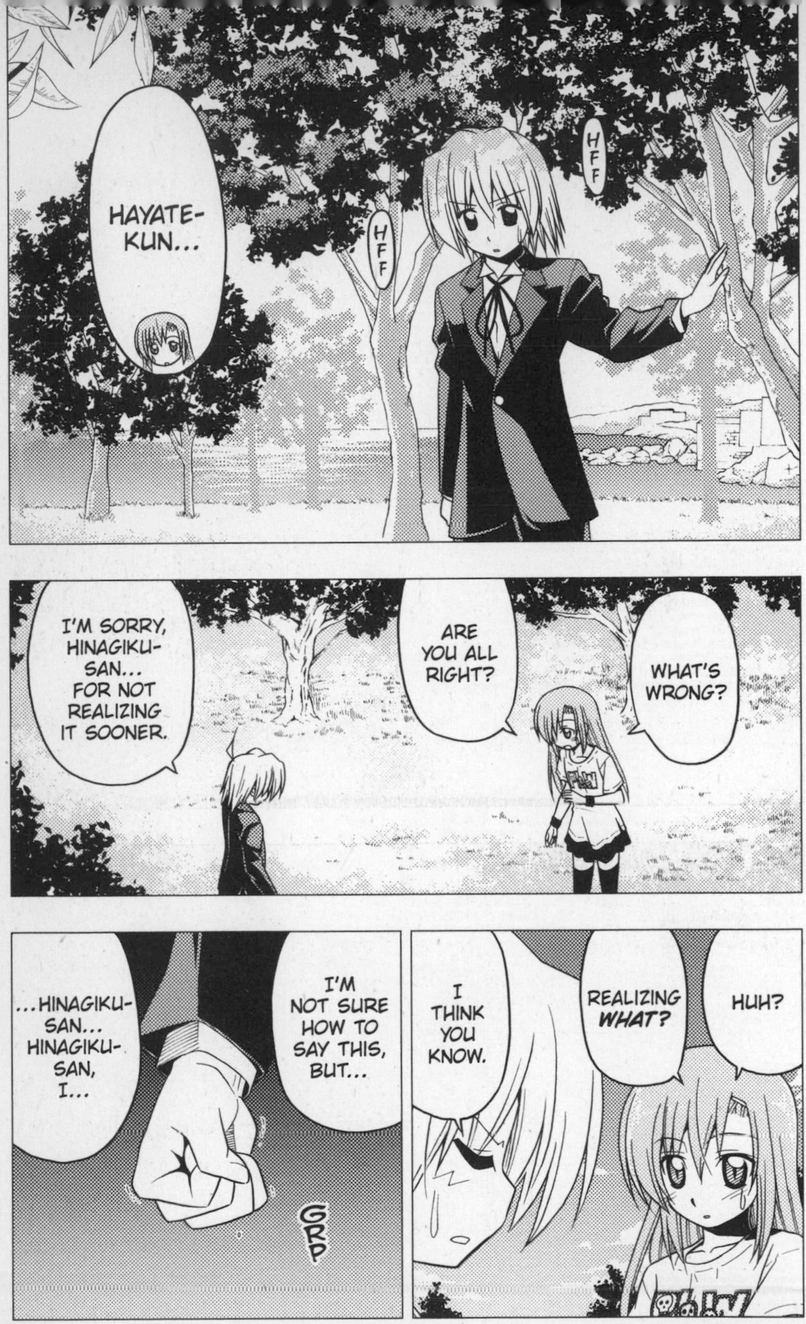
HFF
HFF
HAYATE-KUN...
WHAT'S WRONG?
ARE YOU ALL RIGHT?
I'M SORRY, HINAGIKU-SAN... FOR NOT REALIZING IT SOONER.
HUH?
REALIZING *WHAT?*
I THINK YOU KNOW.
I'M NOT SURE HOW TO SAY THIS, BUT...
...HINAGIKU-SAN... HINAGIKU-SAN, I...
GRP

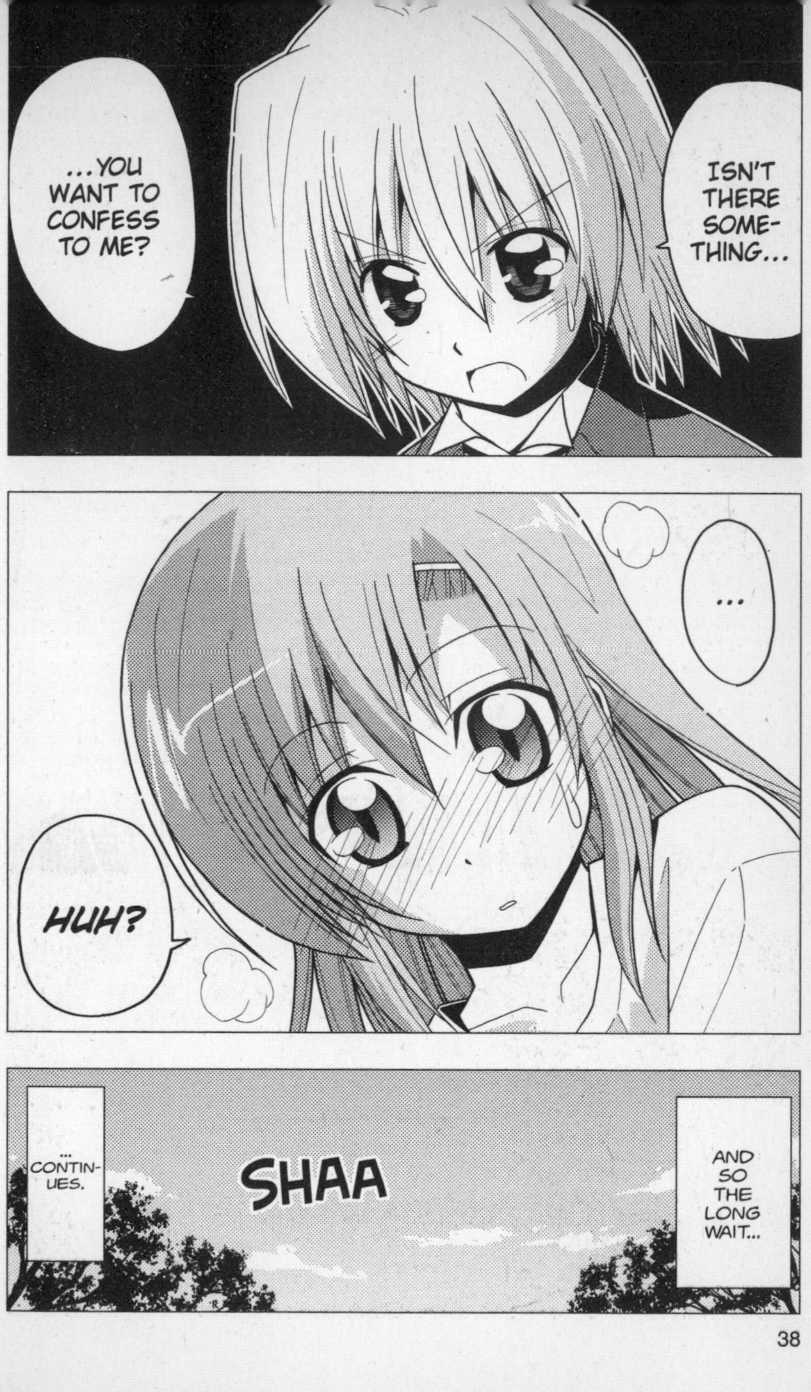
ISN'T THERE SOME-THING...
...YOU WANT TO CONFESS TO ME?
...
HUH?
AND SO THE LONG WAIT...
SHAA
...CONTIN-UES.

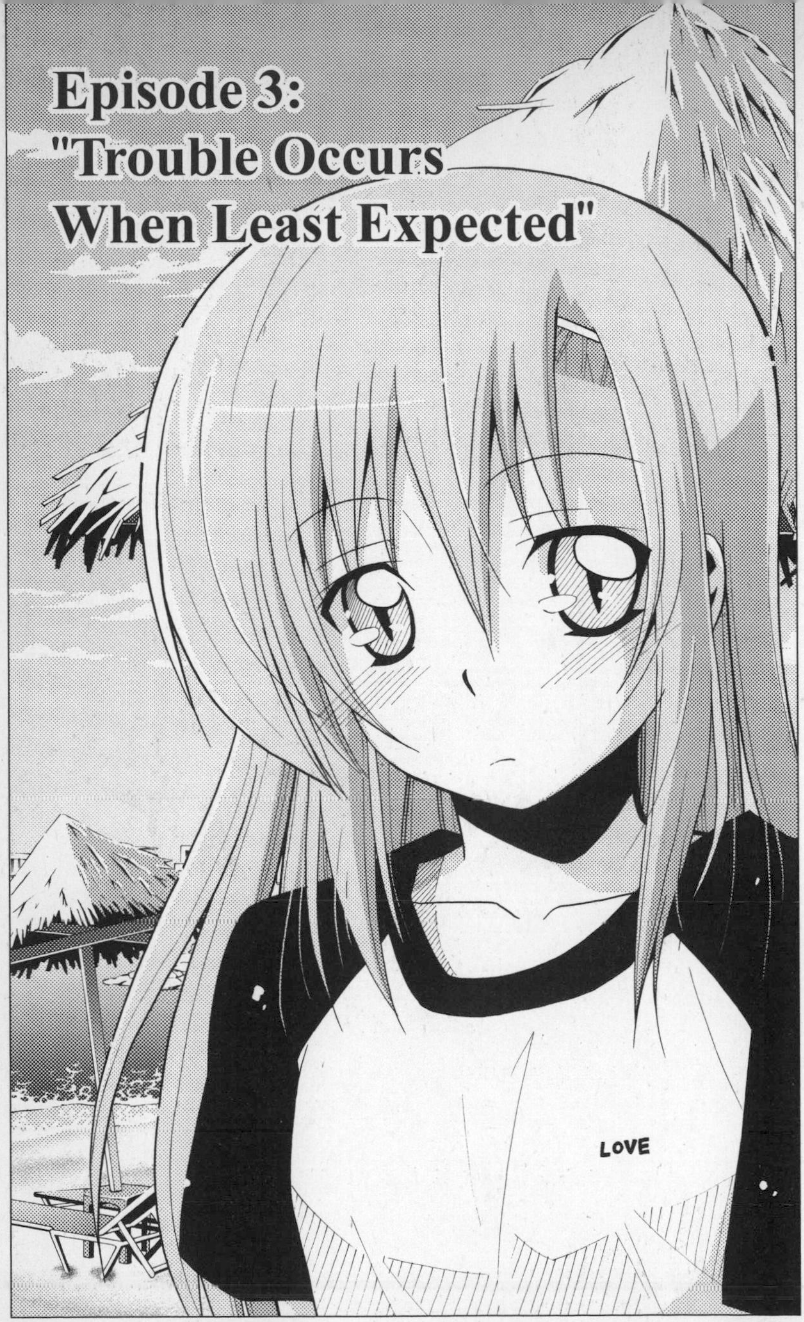
Episode 3:
"Trouble Occurs
When Least Expected"
LOVE

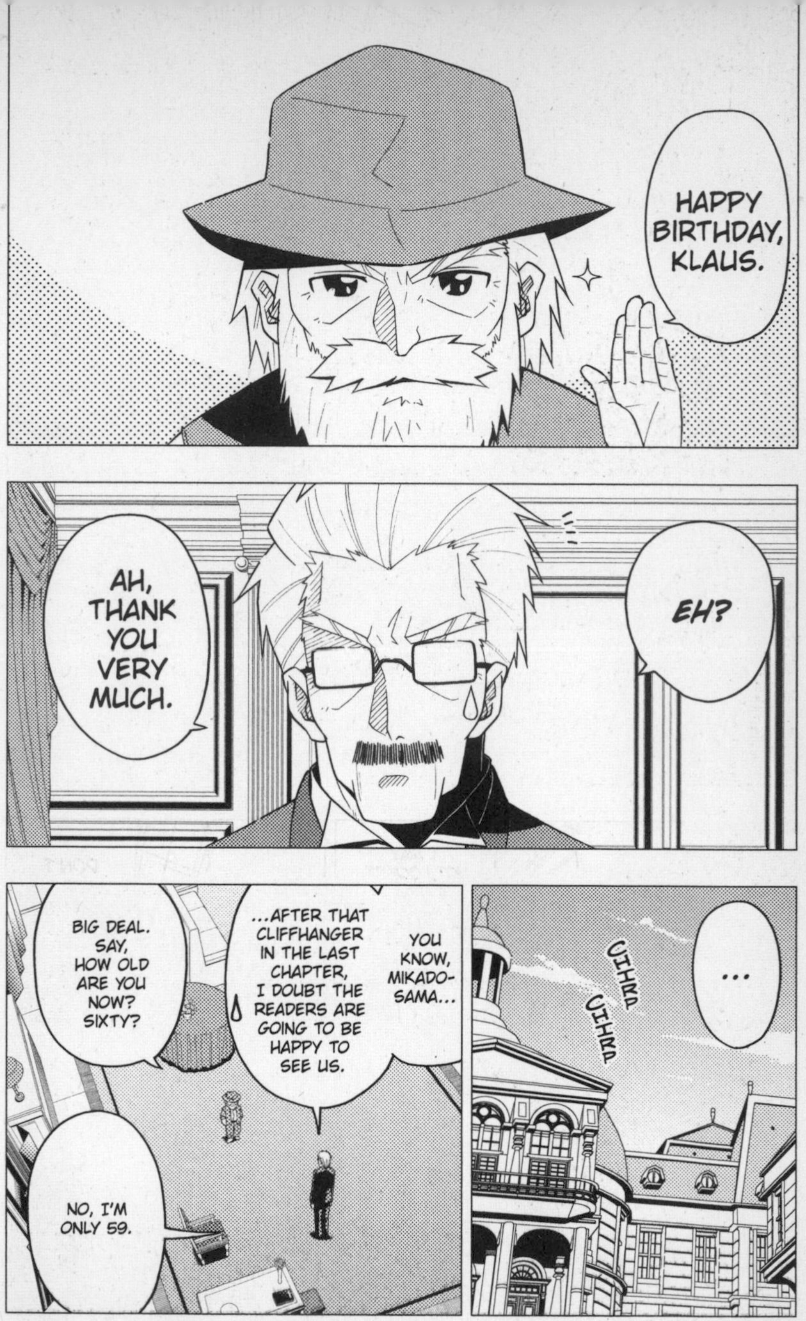
HAPPY BIRTHDAY, KLAUS.
EH?
AH, THANK YOU VERY MUCH.
...
CHIRP
CHIRP
YOU KNOW, MIKADO-SAMA...
...AFTER THAT CLIFFHANGER IN THE LAST CHAPTER, I DOUBT THE READERS ARE GOING TO BE HAPPY TO SEE US.
BIG DEAL. SAY, HOW OLD ARE YOU NOW? SIXTY?
NO, I'M ONLY 59.

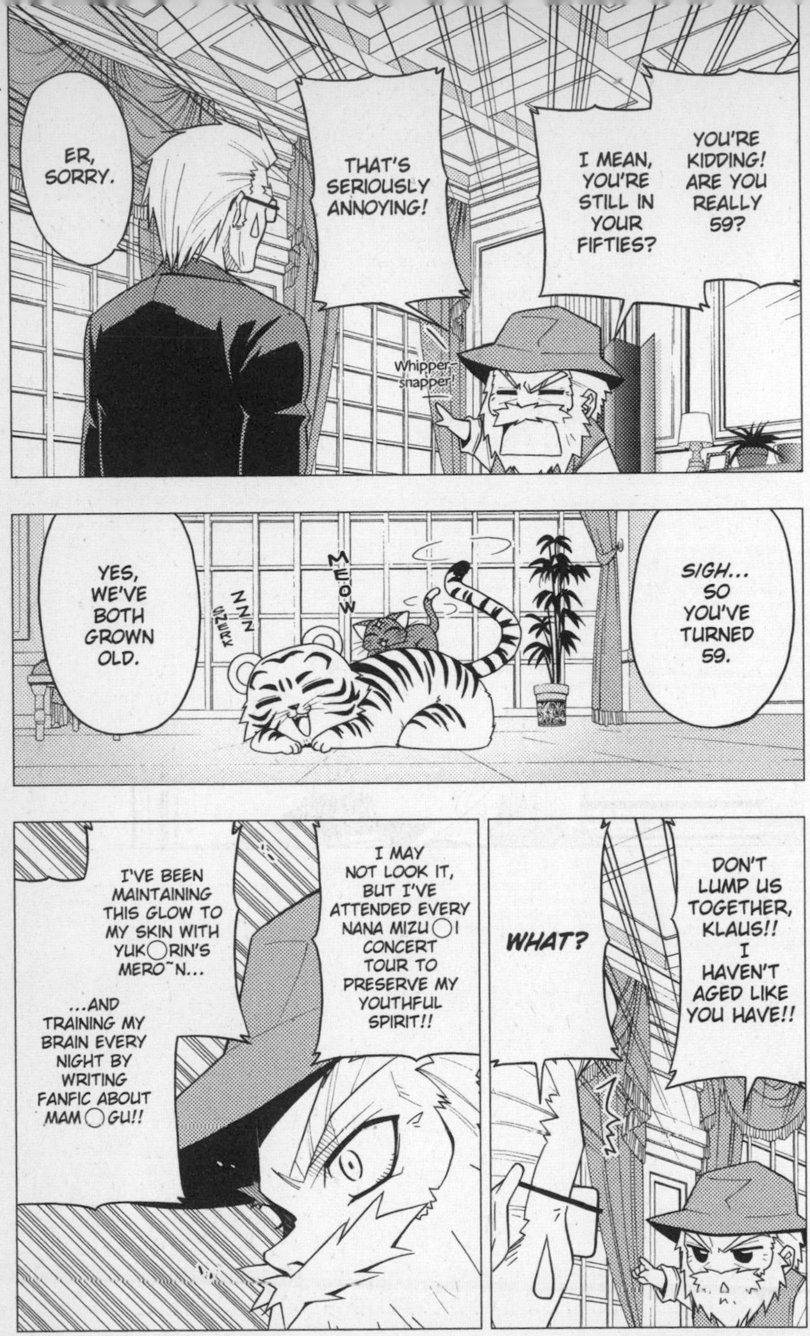
YOU'RE KIDDING! ARE YOU REALLY 59?
I MEAN, YOU'RE STILL IN YOUR FIFTIES?
THAT'S SERIOUSLY ANNOYING!
Whipper-snapper!
ER, SORRY.
SIGH... SO YOU'VE TURNED 59.
MEOW
ZZZ
SNERK
YES, WE'VE BOTH GROWN OLD.
DON'T LUMP US TOGETHER, KLAUS!! I HAVEN'T AGED LIKE YOU HAVE!!
WHAT?
I MAY NOT LOOK IT, BUT I'VE ATTENDED EVERY NANA MIZU◯I CONCERT TOUR TO PRESERVE MY YOUTHFUL SPIRIT!!
I'VE BEEN MAINTAINING THIS GLOW TO MY SKIN WITH YUK◯RIN'S MERO~N...
...AND TRAINING MY BRAIN EVERY NIGHT BY WRITING FANFIC ABOUT MAM◯GU!!

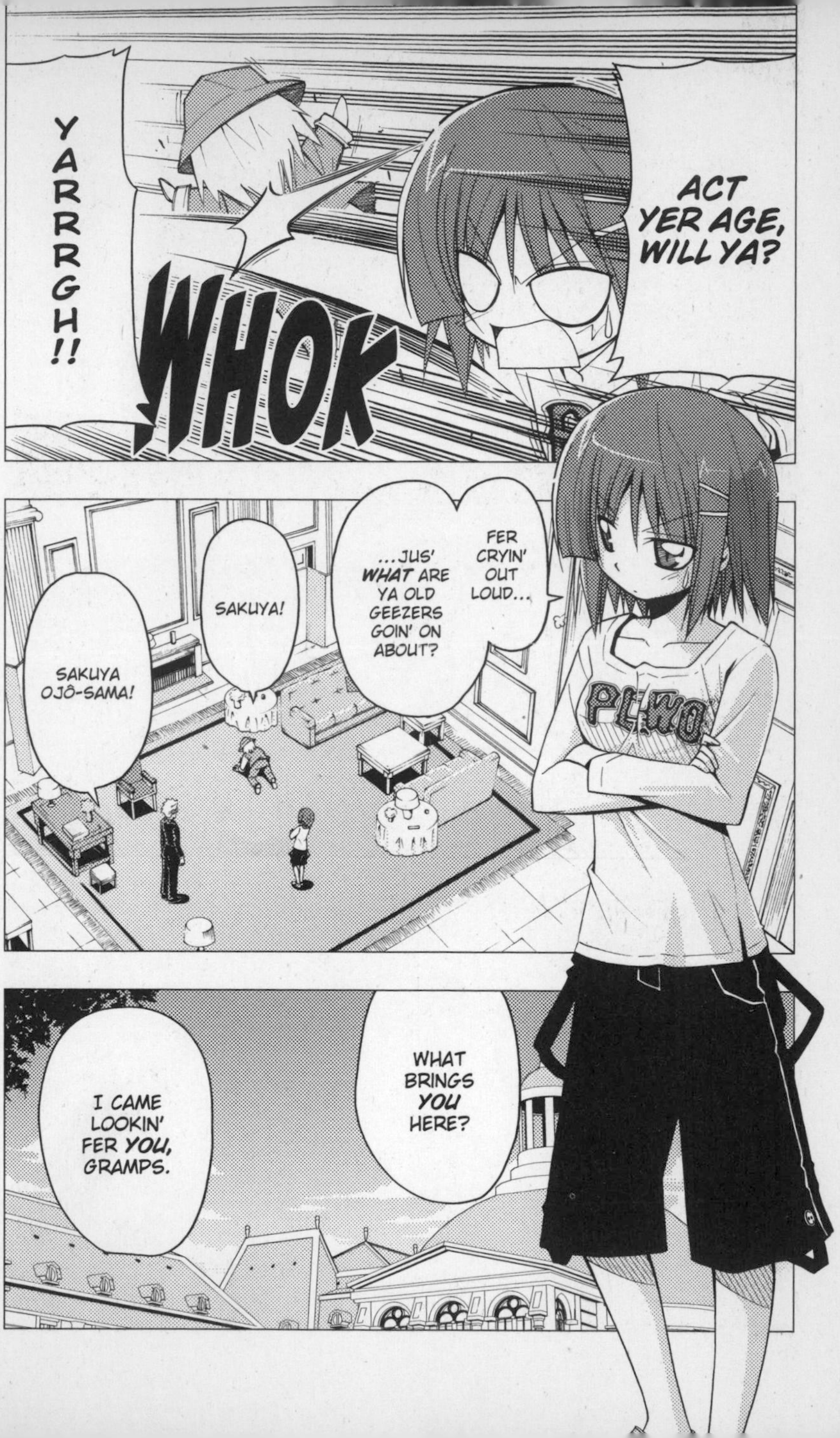
ACT YER AGE, WILL YA?
WHOK
YARRRGH!!
FER CRYIN' OUT LOUD...
...JUS' WHAT ARE YA OLD GEEZERS GOIN' ON ABOUT?
SAKUYA!
SAKUYA OJÔ-SAMA!
WHAT BRINGS YOU HERE?
I CAME LOOKIN' FER YOU, GRAMPS.

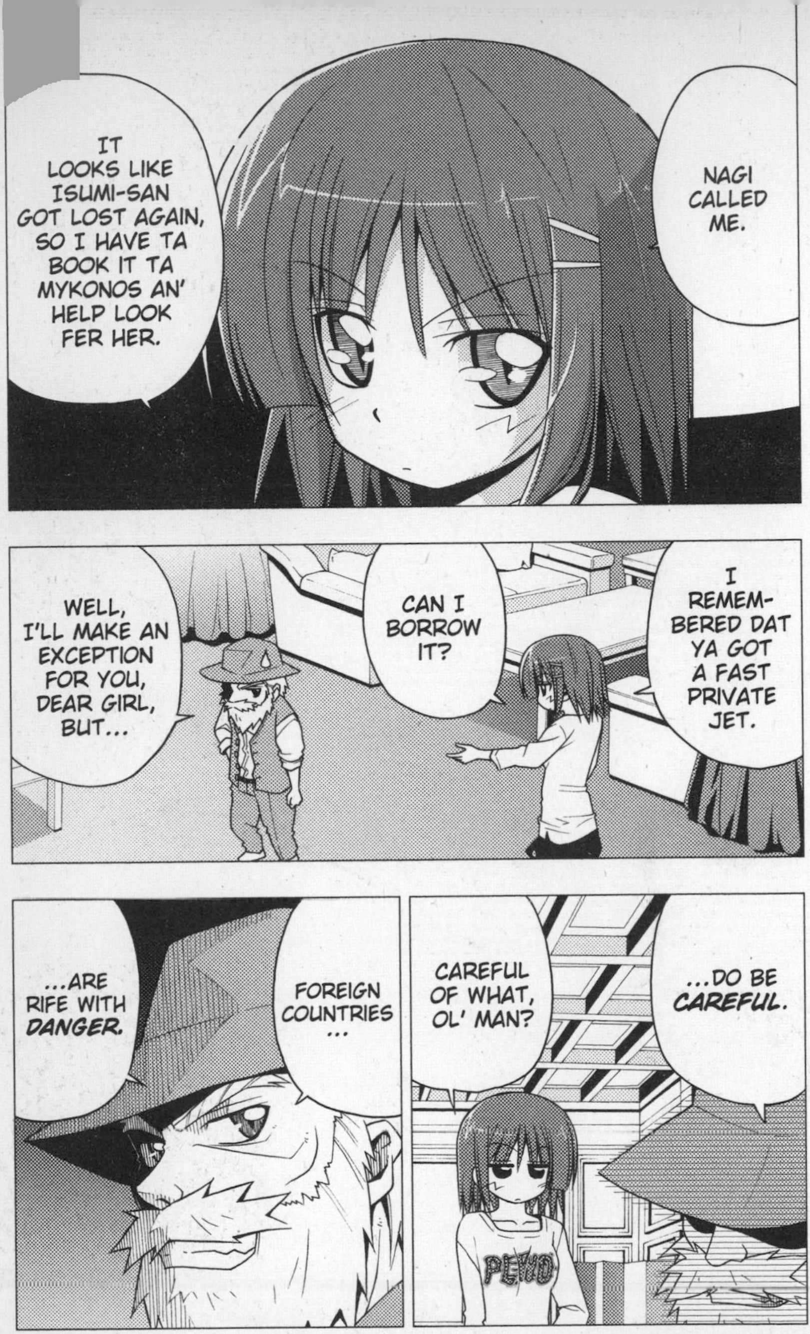
NAGI CALLED ME.
IT LOOKS LIKE ISUMI-SAN GOT LOST AGAIN, SO I HAVE TA BOOK IT TA MYKONOS AN' HELP LOOK FER HER.
I REMEM-BERED DAT YA GOT A FAST PRIVATE JET.
CAN I BORROW IT?
WELL, I'LL MAKE AN EXCEPTION FOR YOU, DEAR GIRL, BUT...
...DO BE *CAREFUL*.
CAREFUL OF WHAT, OL' MAN?
FOREIGN COUNTRIES ...
...ARE RIFE WITH *DANGER*.

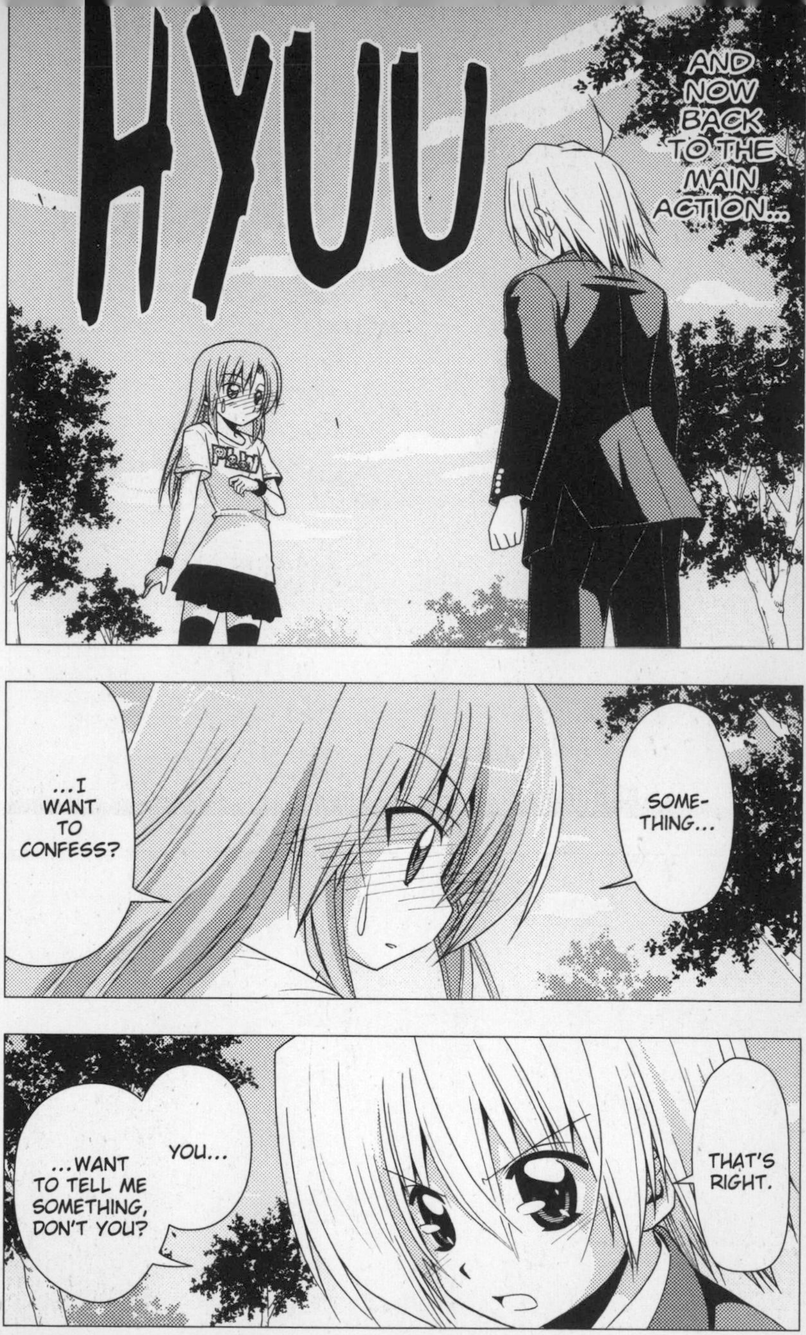
AND NOW BACK TO THE MAIN ACTION...
HYUU
SOME-THING...
...I WANT TO CONFESS?
THAT'S RIGHT.
YOU...
...WANT TO TELL ME SOMETHING, DON'T YOU?

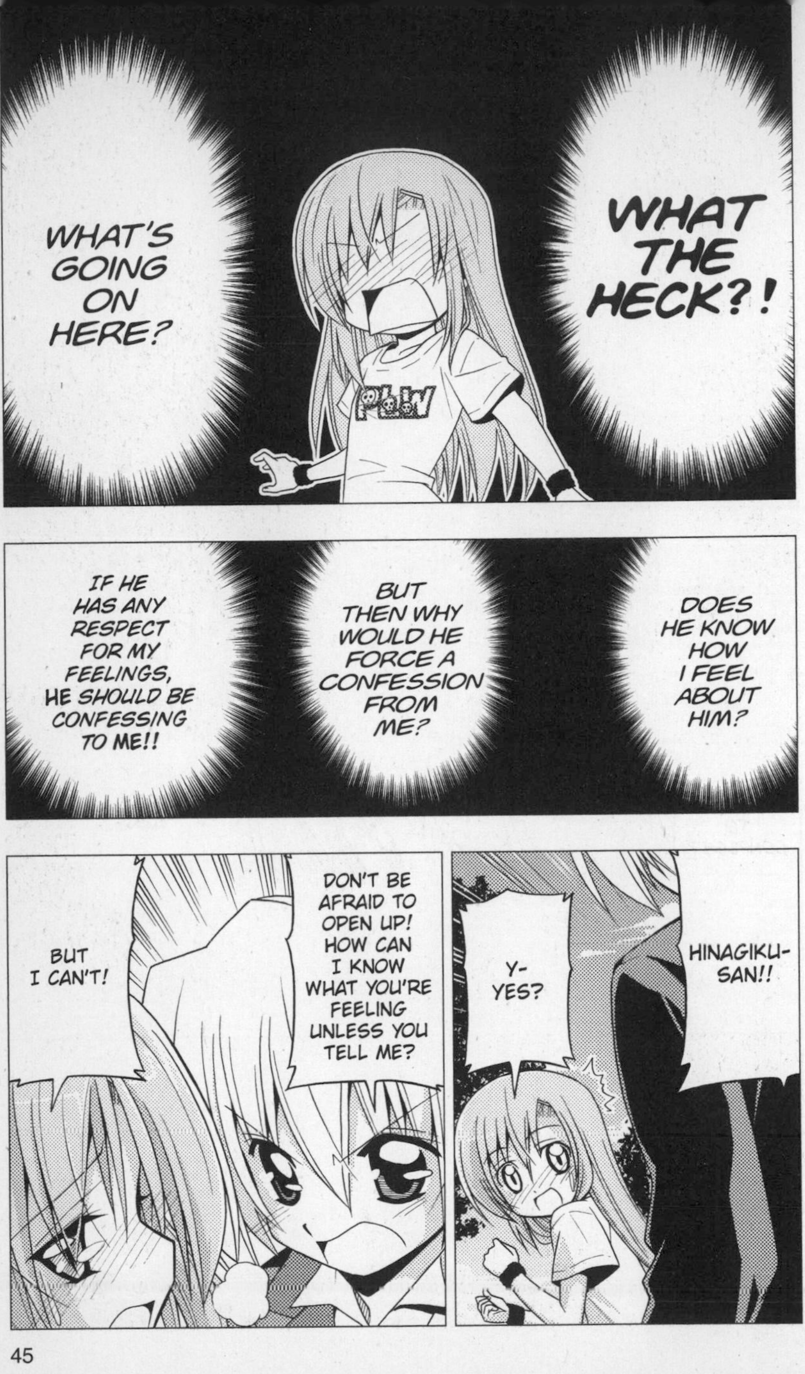
WHAT THE HECK?!
WHAT'S GOING ON HERE?
DOES HE KNOW HOW I FEEL ABOUT HIM?
BUT THEN WHY WOULD HE FORCE A CONFESSION FROM ME?
IF HE HAS ANY RESPECT FOR MY FEELINGS, HE SHOULD BE CONFESSING TO ME!!
HINAGIKU-SAN!!
Y-YES?
DON'T BE AFRAID TO OPEN UP! HOW CAN I KNOW WHAT YOU'RE FEELING UNLESS YOU TELL ME?
BUT I CAN'T!

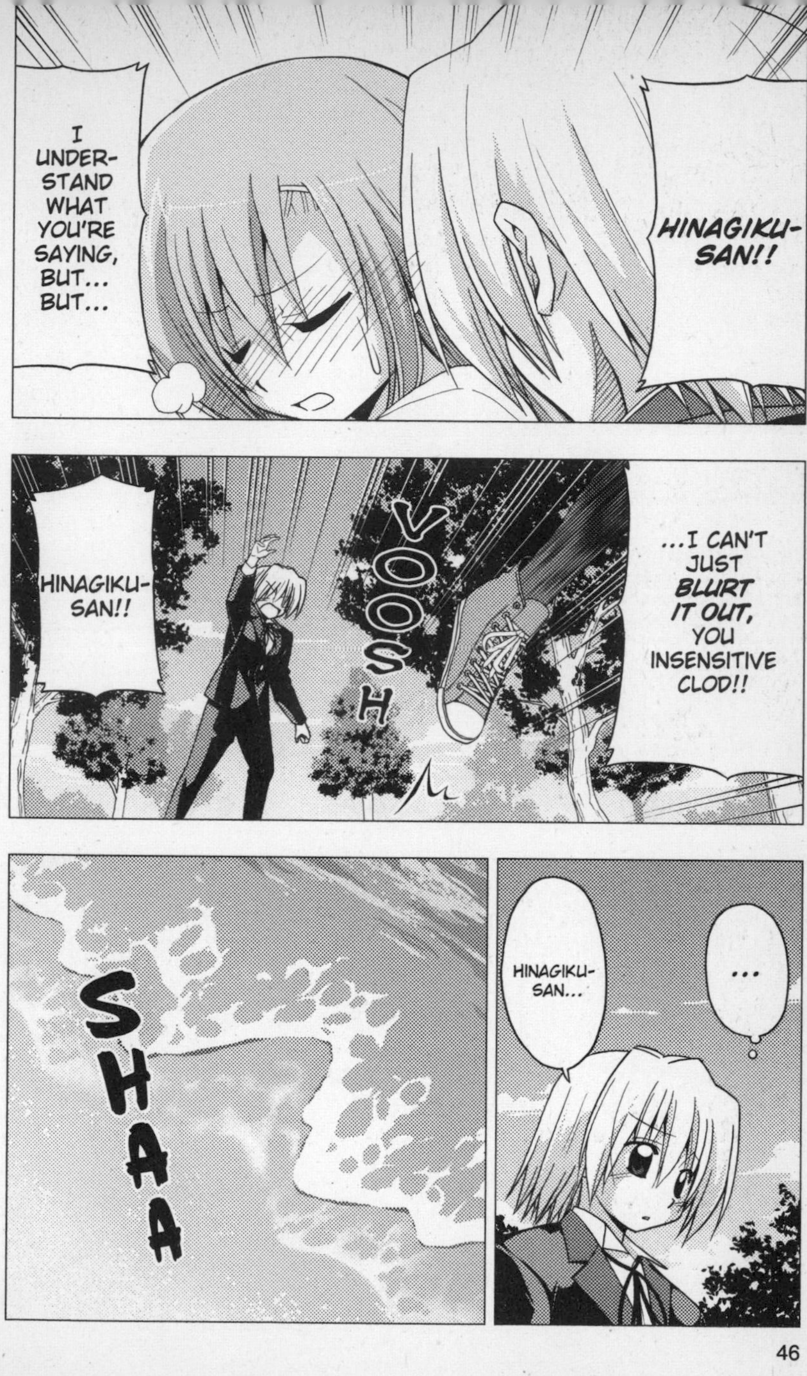
HINAGIKU-SAN!!
I UNDERSTAND WHAT YOU'RE SAYING, BUT... BUT...
...I CAN'T JUST BLURT IT OUT, YOU INSENSITIVE CLOD!!
VOOSH
HINAGIKU-SAN!!
...
HINAGIKU-SAN...
SHAA

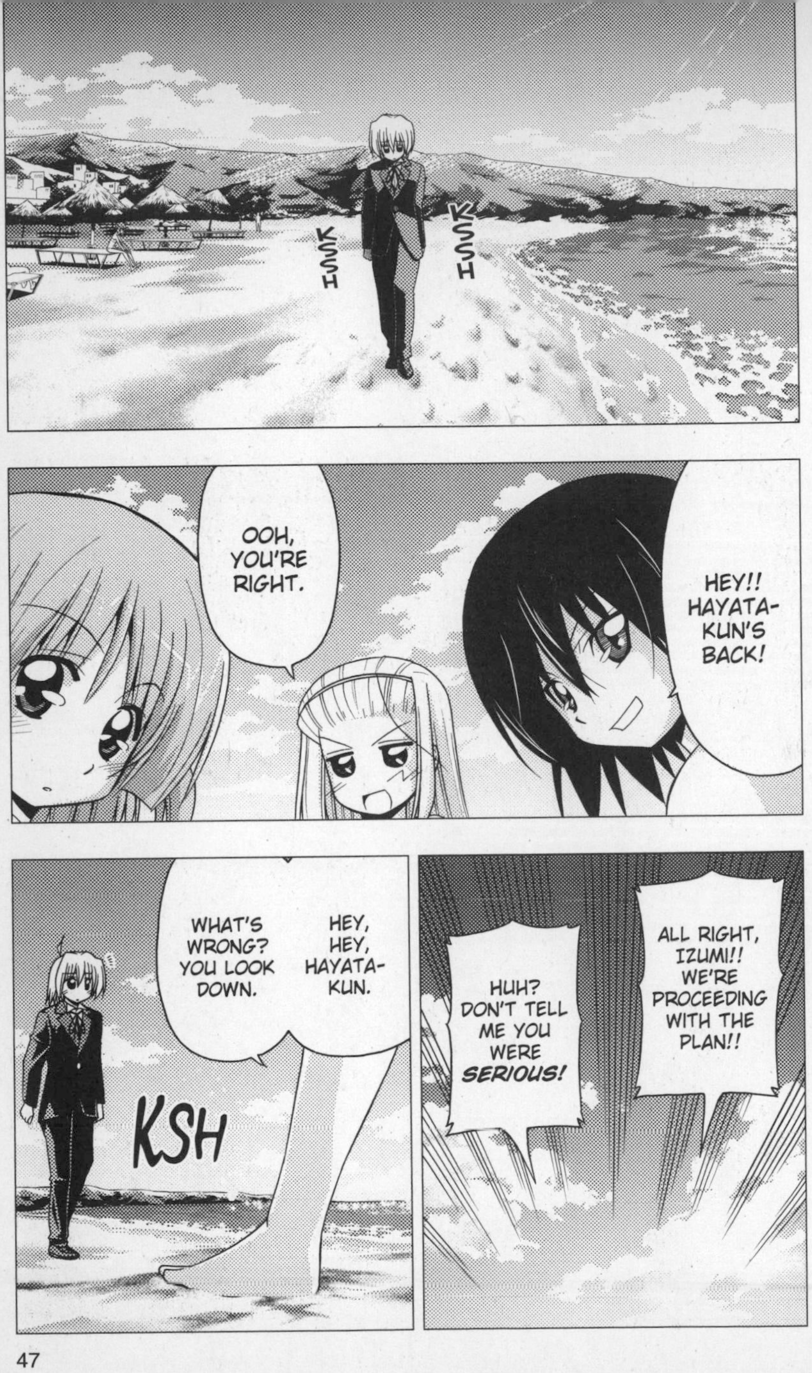
KSSH
KSSH
HEY!! HAYATA-KUN'S BACK!
OOH, YOU'RE RIGHT.
ALL RIGHT, IZUMI!! WE'RE PROCEEDING WITH THE PLAN!!
HUH? DON'T TELL ME YOU WERE SERIOUS!
HEY, HEY, HAYATA-KUN.
WHAT'S WRONG? YOU LOOK DOWN.
KSH

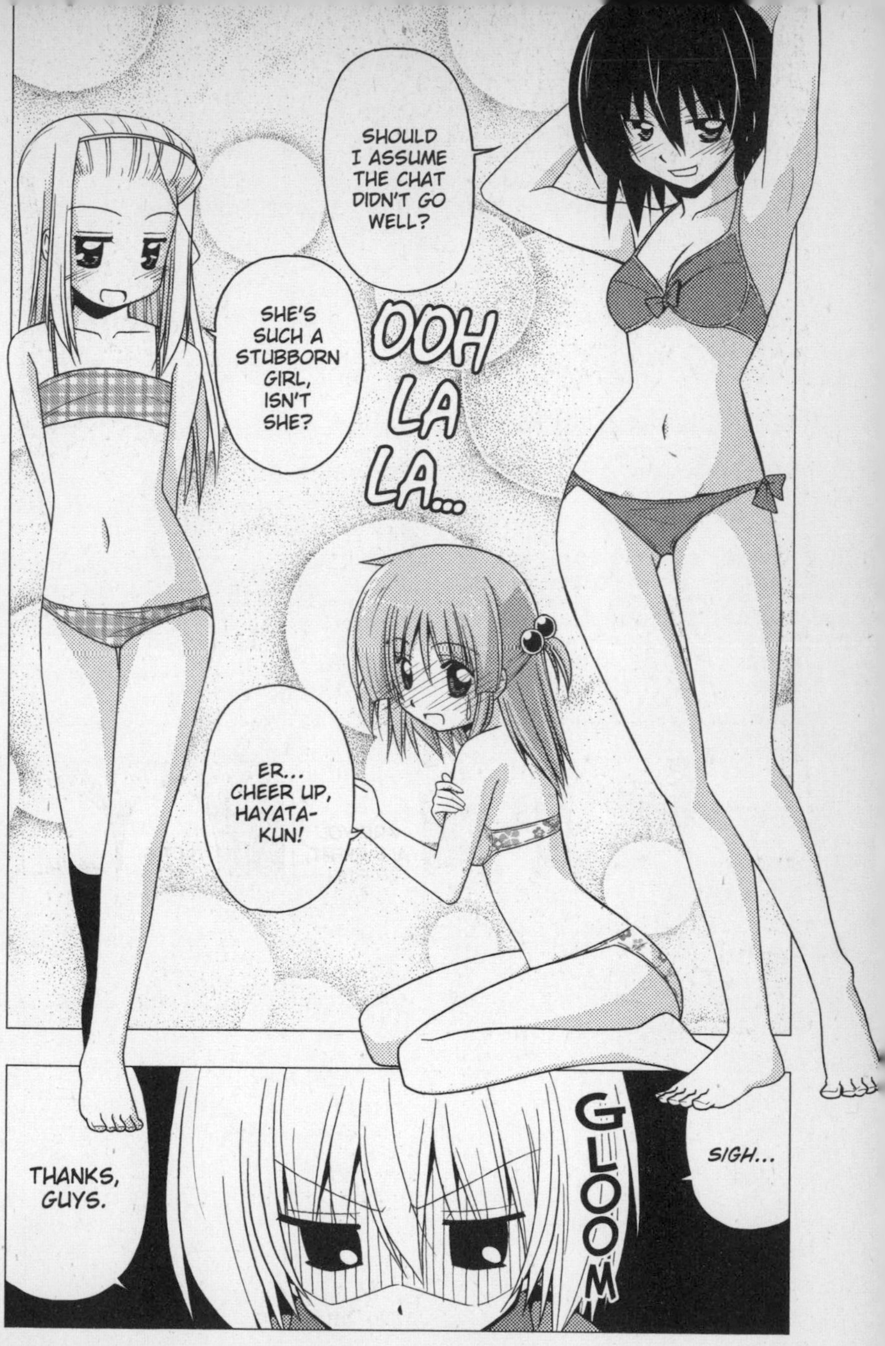
SHOULD I ASSUME THE CHAT DIDN'T GO WELL?
OOH LA LA...
SHE'S SUCH A STUBBORN GIRL, ISN'T SHE?
ER... CHEER UP, HAYATA-KUN!
SIGH...
GLOOM
THANKS, GUYS.

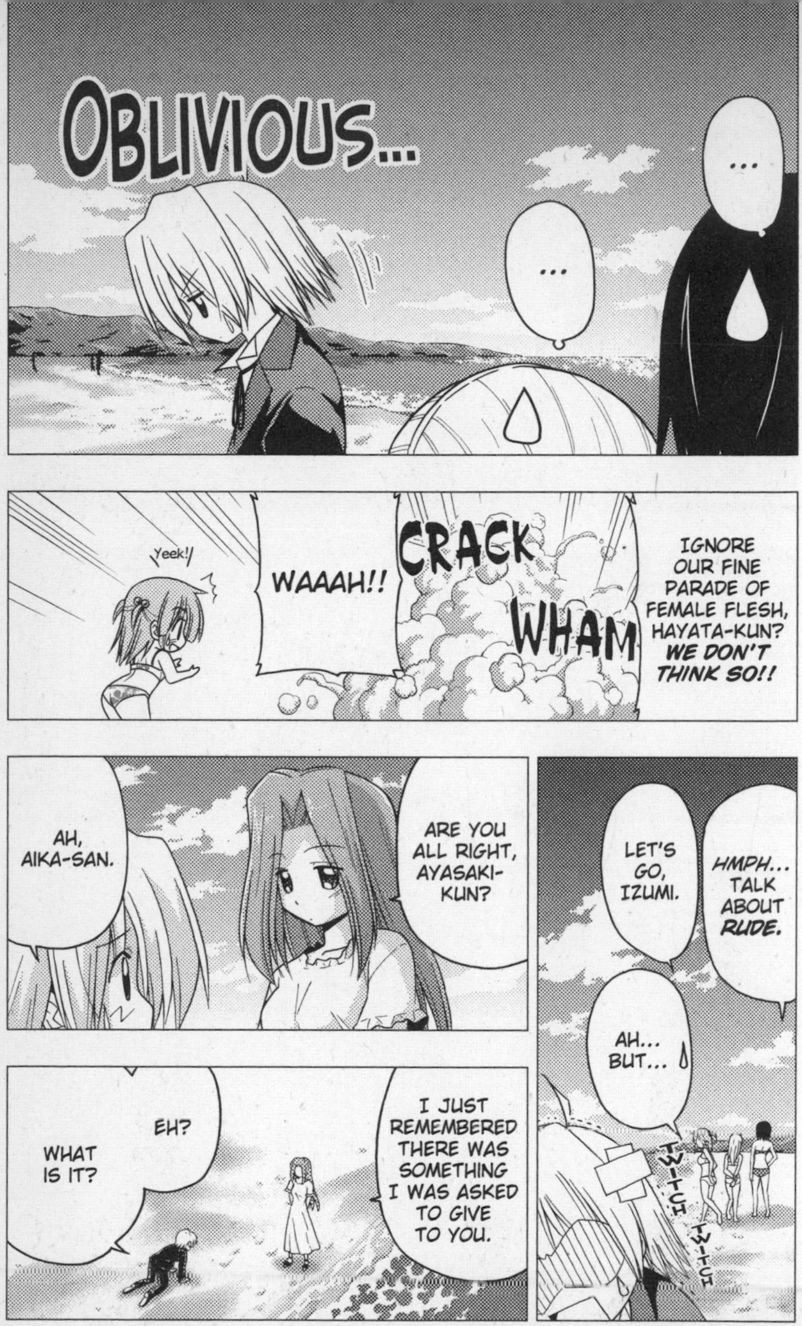
...
OBLIVIOUS...
...
IGNORE OUR FINE PARADE OF FEMALE FLESH, HAYATA-KUN? WE DON'T THINK SO!!
CRACK
WHAM
WAAAH!!
Yeek!
HMPH... TALK ABOUT RUDE.
LET'S GO, IZUMI.
AH... BUT...
TWITCH
TWITCH
ARE YOU ALL RIGHT, AYASAKI-KUN?
AH, AIKA-SAN.
I JUST REMEMBERED THERE WAS SOMETHING I WAS ASKED TO GIVE TO YOU.
EH?
WHAT IS IT?

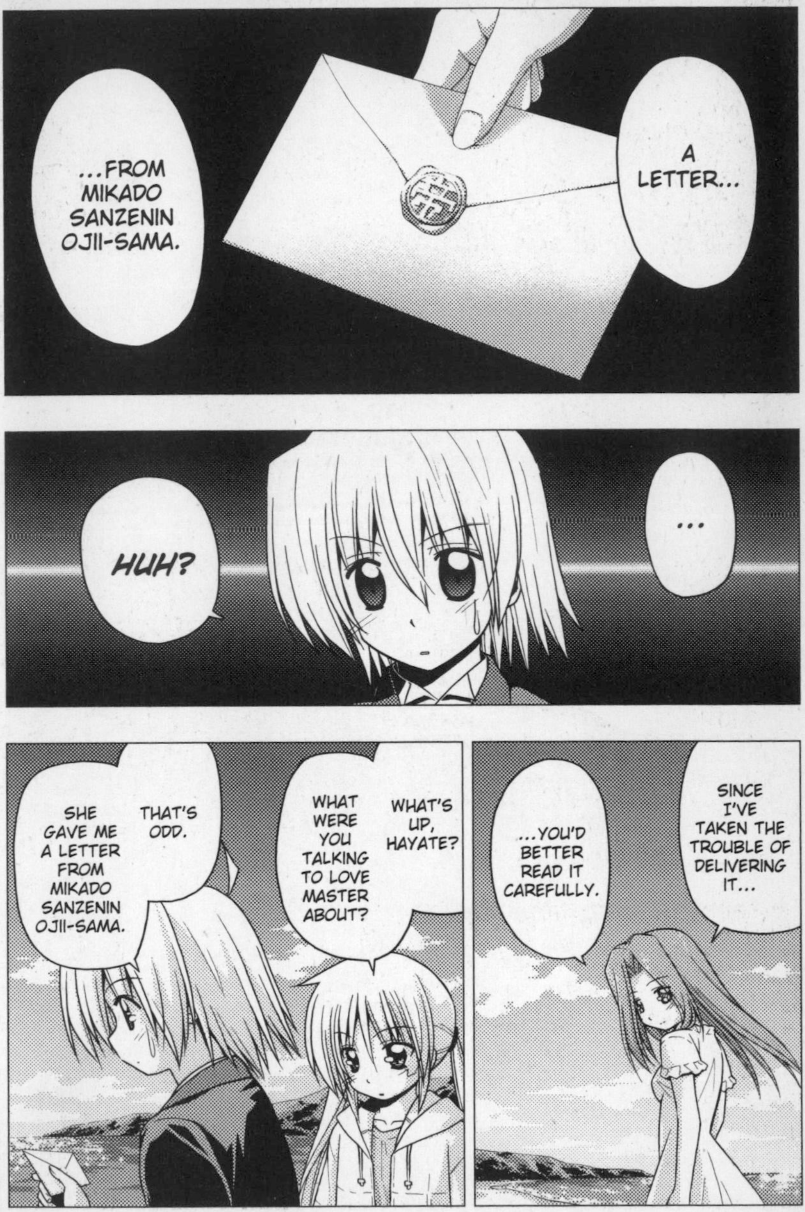
A LETTER...
...FROM MIKADO SANZENIN OJII-SAMA.
...
HUH?
SINCE I'VE TAKEN THE TROUBLE OF DELIVERING IT...
...YOU'D BETTER READ IT CAREFULLY.
WHAT'S UP, HAYATE?
WHAT WERE YOU TALKING TO LOVE MASTER ABOUT?
THAT'S ODD.
SHE GAVE ME A LETTER FROM MIKADO SANZENIN OJII-SAMA.

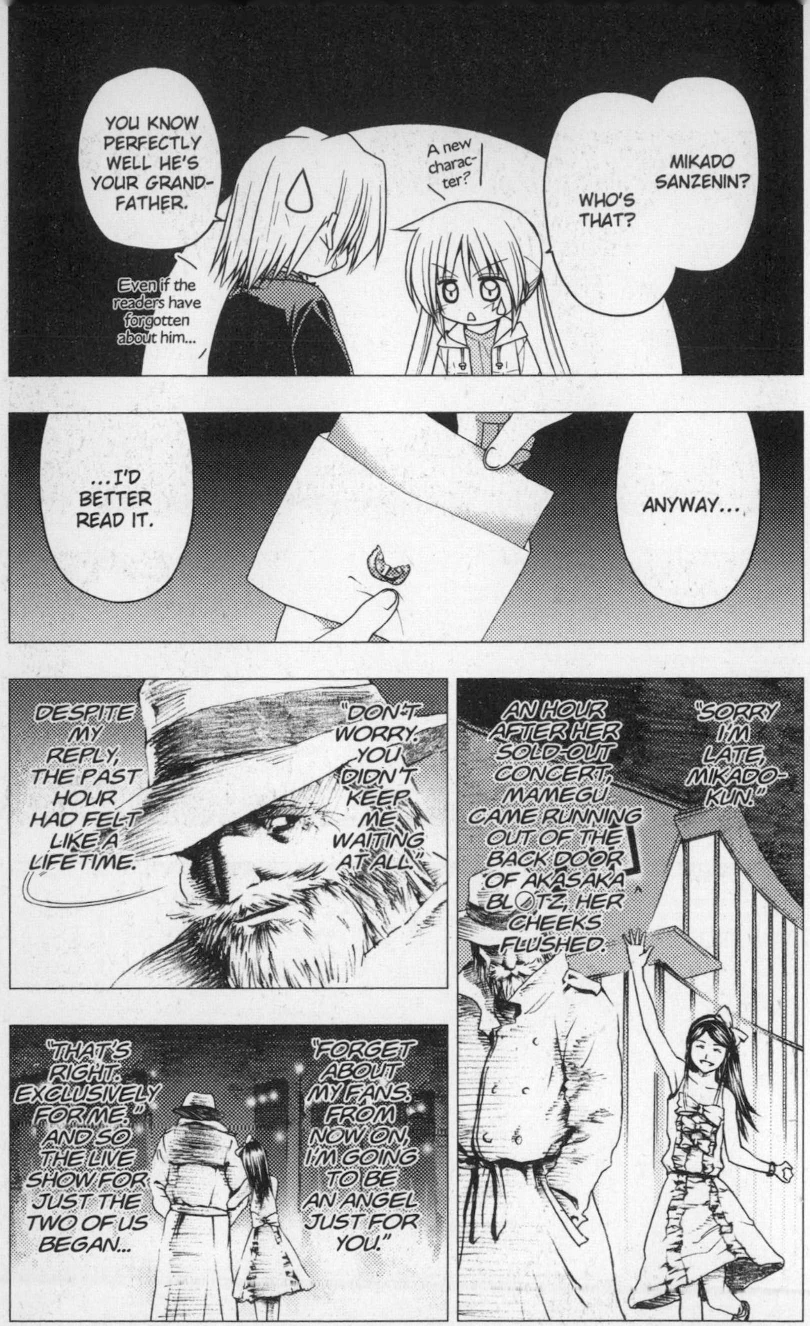
MIKADO SANZENIN?
WHO'S THAT?
A new character?
YOU KNOW PERFECTLY WELL HE'S YOUR GRAND-FATHER.
Even if the readers have forgotten about him...
ANYWAY...
...I'D BETTER READ IT.
"SORRY I'M LATE, MIKADO-KUN."
AN HOUR AFTER HER SOLD-OUT CONCERT, MAMEGU CAME RUNNING OUT OF THE BACK DOOR OF AKASAKA BL○TZ, HER CHEEKS FLUSHED.
"DON'T WORRY. YOU DIDN'T KEEP ME WAITING AT ALL."
DESPITE MY REPLY, THE PAST HOUR HAD FELT LIKE A LIFETIME.
"FORGET ABOUT MY FANS. FROM NOW ON, I'M GOING TO BE AN ANGEL JUST FOR YOU."
"THAT'S RIGHT. EXCLUSIVELY FOR ME." AND SO THE LIVE SHOW FOR JUST THE TWO OF US BEGAN...

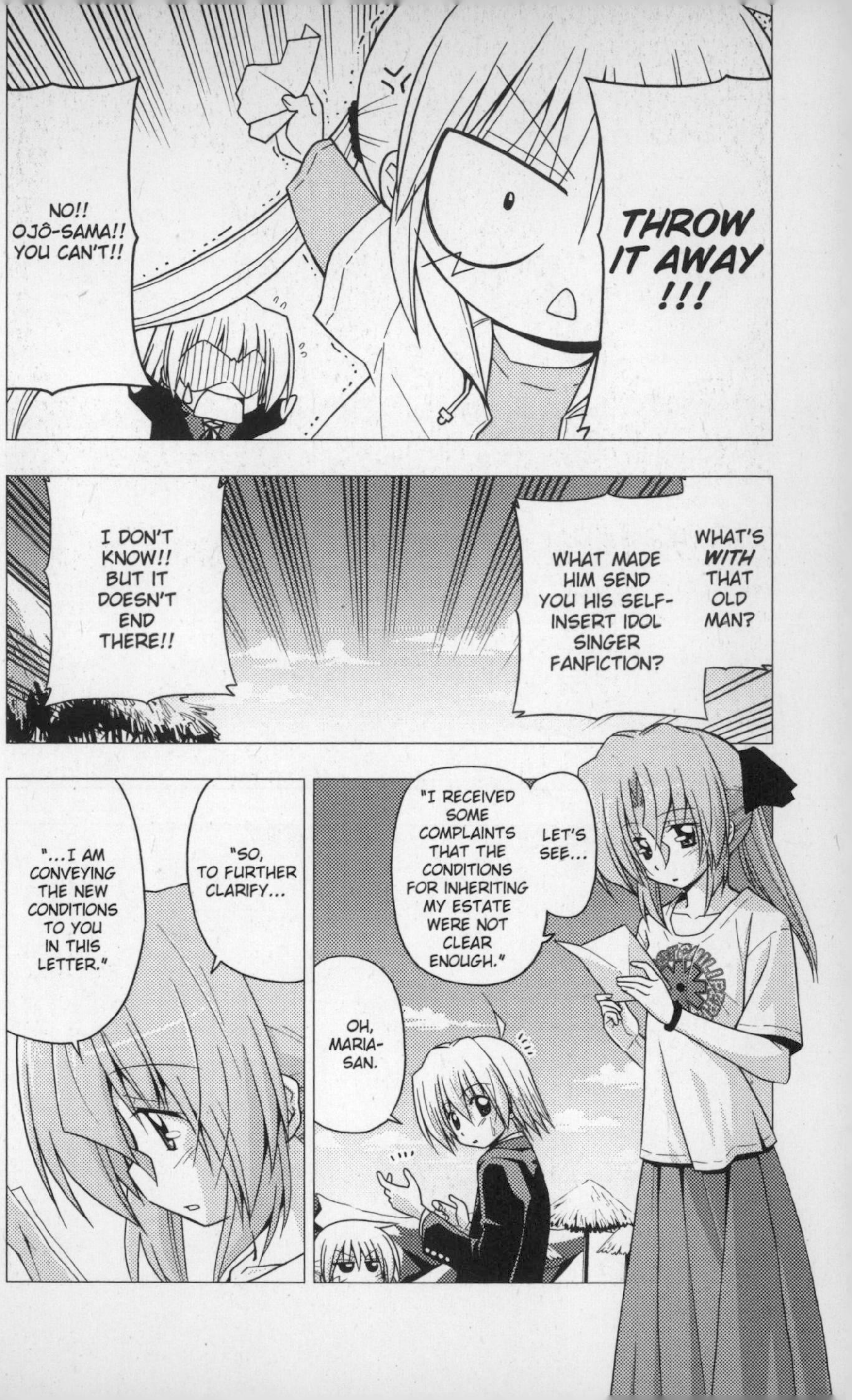
THROW IT AWAY !!!
NO!! OJÔ-SAMA!! YOU CAN'T!!
WHAT'S *WITH* THAT OLD MAN?
WHAT MADE HIM SEND YOU HIS SELF-INSERT IDOL SINGER FANFICTION?
I DON'T KNOW!! BUT IT DOESN'T END THERE!!
LET'S SEE...
"I RECEIVED SOME COMPLAINTS THAT THE CONDITIONS FOR INHERITING MY ESTATE WERE NOT CLEAR ENOUGH."
OH, MARIA-SAN.
"SO, TO FURTHER CLARIFY...
"...I AM CONVEYING THE NEW CONDITIONS TO YOU IN THIS LETTER."

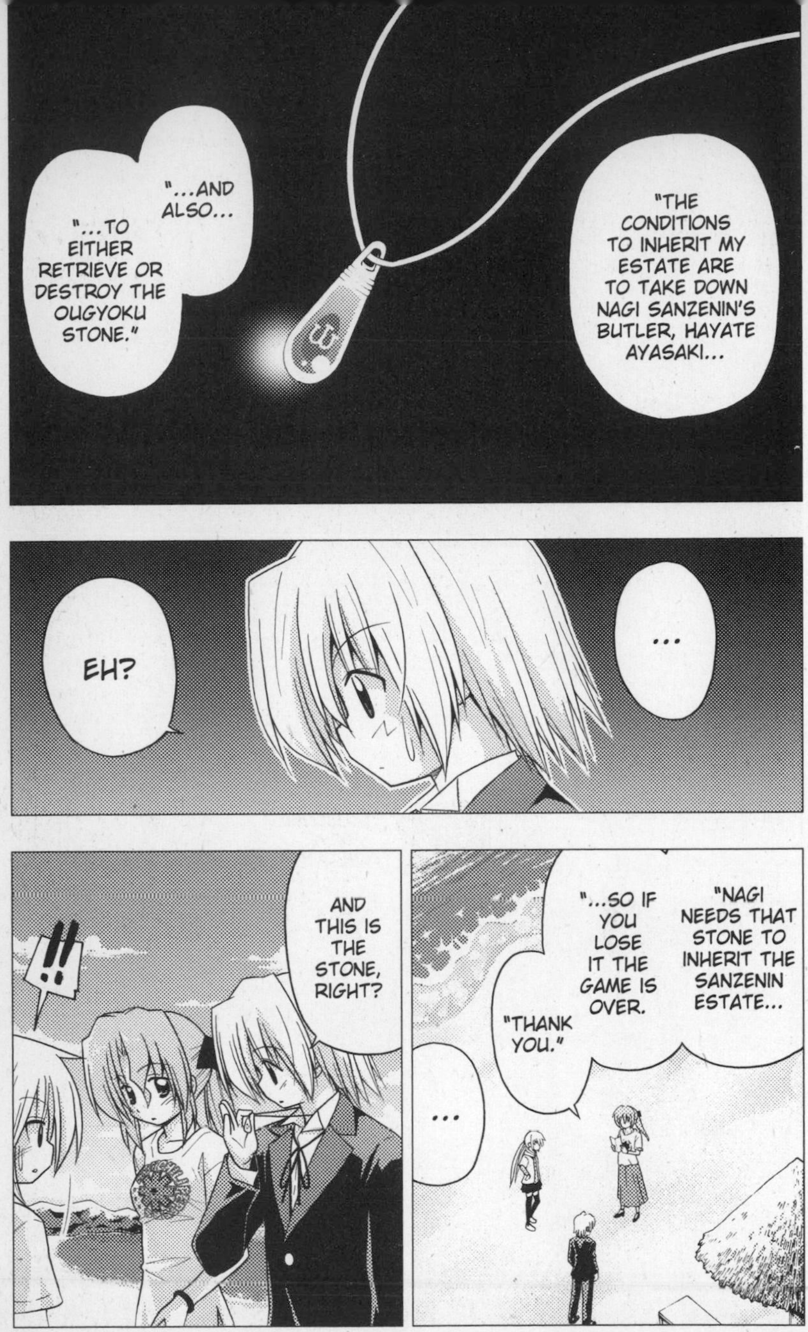
"THE CONDITIONS TO INHERIT MY ESTATE ARE TO TAKE DOWN NAGI SANZENIN'S BUTLER, HAYATE AYASAKI...
"...AND ALSO...
"...TO EITHER RETRIEVE OR DESTROY THE OUGYOKU STONE."
...
EH?
"NAGI NEEDS THAT STONE TO INHERIT THE SANZENIN ESTATE...
"...SO IF YOU LOSE IT THE GAME IS OVER.
"THANK YOU."
...
AND THIS IS THE STONE, RIGHT?
!!

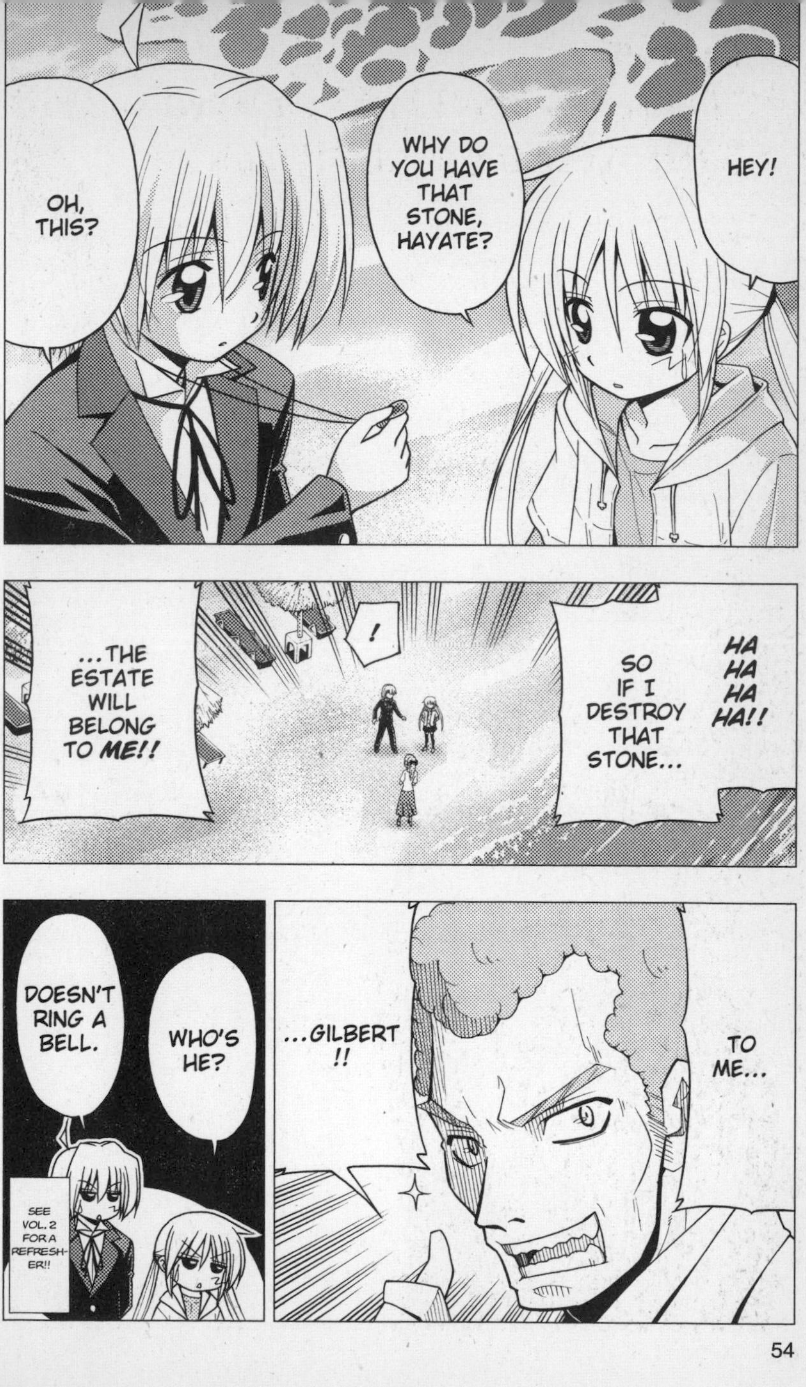
HEY!
WHY DO YOU HAVE THAT STONE, HAYATE?
OH, THIS?
HA HA HA HA!!
SO IF I DESTROY THAT STONE...
!
...THE ESTATE WILL BELONG TO ME!!
TO ME...
...GILBERT !!
WHO'S HE?
DOESN'T RING A BELL.
SEE VOL. 2 FOR A REFRESHER!!

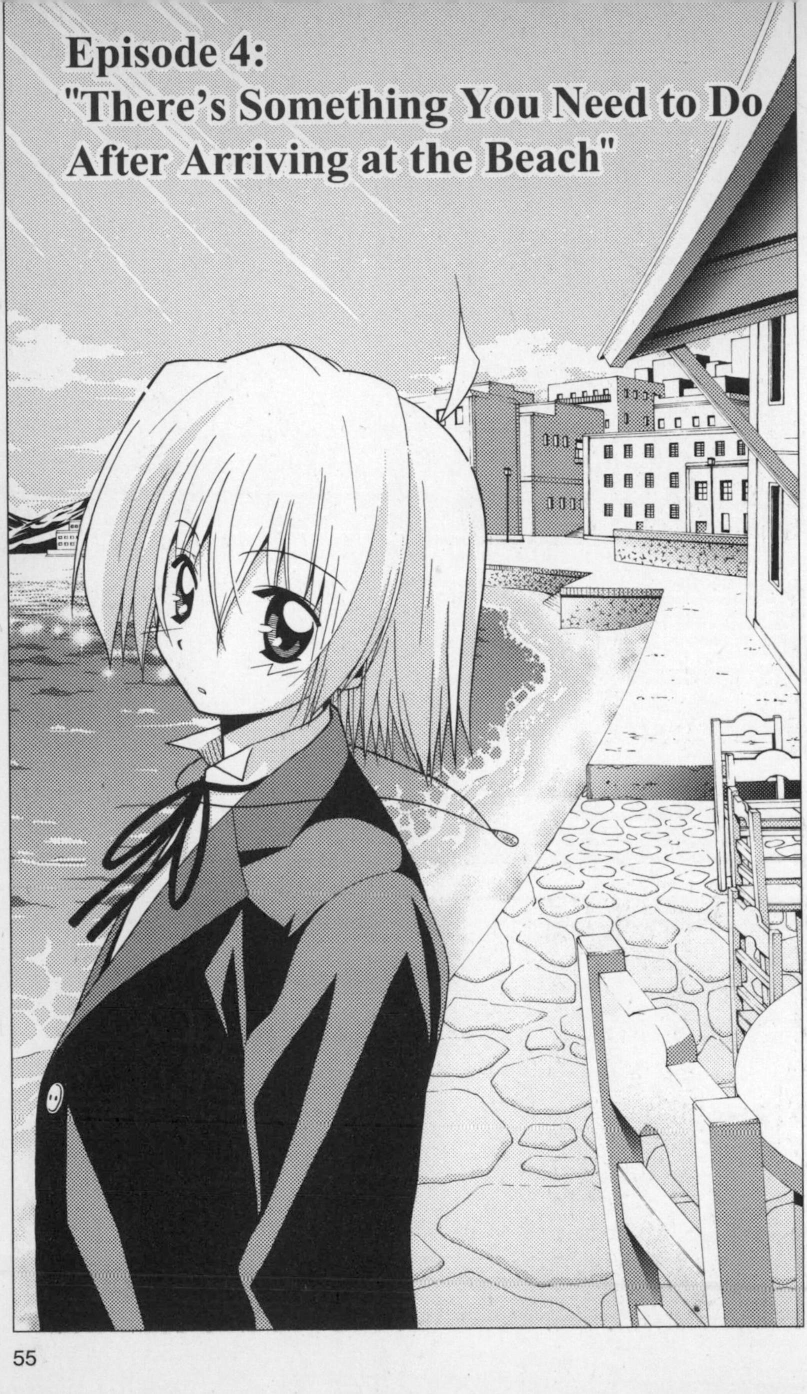
Episode 4:
"There's Something You Need to Do After Arriving at the Beach"
1

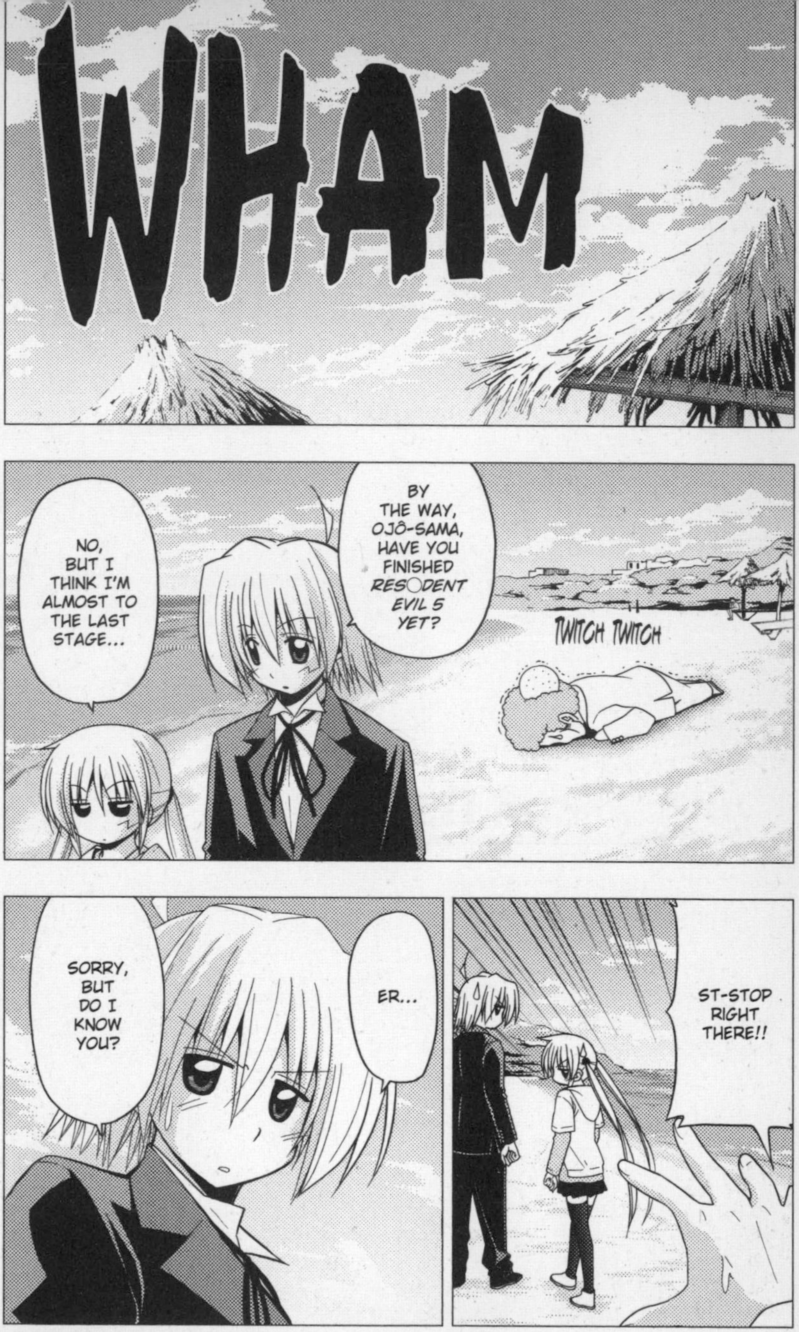
WHAM
BY THE WAY, OJÔ-SAMA, HAVE YOU FINISHED RES◯DENT EVIL 5 YET?
NO, BUT I THINK I'M ALMOST TO THE LAST STAGE...
TWITCH TWITCH
ST-STOP RIGHT THERE!!
ER...
SORRY, BUT DO I KNOW YOU?

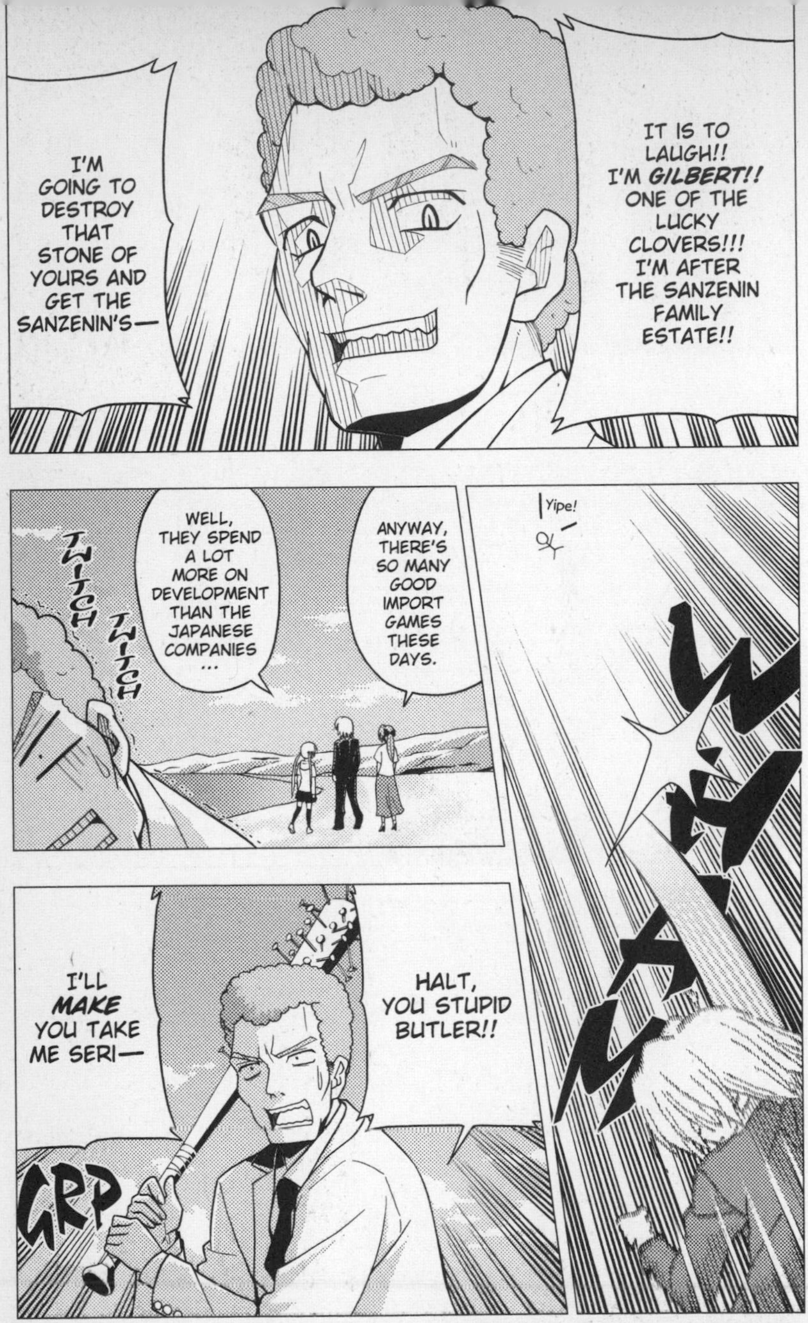
IT IS TO LAUGH!! I'M **GILBERT!!** ONE OF THE LUCKY CLOVERS!!! I'M AFTER THE SANZENIN FAMILY ESTATE!!
I'M GOING TO DESTROY THAT STONE OF YOURS AND GET THE SANZENIN'S—
Yipe!
WHAM
ANYWAY, THERE'S SO MANY GOOD IMPORT GAMES THESE DAYS.
WELL, THEY SPEND A LOT MORE ON DEVELOPMENT THAN THE JAPANESE COMPANIES ...
TWITCH
TWITCH
HALT, YOU STUPID BUTLER!!
I'LL **MAKE** YOU TAKE ME SERI—
GRP

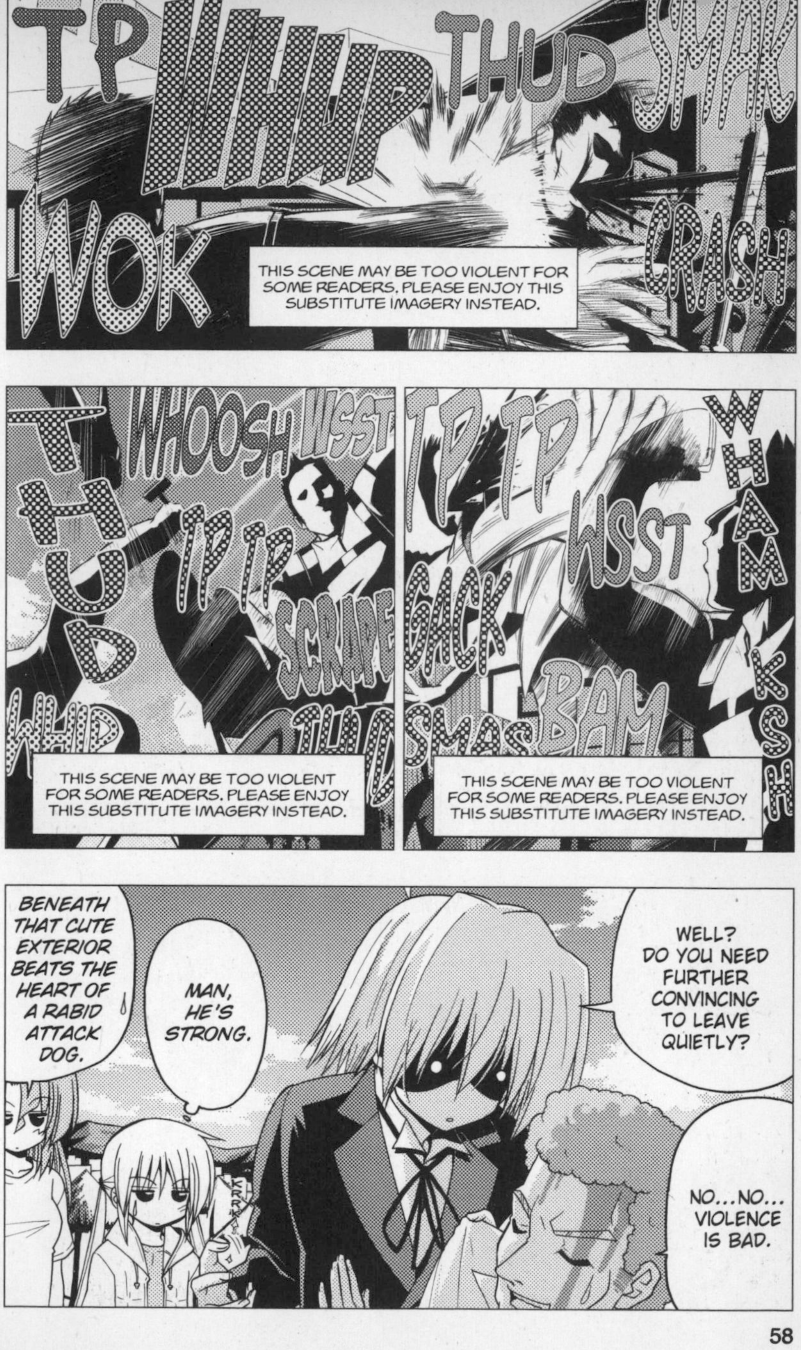
SMAK
THUD
WHHP
TP
CRASH
WOK
THIS SCENE MAY BE TOO VIOLENT FOR SOME READERS. PLEASE ENJOY THIS SUBSTITUTE IMAGERY INSTEAD.
WHAMKSH
TP TP
WSST
GACK
BAM
THIS SCENE MAY BE TOO VIOLENT FOR SOME READERS. PLEASE ENJOY THIS SUBSTITUTE IMAGERY INSTEAD.
WSST
WHOOSH
THUD
TP TP
THIS SCENE MAY BE TOO VIOLENT FOR SOME READERS. PLEASE ENJOY THIS SUBSTITUTE IMAGERY INSTEAD.
WELL? DO YOU NEED FURTHER CONVINCING TO LEAVE QUIETLY?
NO...NO... VIOLENCE IS BAD.
MAN, HE'S STRONG.
BENEATH THAT CUTE EXTERIOR BEATS THE HEART OF A RABID ATTACK DOG.

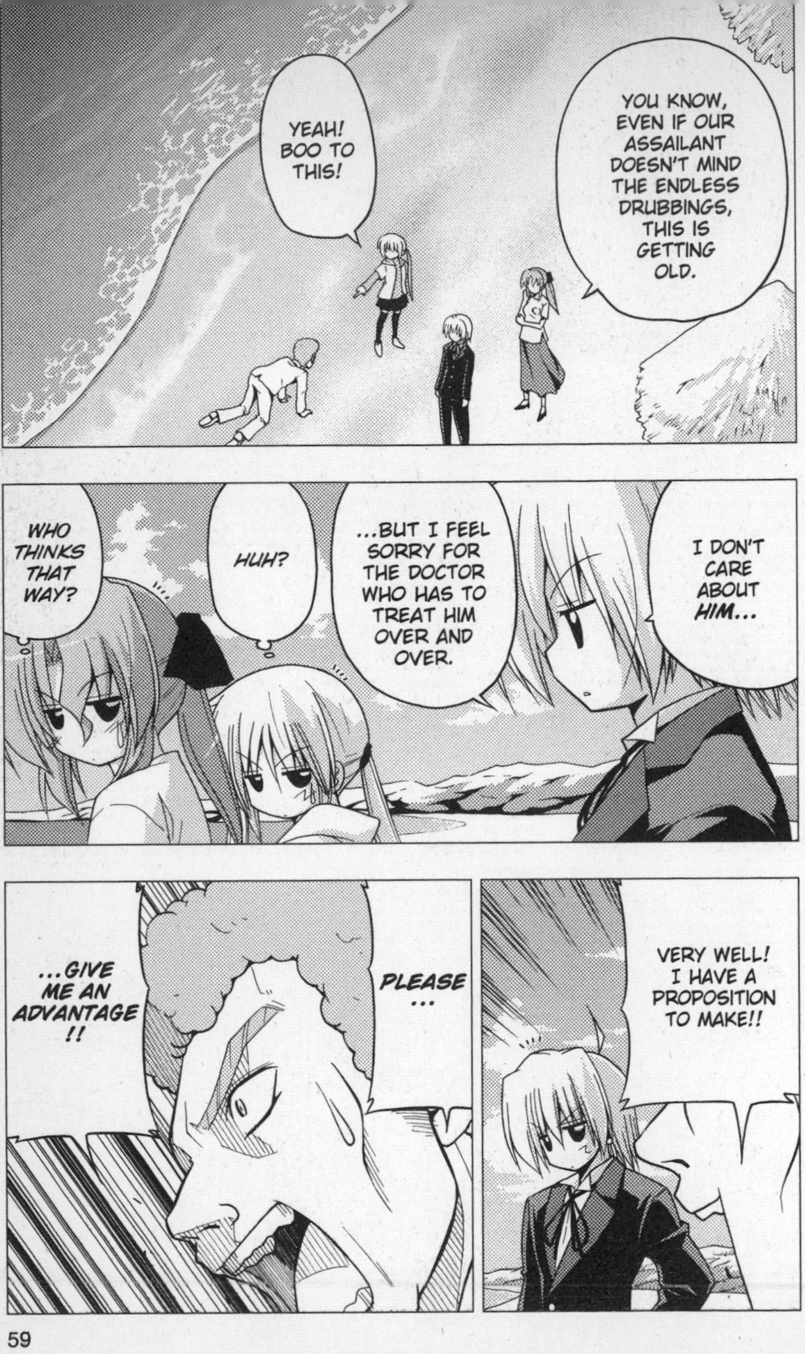
YOU KNOW, EVEN IF OUR ASSAILANT DOESN'T MIND THE ENDLESS DRUBBINGS, THIS IS GETTING OLD.
YEAH! BOO TO THIS!
I DON'T CARE ABOUT *HIM*...
...BUT I FEEL SORRY FOR THE DOCTOR WHO HAS TO TREAT HIM OVER AND OVER.
HUH?
WHO THINKS THAT WAY?
VERY WELL! I HAVE A PROPOSITION TO MAKE!!
PLEASE...
...GIVE ME AN ADVANTAGE!!

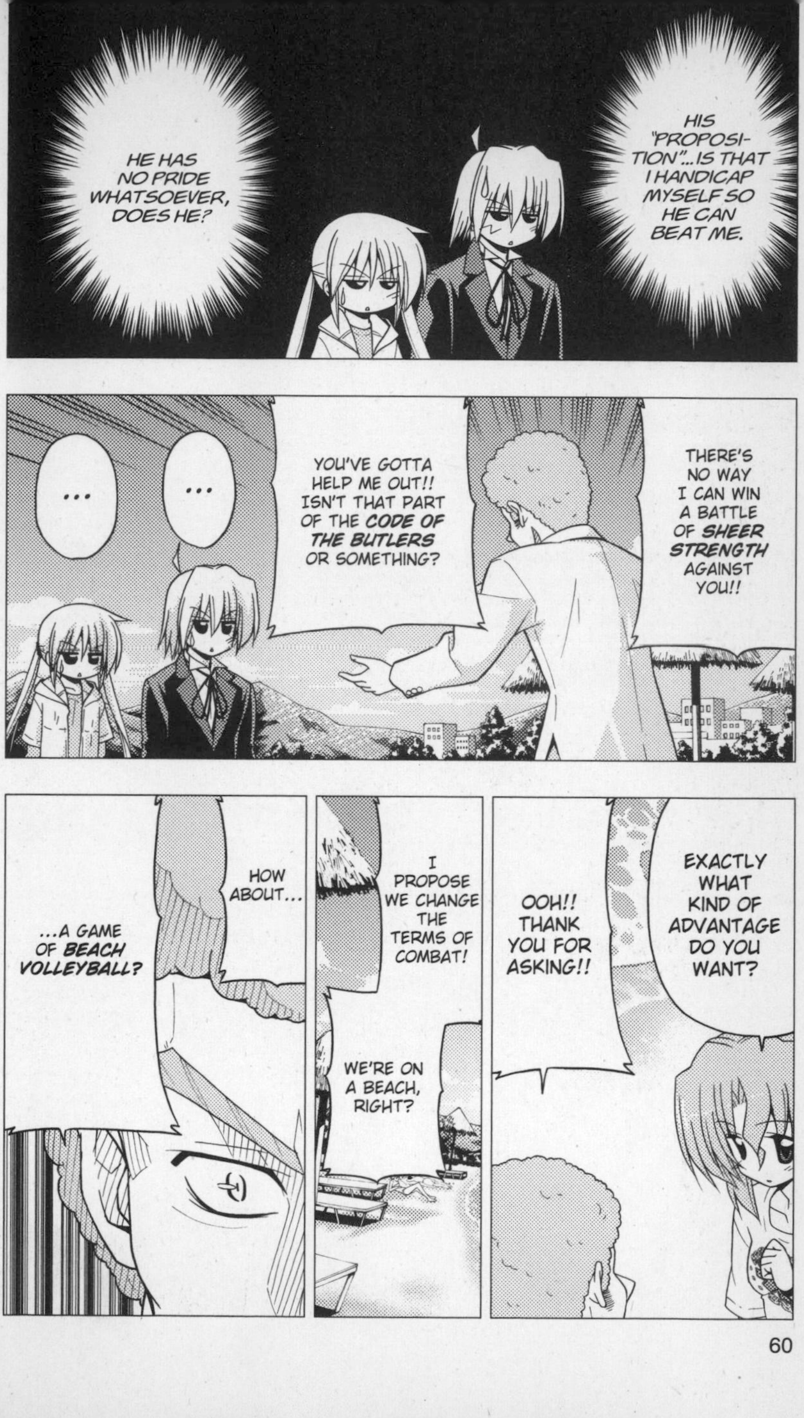
HIS "PROPOSITION"...IS THAT I HANDICAP MYSELF SO HE CAN BEAT ME.
HE HAS NO PRIDE WHATSOEVER, DOES HE?
THERE'S NO WAY I CAN WIN A BATTLE OF **SHEER STRENGTH** AGAINST YOU!!
YOU'VE GOTTA HELP ME OUT!! ISN'T THAT PART OF THE **CODE OF THE BUTLERS** OR SOMETHING?
...
...
EXACTLY WHAT KIND OF ADVANTAGE DO YOU WANT?
OOH!! THANK YOU FOR ASKING!!
I PROPOSE WE CHANGE THE TERMS OF COMBAT!
WE'RE ON A BEACH, RIGHT?
HOW ABOUT...
...A GAME OF **BEACH VOLLEYBALL?**

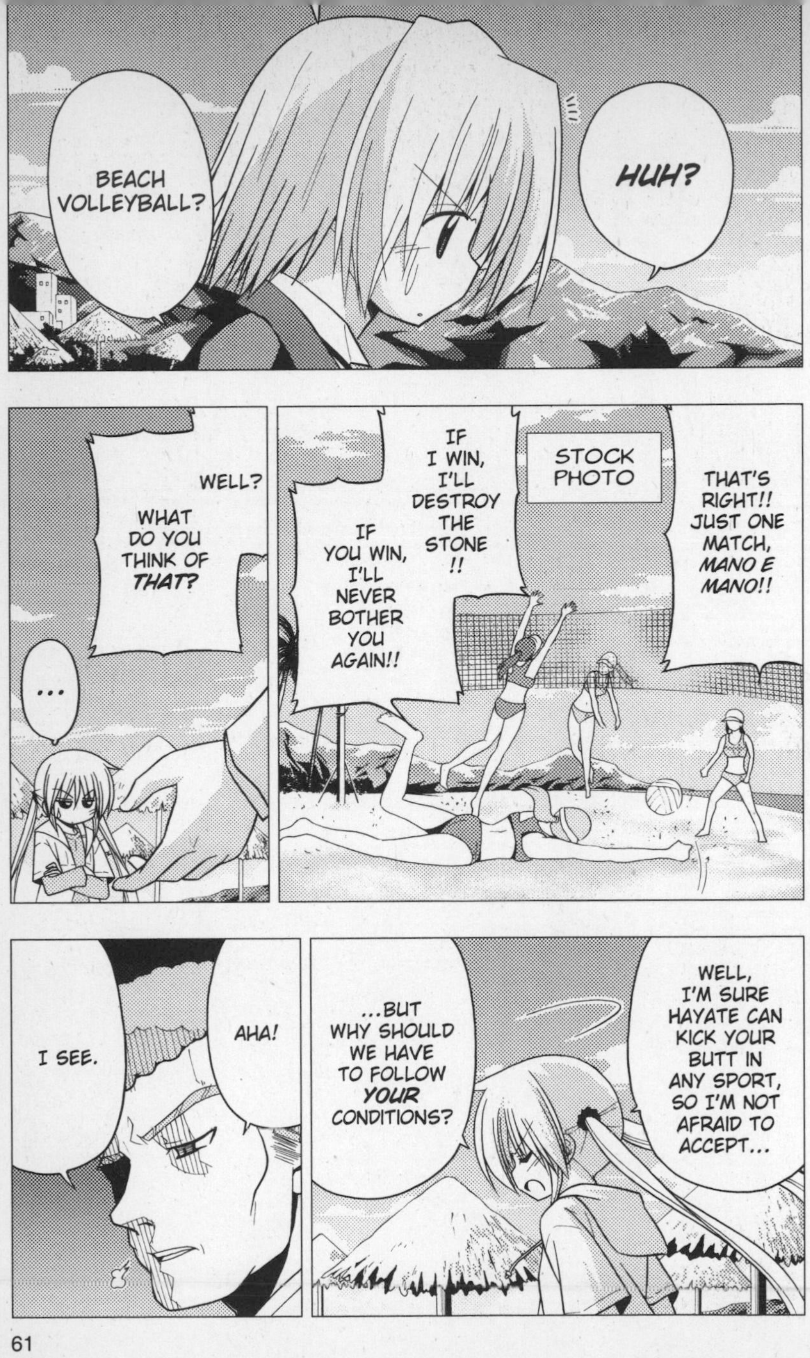
HUH?
BEACH VOLLEYBALL?
STOCK PHOTO
THAT'S RIGHT!! JUST ONE MATCH, *MANO E MANO!!*
IF I WIN, I'LL DESTROY THE STONE !!
IF YOU WIN, I'LL NEVER BOTHER YOU AGAIN!!
WELL?
WHAT DO YOU THINK OF *THAT?*
...
WELL, I'M SURE HAYATE CAN KICK YOUR BUTT IN ANY SPORT, SO I'M NOT AFRAID TO ACCEPT...
...BUT WHY SHOULD WE HAVE TO FOLLOW ***YOUR*** CONDITIONS?
AHA!
I SEE.

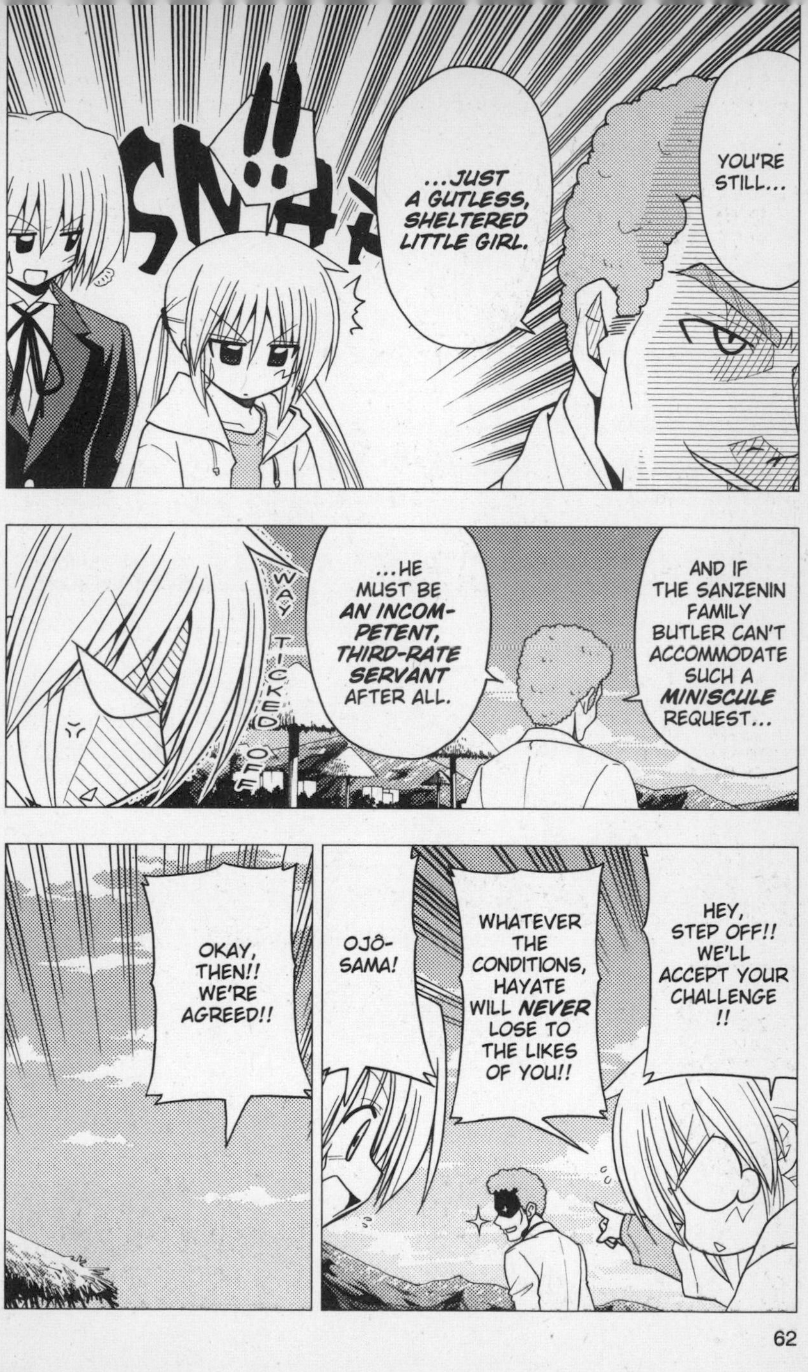
YOU'RE STILL...
...JUST A GUTLESS, SHELTERED LITTLE GIRL.
AND IF THE SANZENIN FAMILY BUTLER CAN'T ACCOMMODATE SUCH A *MINISCULE* REQUEST...
...HE MUST BE *AN INCOMPETENT, THIRD-RATE SERVANT* AFTER ALL.
WAY TICKED OFF
HEY, STEP OFF!! WE'LL ACCEPT YOUR CHALLENGE!!
WHATEVER THE CONDITIONS, HAYATE WILL *NEVER* LOSE TO THE LIKES OF YOU!!
OJÔ-SAMA!
OKAY, THEN!! WE'RE AGREED!!

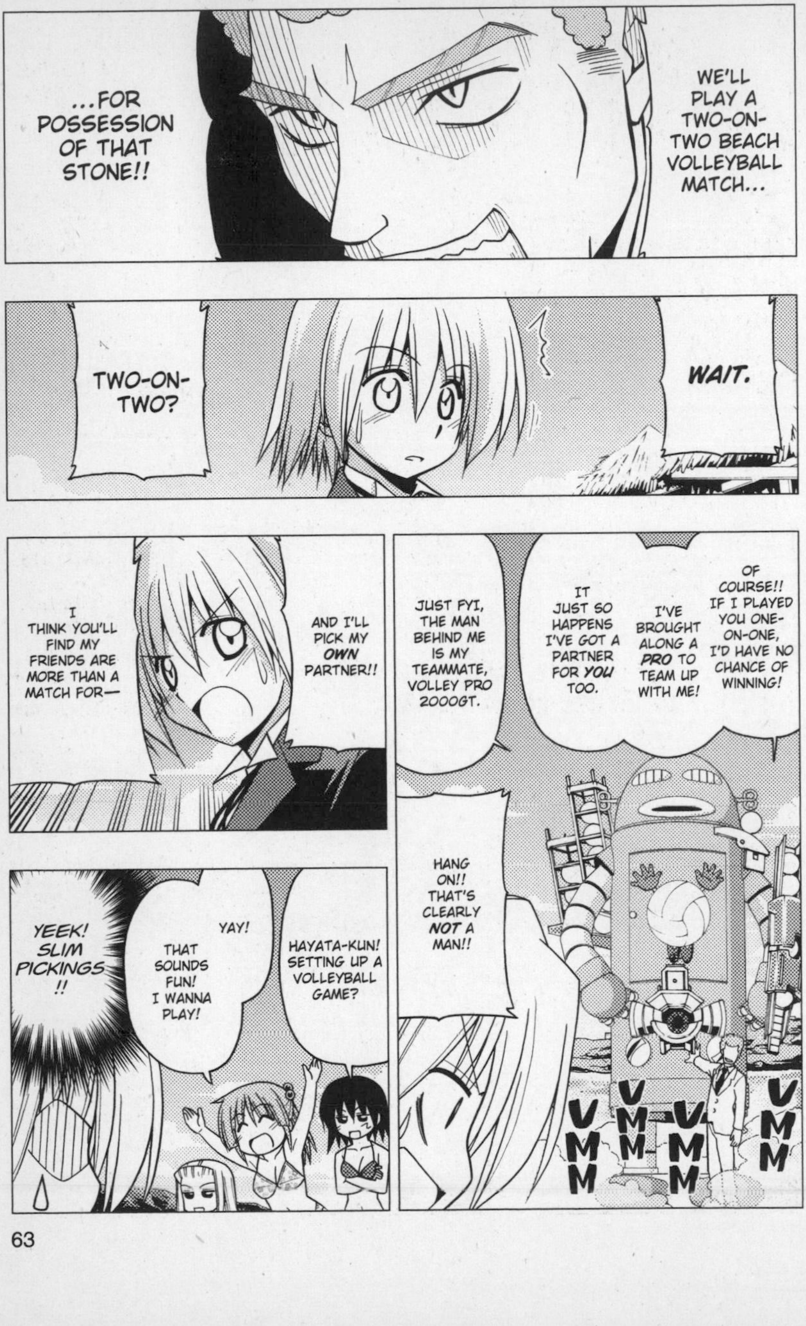
WE'LL PLAY A TWO-ON-TWO BEACH VOLLEYBALL MATCH...
...FOR POSSESSION OF THAT STONE!!
WAIT.
TWO-ON-TWO?
OF COURSE!! IF I PLAYED YOU ONE-ON-ONE, I'D HAVE NO CHANCE OF WINNING!
I'VE BROUGHT ALONG A PRO TO TEAM UP WITH ME!
IT JUST SO HAPPENS I'VE GOT A PARTNER FOR YOU TOO.
JUST FYI, THE MAN BEHIND ME IS MY TEAMMATE, VOLLEY PRO 2000GT.
HANG ON!! THAT'S CLEARLY NOT A MAN!!
VMM
VMMM
VMM-
VMMM
AND I'LL PICK MY OWN PARTNER!!
I THINK YOU'LL FIND MY FRIENDS ARE MORE THAN A MATCH FOR—
HAYATA-KUN! SETTING UP A VOLLEYBALL GAME?
YAY! THAT SOUNDS FUN! I WANNA PLAY!
YEEK! SLIM PICKINGS!!

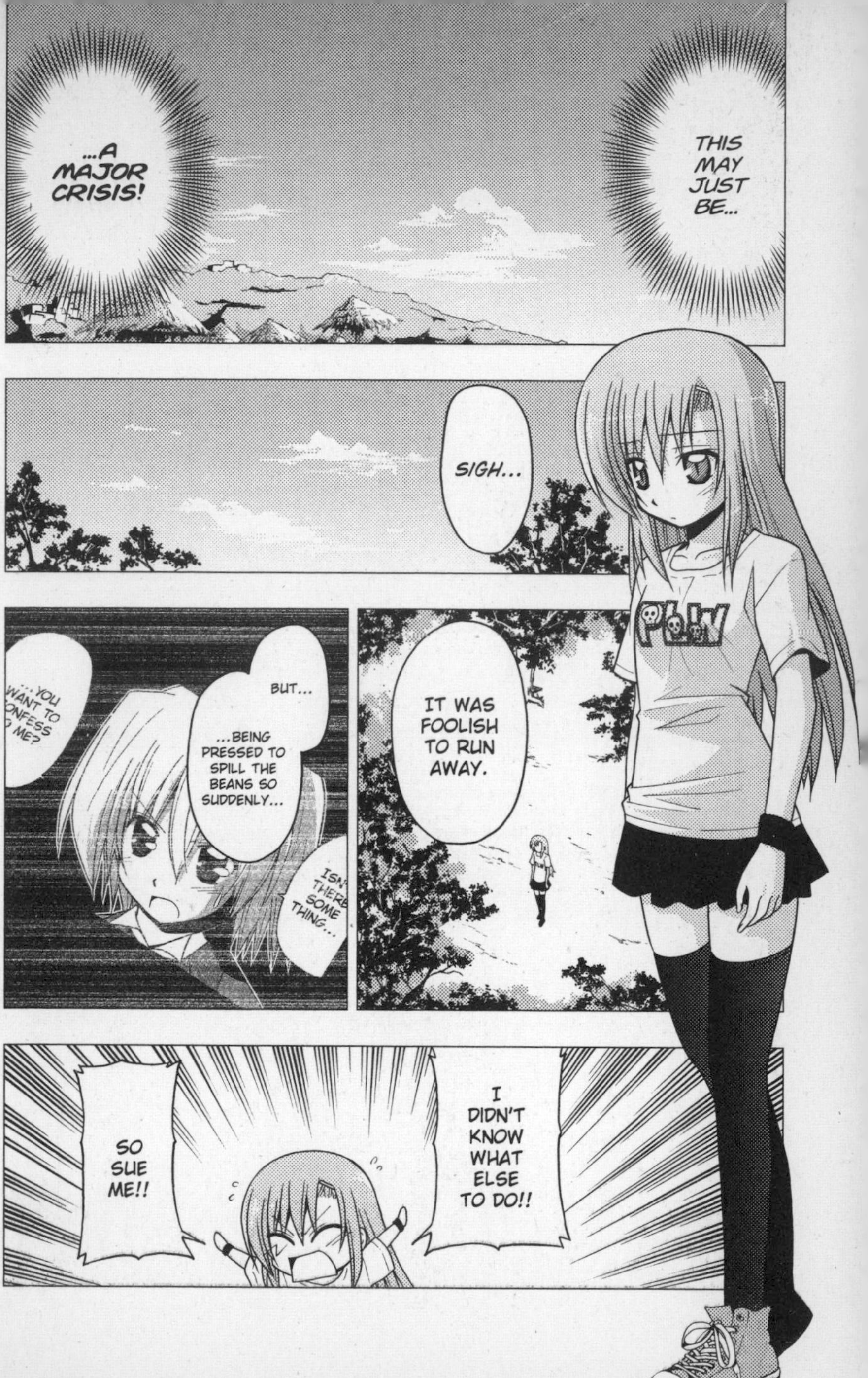
THIS MAY JUST BE...
...A MAJOR CRISIS!
SIGH...
IT WAS FOOLISH TO RUN AWAY.
BUT...
...BEING PRESSED TO SPILL THE BEANS SO SUDDENLY...
...YOU WANT TO ONFESS O ME?
ISN THERE SOME THING...
I DIDN'T KNOW WHAT ELSE TO DO!!
SO SUE ME!!

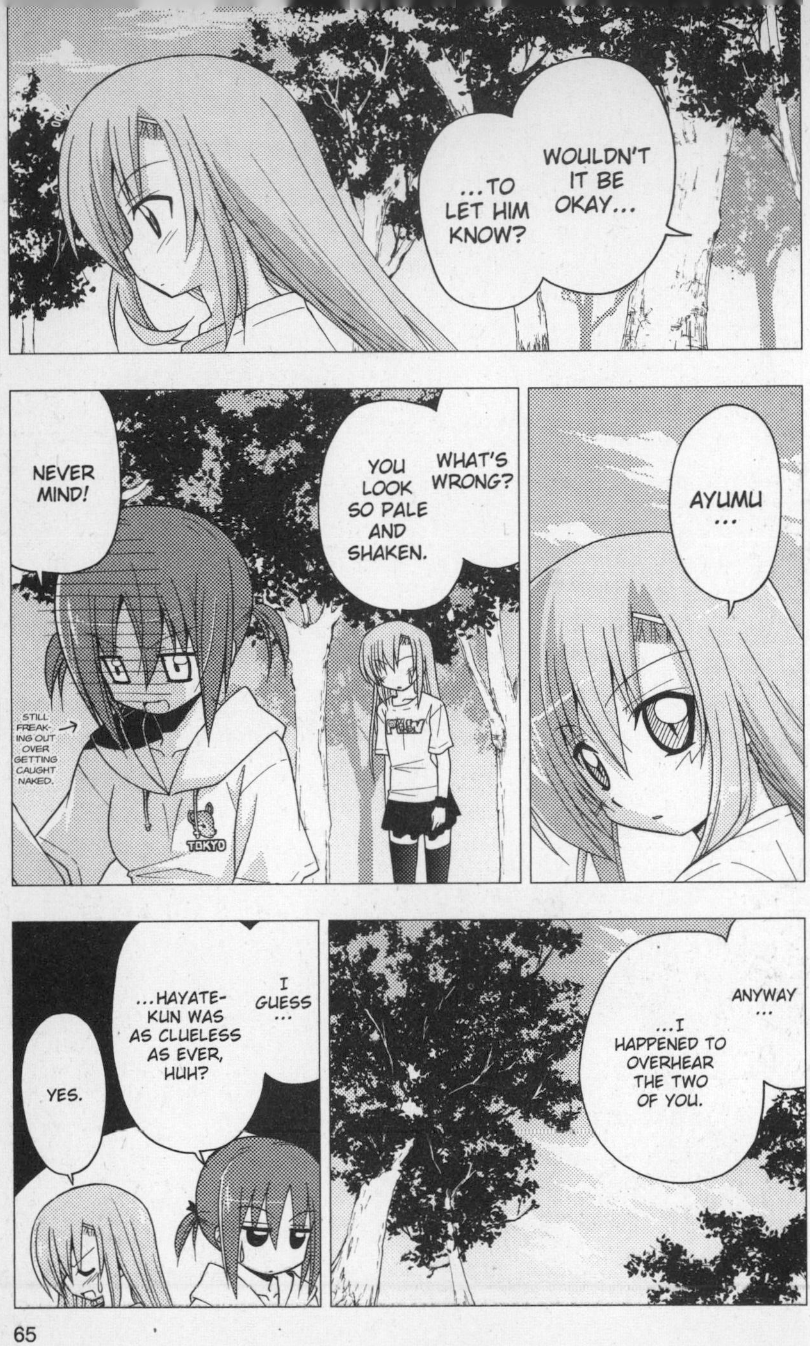
WOULDN'T IT BE OKAY...
...TO LET HIM KNOW?
AYUMU ...
WHAT'S WRONG?
YOU LOOK SO PALE AND SHAKEN.
NEVER MIND!
STILL FREAKING OUT OVER GETTING CAUGHT NAKED.
ANYWAY ...
...I HAPPENED TO OVERHEAR THE TWO OF YOU.
I GUESS ...
...HAYATE-KUN WAS AS CLUELESS AS EVER, HUH?
YES.

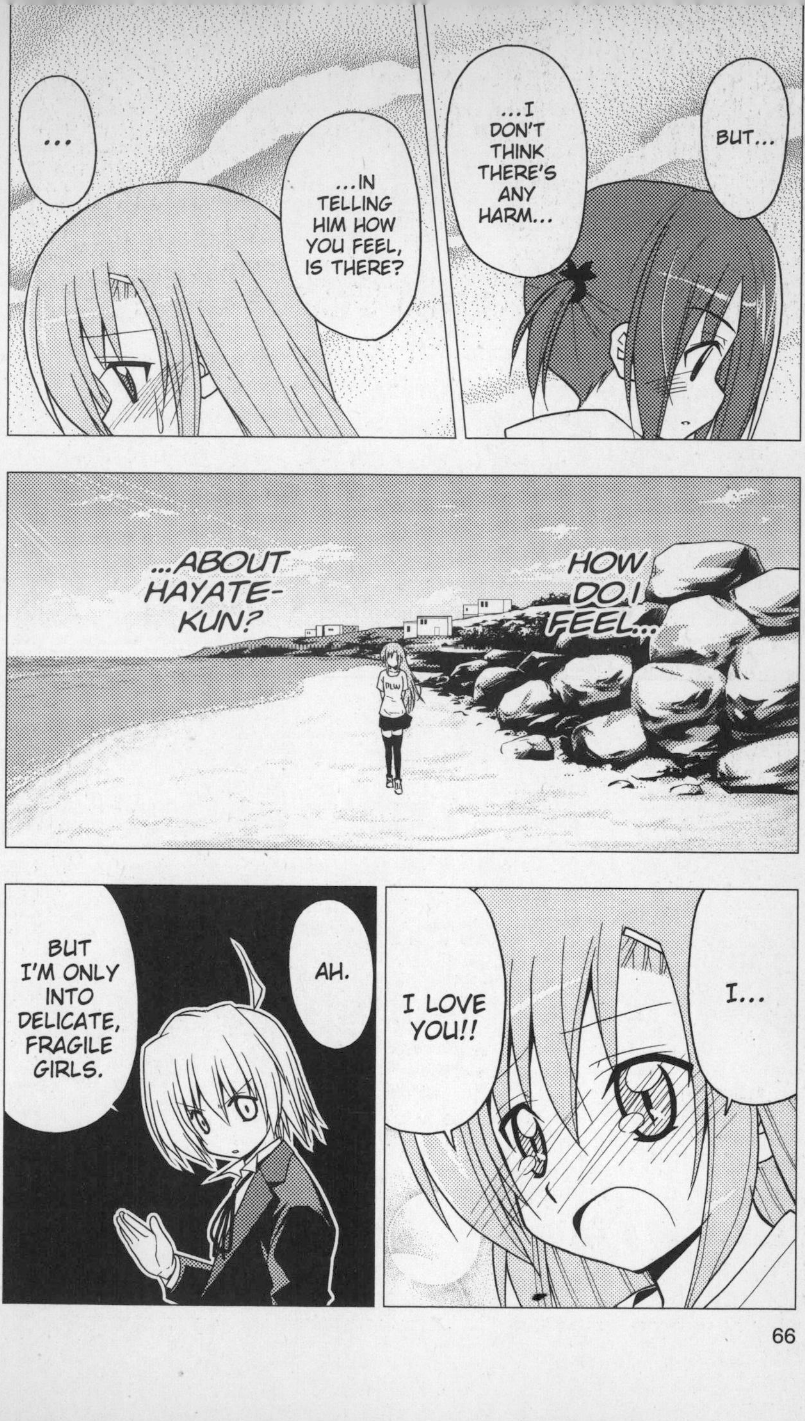
BUT...
...I DON'T THINK THERE'S ANY HARM...
...IN TELLING HIM HOW YOU FEEL, IS THERE?
...
HOW DO I FEEL...
...ABOUT HAYATE-KUN?
I...
I LOVE YOU!!
AH.
BUT I'M ONLY INTO DELICATE, FRAGILE GIRLS.

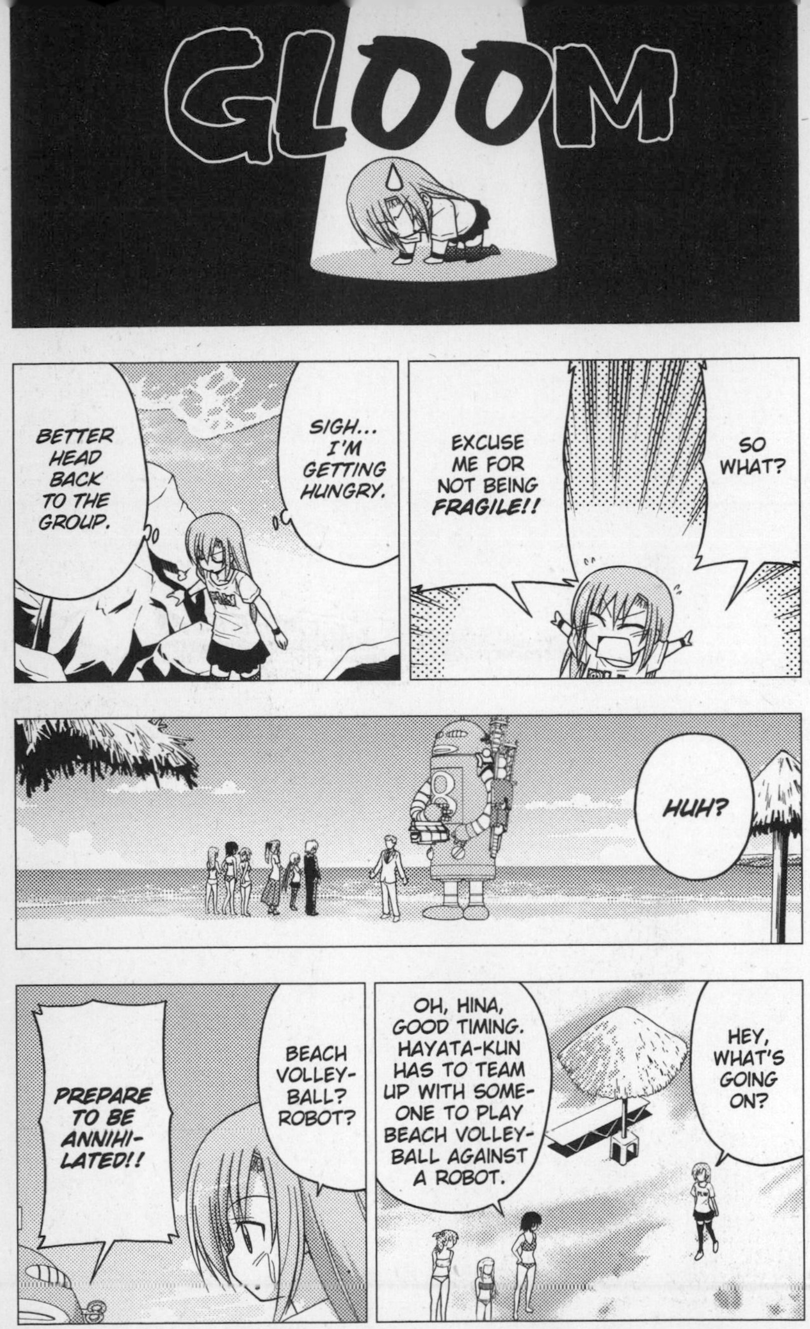
GLOOM
SO WHAT?
EXCUSE ME FOR NOT BEING FRAGILE!!
SIGH... I'M GETTING HUNGRY.
BETTER HEAD BACK TO THE GROUP.
HUH?
HEY, WHAT'S GOING ON?
OH, HINA, GOOD TIMING. HAYATA-KUN HAS TO TEAM UP WITH SOME-ONE TO PLAY BEACH VOLLEY-BALL AGAINST A ROBOT.
BEACH VOLLEY-BALL? ROBOT?
PREPARE TO BE ANNIHI-LATED!!

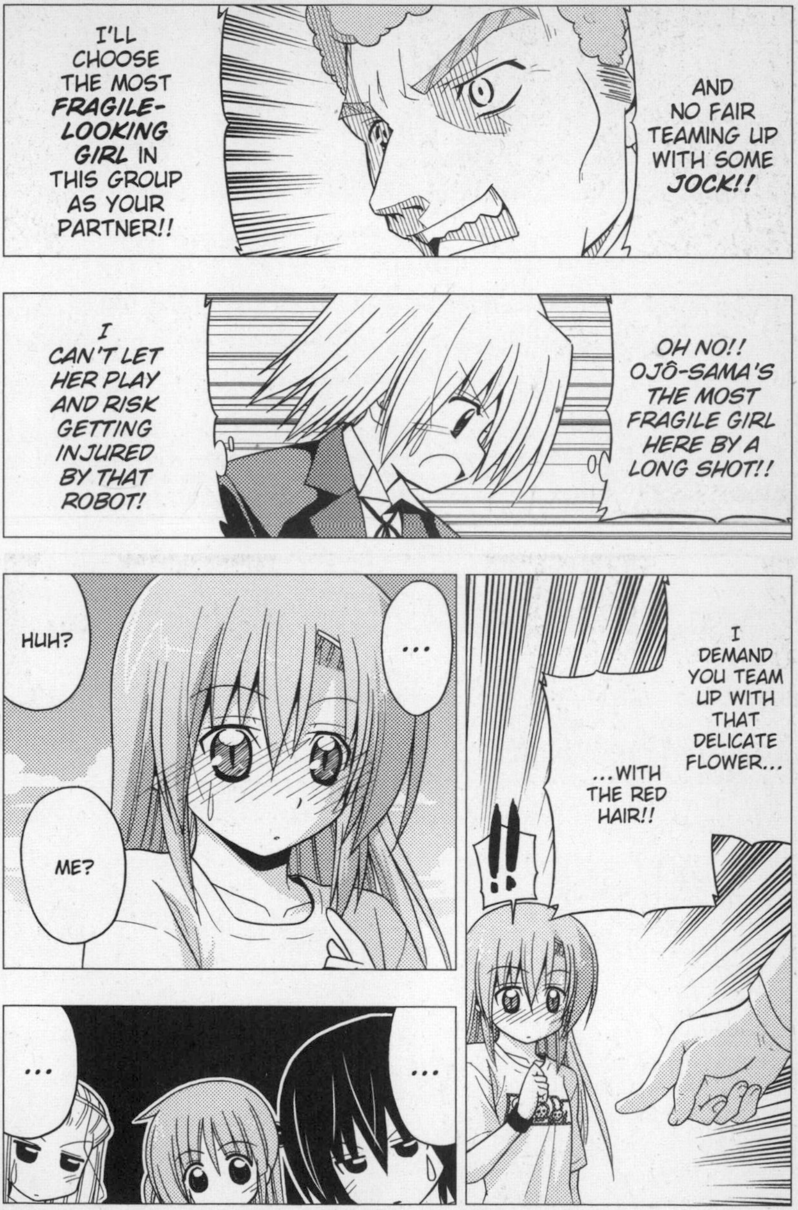
I'LL CHOOSE THE MOST FRAGILE-LOOKING GIRL IN THIS GROUP AS YOUR PARTNER!!
AND NO FAIR TEAMING UP WITH SOME JOCK!!
OH NO!! OJÔ-SAMA'S THE MOST FRAGILE GIRL HERE BY A LONG SHOT!!
I CAN'T LET HER PLAY AND RISK GETTING INJURED BY THAT ROBOT!
I DEMAND YOU TEAM UP WITH THAT DELICATE FLOWER...
...WITH THE RED HAIR!!
!!
...
HUH?
ME?
...
...

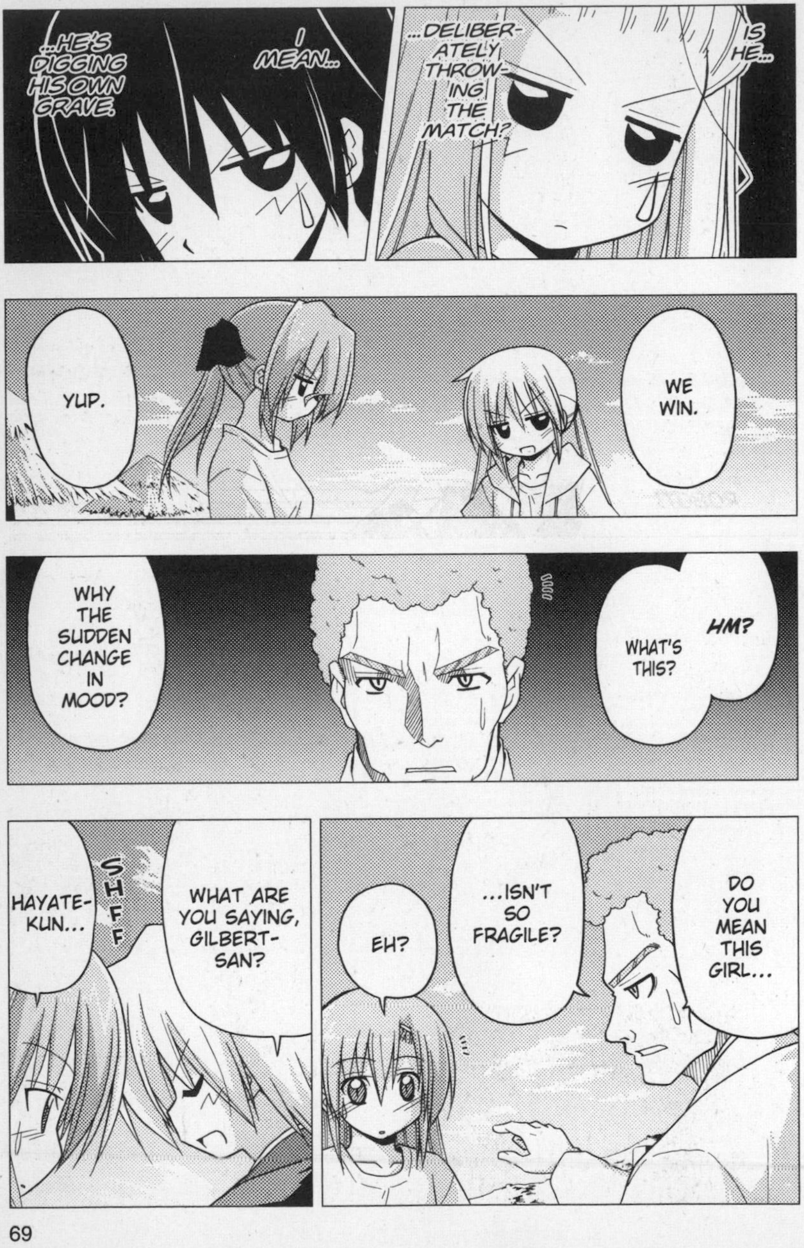
IS HE...
...DELIBER-ATELY THROW-ING THE MATCH?
I MEAN...
...HE'S DIGGING HIS OWN GRAVE.
WE WIN.
YUP.
HM?
WHAT'S THIS?
WHY THE SUDDEN CHANGE IN MOOD?
DO YOU MEAN THIS GIRL...
...ISN'T SO FRAGILE?
EH?
WHAT ARE YOU SAYING, GILBERT-SAN?
SHFF
HAYATE-KUN...

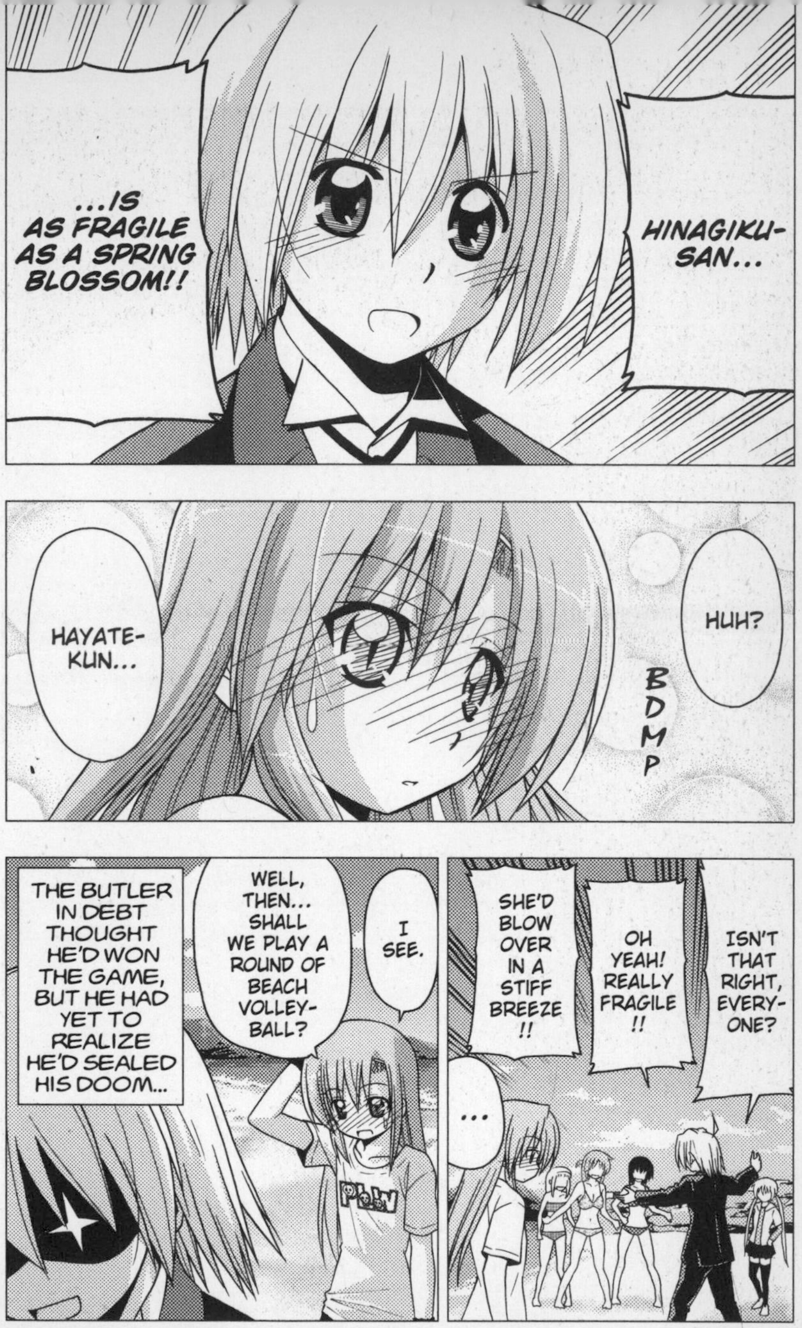
HINAGIKU-SAN...
...IS AS FRAGILE AS A SPRING BLOSSOM!!
HUH?
BDMP
HAYATE-KUN...
ISN'T THAT RIGHT, EVERYONE?
OH YEAH! REALLY FRAGILE!!
SHE'D BLOW OVER IN A STIFF BREEZE!!
...
I SEE.
WELL, THEN... SHALL WE PLAY A ROUND OF BEACH VOLLEY-BALL?
THE BUTLER IN DEBT THOUGHT HE'D WON THE GAME, BUT HE HAD YET TO REALIZE HE'D SEALED HIS DOOM...

Episode 5:
"Love Makes a Person Run in Strange Directions, Then Want to Die"

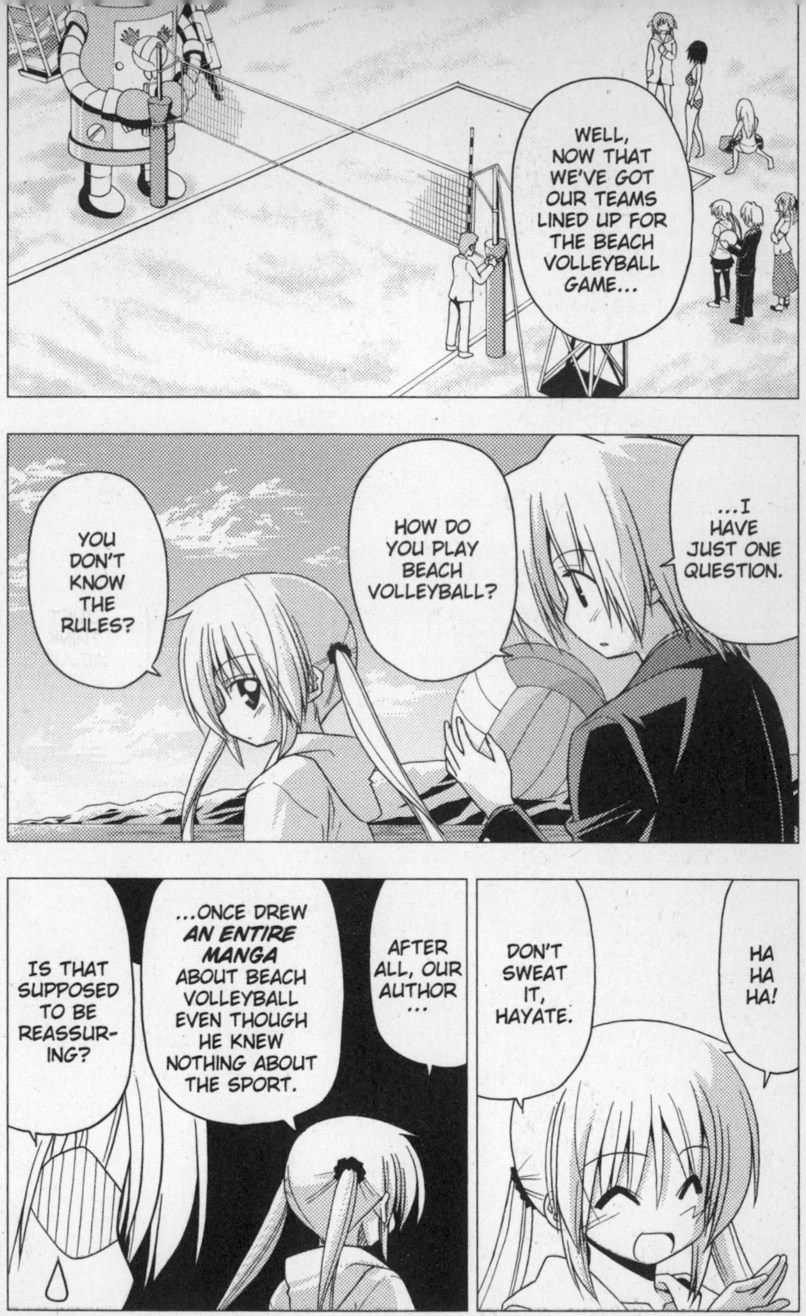
WELL, NOW THAT WE'VE GOT OUR TEAMS LINED UP FOR THE BEACH VOLLEYBALL GAME...
...I HAVE JUST ONE QUESTION.
HOW DO YOU PLAY BEACH VOLLEYBALL?
YOU DON'T KNOW THE RULES?
HA HA HA!
DON'T SWEAT IT, HAYATE.
AFTER ALL, OUR AUTHOR...
...ONCE DREW ***AN ENTIRE MANGA*** ABOUT BEACH VOLLEYBALL EVEN THOUGH HE KNEW NOTHING ABOUT THE SPORT.
IS THAT SUPPOSED TO BE REASSUR-ING?

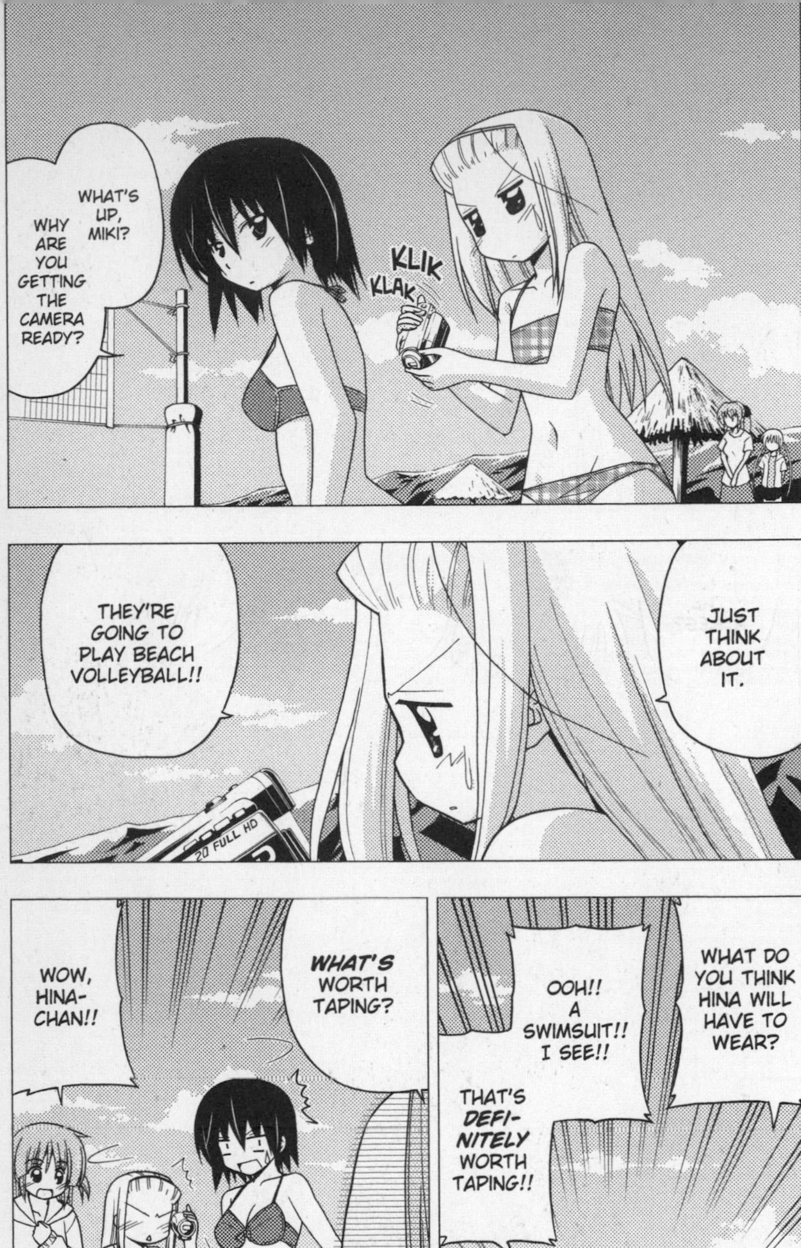
KLIK
KLAK
WHAT'S UP, MIKI? WHY ARE YOU GETTING THE CAMERA READY?
JUST THINK ABOUT IT.
THEY'RE GOING TO PLAY BEACH VOLLEYBALL!!
20 FULL HD
WHAT DO YOU THINK HINA WILL HAVE TO WEAR?
OOH!! A SWIMSUIT!! I SEE!!
THAT'S DEFINITELY WORTH TAPING!!
WHAT'S WORTH TAPING?
WOW, HINA-CHAN!!

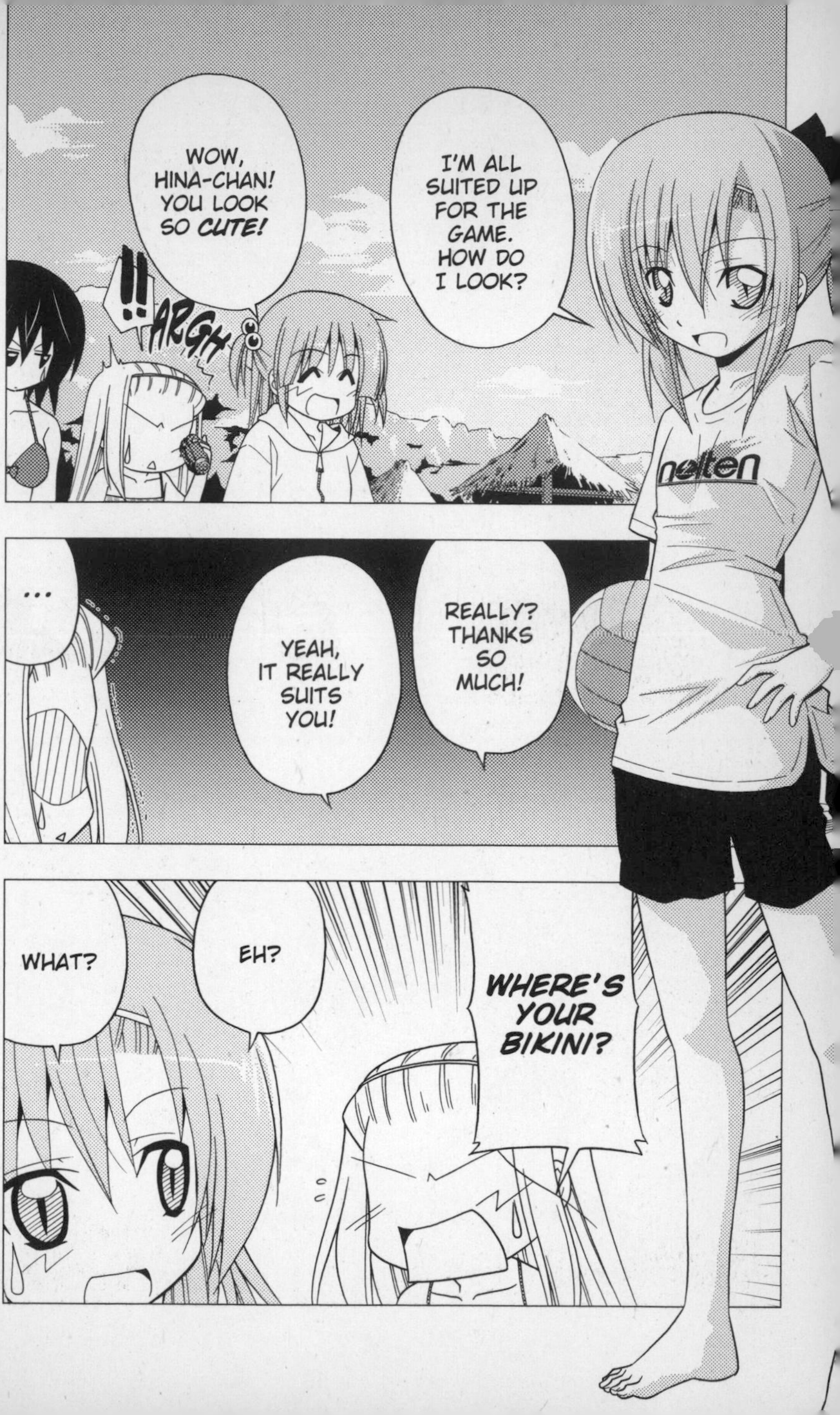
I'M ALL SUITED UP FOR THE GAME. HOW DO I LOOK?
WOW, HINA-CHAN! YOU LOOK SO CUTE!
!!
ARGH
REALLY? THANKS SO MUCH!
YEAH, IT REALLY SUITS YOU!
...
WHERE'S YOUR BIKINI?
EH?
WHAT?

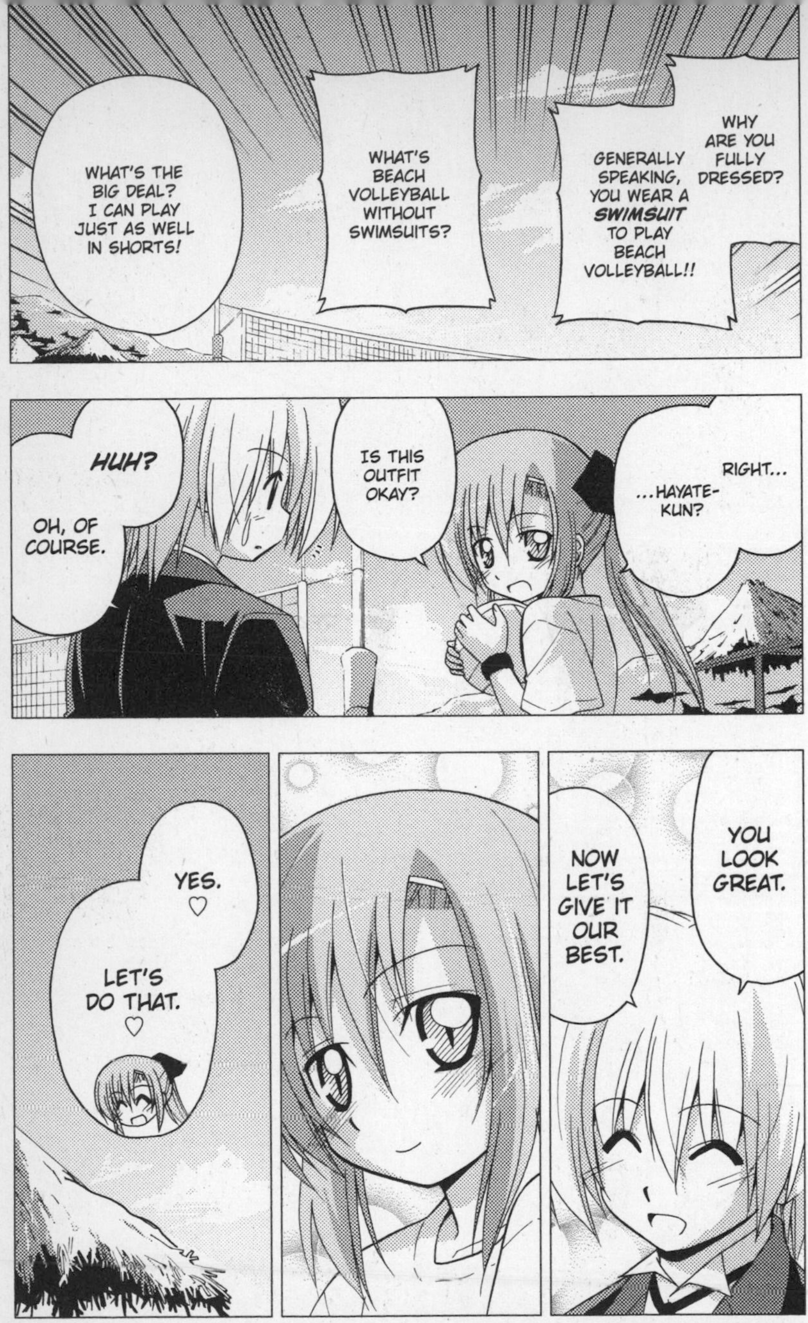
WHY ARE YOU FULLY DRESSED?
GENERALLY SPEAKING, YOU WEAR A ***SWIMSUIT*** TO PLAY BEACH VOLLEYBALL!!
WHAT'S BEACH VOLLEYBALL WITHOUT SWIMSUITS?
WHAT'S THE BIG DEAL? I CAN PLAY JUST AS WELL IN SHORTS!
RIGHT... ...HAYATE-KUN?
IS THIS OUTFIT OKAY?
HUH?
OH, OF COURSE.
YOU LOOK GREAT.
NOW LET'S GIVE IT OUR BEST.
YES. ♡
LET'S DO THAT. ♡

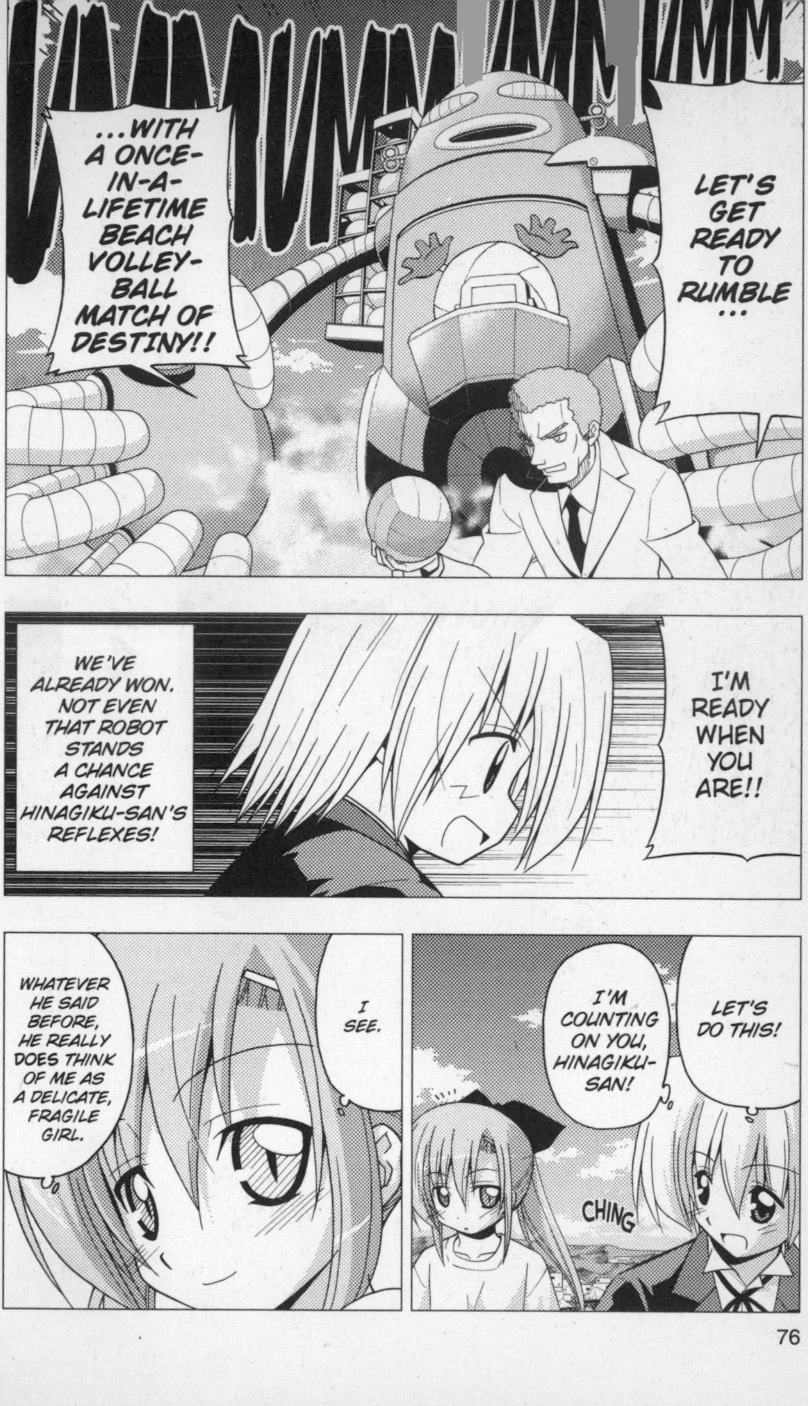
LET'S GET READY TO RUMBLE...
...WITH A ONCE-IN-A-LIFETIME BEACH VOLLEY-BALL MATCH OF DESTINY!!
I'M READY WHEN YOU ARE!!
WE'VE ALREADY WON. NOT EVEN THAT ROBOT STANDS A CHANCE AGAINST HINAGIKU-SAN'S REFLEXES!
LET'S DO THIS!
I'M COUNTING ON YOU, HINAGIKU-SAN!
CHING
I SEE.
WHATEVER HE SAID BEFORE, HE REALLY DOES THINK OF ME AS A DELICATE, FRAGILE GIRL.

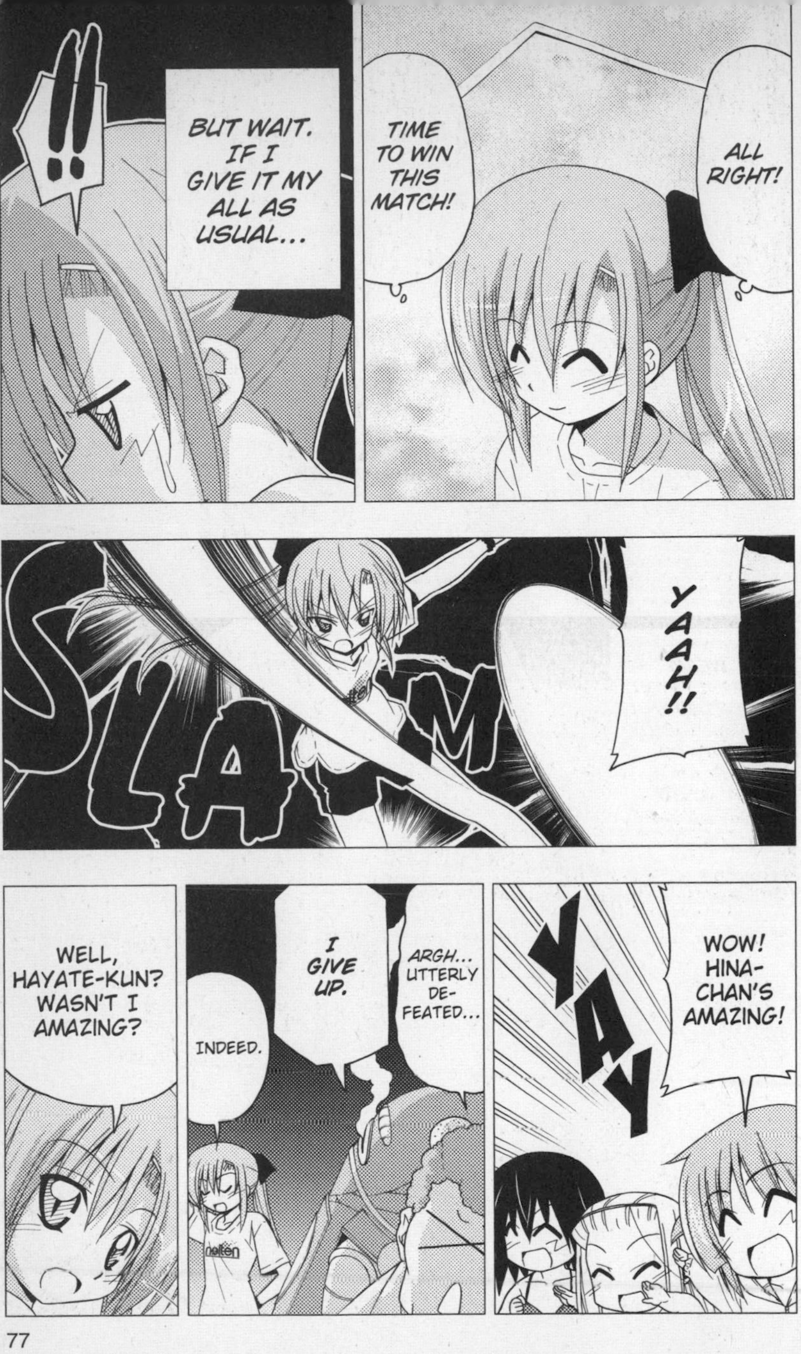
ALL RIGHT!
TIME TO WIN THIS MATCH!
BUT WAIT. IF I GIVE IT MY ALL AS USUAL...
!!
YAAH!!
SLAM
WOW! HINA-CHAN'S AMAZING!
YAY
ARGH... UTTERLY DE-FEATED...
I GIVE UP.
INDEED.
WELL, HAYATE-KUN? WASN'T I AMAZING?

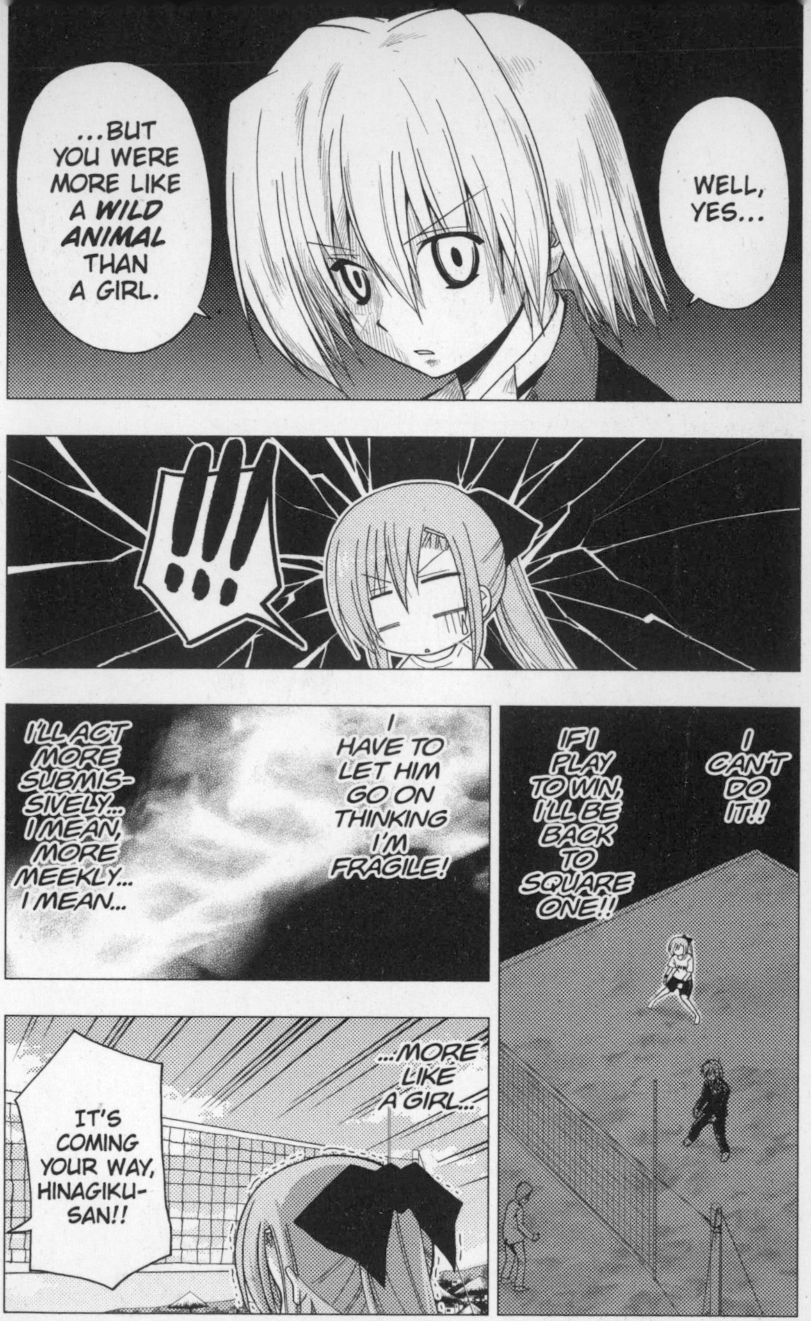
WELL, YES...
...BUT YOU WERE MORE LIKE A ***WILD ANIMAL*** THAN A GIRL.
!!!
I CAN'T DO IT!!
IF I PLAY TO WIN, I'LL BE BACK TO SQUARE ONE!!
I HAVE TO LET HIM GO ON THINKING I'M FRAGILE!
I'LL ACT MORE SUBMIS-SIVELY... I MEAN, MORE MEEKLY... I MEAN...
...MORE LIKE A GIRL...
IT'S COMING YOUR WAY, HINAGIKU-SAN!!

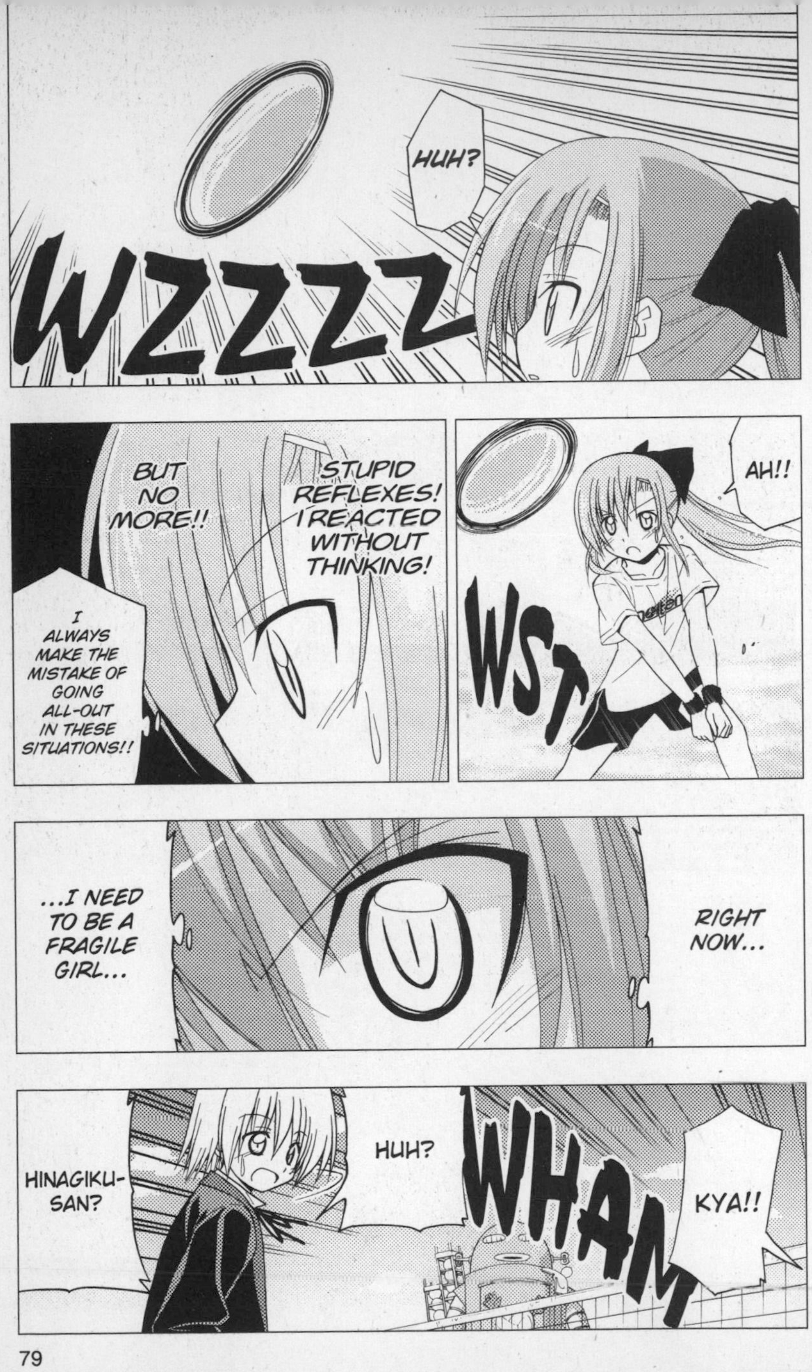
HUH?
WZZZZ
AH!!
WST
STUPID REFLEXES! I REACTED WITHOUT THINKING!
BUT NO MORE!!
I ALWAYS MAKE THE MISTAKE OF GOING ALL-OUT IN THESE SITUATIONS!!
RIGHT NOW...
...I NEED TO BE A FRAGILE GIRL...
KYA!!
WHAM
HUH?
HINAGIKU-SAN?

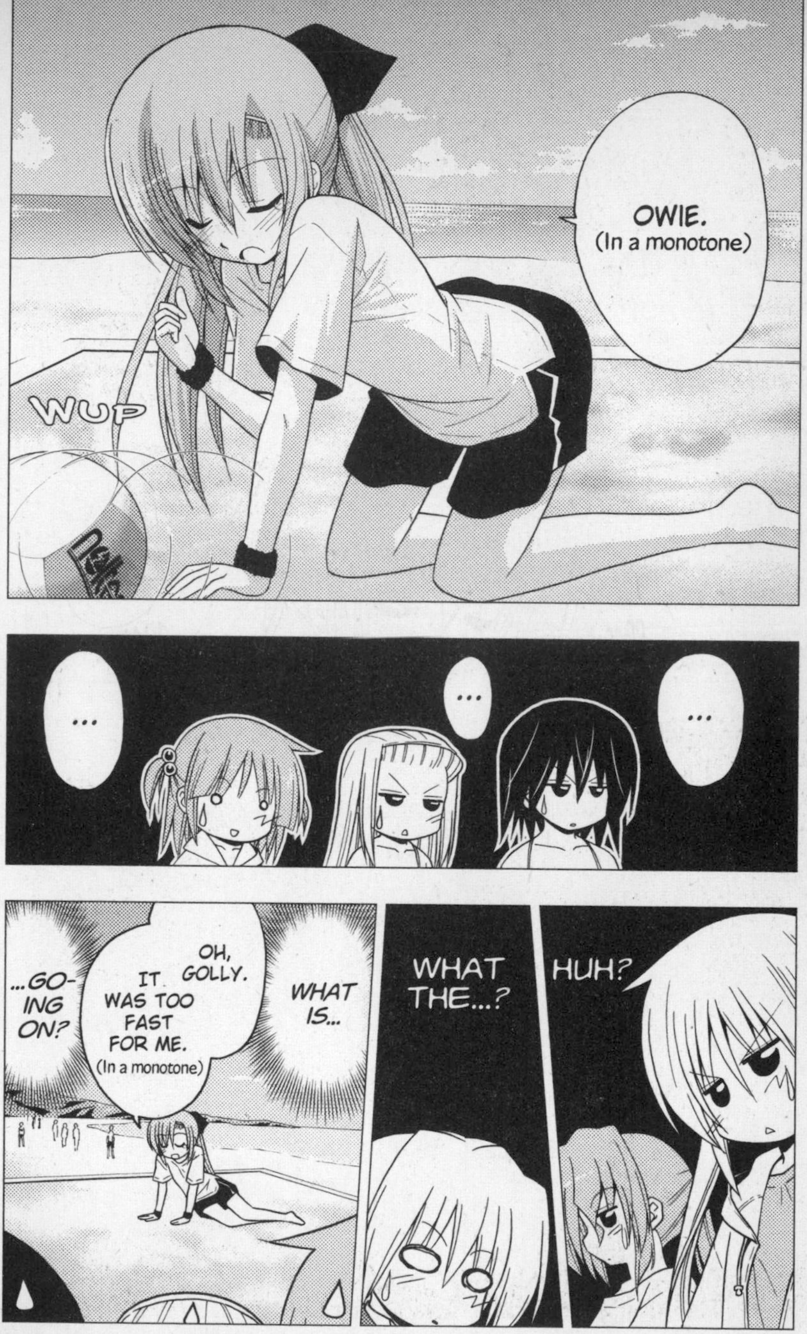
OWIE.
(In a monotone)
WUP
...
...
...
HUH?
WHAT THE...?
WHAT IS...
OH, GOLLY. IT WAS TOO FAST FOR ME.
(In a monotone)
...GO-ING ON?

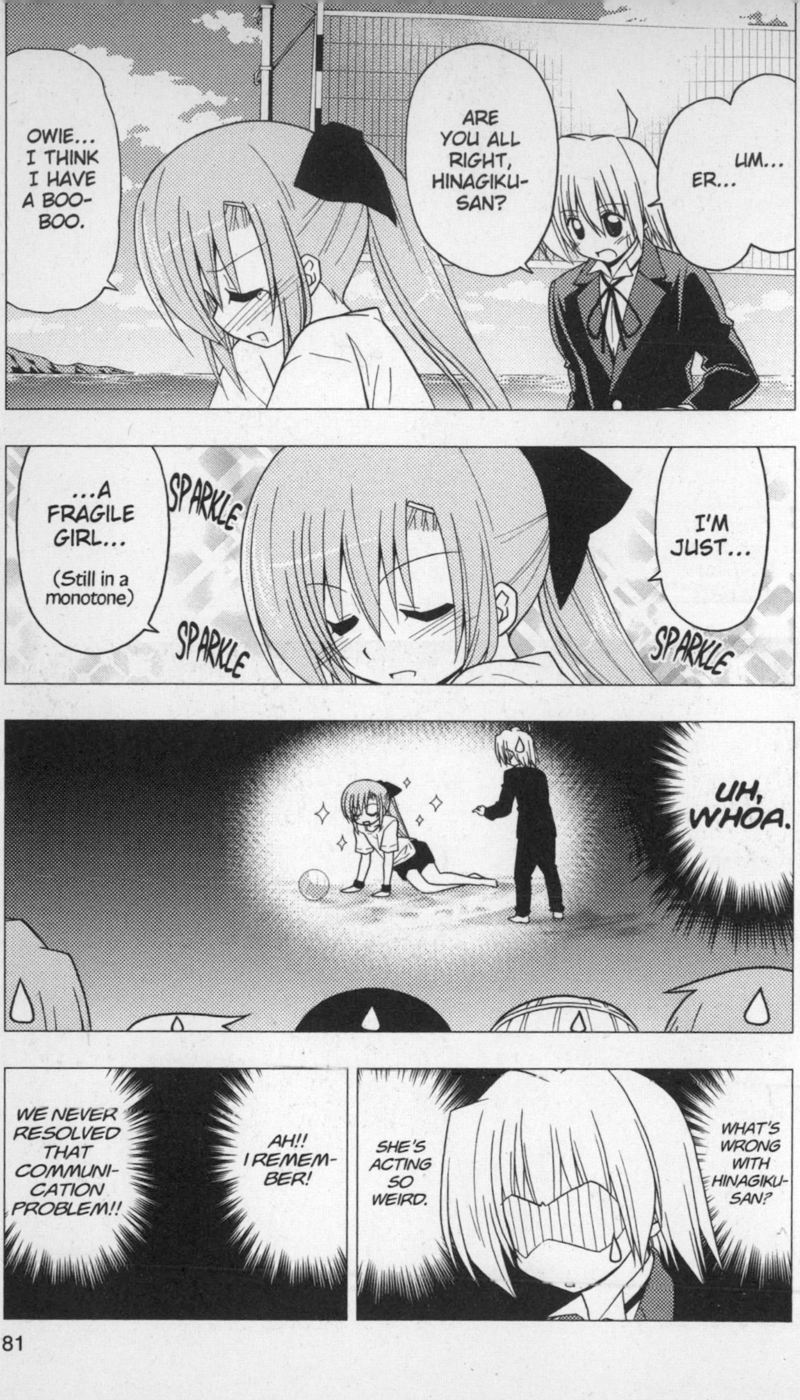
UM... ER...
ARE YOU ALL RIGHT, HINAGIKU-SAN?
OWIE... I THINK I HAVE A BOO-BOO.
I'M JUST...
SPARKLE
SPARKLE
SPARKLE
...A FRAGILE GIRL...
(Still in a monotone)
UH, WHOA.
WHAT'S WRONG WITH HINAGIKU-SAN?
SHE'S ACTING SO WEIRD.
AH!! I REMEMBER!
WE NEVER RESOLVED THAT COMMUNICATION PROBLEM!!

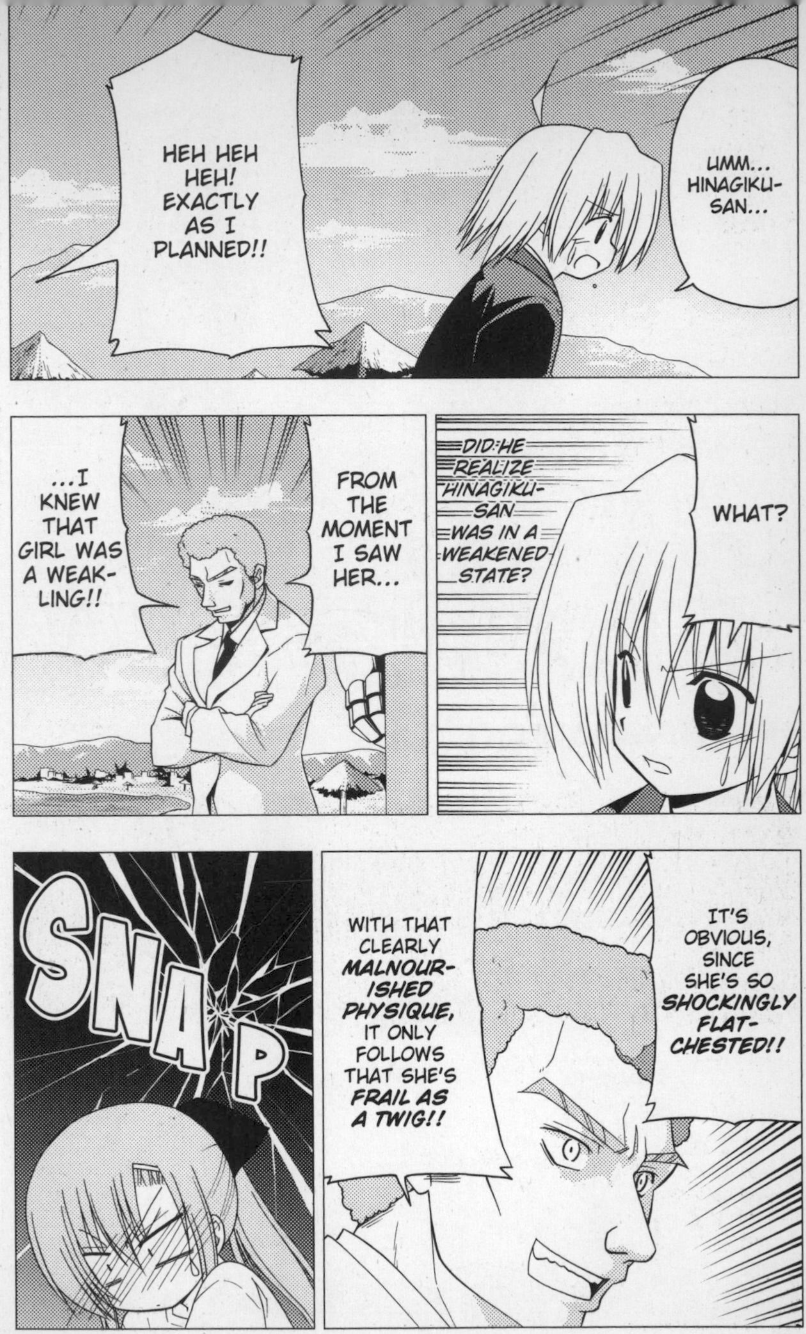
UMM... HINAGIKU-SAN...
HEH HEH HEH! EXACTLY AS I PLANNED!!
WHAT?
DID HE REALIZE HINAGIKU-SAN WAS IN A WEAKENED STATE?
FROM THE MOMENT I SAW HER...
...I KNEW THAT GIRL WAS A WEAK-LING!!
IT'S OBVIOUS, SINCE SHE'S SO *SHOCKINGLY FLAT-CHESTED!!*
WITH THAT CLEARLY *MALNOUR-ISHED PHYSIQUE,* IT ONLY FOLLOWS THAT SHE'S *FRAIL AS A TWIG!!*
SNAP

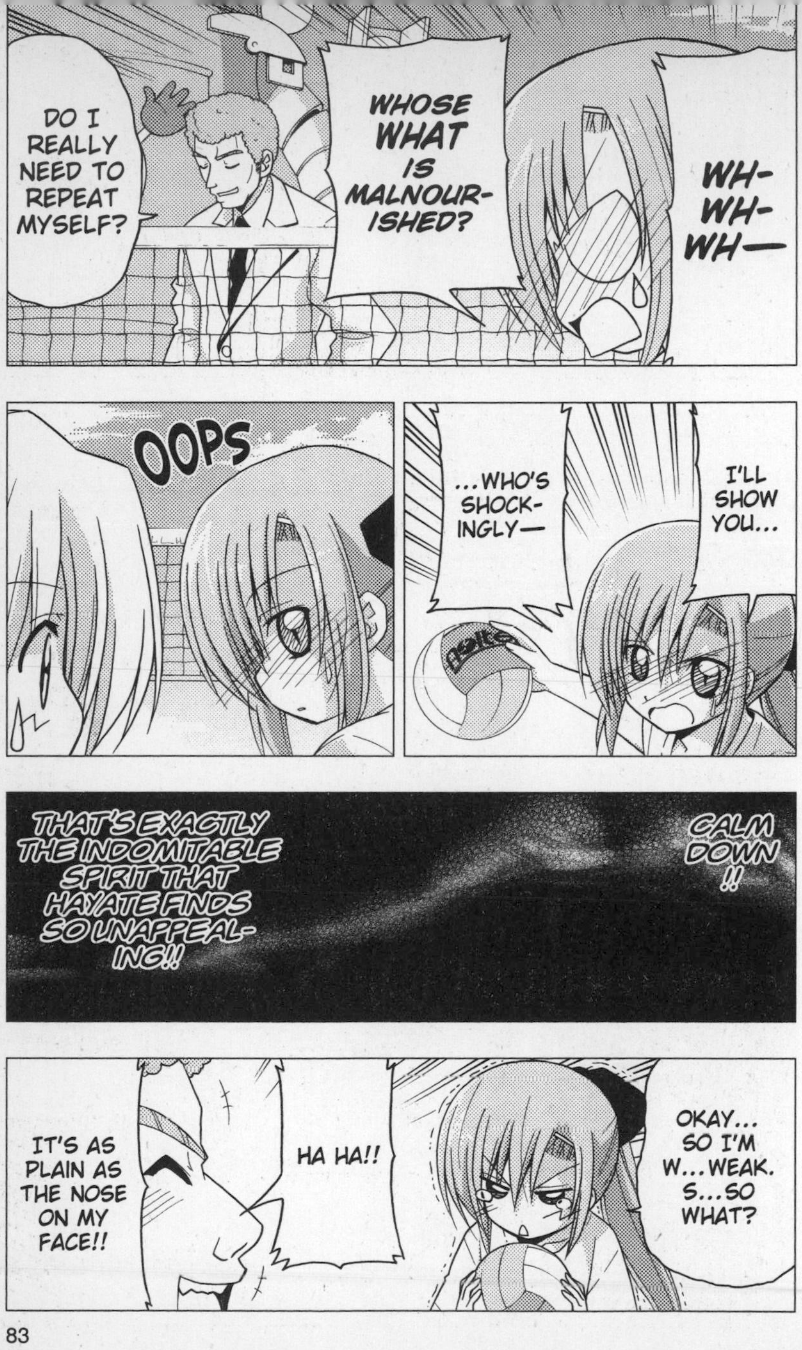
WH-WH-WH—
WHOSE WHAT IS MALNOUR-ISHED?
DO I REALLY NEED TO REPEAT MYSELF?
I'LL SHOW YOU...
...WHO'S SHOCK-INGLY—
OOPS
CALM DOWN!!
THAT'S EXACTLY THE INDOMITABLE SPIRIT THAT HAYATE FINDS SO UNAPPEAL-ING!!
OKAY... SO I'M W...WEAK. S...SO WHAT?
HA HA!!
IT'S AS PLAIN AS THE NOSE ON MY FACE!!

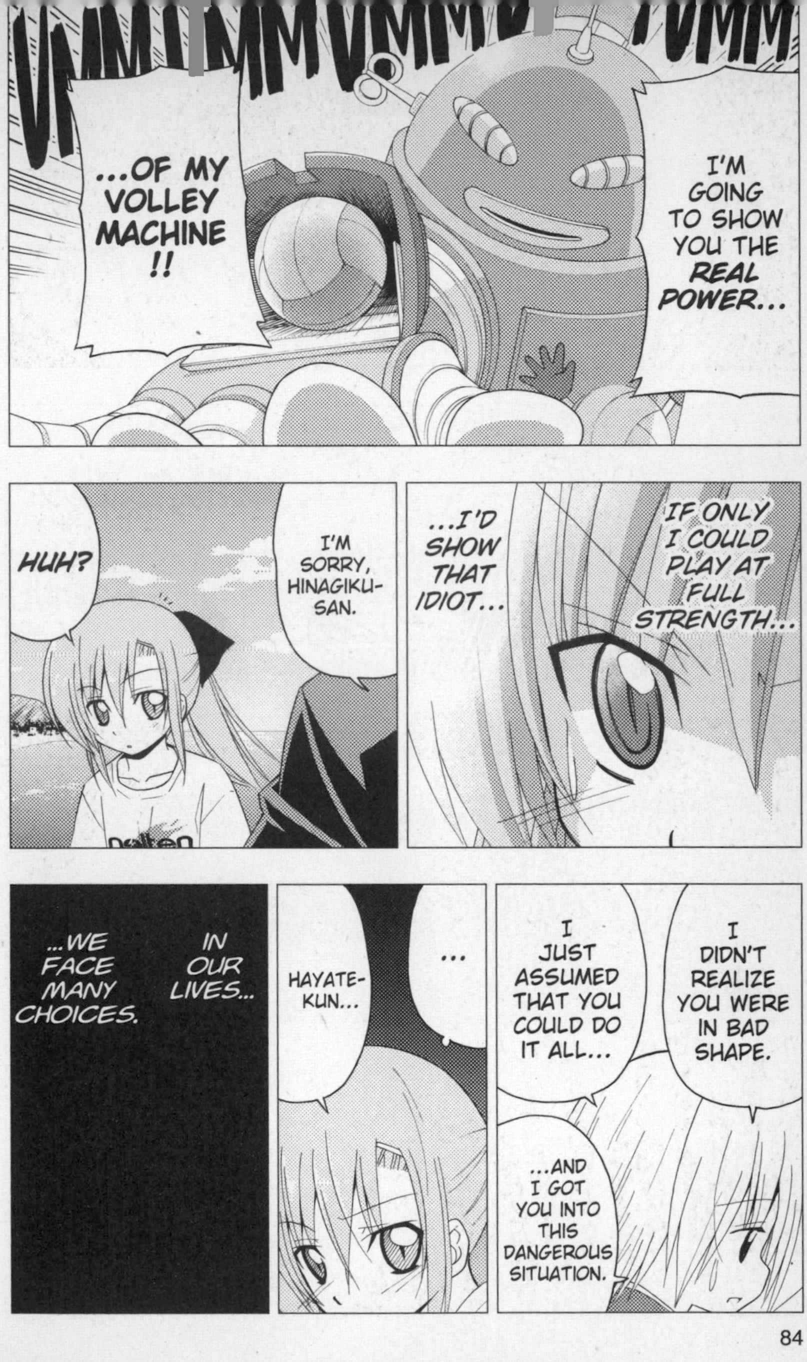
I'M GOING TO SHOW YOU THE REAL POWER...
...OF MY VOLLEY MACHINE !!
IF ONLY I COULD PLAY AT FULL STRENGTH...
...I'D SHOW THAT IDIOT...
I'M SORRY, HINAGIKU-SAN.
HUH?
I DIDN'T REALIZE YOU WERE IN BAD SHAPE.
I JUST ASSUMED THAT YOU COULD DO IT ALL...
...AND I GOT YOU INTO THIS DANGEROUS SITUATION.
...
HAYATE-KUN...
IN OUR LIVES...
...WE FACE MANY CHOICES.

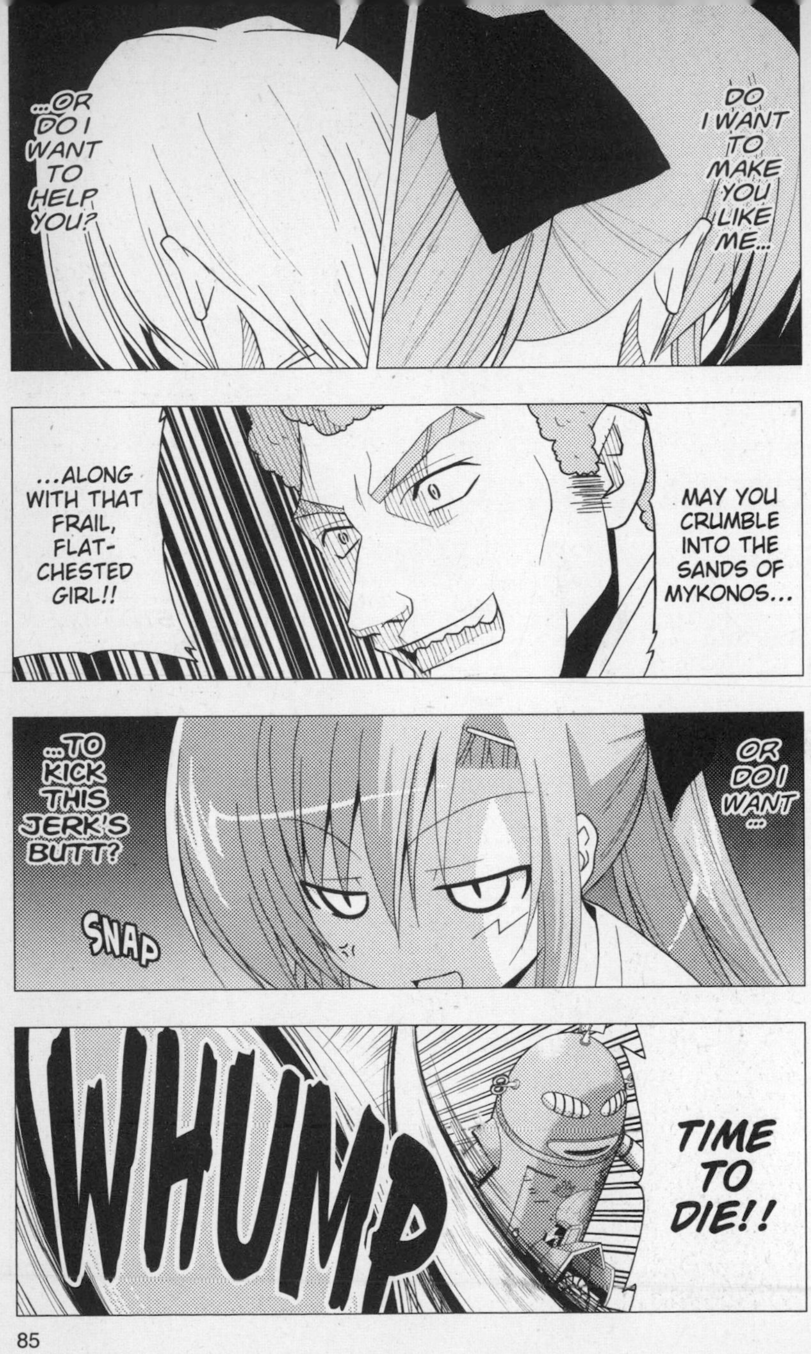
DO I WANT TO MAKE YOU LIKE ME...
...OR DO I WANT TO HELP YOU?
MAY YOU CRUMBLE INTO THE SANDS OF MYKONOS...
...ALONG WITH THAT FRAIL, FLAT-CHESTED GIRL!!
OR DO I WANT...
...TO KICK THIS JERK'S BUTT?
SNAP
TIME TO DIE!!
WHUMP

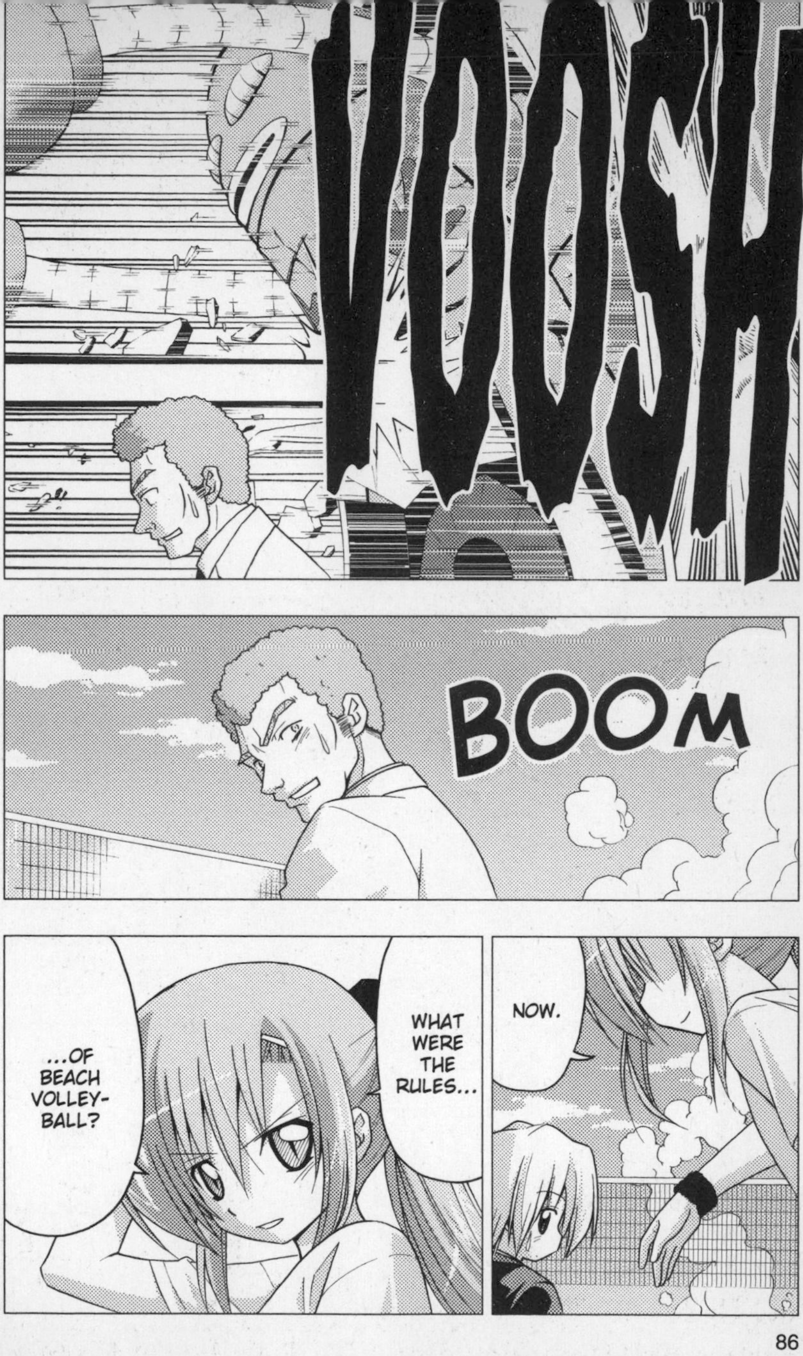
VOOSH
BOOM
NOW.
WHAT WERE THE RULES...
...OF BEACH VOLLEY-BALL?

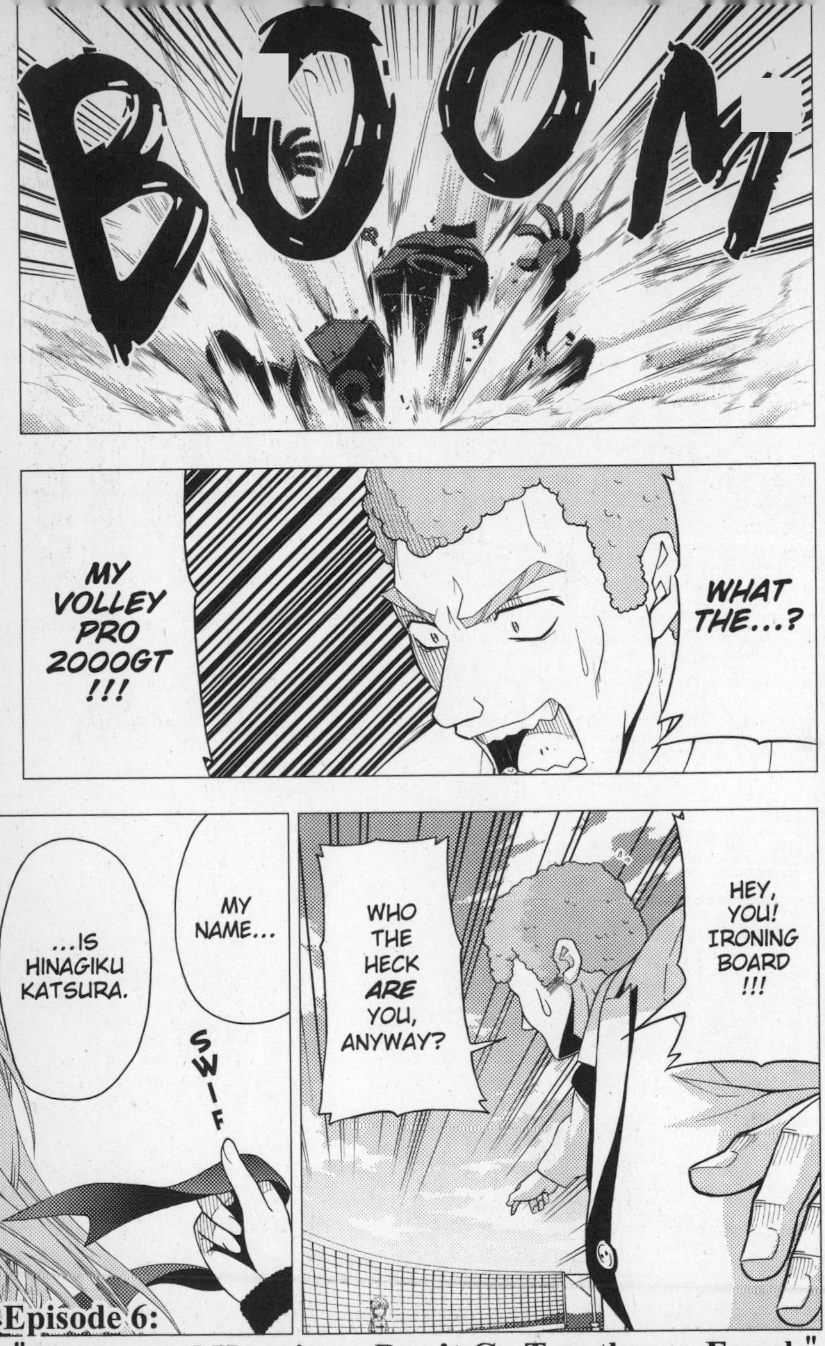
BOOM
WHAT THE...?
MY VOLLEY PRO 2000GT !!!
HEY, YOU! IRONING BOARD !!!
WHO THE HECK *ARE* YOU, ANYWAY?
MY NAME...
...IS HINAGIKU KATSURA.
SWIF

Episode 6: "Victory and Happiness Don't Go Together as Equals"

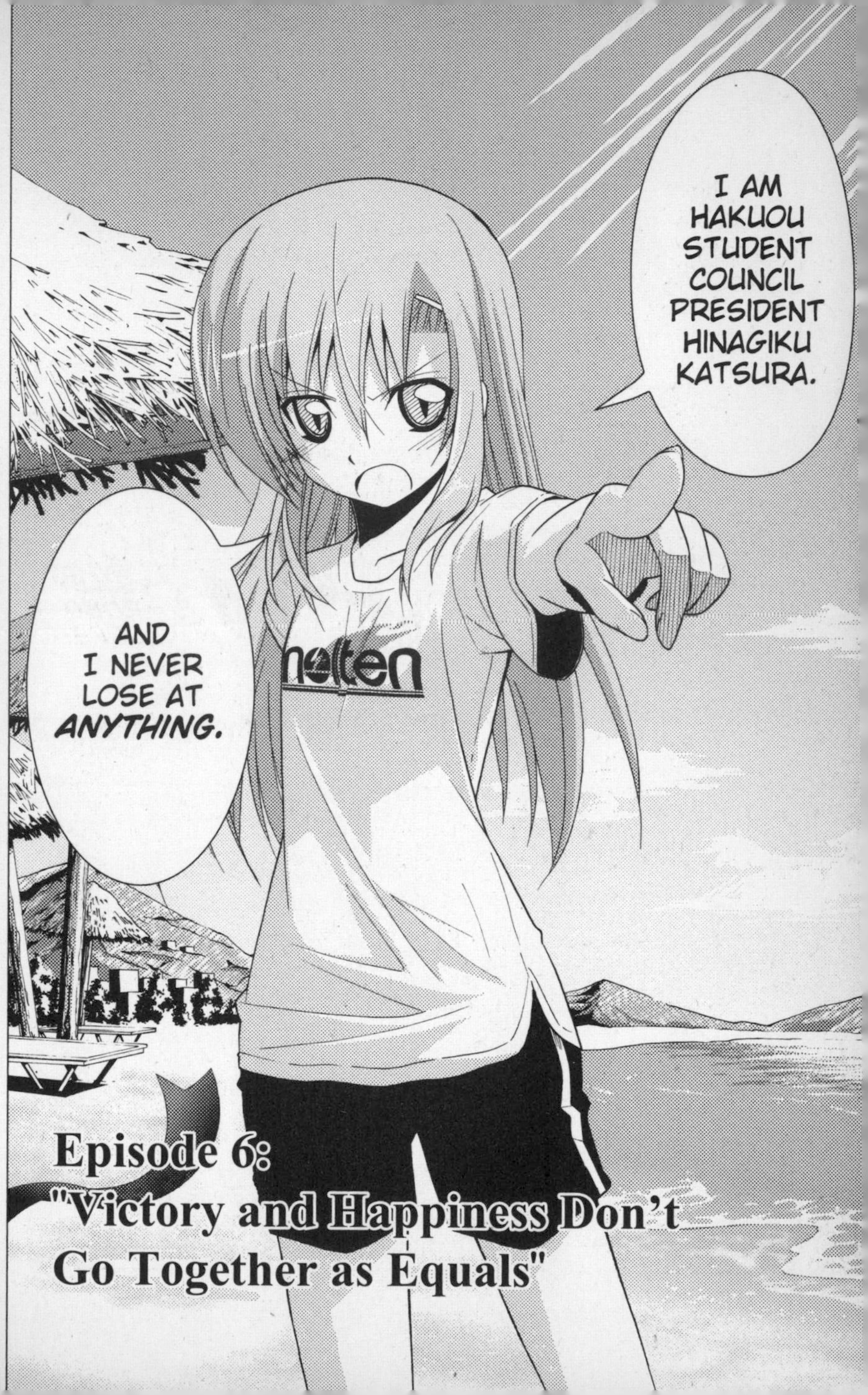
I AM HAKUOU STUDENT COUNCIL PRESIDENT HINAGIKU KATSURA.
AND I NEVER LOSE AT ANYTHING.
Episode 6:
"Victory and Happiness Don't Go Together as Equals"

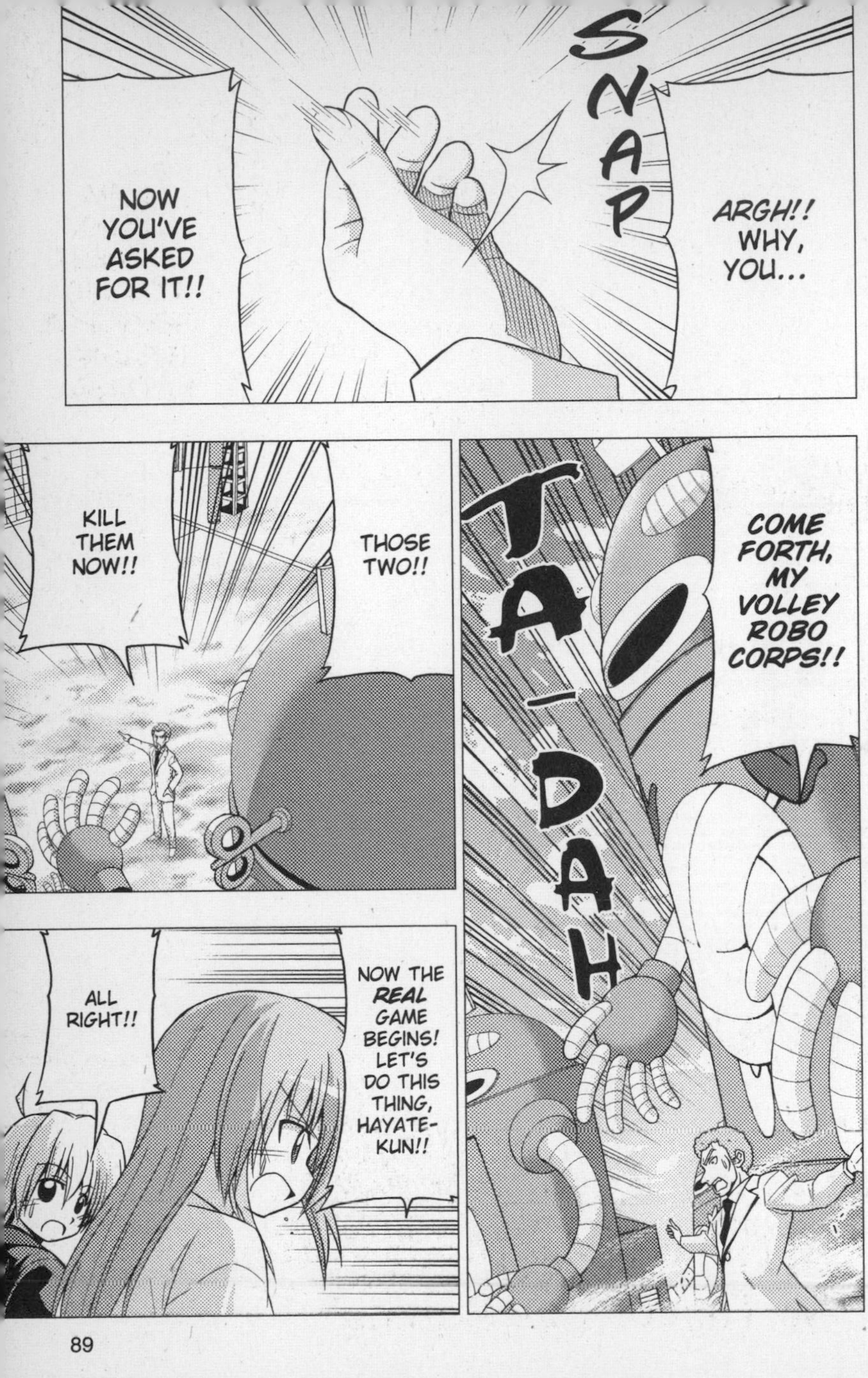
ARGH!! WHY, YOU...
SNAP
NOW YOU'VE ASKED FOR IT!!
COME FORTH, MY VOLLEY ROBO CORPS!!
TA-DAH
THOSE TWO!!
KILL THEM NOW!!
NOW THE *REAL* GAME BEGINS! LET'S DO THIS THING, HAYATE-KUN!!
ALL RIGHT!!

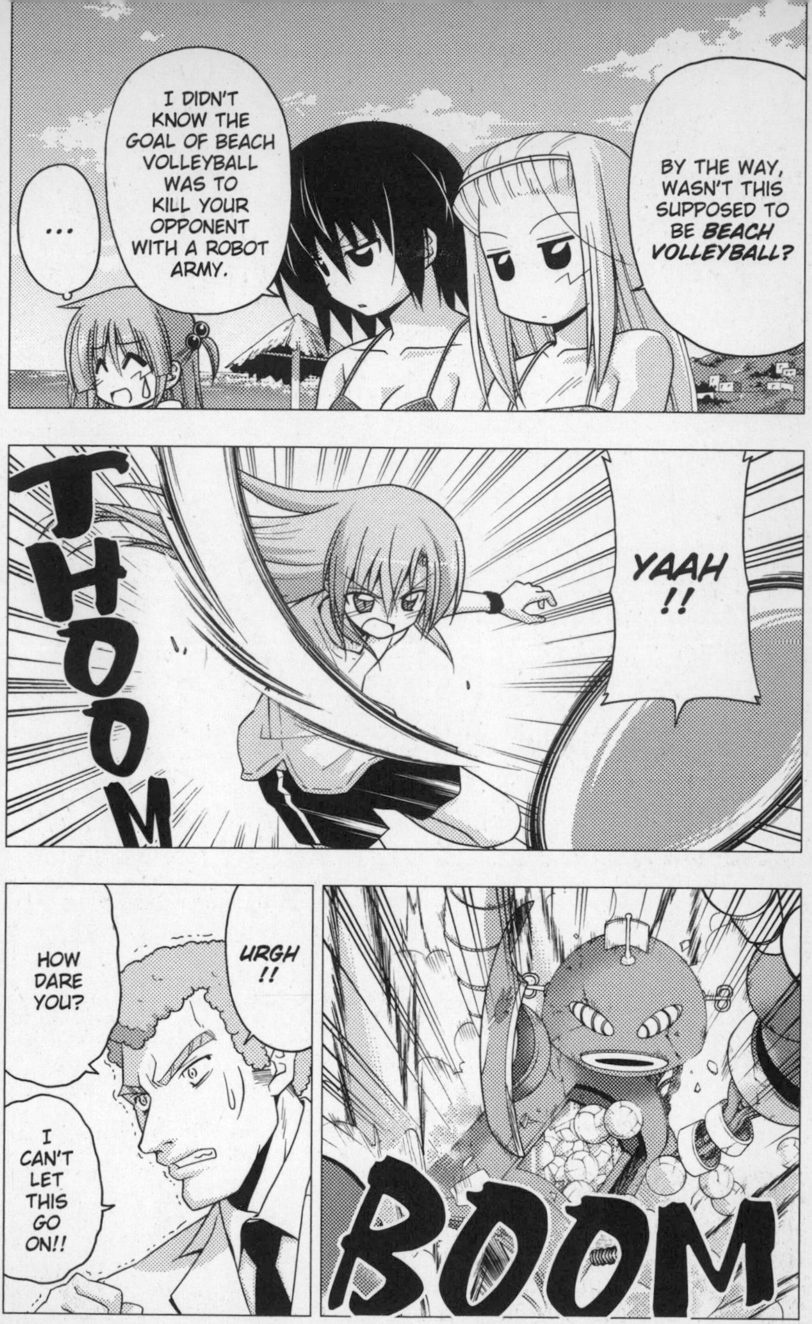
BY THE WAY, WASN'T THIS SUPPOSED TO BE BEACH VOLLEYBALL?
I DIDN'T KNOW THE GOAL OF BEACH VOLLEYBALL WAS TO KILL YOUR OPPONENT WITH A ROBOT ARMY.
...
YAAH !!
THOOM
BOOM
URGH !!
HOW DARE YOU?
I CAN'T LET THIS GO ON!!

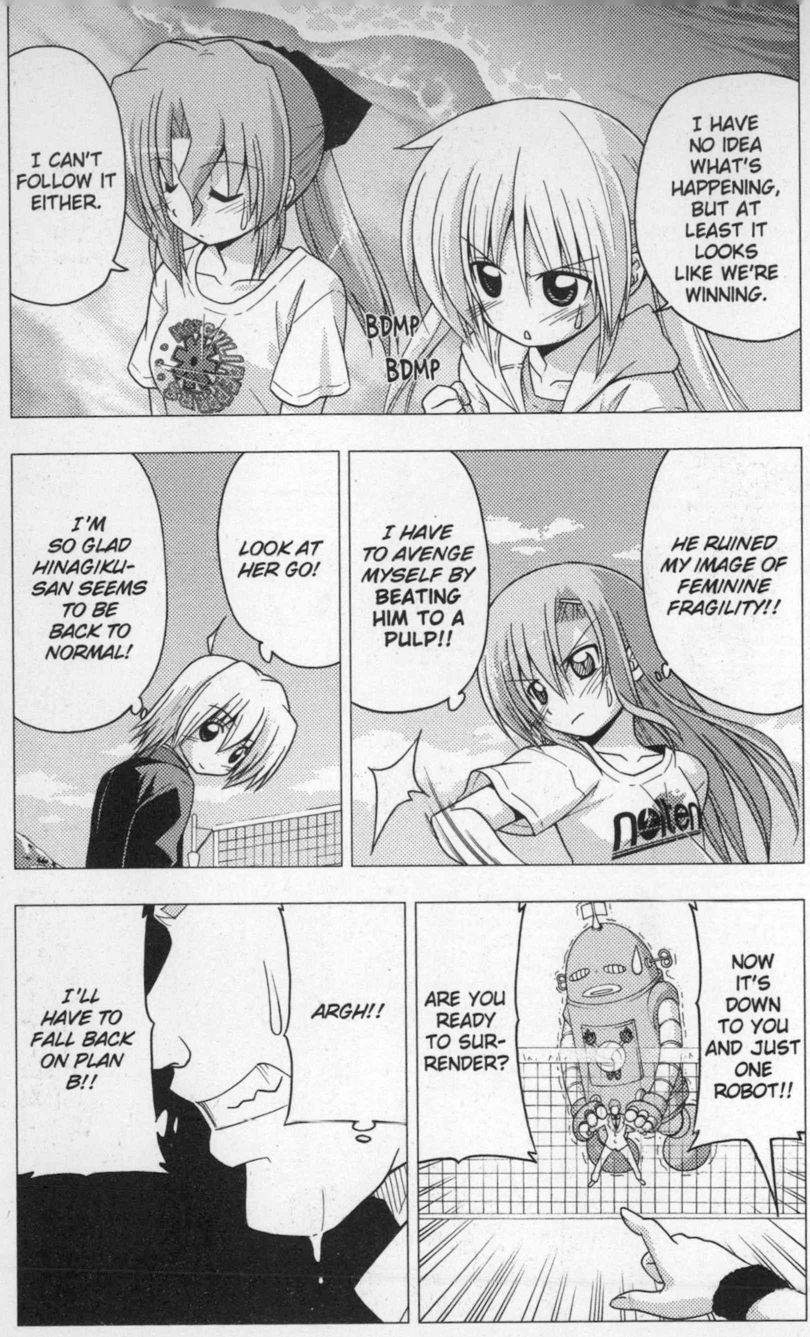
I HAVE NO IDEA WHAT'S HAPPENING, BUT AT LEAST IT LOOKS LIKE WE'RE WINNING.
BDMP
BDMP
I CAN'T FOLLOW IT EITHER.
HE RUINED MY IMAGE OF FEMININE FRAGILITY!!
I HAVE TO AVENGE MYSELF BY BEATING HIM TO A PULP!!
LOOK AT HER GO!
I'M SO GLAD HINAGIKU-SAN SEEMS TO BE BACK TO NORMAL!
NOW IT'S DOWN TO YOU AND JUST ONE ROBOT!!
ARE YOU READY TO SUR-RENDER?
ARGH!!
I'LL HAVE TO FALL BACK ON PLAN B!!

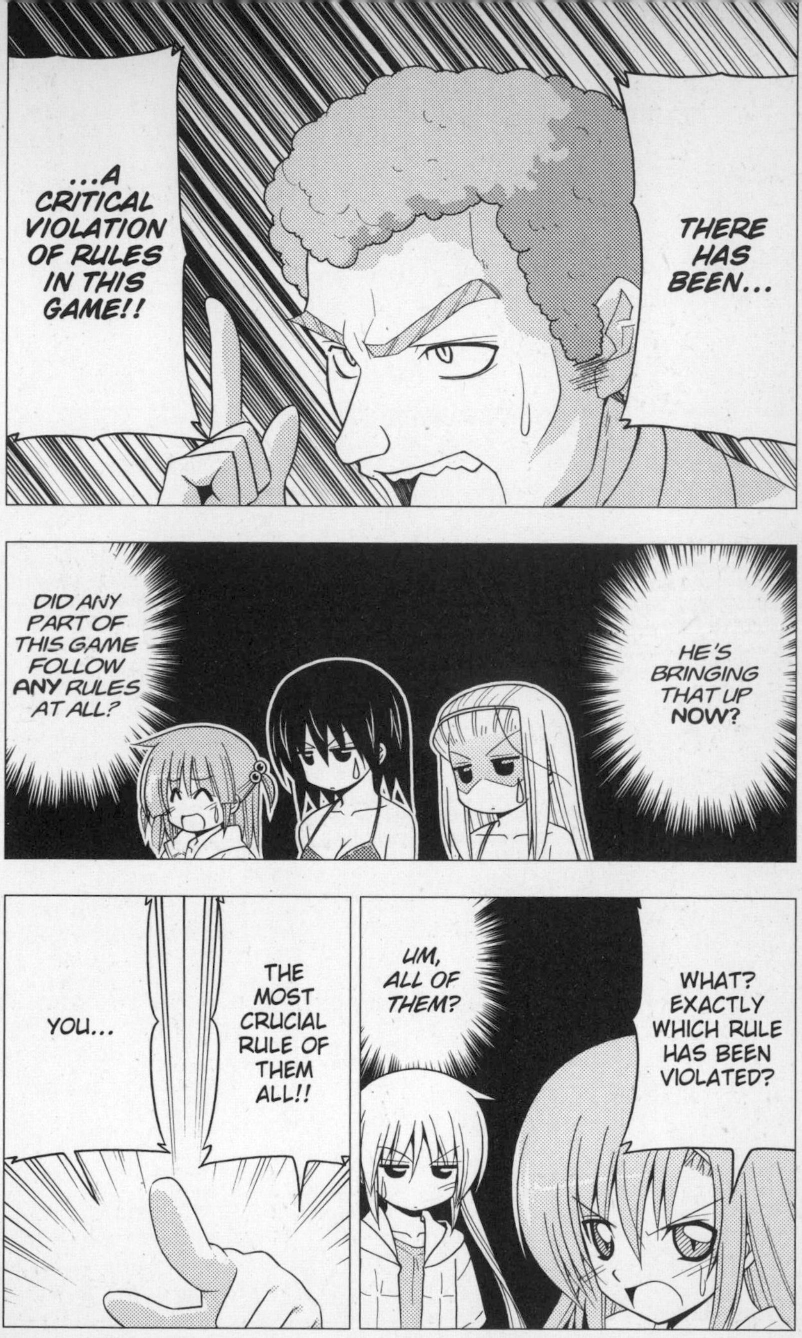
THERE HAS BEEN...
...A CRITICAL VIOLATION OF RULES IN THIS GAME!!
HE'S BRINGING THAT UP NOW?
DID ANY PART OF THIS GAME FOLLOW ANY RULES AT ALL?
WHAT? EXACTLY WHICH RULE HAS BEEN VIOLATED?
UM, ALL OF THEM?
THE MOST CRUCIAL RULE OF THEM ALL!!
YOU...

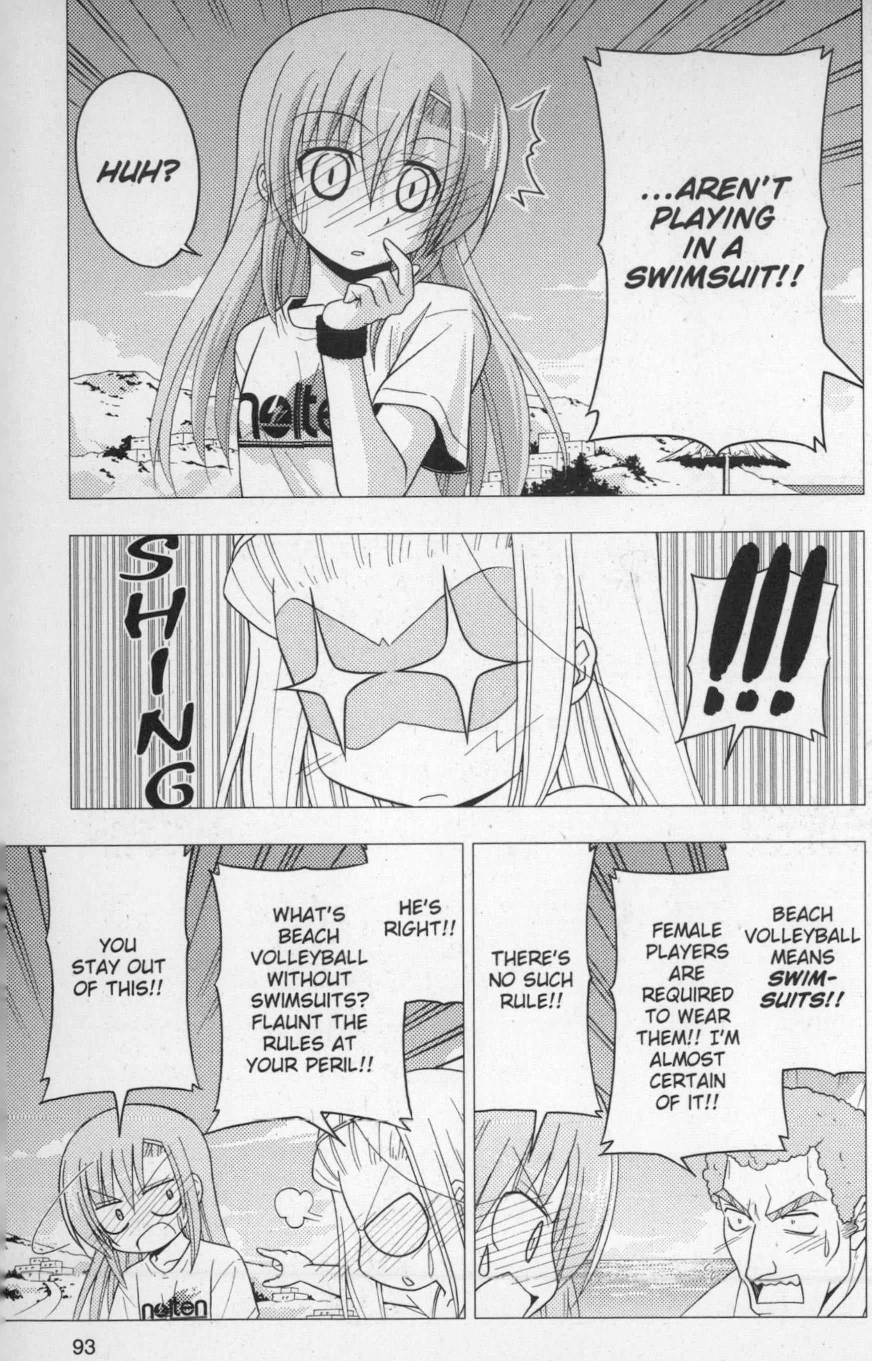
...AREN'T PLAYING IN A SWIMSUIT!!
HUH?
!!!
SHING
BEACH VOLLEYBALL MEANS SWIM-SUITS!!
FEMALE PLAYERS ARE REQUIRED TO WEAR THEM!! I'M ALMOST CERTAIN OF IT!!
THERE'S NO SUCH RULE!!
HE'S RIGHT!!
WHAT'S BEACH VOLLEYBALL WITHOUT SWIMSUITS? FLAUNT THE RULES AT YOUR PERIL!!
YOU STAY OUT OF THIS!!

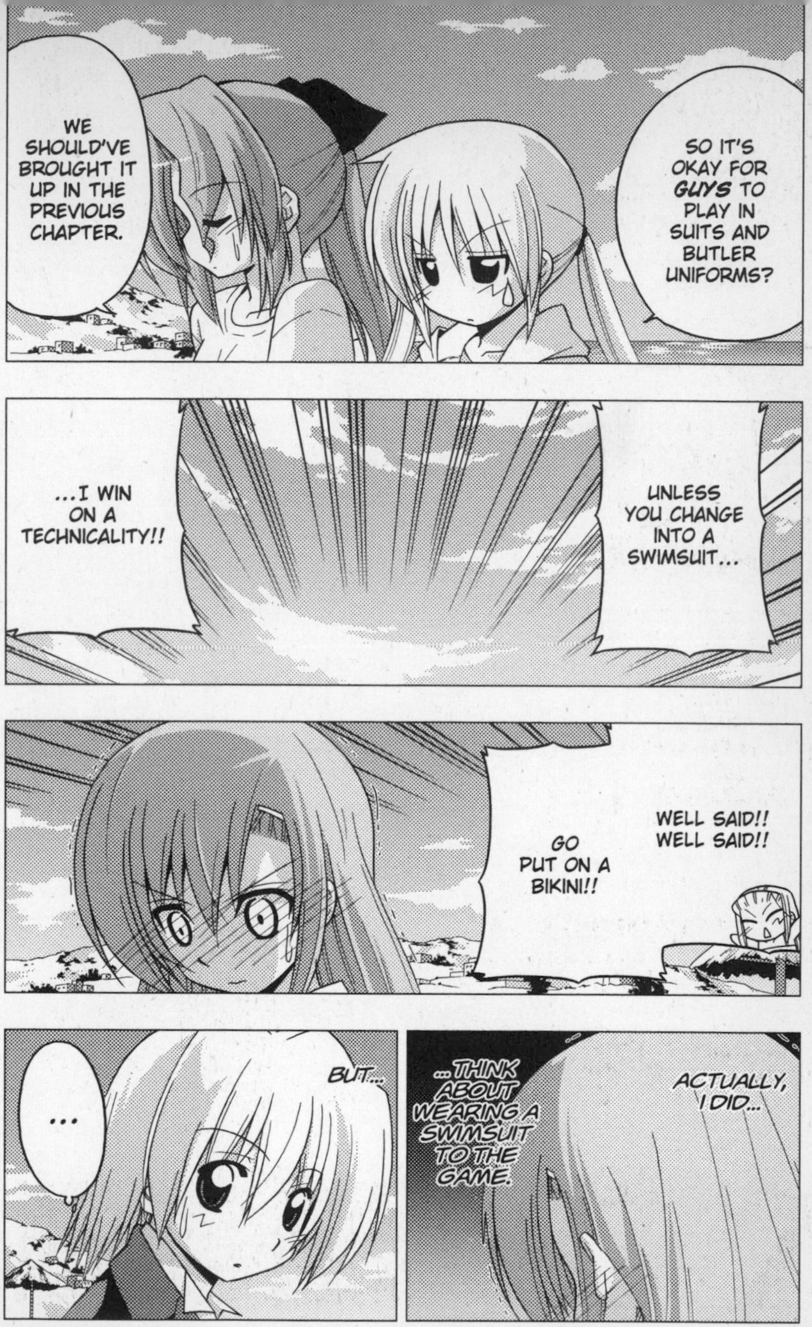
SO IT'S OKAY FOR **GUYS** TO PLAY IN SUITS AND BUTLER UNIFORMS?
WE SHOULD'VE BROUGHT IT UP IN THE PREVIOUS CHAPTER.
UNLESS YOU CHANGE INTO A SWIMSUIT...
...I WIN ON A TECHNICALITY!!
WELL SAID!! WELL SAID!!
GO PUT ON A BIKINI!!
ACTUALLY, I DID...
...THINK ABOUT WEARING A SWIMSUIT TO THE GAME.
BUT...
...

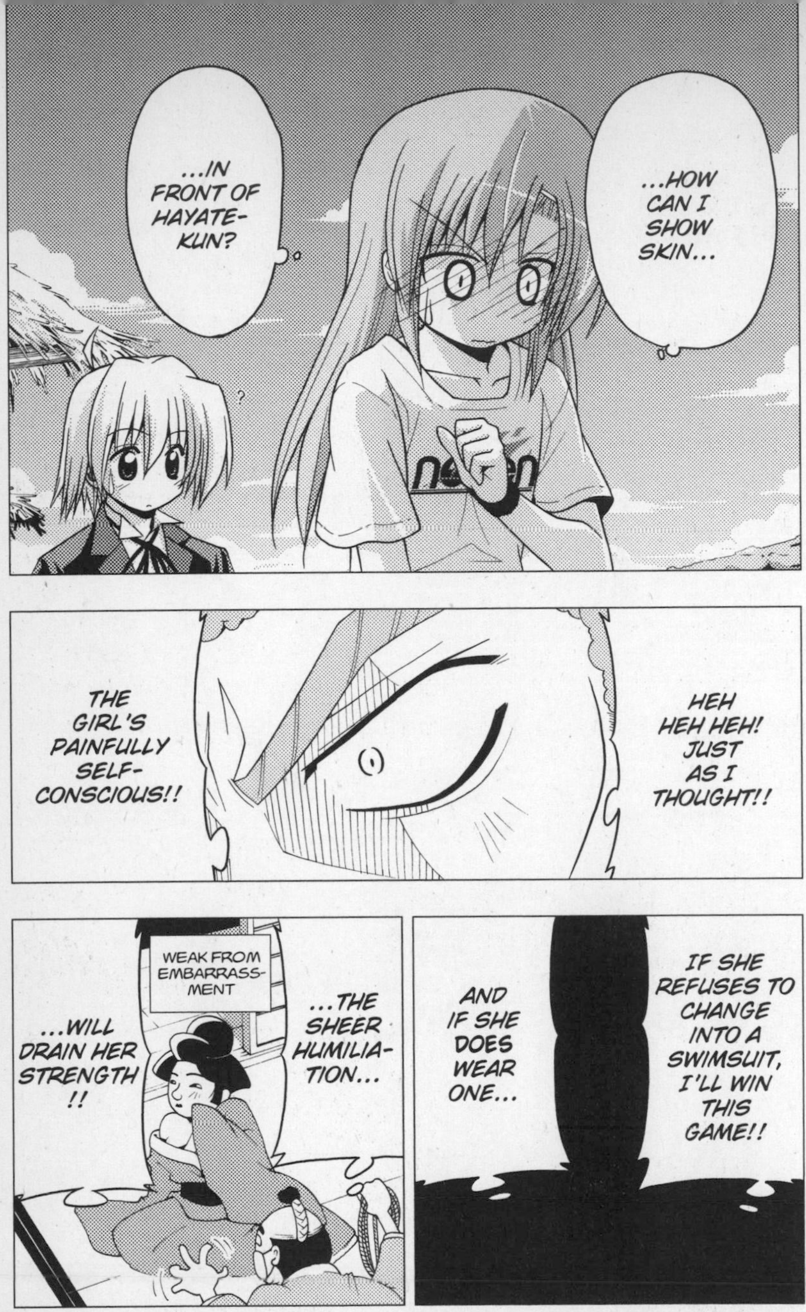
...HOW CAN I SHOW SKIN...
...IN FRONT OF HAYATE-KUN?
?
HEH HEH HEH! JUST AS I THOUGHT!!
THE GIRL'S PAINFULLY SELF-CONSCIOUS!!
IF SHE REFUSES TO CHANGE INTO A SWIMSUIT, I'LL WIN THIS GAME!!
AND IF SHE DOES WEAR ONE...
WEAK FROM EMBARRASSMENT
...THE SHEER HUMILIATION...
...WILL DRAIN HER STRENGTH!!

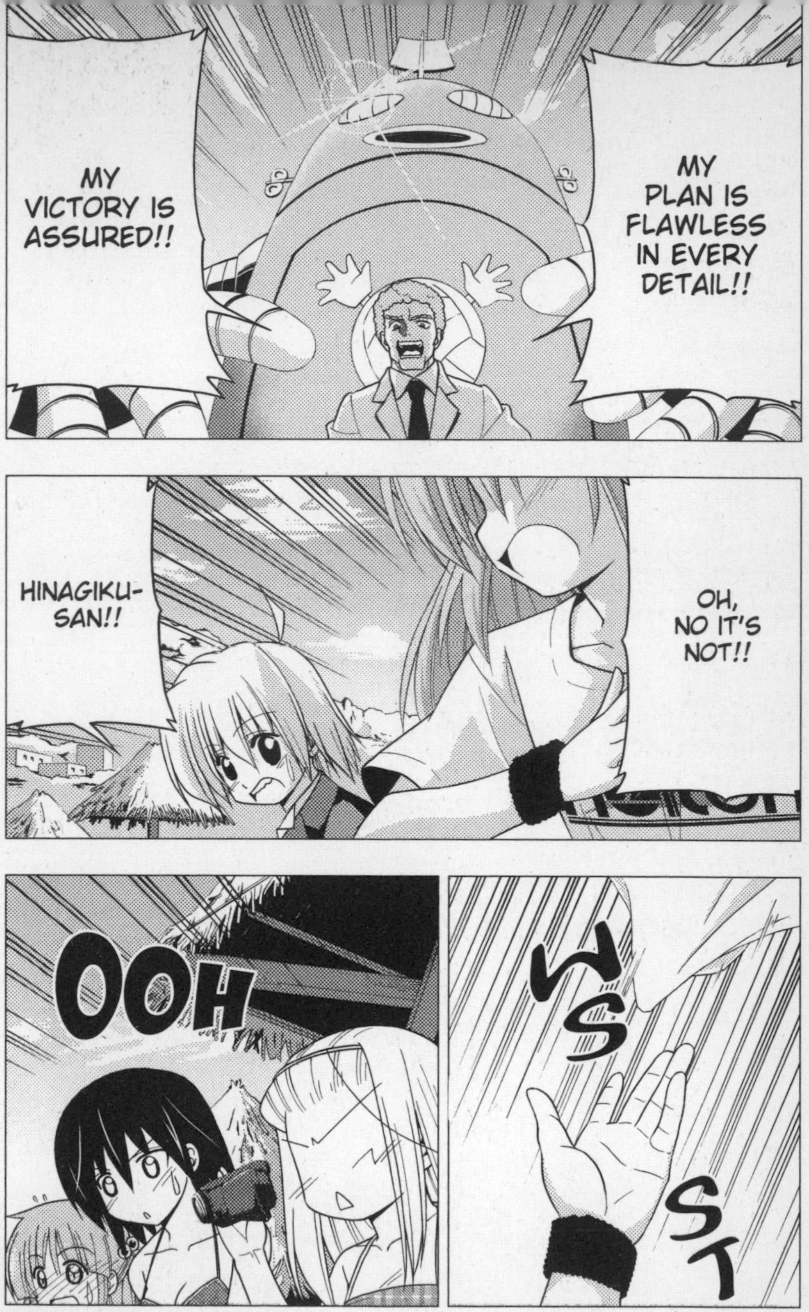
MY PLAN IS FLAWLESS IN EVERY DETAIL!!
MY VICTORY IS ASSURED!!
OH, NO IT'S NOT!!
HINAGIKU-SAN!!
WSST
OOH

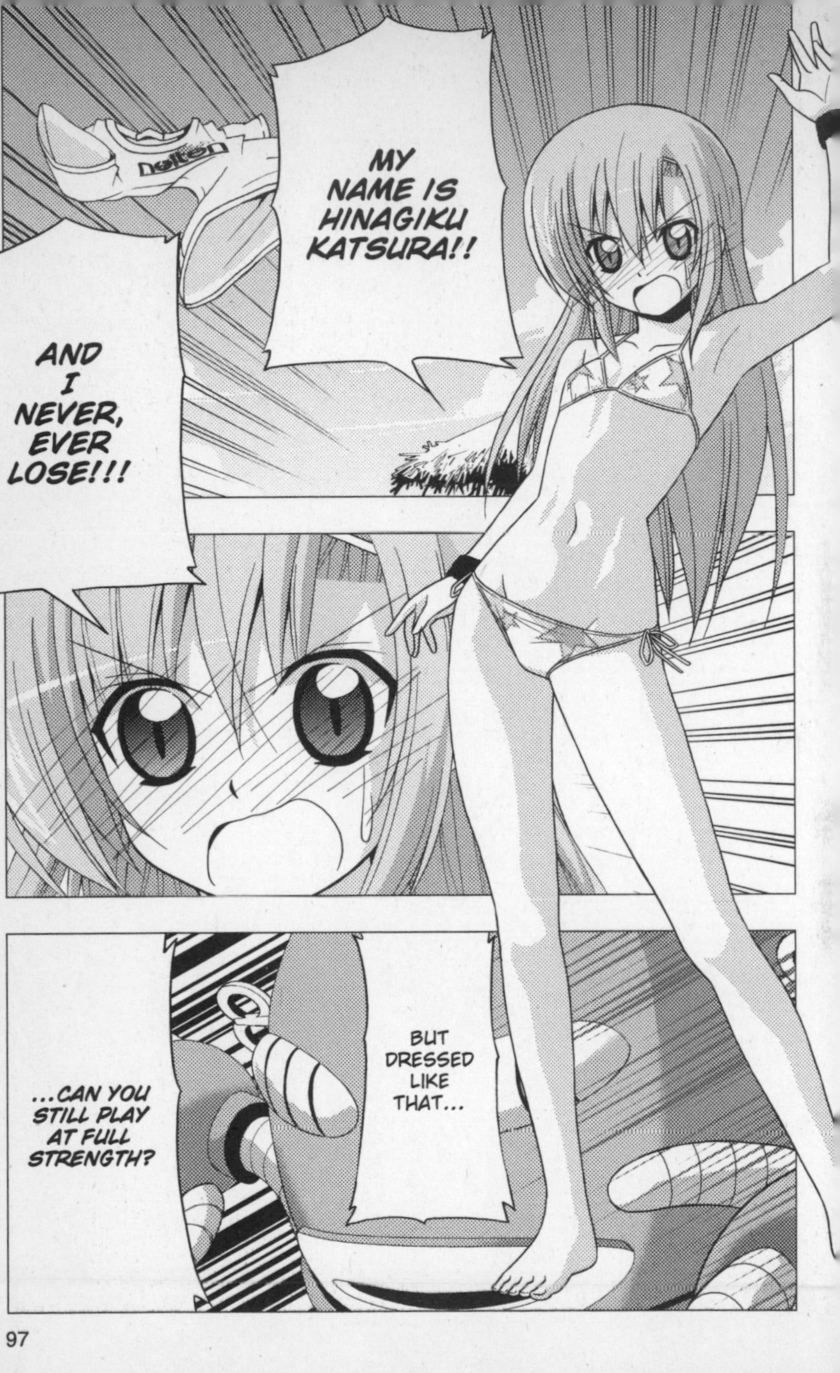
MY NAME IS HINAGIKU KATSURA!!
AND I NEVER, EVER LOSE!!!
BUT DRESSED LIKE THAT...
...CAN YOU STILL PLAY AT FULL STRENGTH?

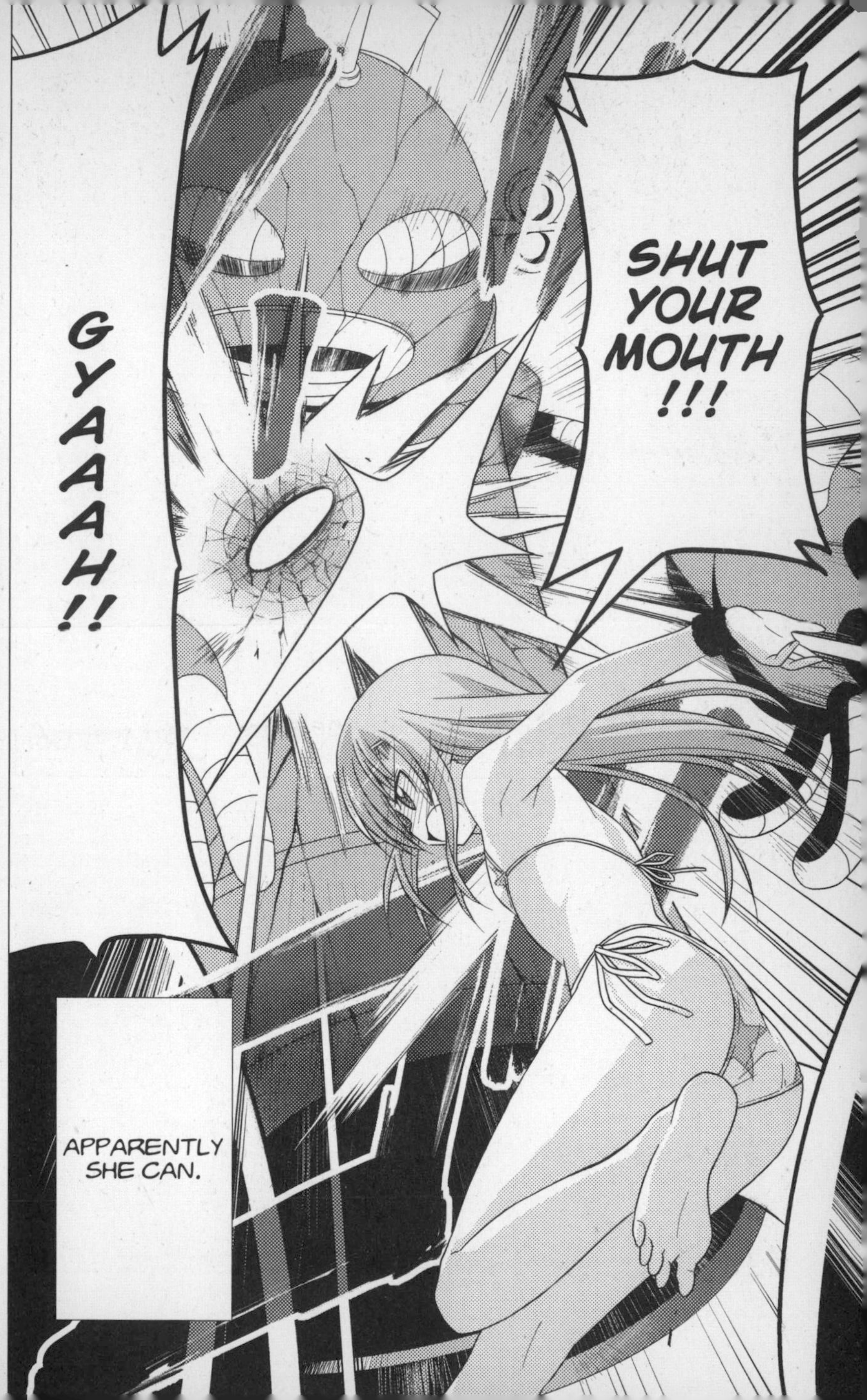
SHUT YOUR MOUTH !!!
GYAAAAH!!
APPARENTLY SHE CAN.

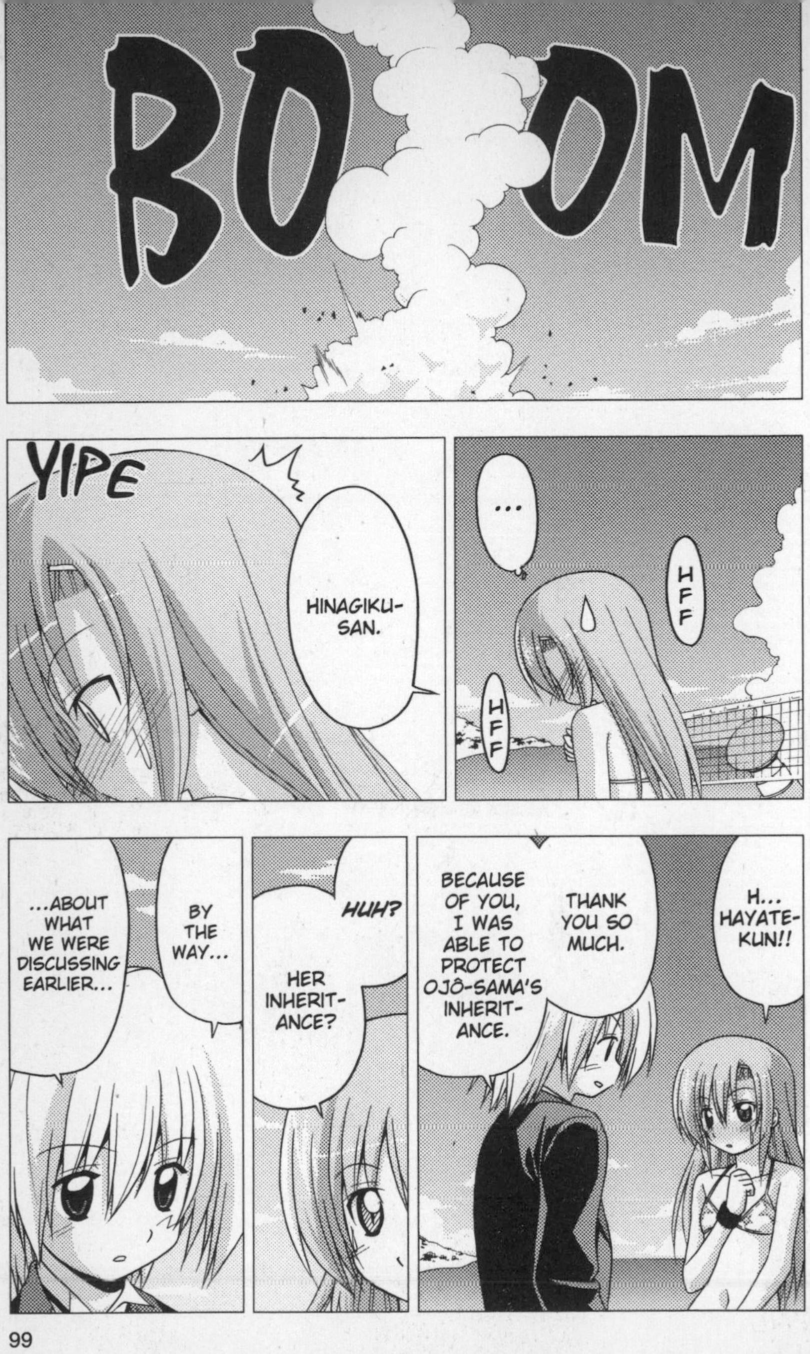
BOOM
...
HFF
HFF
YIPE
HINAGIKU-SAN.
H... HAYATE-KUN!!
THANK YOU SO MUCH.
BECAUSE OF YOU, I WAS ABLE TO PROTECT OJÔ-SAMA'S INHERITANCE.
HUH?
HER INHERITANCE?
BY THE WAY...
...ABOUT WHAT WE WERE DISCUSSING EARLIER...

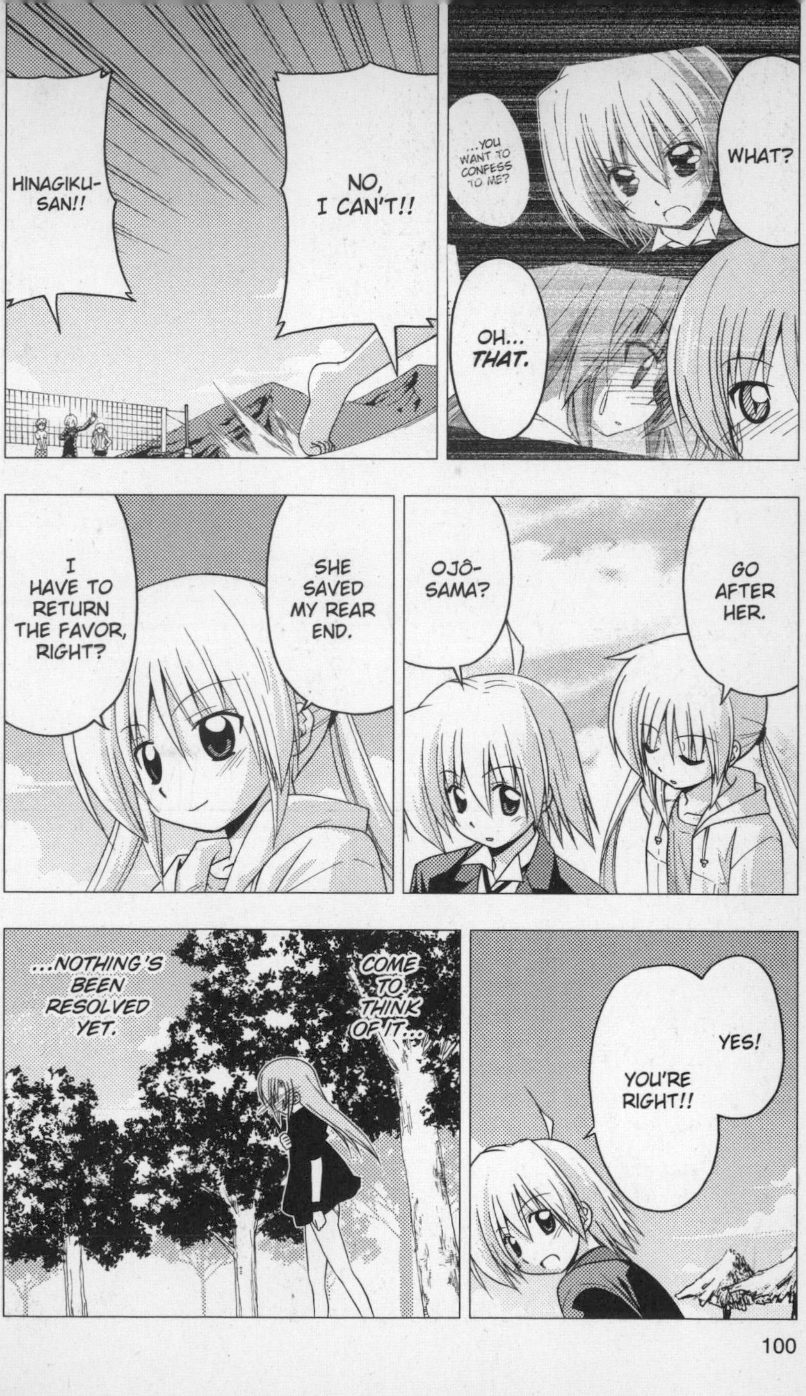
WHAT?
...YOU WANT TO CONFESS TO ME?
OH... THAT.
NO, I CAN'T!!
HINAGIKU-SAN!!
GO AFTER HER.
OJÔ-SAMA?
SHE SAVED MY REAR END.
I HAVE TO RETURN THE FAVOR, RIGHT?
YES!
YOU'RE RIGHT!!
COME TO THINK OF IT...
...NOTHING'S BEEN RESOLVED YET.

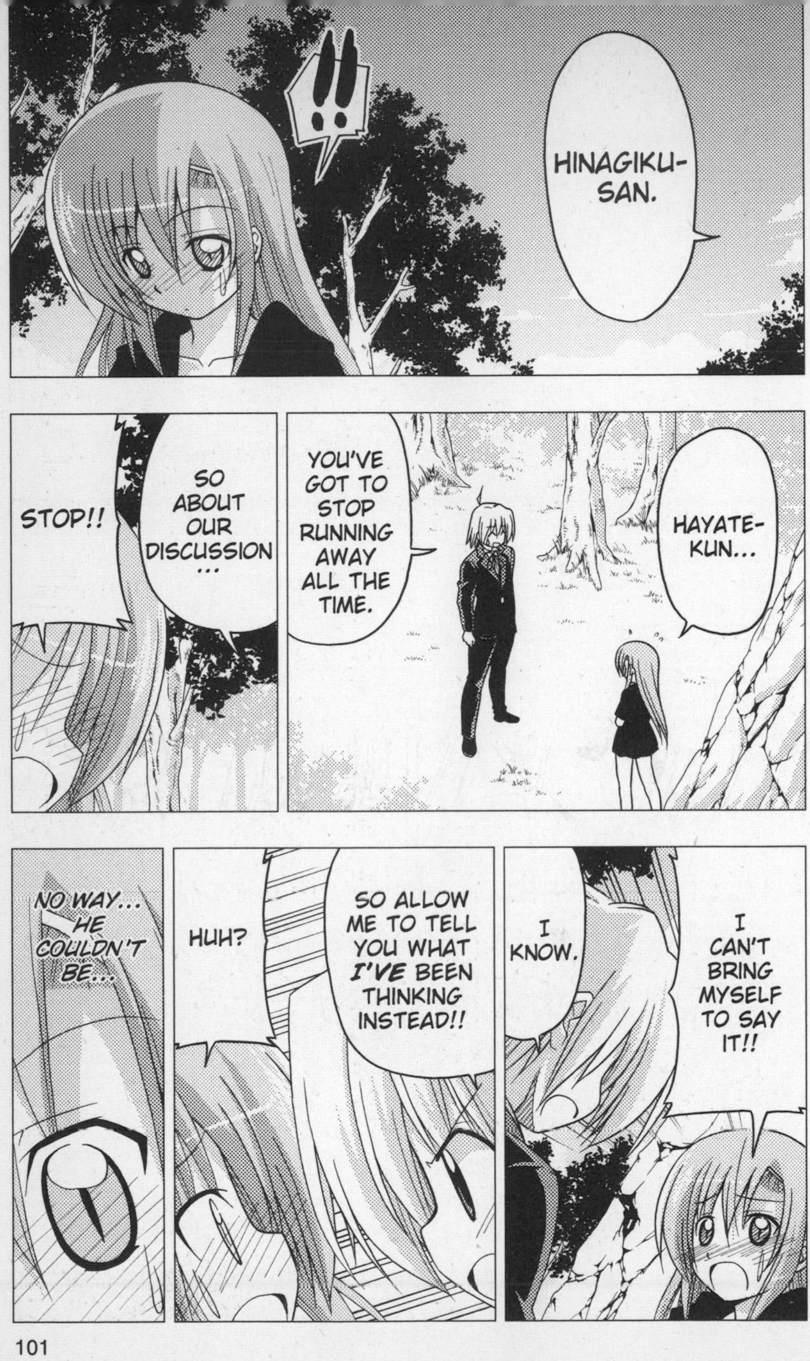
HINAGIKU-SAN.
!!
HAYATE-KUN...
YOU'VE GOT TO STOP RUNNING AWAY ALL THE TIME.
SO ABOUT OUR DISCUSSION...
STOP!!
I CAN'T BRING MYSELF TO SAY IT!!
I KNOW.
SO ALLOW ME TO TELL YOU WHAT *I'VE* BEEN THINKING INSTEAD!!
HUH?
NO WAY... HE COULDN'T BE...

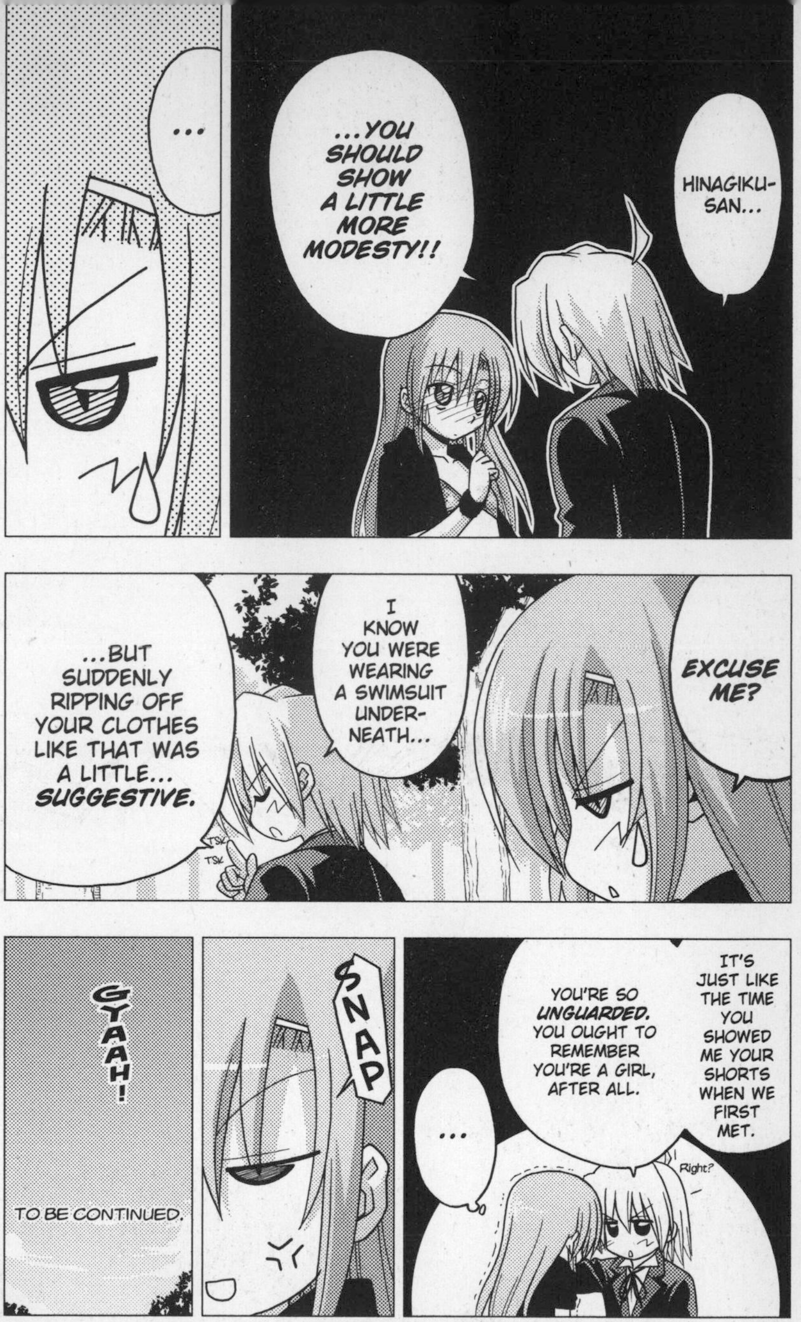
HINAGIKU-SAN...
...YOU SHOULD SHOW A LITTLE MORE MODESTY!!
...
EXCUSE ME?
I KNOW YOU WERE WEARING A SWIMSUIT UNDERNEATH...
TSK TSK
...BUT SUDDENLY RIPPING OFF YOUR CLOTHES LIKE THAT WAS A LITTLE... SUGGESTIVE.
IT'S JUST LIKE THE TIME YOU SHOWED ME YOUR SHORTS WHEN WE FIRST MET.
YOU'RE SO UNGUARDED. YOU OUGHT TO REMEMBER YOU'RE A GIRL, AFTER ALL.
Right?
...
SNAP
GYAAH!
TO BE CONTINUED.

Episode 7: "It Takes a Lot of Effort to Please Girls, But It's Worth It"

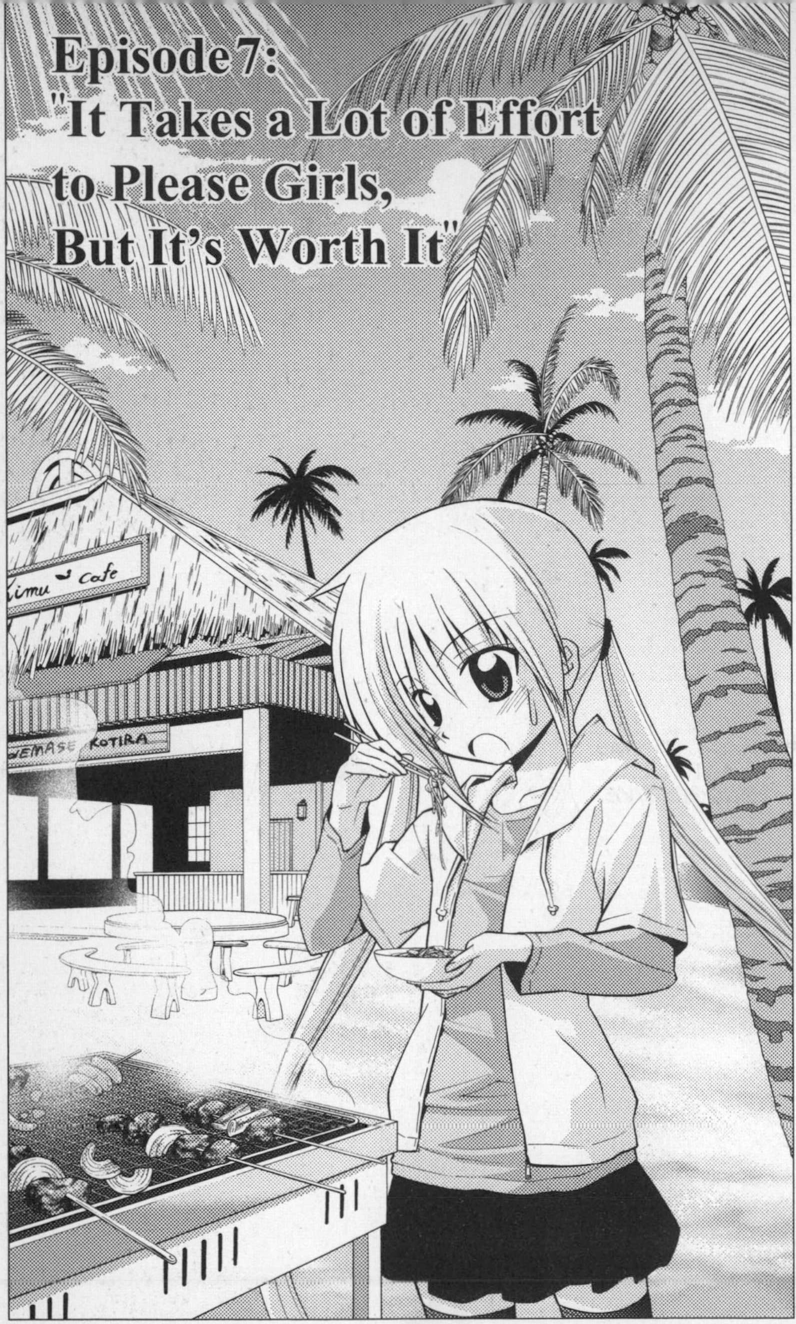

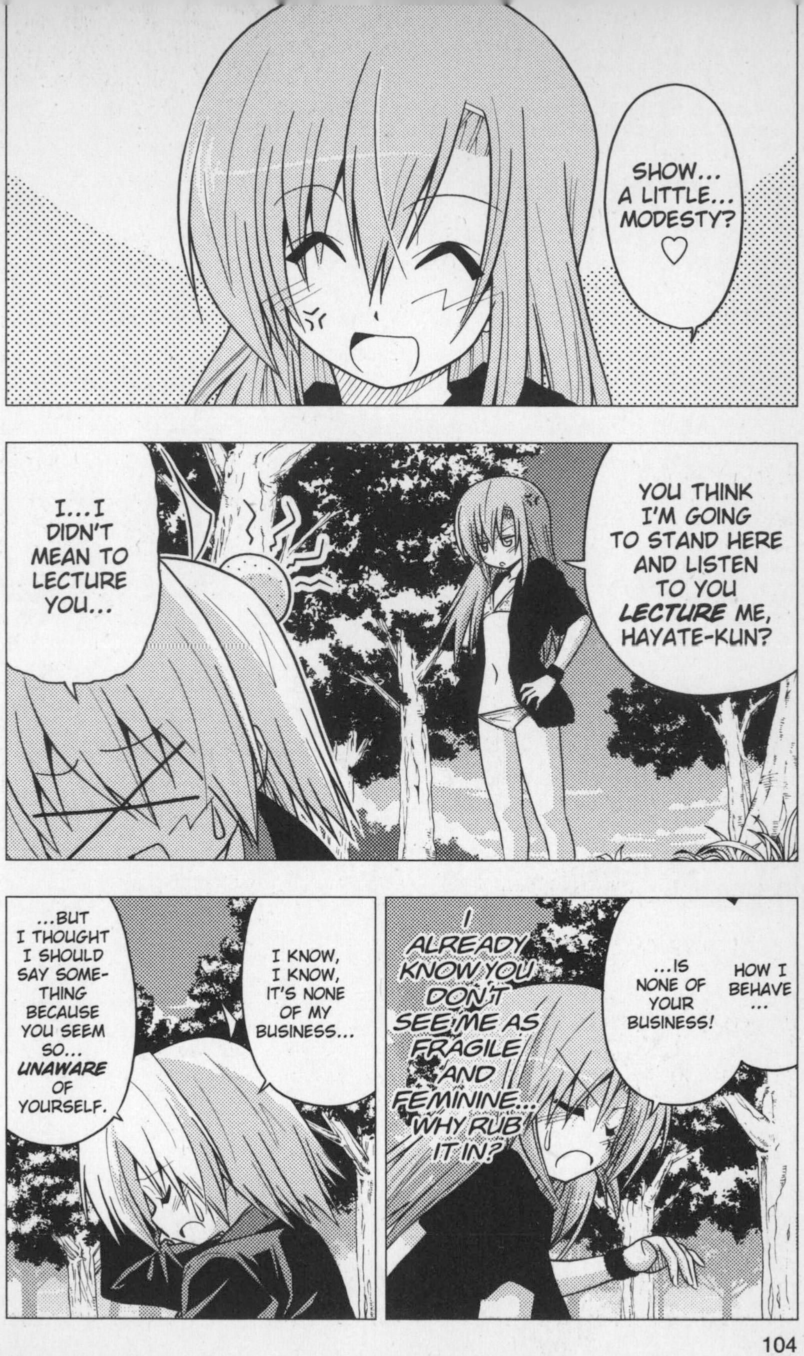
SHOW... A LITTLE... MODESTY? ♡
YOU THINK I'M GOING TO STAND HERE AND LISTEN TO YOU *LECTURE* ME, HAYATE-KUN?
I...I DIDN'T MEAN TO LECTURE YOU...
HOW I BEHAVE ...
...IS NONE OF YOUR BUSINESS!
I ALREADY KNOW YOU DON'T SEE ME AS FRAGILE AND FEMININE... WHY RUB IT IN?
I KNOW, I KNOW, IT'S NONE OF MY BUSINESS...
...BUT I THOUGHT I SHOULD SAY SOME-THING BECAUSE YOU SEEM SO... *UNAWARE* OF YOURSELF.

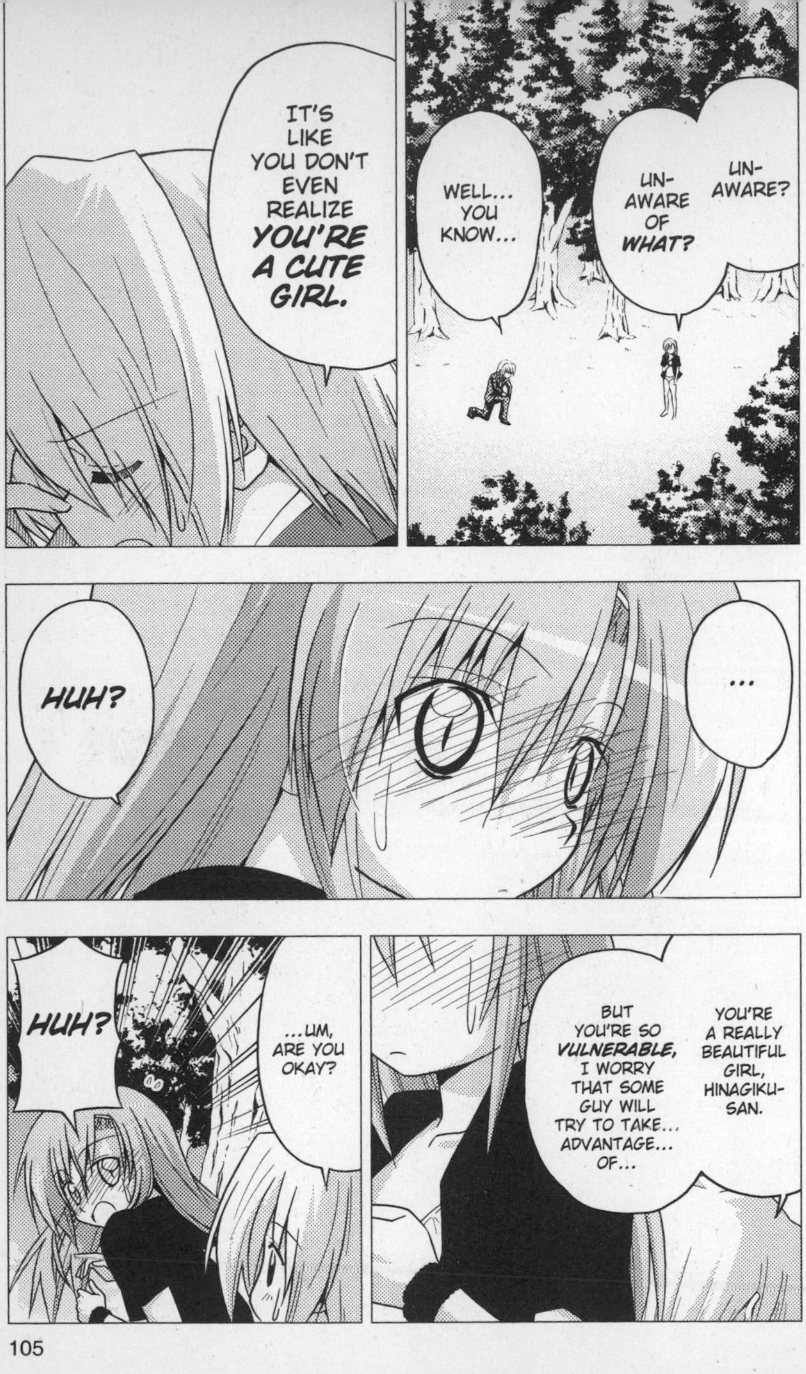
UN-AWARE?
UN-AWARE OF WHAT?
WELL... YOU KNOW...
IT'S LIKE YOU DON'T EVEN REALIZE YOU'RE A CUTE GIRL.
...
HUH?
YOU'RE A REALLY BEAUTIFUL GIRL, HINAGIKU-SAN.
BUT YOU'RE SO VULNERABLE, I WORRY THAT SOME GUY WILL TRY TO TAKE... ADVANTAGE... OF...
...UM, ARE YOU OKAY?
HUH?

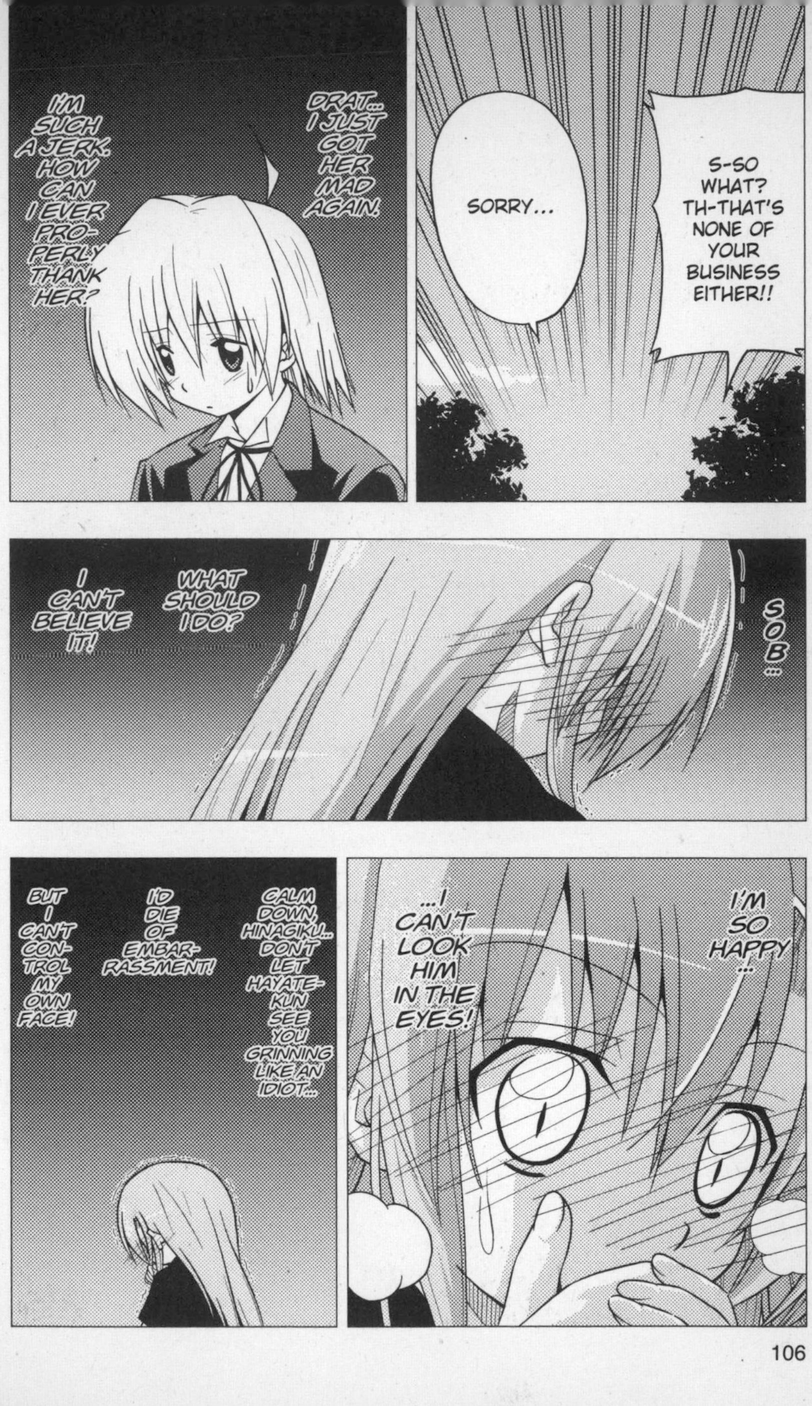
S-SO WHAT? TH-THAT'S NONE OF YOUR BUSINESS EITHER!!
SORRY...
DRAT... I JUST GOT HER MAD AGAIN.
I'M SUCH A JERK. HOW CAN I EVER PROPERLY THANK HER?
SOB...
WHAT SHOULD I DO?
I CAN'T BELIEVE IT!
I'M SO HAPPY...
...I CAN'T LOOK HIM IN THE EYES!
CALM DOWN, HINAGIKU... DON'T LET HAYATE-KUN SEE YOU GRINNING LIKE AN IDIOT...
I'D DIE OF EMBARRASSMENT!
BUT I CAN'T CONTROL MY OWN FACE!

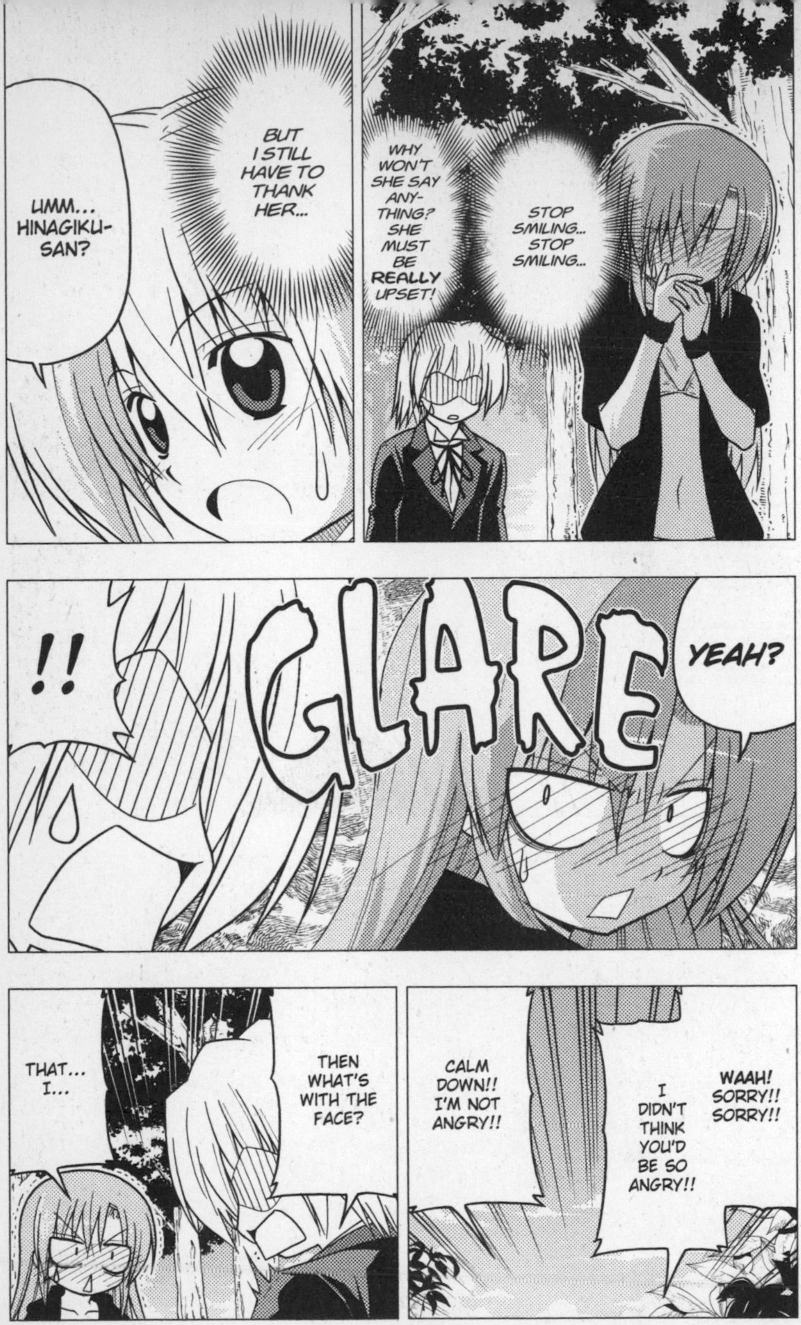
STOP SMILING... STOP SMILING...
WHY WON'T SHE SAY ANYTHING? SHE MUST BE **REALLY** UPSET!
BUT I STILL HAVE TO THANK HER...
UMM... HINAGIKU-SAN?
YEAH?
GLARE
!!
WAAH! SORRY!! SORRY!!
I DIDN'T THINK YOU'D BE SO ANGRY!!
CALM DOWN!! I'M NOT ANGRY!!
THEN WHAT'S WITH THE FACE?
THAT... I...

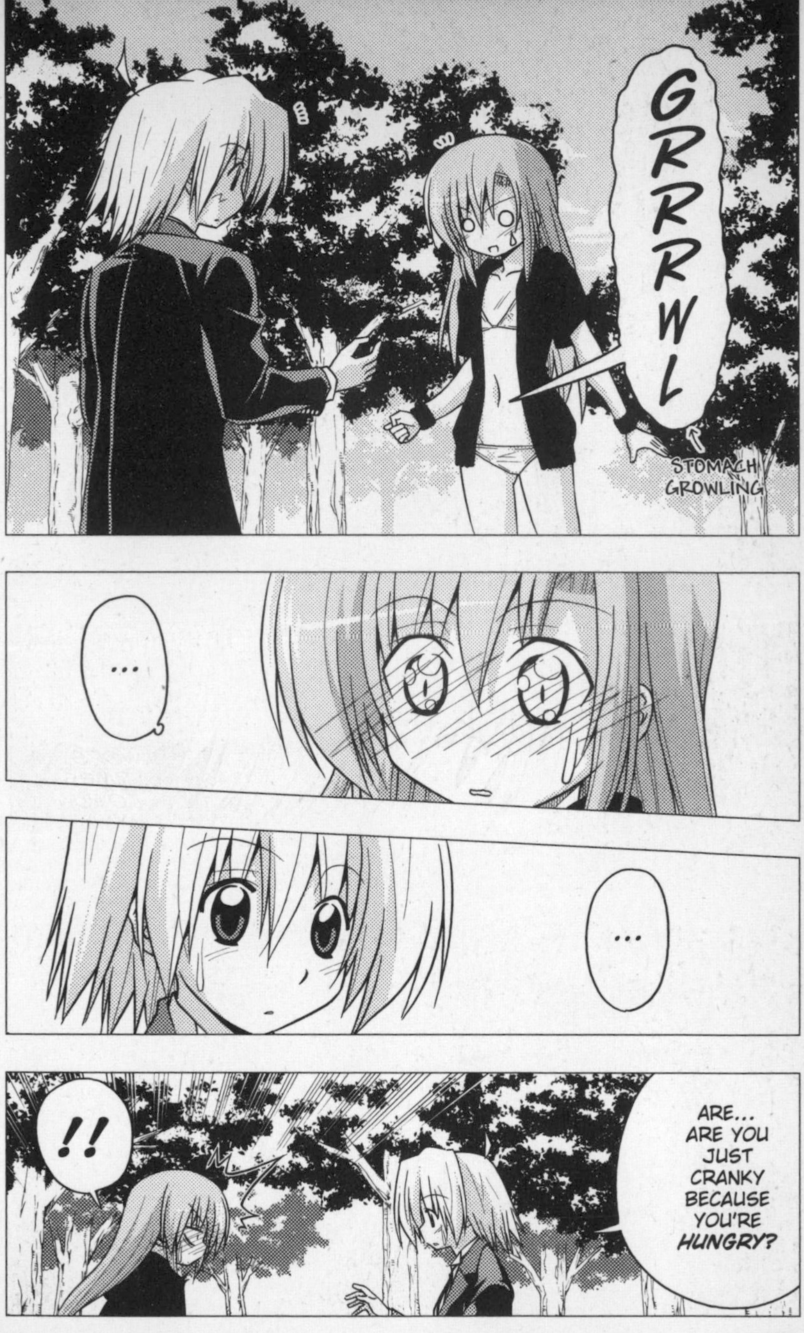
GRRRWL
STOMACH GROWLING
...
...
ARE... ARE YOU JUST CRANKY BECAUSE YOU'RE HUNGRY?
!!

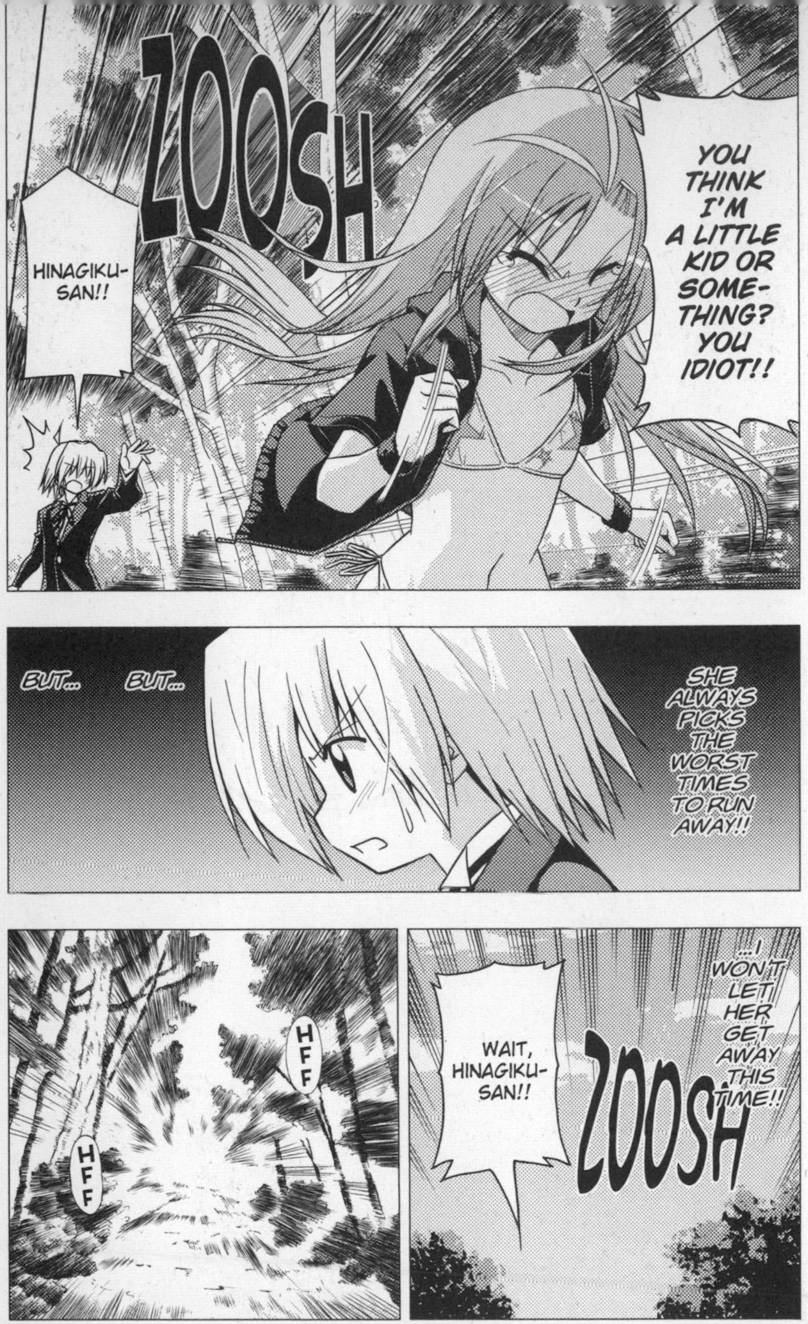
YOU THINK I'M A LITTLE KID OR SOMETHING? YOU IDIOT!!
ZOOSH
HINAGIKU-SAN!!
SHE ALWAYS PICKS THE WORST TIMES TO RUN AWAY!!
BUT... BUT...
...I WON'T LET HER GET AWAY THIS TIME!!
ZOOSH
WAIT, HINAGIKU-SAN!!
HFF
HFF

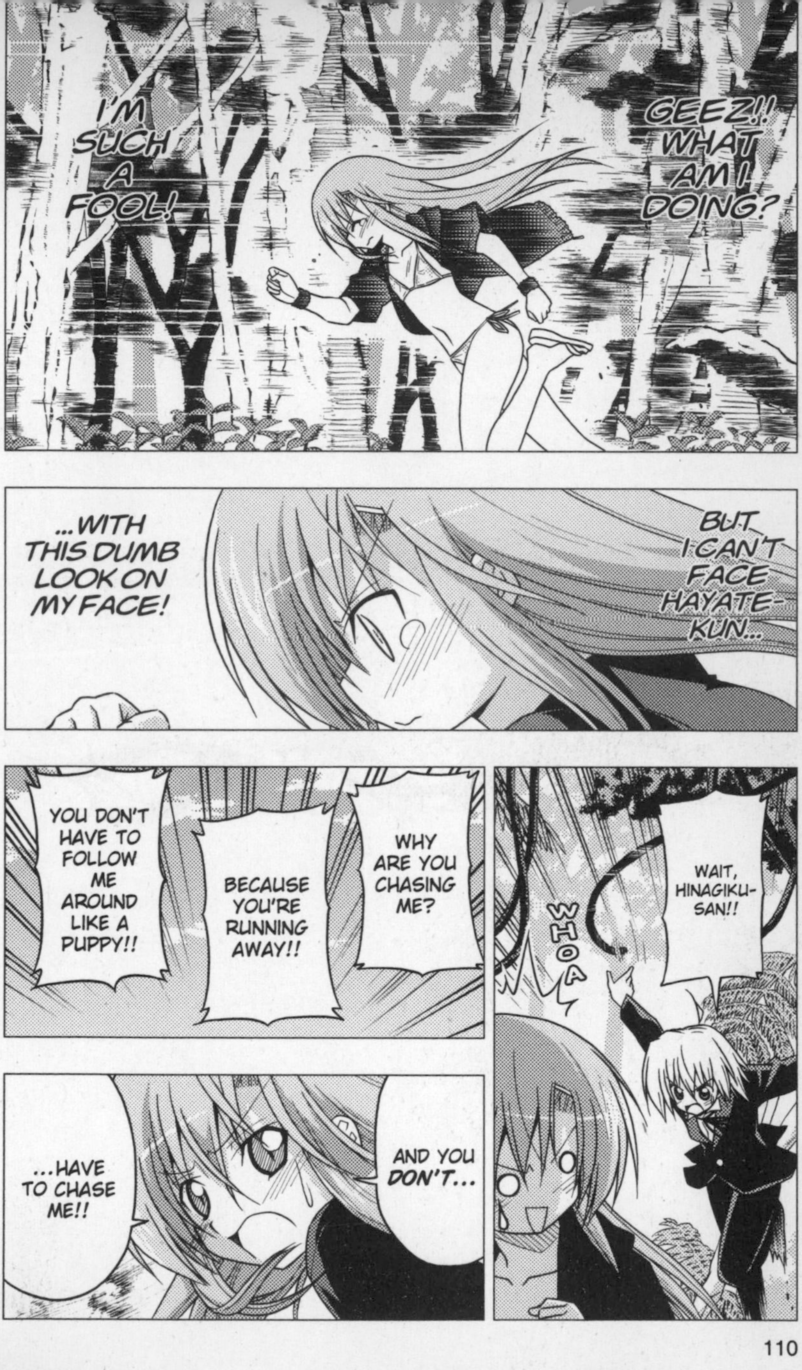
GEEZ!! WHAT AM I DOING?
I'M SUCH A FOOL!
BUT I CAN'T FACE HAYATE-KUN...
...WITH THIS DUMB LOOK ON MY FACE!
WAIT, HINAGIKU-SAN!!
WHOA
WHY ARE YOU CHASING ME?
BECAUSE YOU'RE RUNNING AWAY!!
YOU DON'T HAVE TO FOLLOW ME AROUND LIKE A PUPPY!!
AND YOU DON'T...
...HAVE TO CHASE ME!!

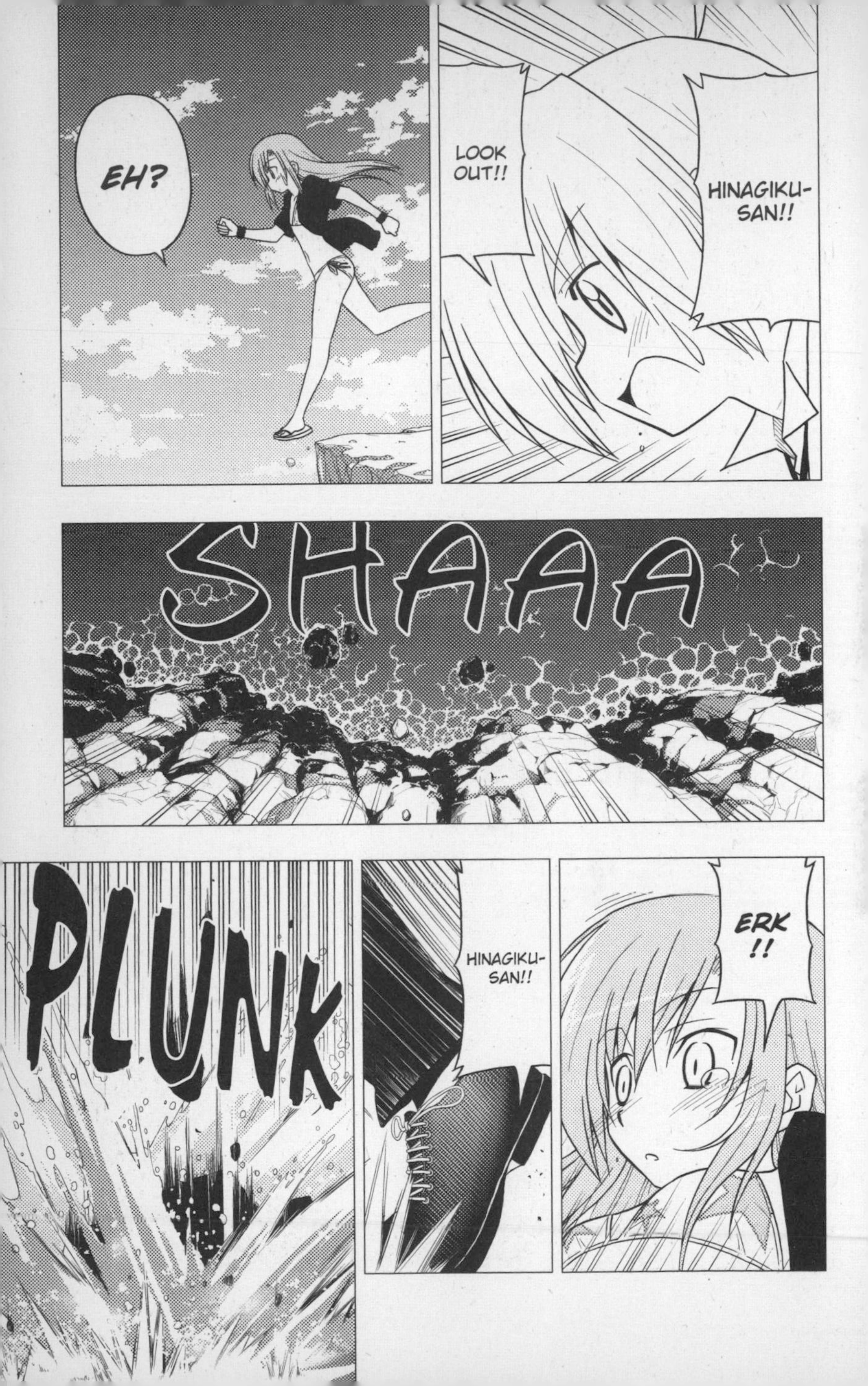
HINAGIKU-SAN!!
LOOK OUT!!
EH?
SHAAAA
ERK !!
HINAGIKU-SAN!!
PLUNK

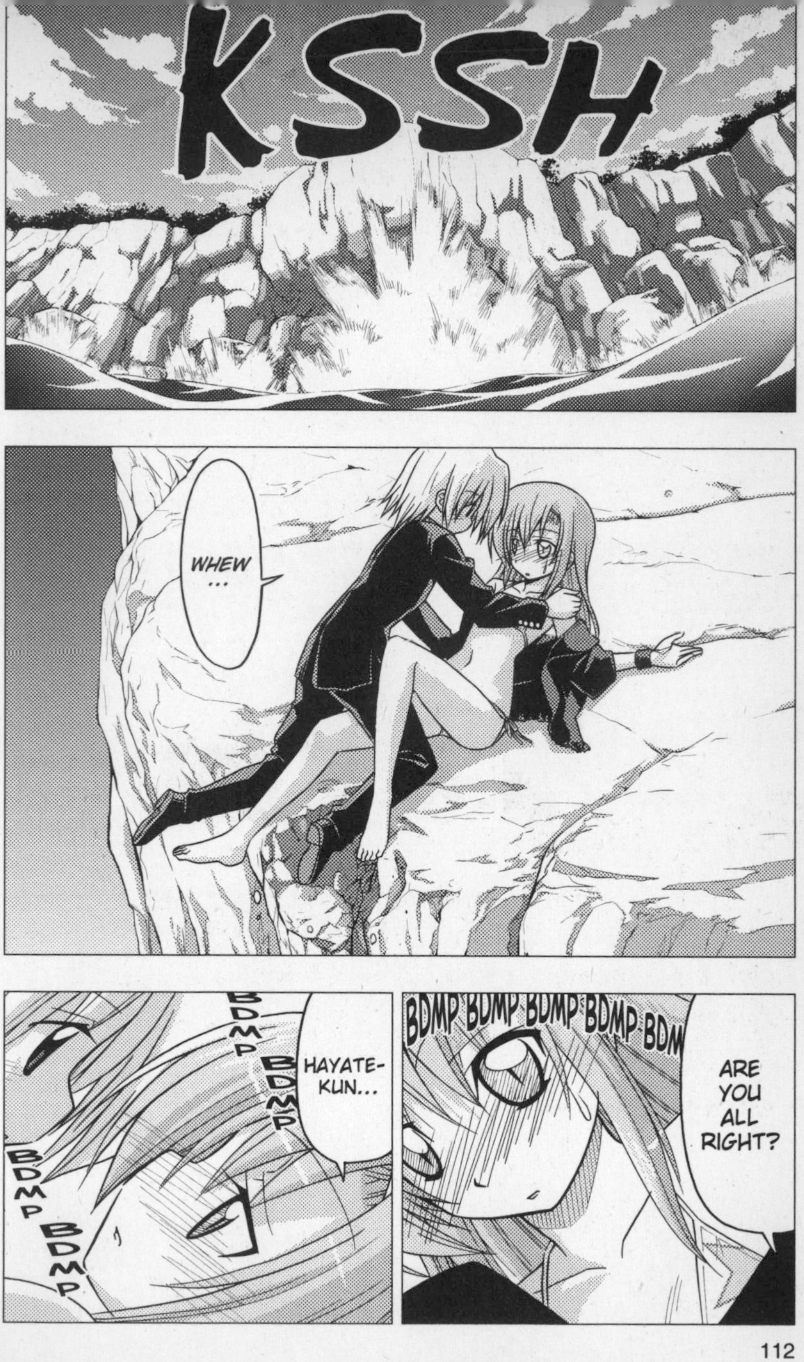
KSSH
WHEW...
BDMP BDMP BDMP BDMP BDM
ARE YOU ALL RIGHT?
BDMP
HAYATE-KUN...
BDMP
BDMP
BDMP

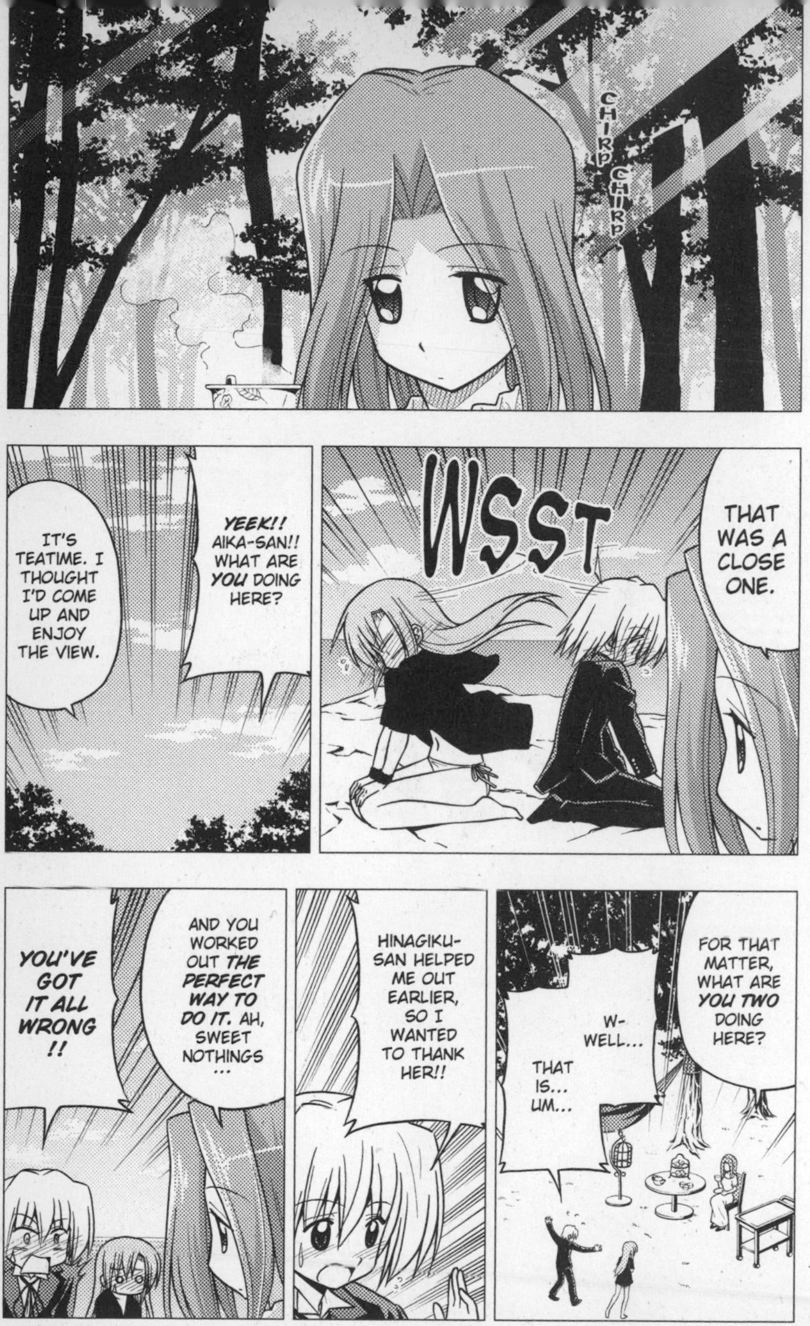
CHIRP CHIRP
WSST
THAT WAS A CLOSE ONE.
YEEK!! AIKA-SAN!! WHAT ARE YOU DOING HERE?
IT'S TEATIME. I THOUGHT I'D COME UP AND ENJOY THE VIEW.
FOR THAT MATTER, WHAT ARE YOU TWO DOING HERE?
W-WELL...
THAT IS... UM...
HINAGIKU-SAN HELPED ME OUT EARLIER, SO I WANTED TO THANK HER!!
AND YOU WORKED OUT THE PERFECT WAY TO DO IT. AH, SWEET NOTHINGS...
YOU'VE GOT IT ALL WRONG!!

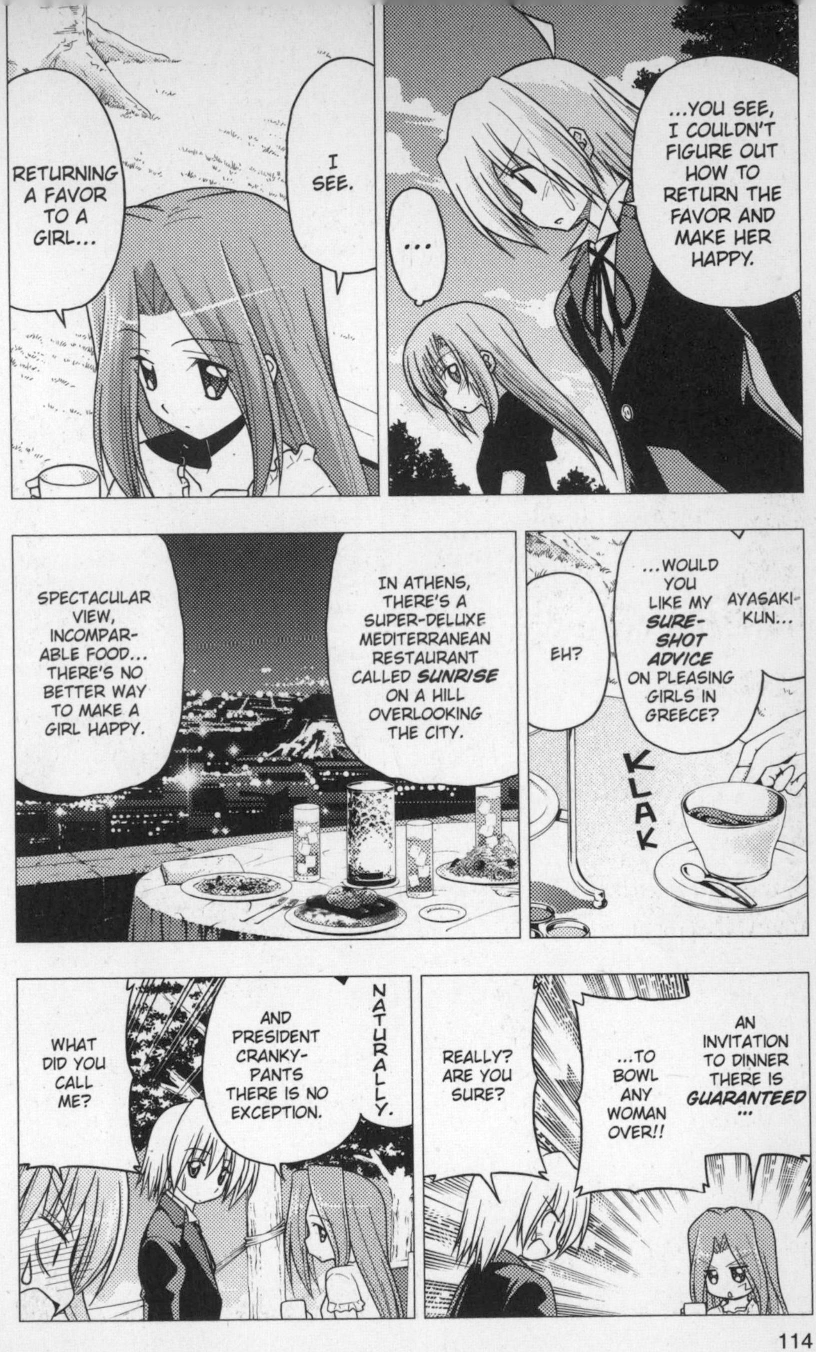
...YOU SEE, I COULDN'T FIGURE OUT HOW TO RETURN THE FAVOR AND MAKE HER HAPPY.
...
I SEE.
RETURNING A FAVOR TO A GIRL...
AYASAKI-KUN...
...WOULD YOU LIKE MY SURE-SHOT ADVICE ON PLEASING GIRLS IN GREECE?
EH?
KLAK
IN ATHENS, THERE'S A SUPER-DELUXE MEDITERRANEAN RESTAURANT CALLED SUNRISE ON A HILL OVERLOOKING THE CITY.
SPECTACULAR VIEW, INCOMPARABLE FOOD... THERE'S NO BETTER WAY TO MAKE A GIRL HAPPY.
AN INVITATION TO DINNER THERE IS GUARANTEED...
...TO BOWL ANY WOMAN OVER!!
REALLY? ARE YOU SURE?
NATURALLY.
AND PRESIDENT CRANKY-PANTS THERE IS NO EXCEPTION.
WHAT DID YOU CALL ME?

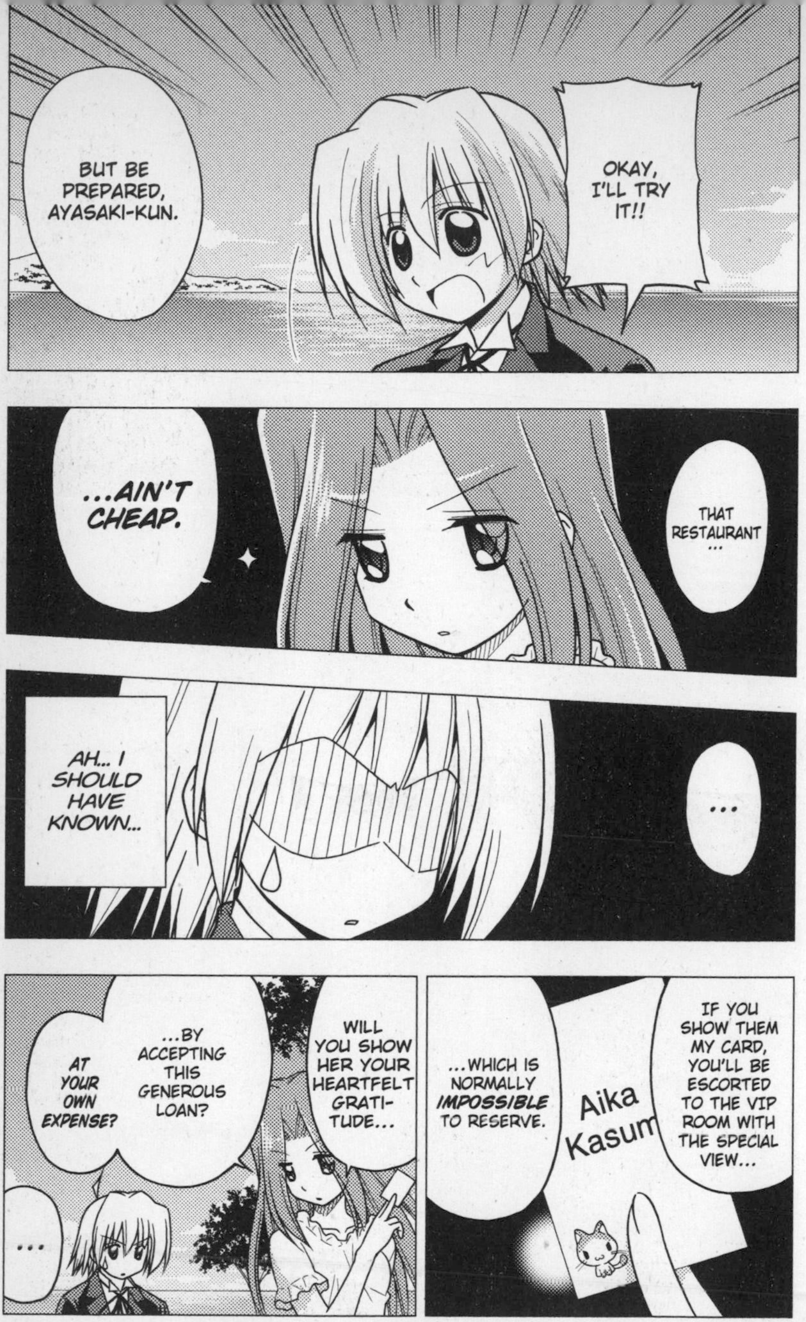
OKAY, I'LL TRY IT!!
BUT BE PREPARED, AYASAKI-KUN.
THAT RESTAURANT ...
...AIN'T CHEAP.
...
AH... I SHOULD HAVE KNOWN...
IF YOU SHOW THEM MY CARD, YOU'LL BE ESCORTED TO THE VIP ROOM WITH THE SPECIAL VIEW...
Aika Kasum
...WHICH IS NORMALLY IMPOSSIBLE TO RESERVE.
WILL YOU SHOW HER YOUR HEARTFELT GRATITUDE...
...BY ACCEPTING THIS GENEROUS LOAN?
AT YOUR OWN EXPENSE?
...

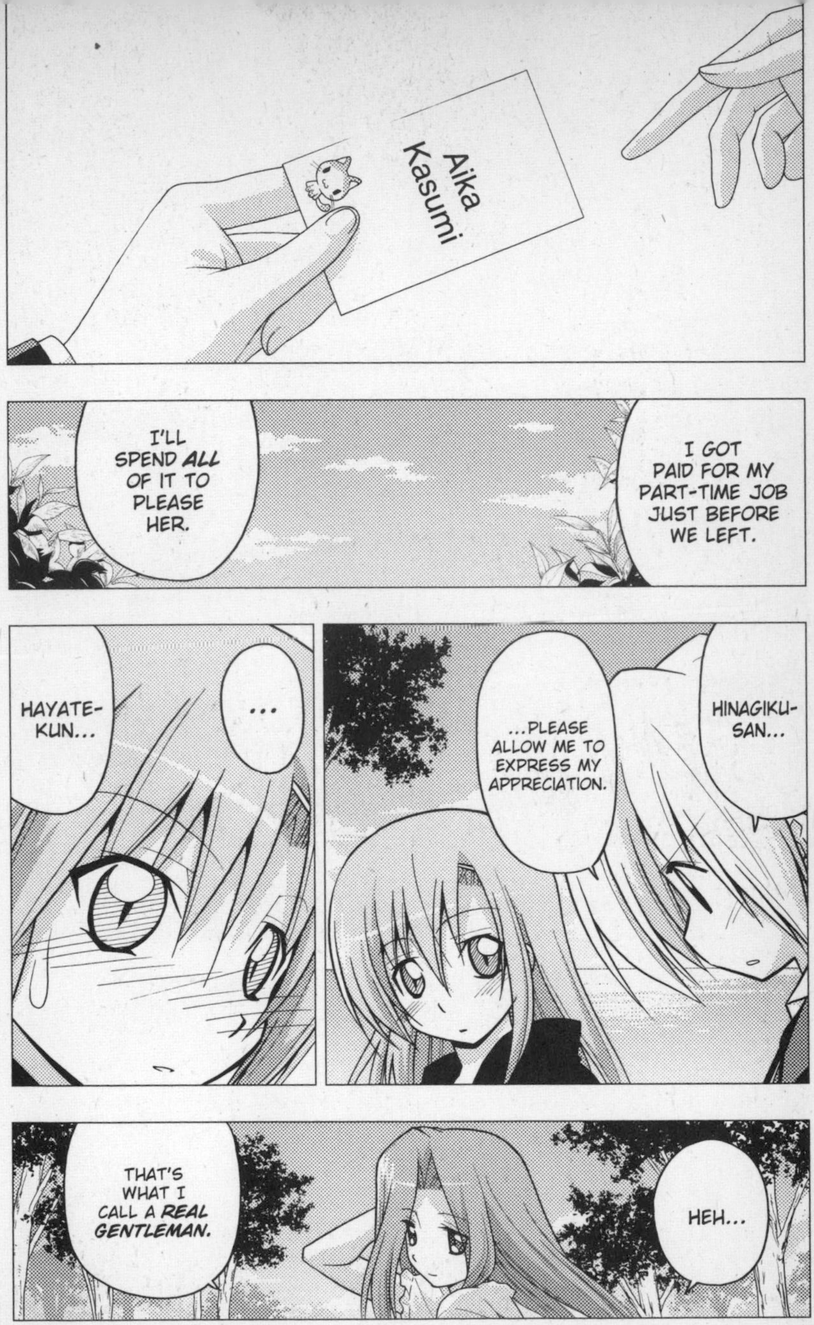

Aika Kasumi
I GOT PAID FOR MY PART-TIME JOB JUST BEFORE WE LEFT.
I'LL SPEND ALL OF IT TO PLEASE HER.
HINAGIKU-SAN...
...PLEASE ALLOW ME TO EXPRESS MY APPRECIATION.
...
HAYATE-KUN...
HEH...
THAT'S WHAT I CALL A REAL GENTLEMAN.

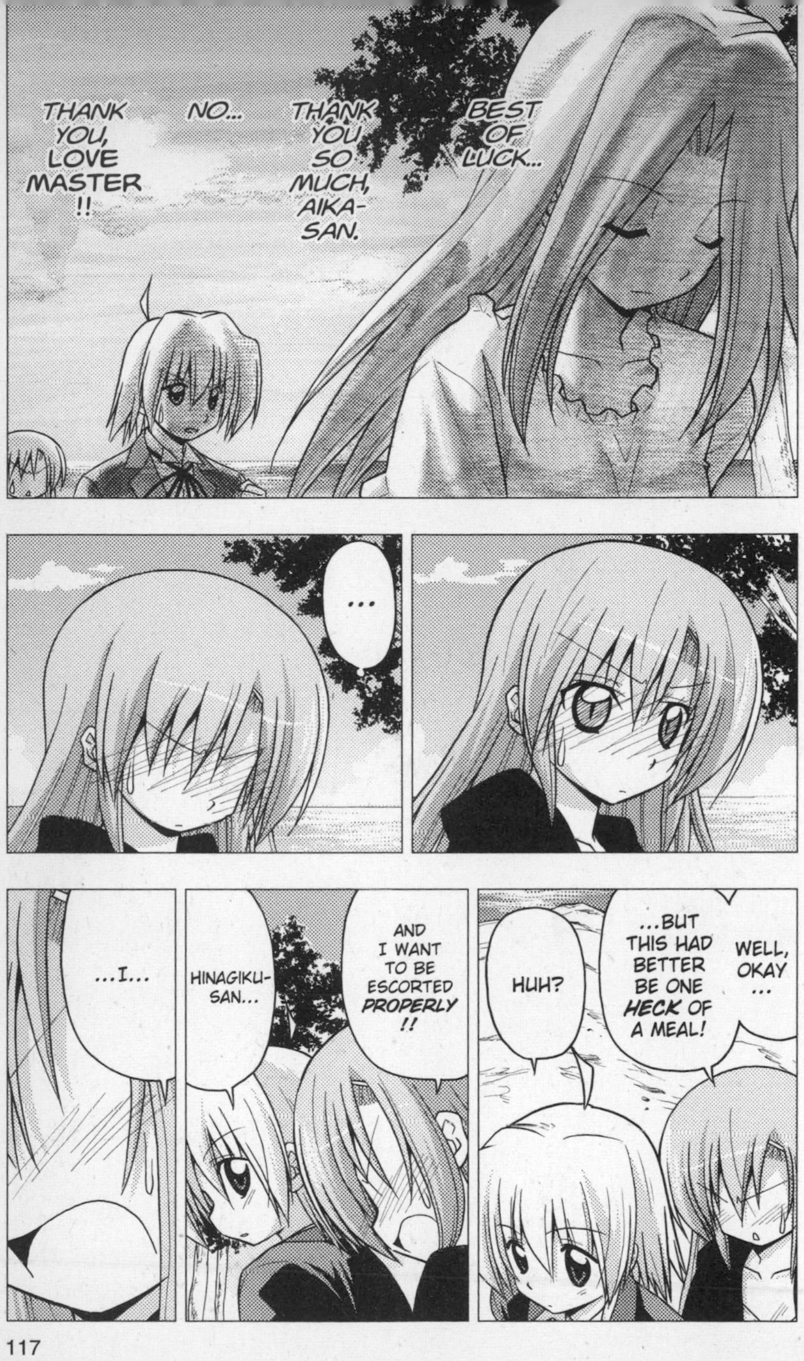
BEST OF LUCK...
THANK YOU SO MUCH, AIKA-SAN.
NO...
THANK YOU, LOVE MASTER!!
...
WELL, OKAY ...
...BUT THIS HAD BETTER BE ONE HECK OF A MEAL!
HUH?
AND I WANT TO BE ESCORTED PROPERLY!!
HINAGIKU-SAN...
...I...

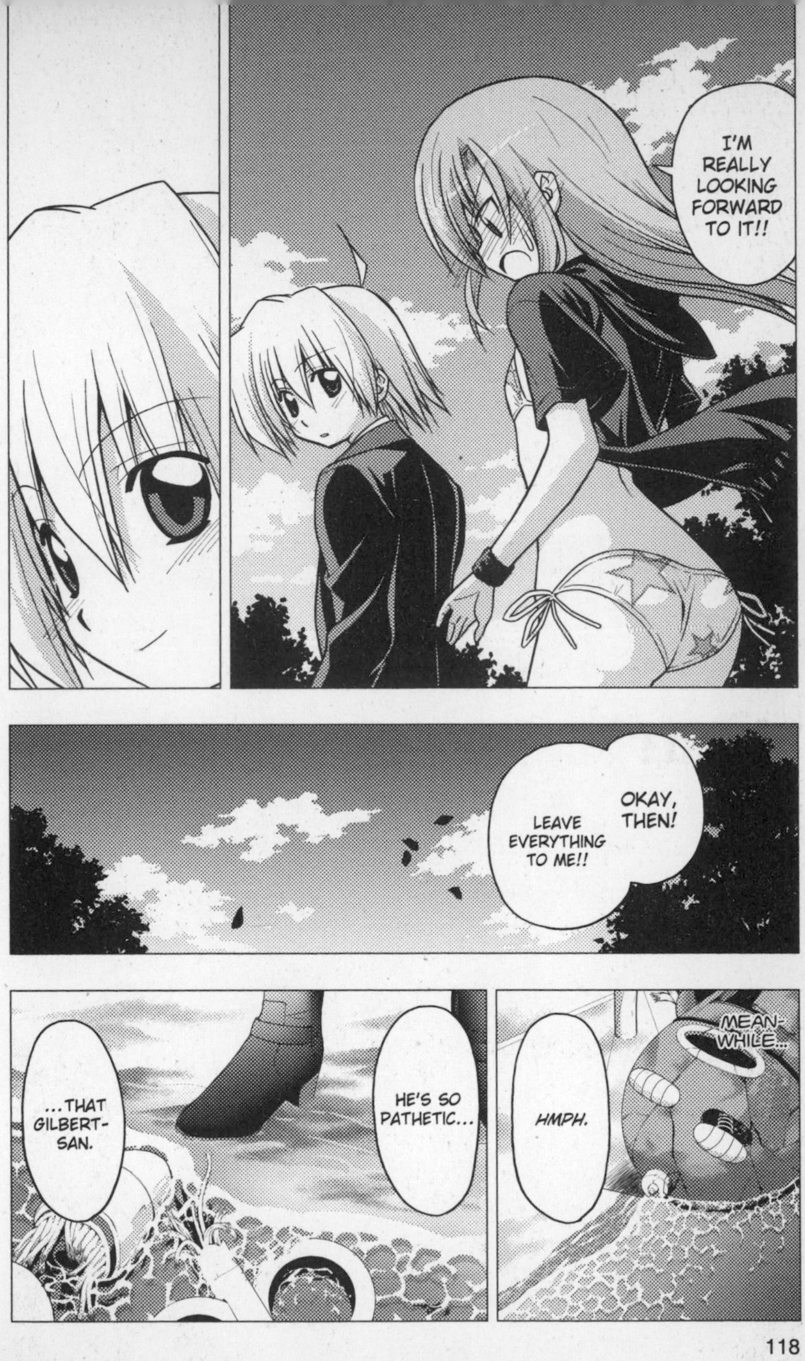
I'M REALLY LOOKING FORWARD TO IT!!
OKAY, THEN!
LEAVE EVERYTHING TO ME!!
MEAN-WHILE...
HMPH.
HE'S SO PATHETIC...
...THAT GILBERT-SAN.

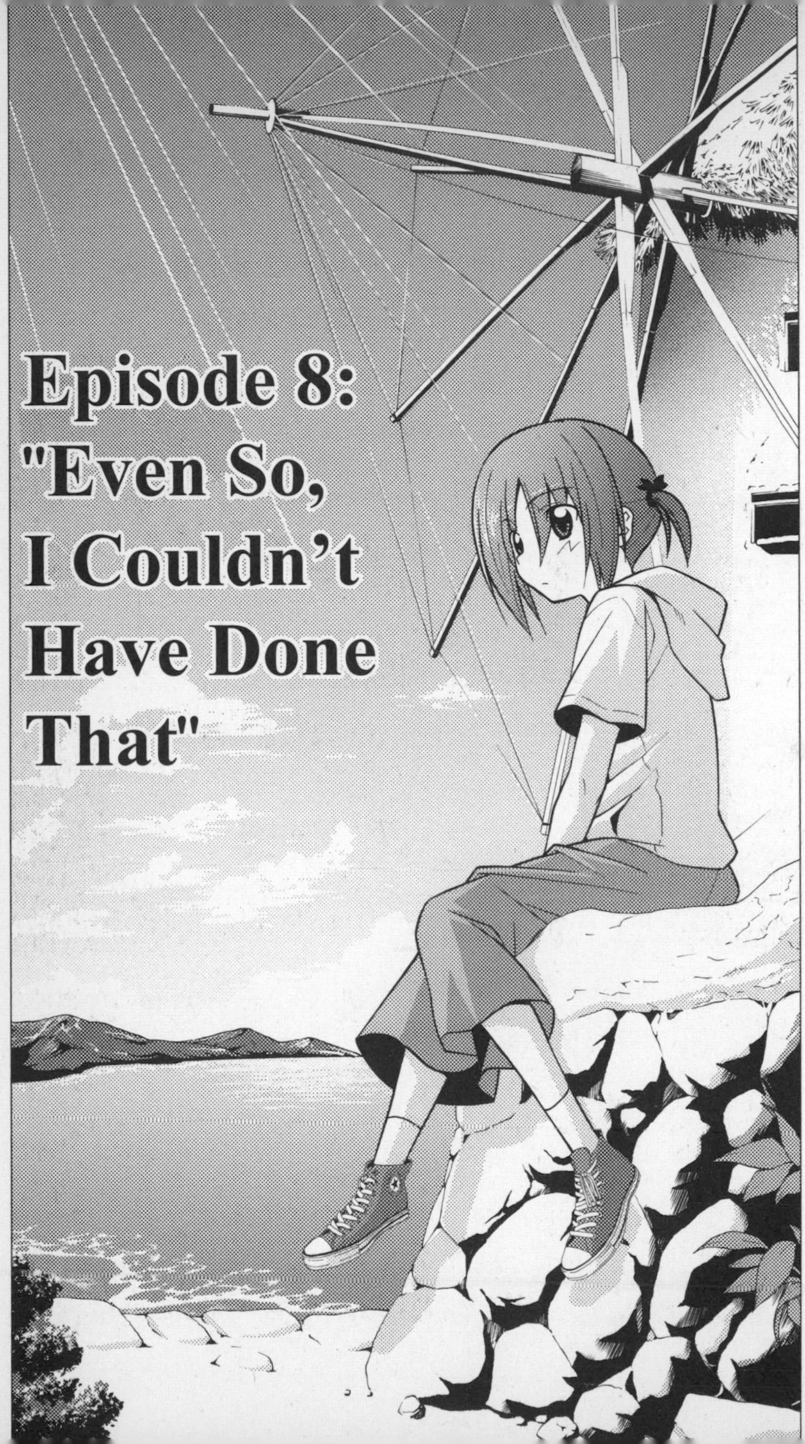
Episode 8:
"Even So, I Couldn't Have Done That"

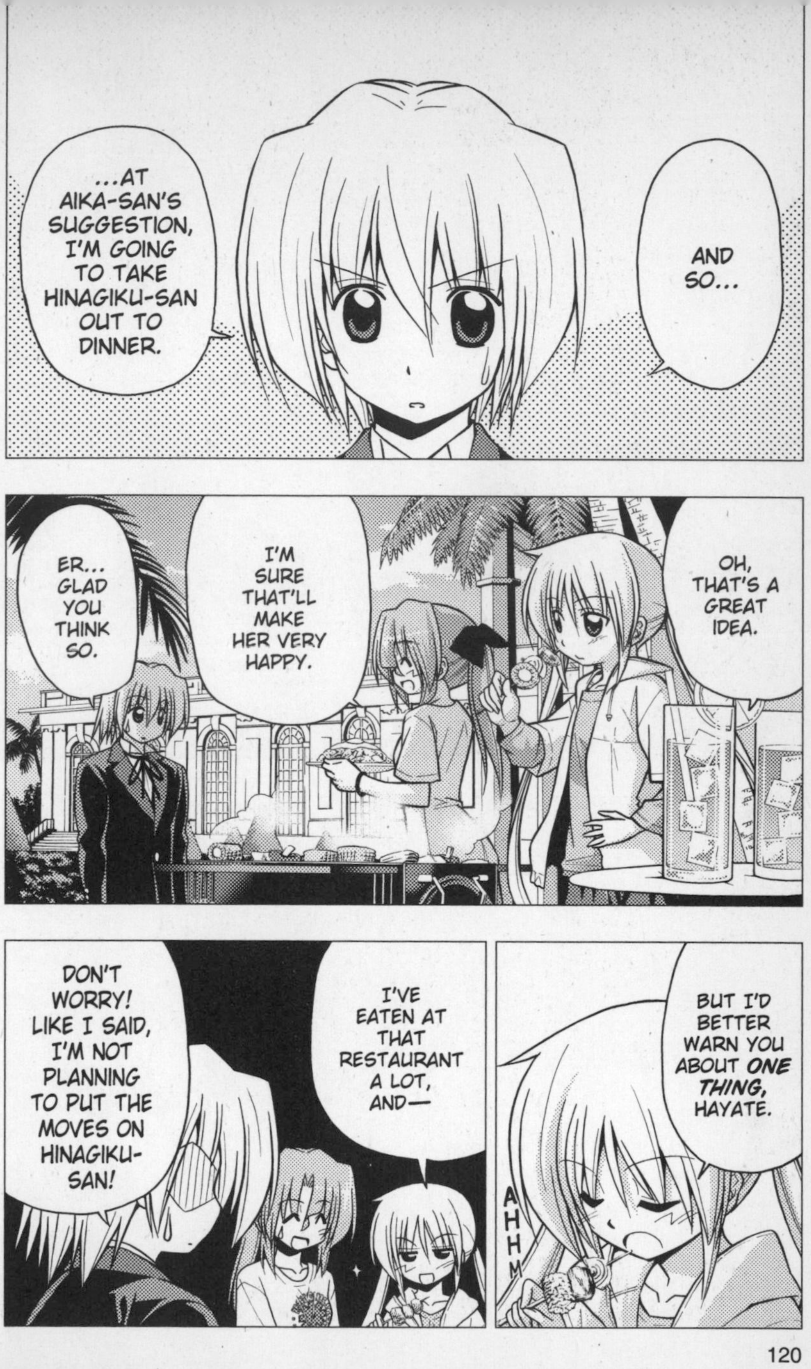
AND SO...
...AT AIKA-SAN'S SUGGESTION, I'M GOING TO TAKE HINAGIKU-SAN OUT TO DINNER.
OH, THAT'S A GREAT IDEA.
I'M SURE THAT'LL MAKE HER VERY HAPPY.
ER... GLAD YOU THINK SO.
BUT I'D BETTER WARN YOU ABOUT *ONE THING,* HAYATE.
AHHM
I'VE EATEN AT THAT RESTAURANT A LOT, AND—
DON'T WORRY! LIKE I SAID, I'M NOT PLANNING TO PUT THE MOVES ON HINAGIKU-SAN!

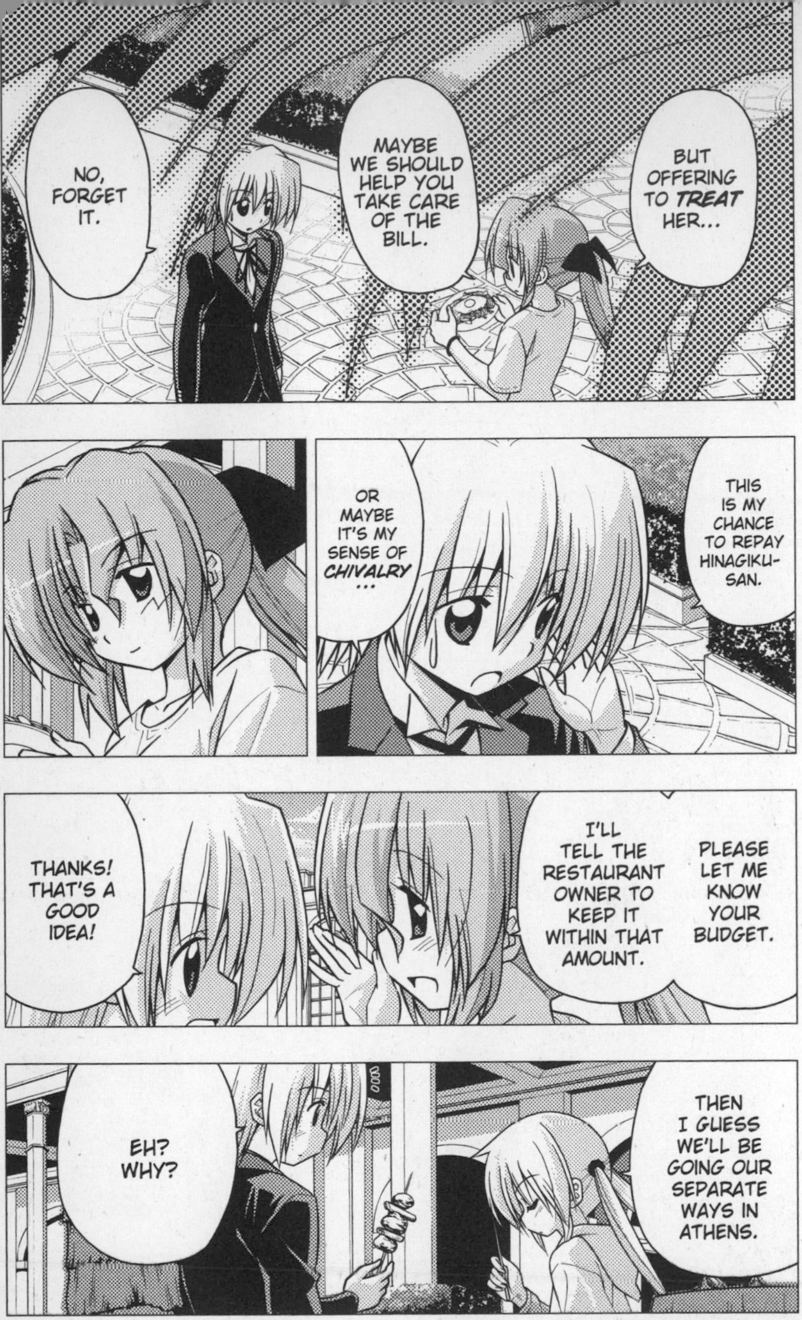
BUT OFFERING TO TREAT HER...
MAYBE WE SHOULD HELP YOU TAKE CARE OF THE BILL.
NO, FORGET IT.
THIS IS MY CHANCE TO REPAY HINAGIKU-SAN.
OR MAYBE IT'S MY SENSE OF CHIVALRY...
PLEASE LET ME KNOW YOUR BUDGET.
I'LL TELL THE RESTAURANT OWNER TO KEEP IT WITHIN THAT AMOUNT.
THANKS! THAT'S A GOOD IDEA!
THEN I GUESS WE'LL BE GOING OUR SEPARATE WAYS IN ATHENS.
EH? WHY?

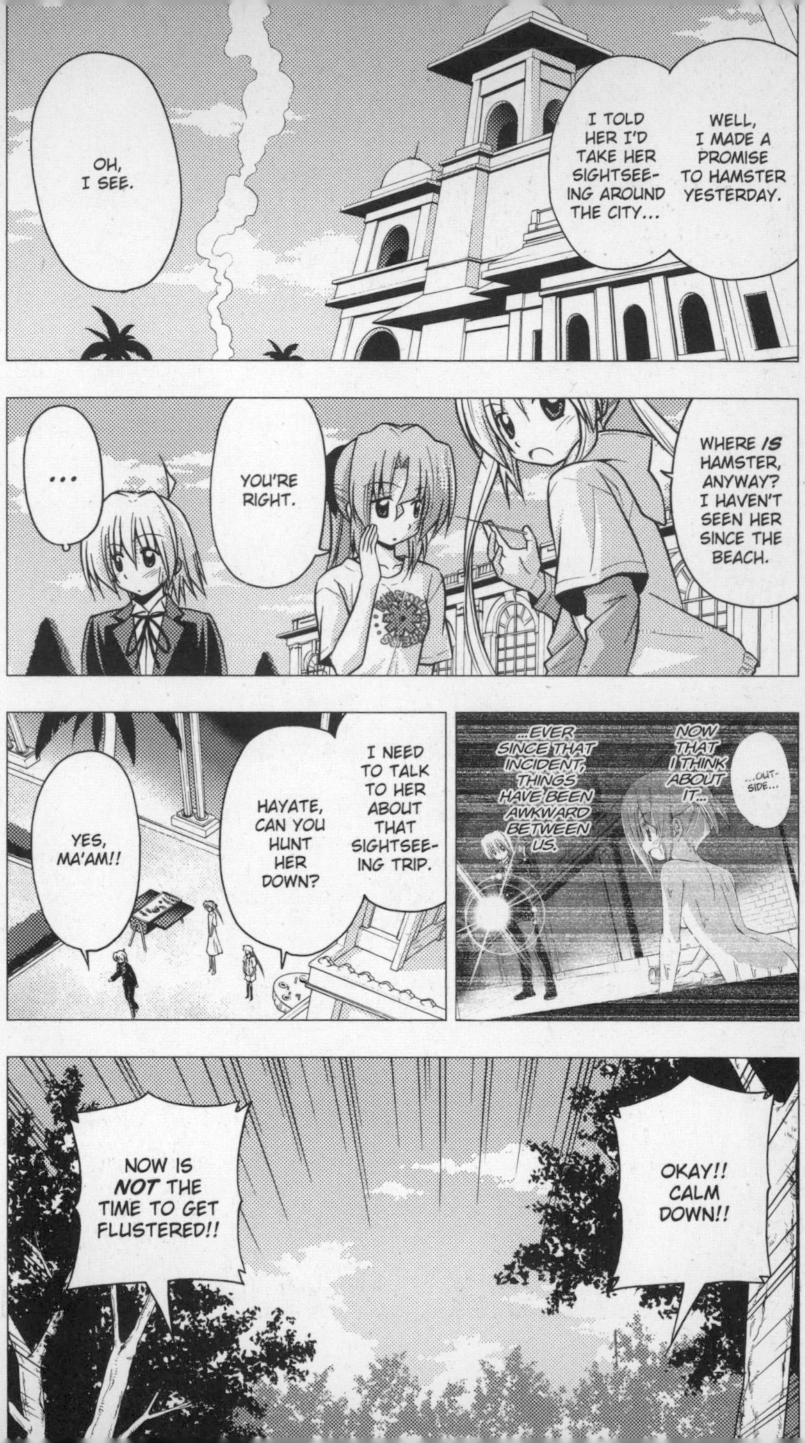
WELL, I MADE A PROMISE TO HAMSTER YESTERDAY.
I TOLD HER I'D TAKE HER SIGHTSEE-ING AROUND THE CITY...
OH, I SEE.
WHERE *IS* HAMSTER, ANYWAY? I HAVEN'T SEEN HER SINCE THE BEACH.
YOU'RE RIGHT.
...
NOW THAT I THINK ABOUT IT...
...EVER SINCE THAT INCIDENT, THINGS HAVE BEEN AWKWARD BETWEEN US.
...OUT-SIDE...
I NEED TO TALK TO HER ABOUT THAT SIGHTSEE-ING TRIP.
HAYATE, CAN YOU HUNT HER DOWN?
YES, MA'AM!!
OKAY!! CALM DOWN!!
NOW IS ***NOT*** THE TIME TO GET FLUSTERED!!

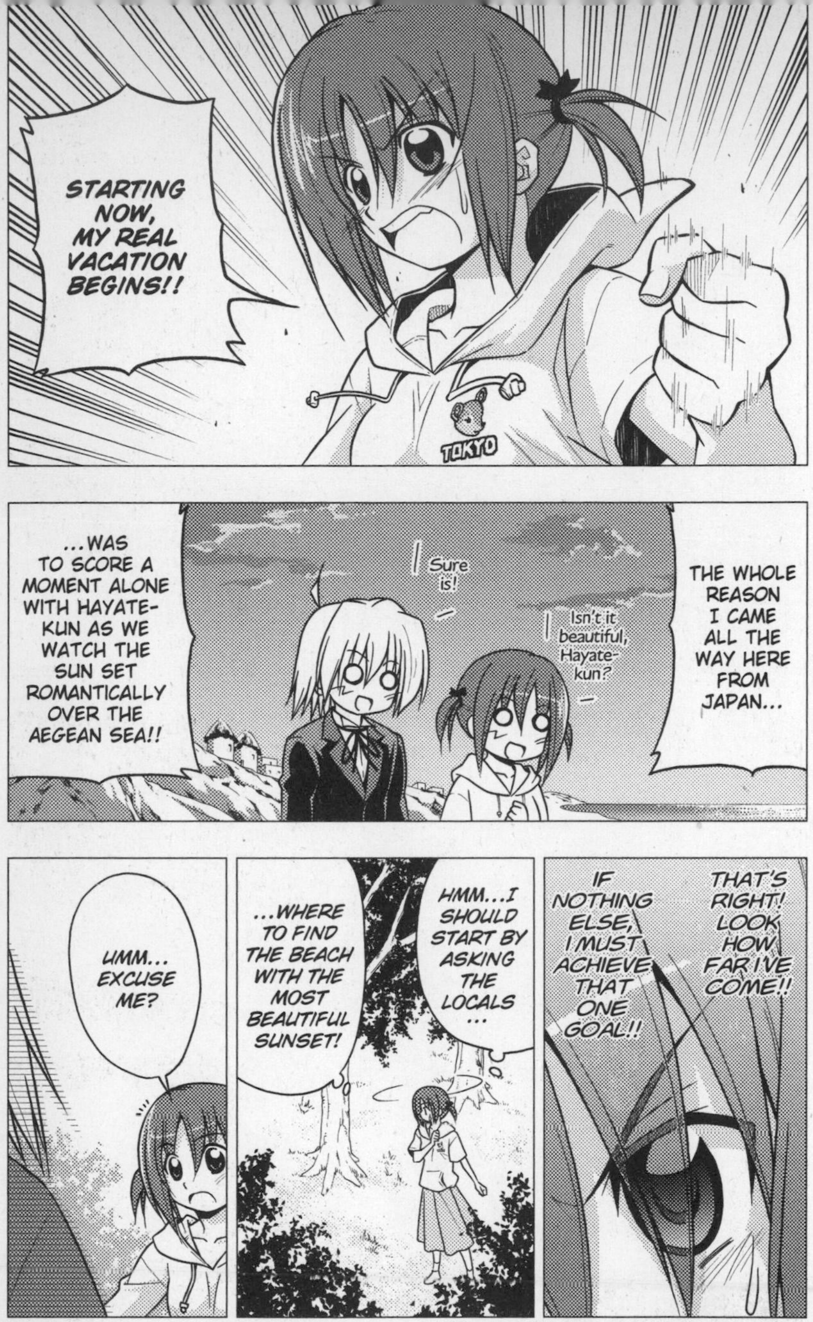
STARTING NOW, MY REAL VACATION BEGINS!!
TOKYO
THE WHOLE REASON I CAME ALL THE WAY HERE FROM JAPAN...
Isn't it beautiful, Hayate-kun?
Sure is!
...WAS TO SCORE A MOMENT ALONE WITH HAYATE-KUN AS WE WATCH THE SUN SET ROMANTICALLY OVER THE AEGEAN SEA!!
THAT'S RIGHT! LOOK HOW FAR I'VE COME!!
IF NOTHING ELSE, I MUST ACHIEVE THAT ONE GOAL!!
HMM...I SHOULD START BY ASKING THE LOCALS...
...WHERE TO FIND THE BEACH WITH THE MOST BEAUTIFUL SUNSET!
UMM... EXCUSE ME?

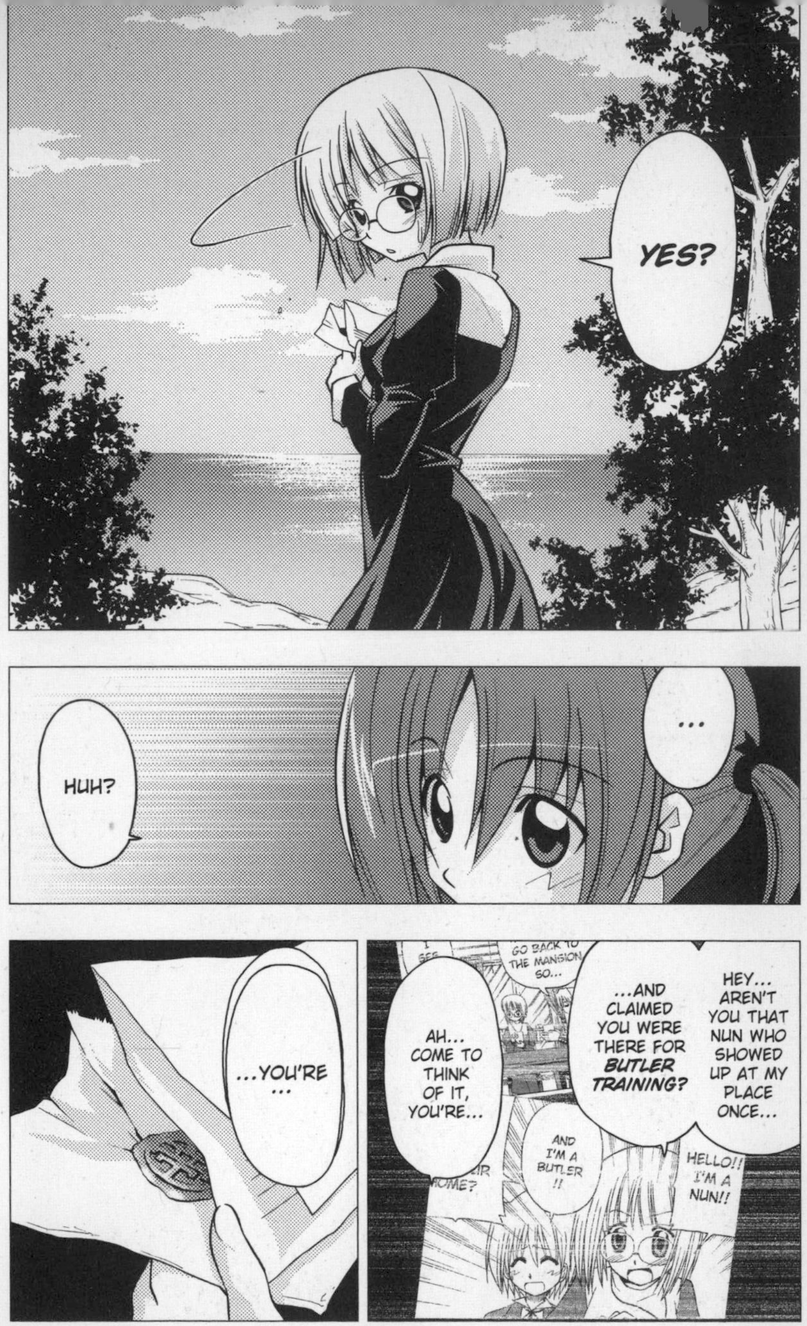
YES?
...
HUH?
HEY... AREN'T YOU THAT NUN WHO SHOWED UP AT MY PLACE ONCE...
...AND CLAIMED YOU WERE THERE FOR BUTLER TRAINING?
GO BACK TO THE MANSION SO...
HELLO!! I'M A NUN!!
AND I'M A BUTLER !!
AH... COME TO THINK OF IT, YOU'RE...
...YOU'RE ...

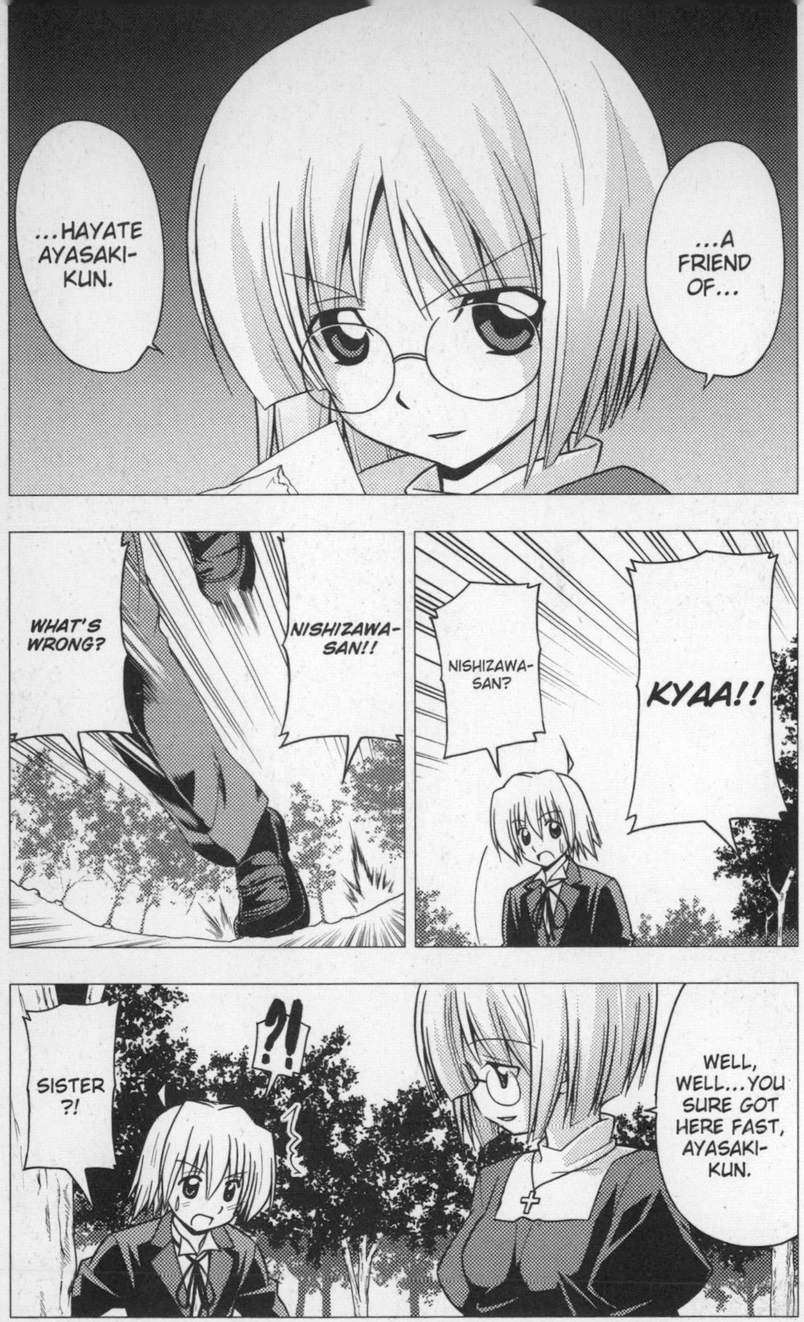

...A FRIEND OF...
...HAYATE AYASAKI-KUN.
KYAA!!
NISHIZAWA-SAN?
NISHIZAWA-SAN!!
WHAT'S WRONG?
WELL, WELL...YOU SURE GOT HERE FAST, AYASAKI-KUN.
?!
SISTER?!

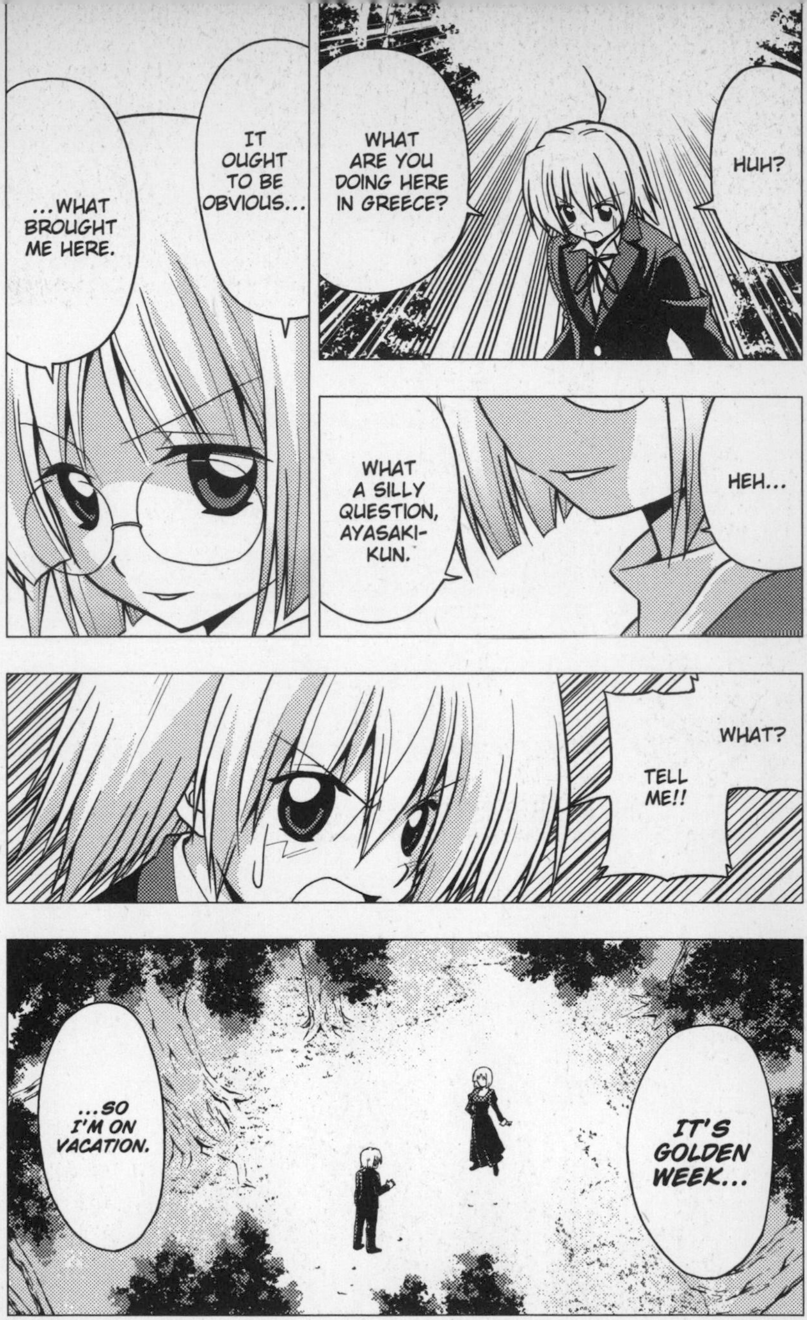
HUH?
WHAT ARE YOU DOING HERE IN GREECE?
HEH...
WHAT A SILLY QUESTION, AYASAKI-KUN.
IT OUGHT TO BE OBVIOUS...
...WHAT BROUGHT ME HERE.
WHAT?
TELL ME!!
IT'S GOLDEN WEEK...
...SO I'M ON VACATION.

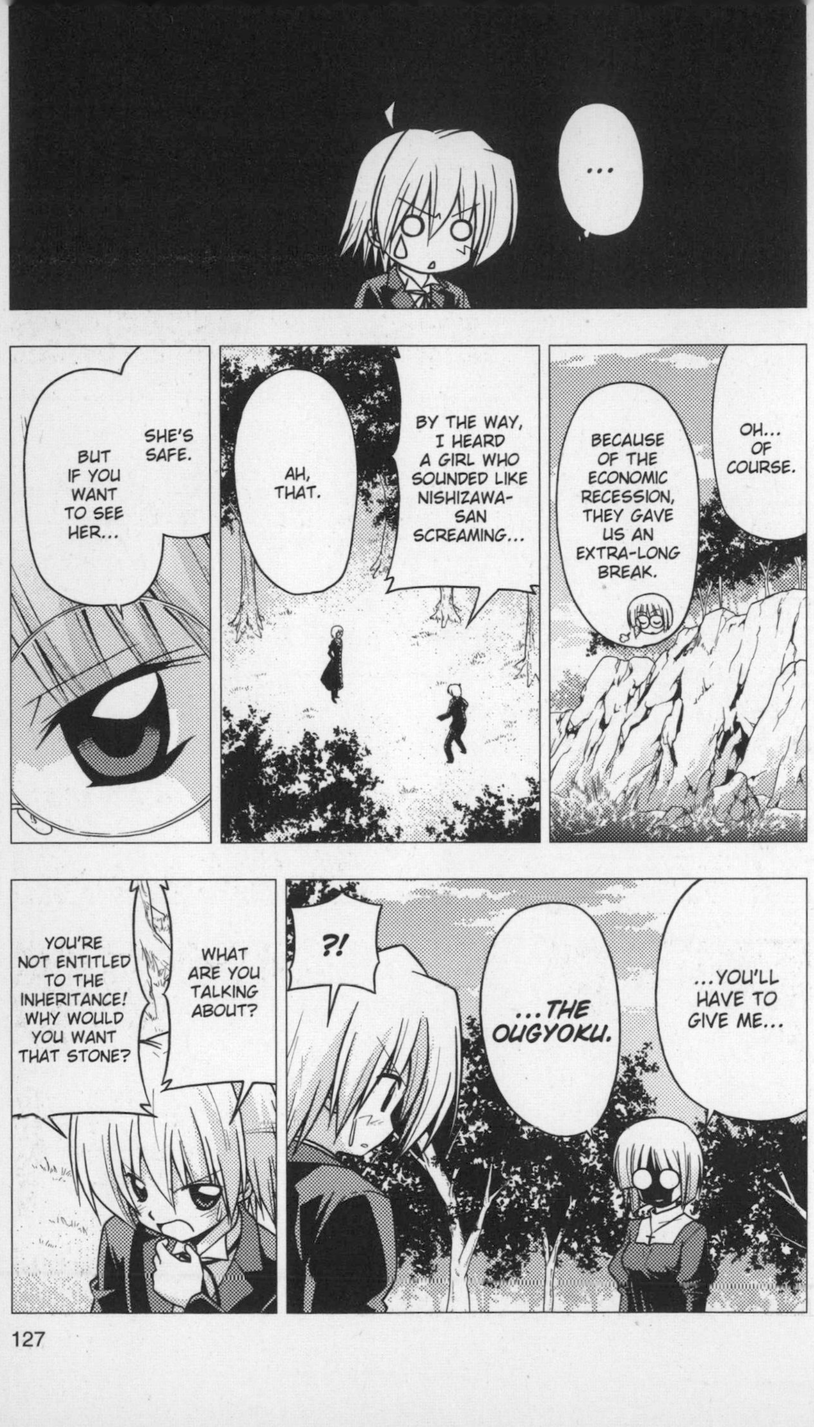
...
OH... OF COURSE.
BECAUSE OF THE ECONOMIC RECESSION, THEY GAVE US AN EXTRA-LONG BREAK.
BY THE WAY, I HEARD A GIRL WHO SOUNDED LIKE NISHIZAWA-SAN SCREAMING...
AH, THAT.
SHE'S SAFE.
BUT IF YOU WANT TO SEE HER...
...YOU'LL HAVE TO GIVE ME...
...THE OUGYOKU.
?!
WHAT ARE YOU TALKING ABOUT?
YOU'RE NOT ENTITLED TO THE INHERITANCE! WHY WOULD YOU WANT THAT STONE?

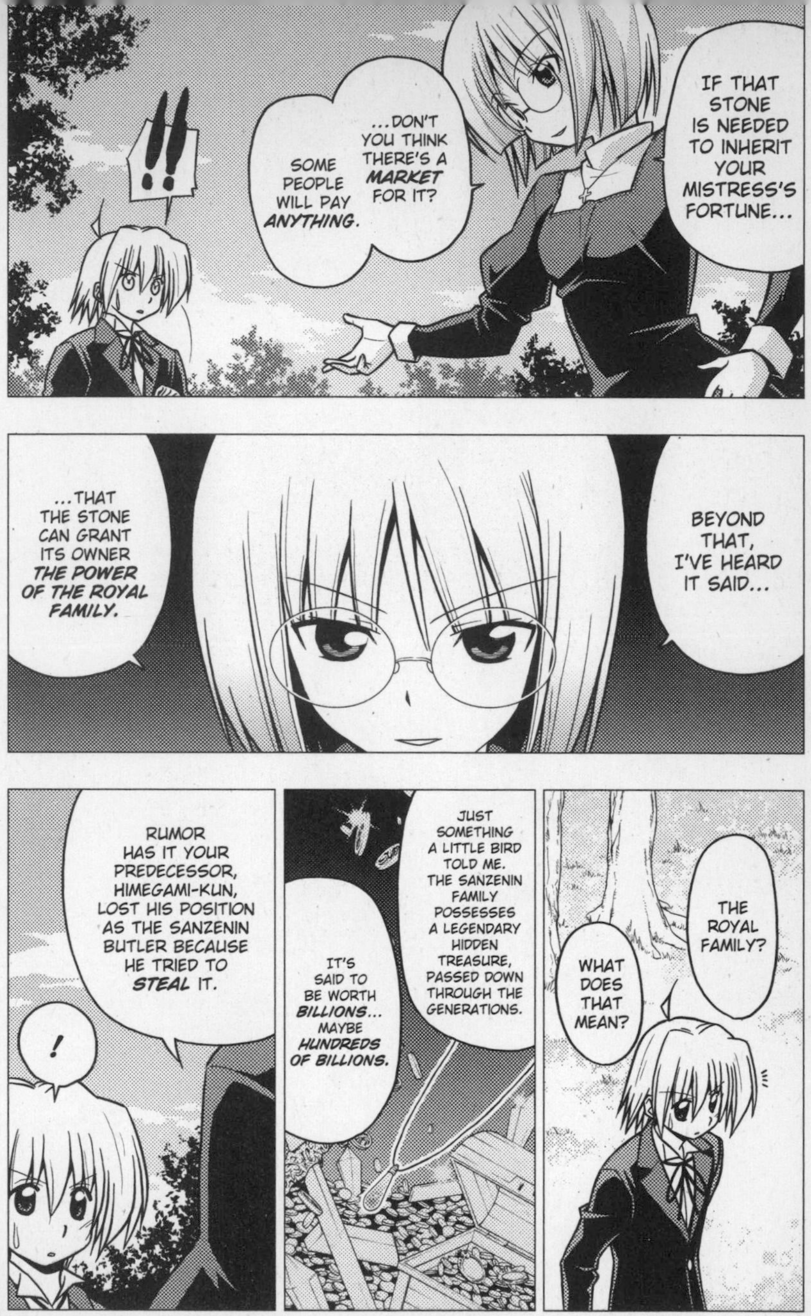
IF THAT STONE IS NEEDED TO INHERIT YOUR MISTRESS'S FORTUNE...
...DON'T YOU THINK THERE'S A MARKET FOR IT?
SOME PEOPLE WILL PAY ANYTHING.
!!
BEYOND THAT, I'VE HEARD IT SAID...
...THAT THE STONE CAN GRANT ITS OWNER THE POWER OF THE ROYAL FAMILY.
THE ROYAL FAMILY?
WHAT DOES THAT MEAN?
JUST SOMETHING A LITTLE BIRD TOLD ME. THE SANZENIN FAMILY POSSESSES A LEGENDARY HIDDEN TREASURE, PASSED DOWN THROUGH THE GENERATIONS.
IT'S SAID TO BE WORTH BILLIONS... MAYBE HUNDREDS OF BILLIONS.
RUMOR HAS IT YOUR PREDECESSOR, HIMEGAMI-KUN, LOST HIS POSITION AS THE SANZENIN BUTLER BECAUSE HE TRIED TO STEAL IT.
!

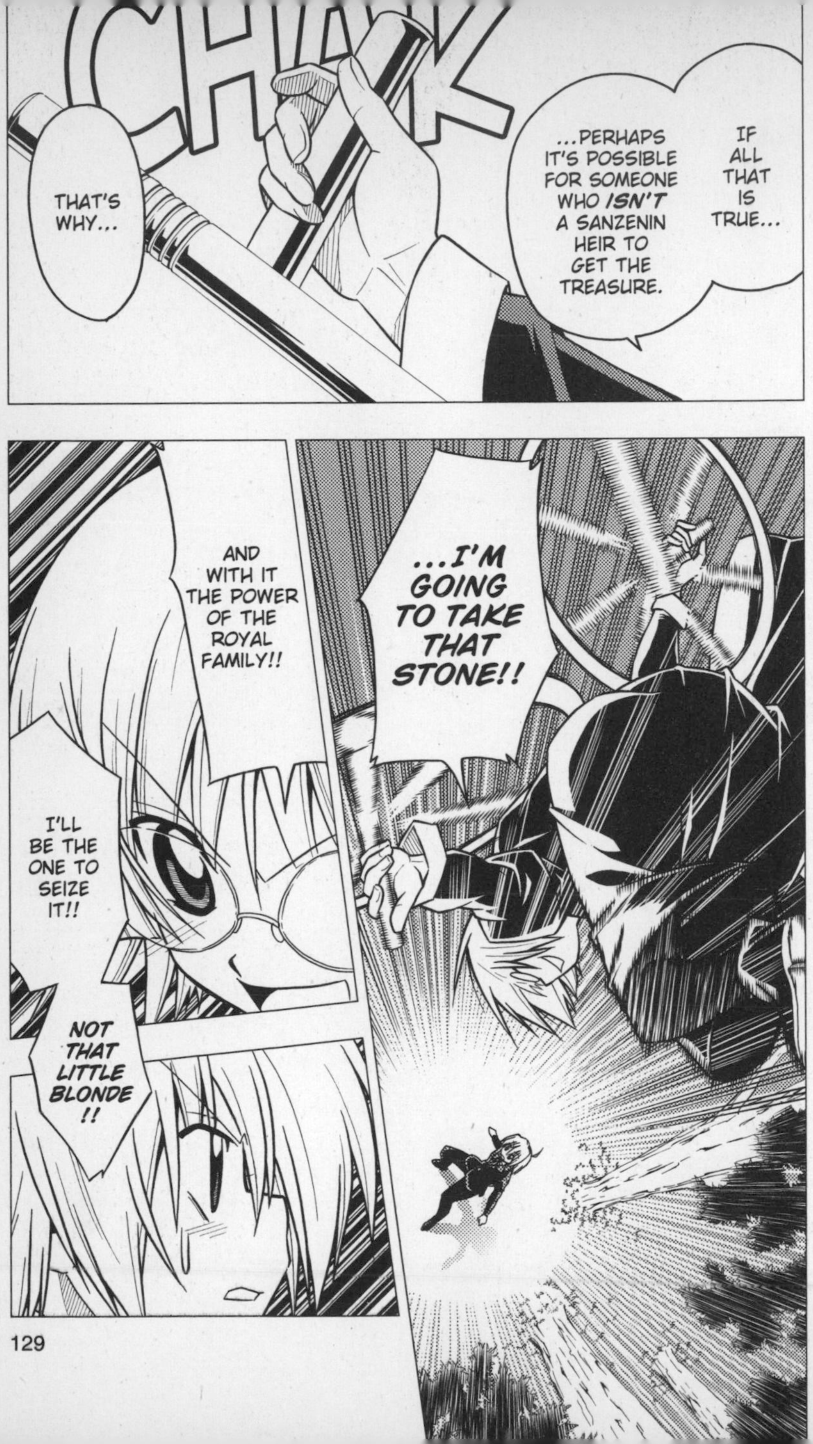
CHAK
IF ALL THAT IS TRUE...
...PERHAPS IT'S POSSIBLE FOR SOMEONE WHO *ISN'T* A SANZENIN HEIR TO GET THE TREASURE.
THAT'S WHY...
...I'M GOING TO TAKE THAT STONE!!
AND WITH IT THE POWER OF THE ROYAL FAMILY!!
I'LL BE THE ONE TO SEIZE IT!!
NOT THAT LITTLE BLONDE!!

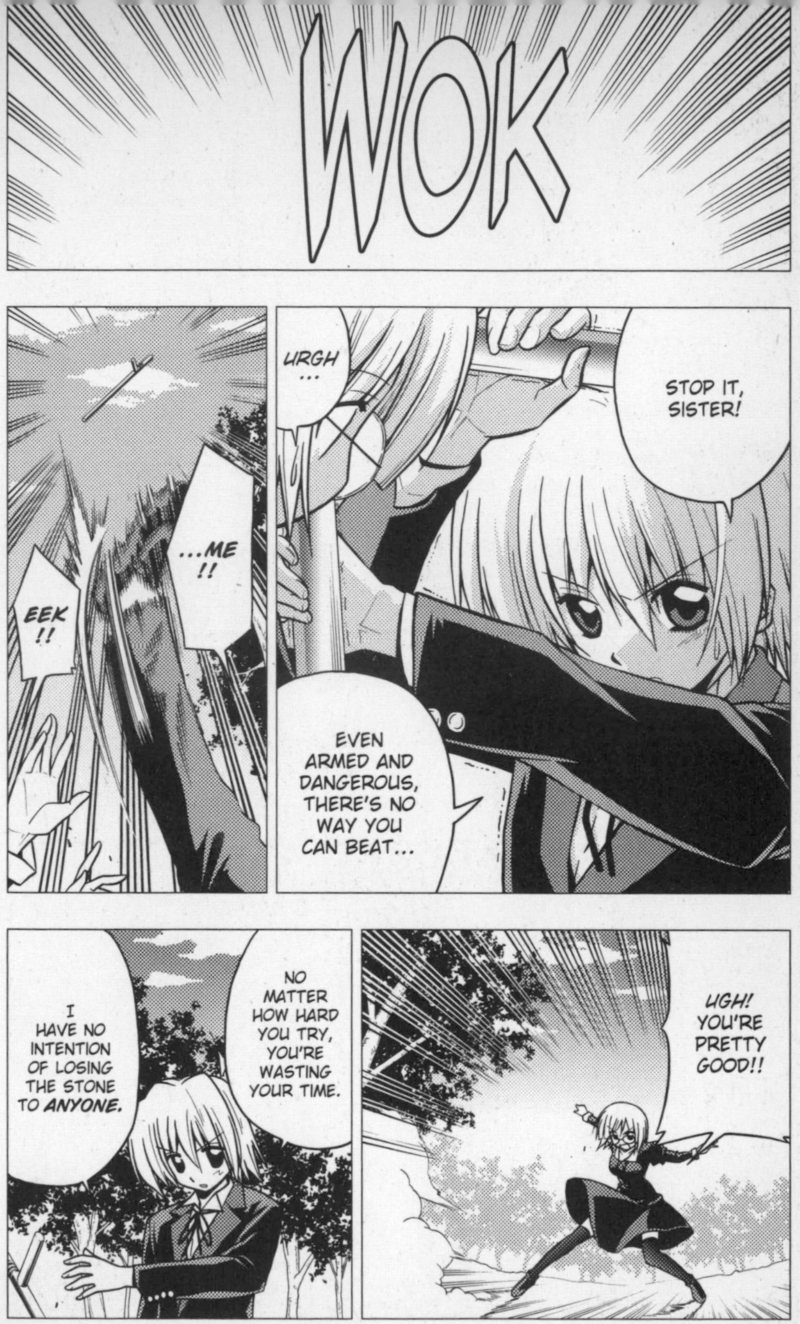
WOK
STOP IT, SISTER!
URGH ...
EVEN ARMED AND DANGEROUS, THERE'S NO WAY YOU CAN BEAT...
...ME !!
EEK !!
UGH! YOU'RE PRETTY GOOD!!
NO MATTER HOW HARD YOU TRY, YOU'RE WASTING YOUR TIME.
I HAVE NO INTENTION OF LOSING THE STONE TO ANYONE.

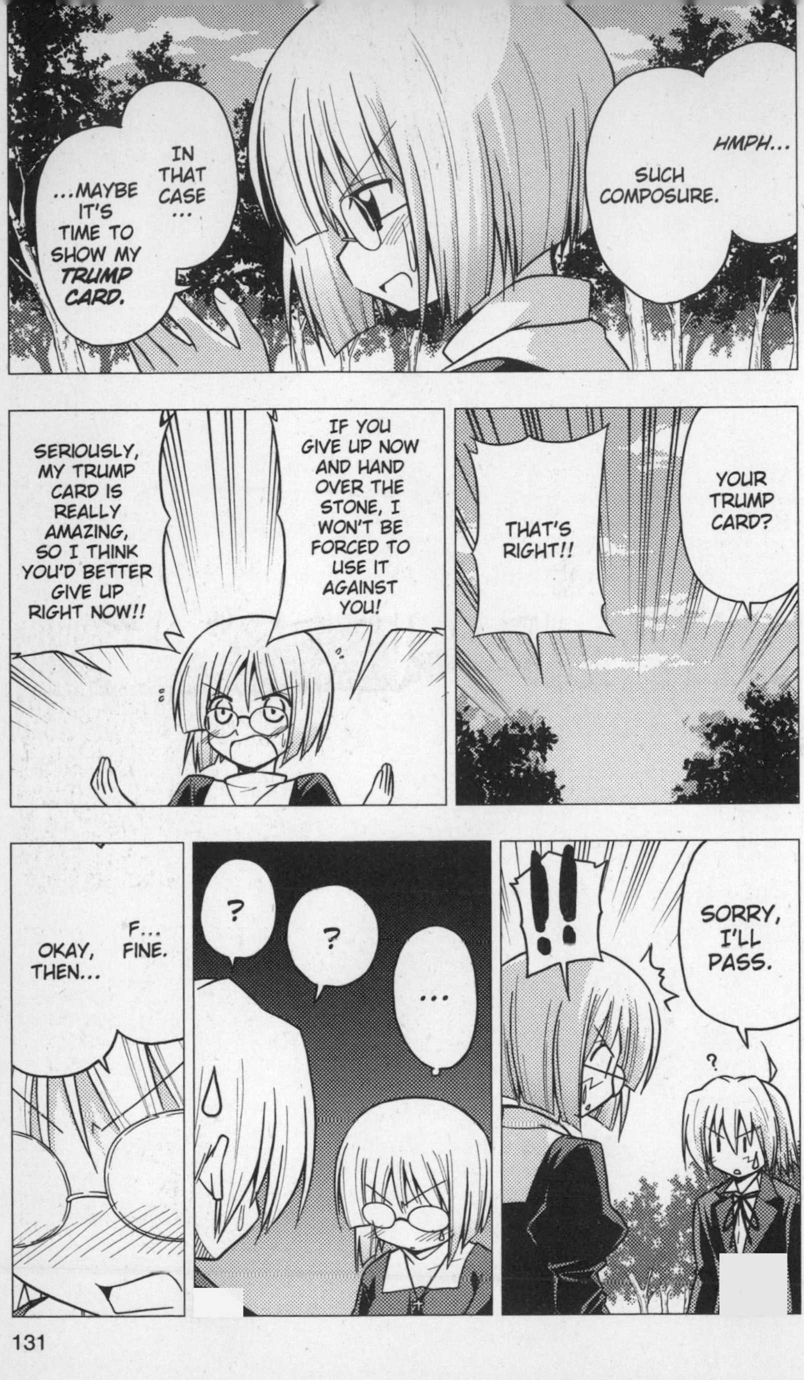
HMPH...
SUCH COMPOSURE.
IN THAT CASE...
...MAYBE IT'S TIME TO SHOW MY TRUMP CARD.
YOUR TRUMP CARD?
THAT'S RIGHT!!
IF YOU GIVE UP NOW AND HAND OVER THE STONE, I WON'T BE FORCED TO USE IT AGAINST YOU!
SERIOUSLY, MY TRUMP CARD IS REALLY AMAZING, SO I THINK YOU'D BETTER GIVE UP RIGHT NOW!!
!!
SORRY, I'LL PASS.
?
?
?
...
F... FINE.
OKAY, THEN...

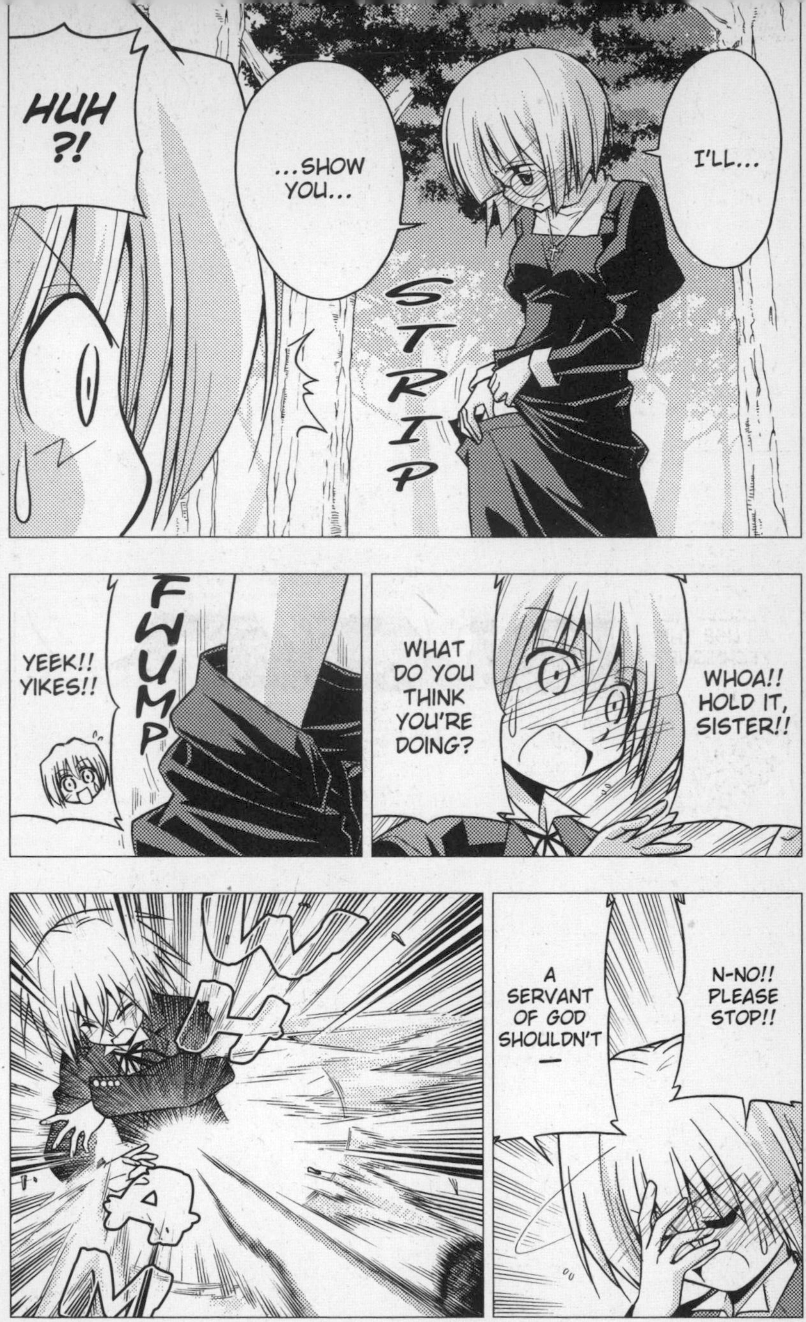
I'LL...
...SHOW YOU...
STRIP
HUH ?!
WHOA!! HOLD IT, SISTER!!
WHAT DO YOU THINK YOU'RE DOING?
FWUMP
YEEK!! YIKES!!
N-NO!! PLEASE STOP!!
A SERVANT OF GOD SHOULDN'T —

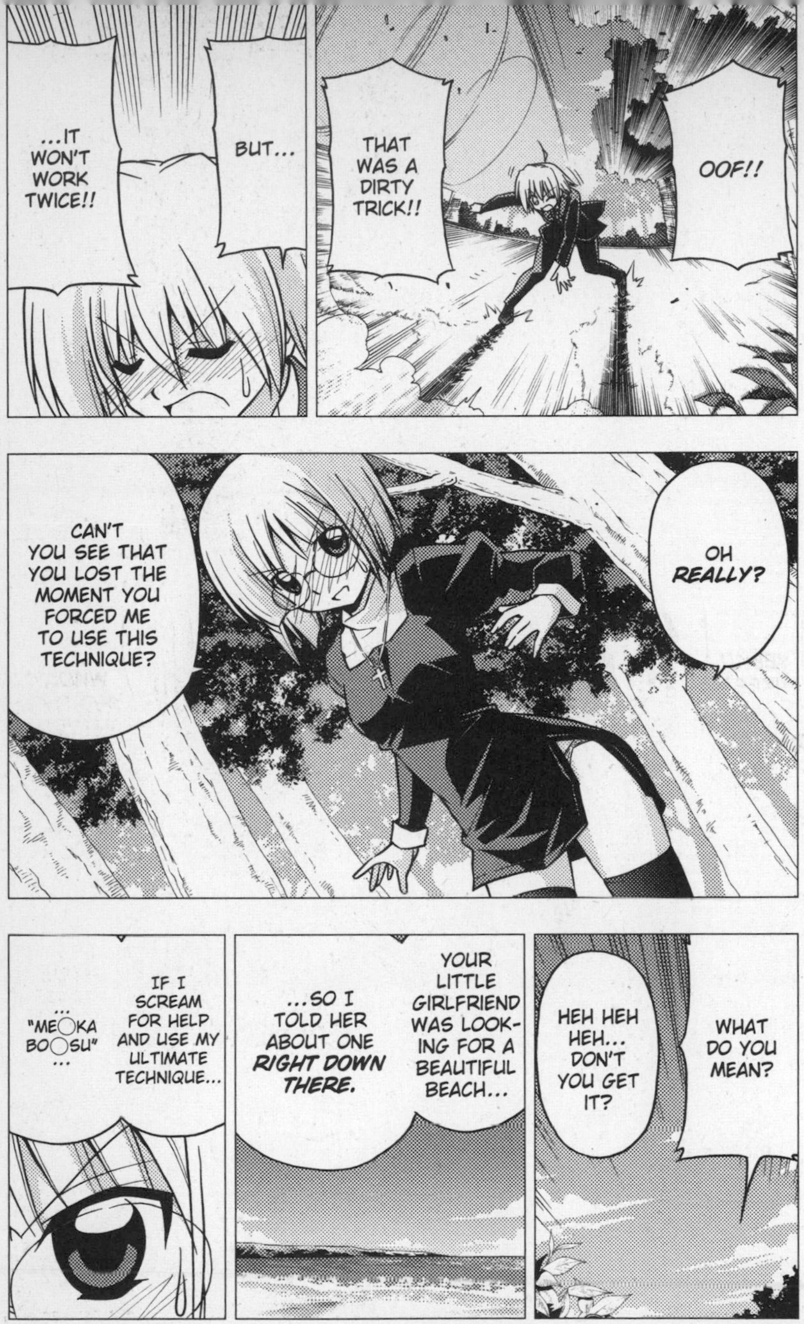
OOF!!
THAT WAS A DIRTY TRICK!!
BUT...
...IT WON'T WORK TWICE!!
OH *REALLY?*
CAN'T YOU SEE THAT YOU LOST THE MOMENT YOU FORCED ME TO USE THIS TECHNIQUE?
WHAT DO YOU MEAN?
HEH HEH HEH... DON'T YOU GET IT?
YOUR LITTLE GIRLFRIEND WAS LOOK-ING FOR A BEAUTIFUL BEACH...
...SO I TOLD HER ABOUT ONE *RIGHT DOWN THERE.*
IF I SCREAM FOR HELP AND USE MY ULTIMATE TECHNIQUE...
... "ME◯KA BO◯SU" ...

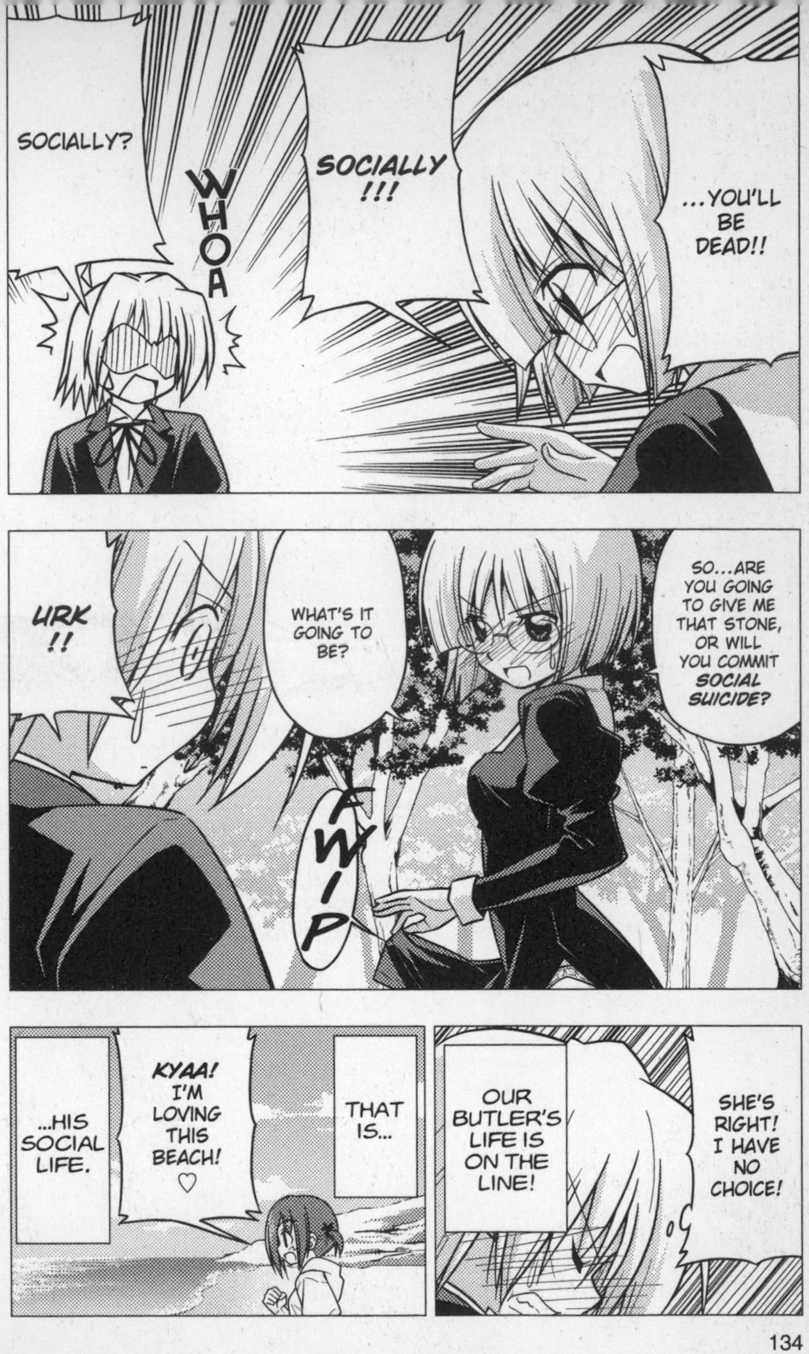
...YOU'LL BE DEAD!!
SOCIALLY !!!
WHOA
SOCIALLY?
SO...ARE YOU GOING TO GIVE ME THAT STONE, OR WILL YOU COMMIT SOCIAL SUICIDE?
WHAT'S IT GOING TO BE?
URK !!
FWIP
SHE'S RIGHT! I HAVE NO CHOICE!
OUR BUTLER'S LIFE IS ON THE LINE!
THAT IS...
KYAA! I'M LOVING THIS BEACH! ♡
...HIS SOCIAL LIFE.

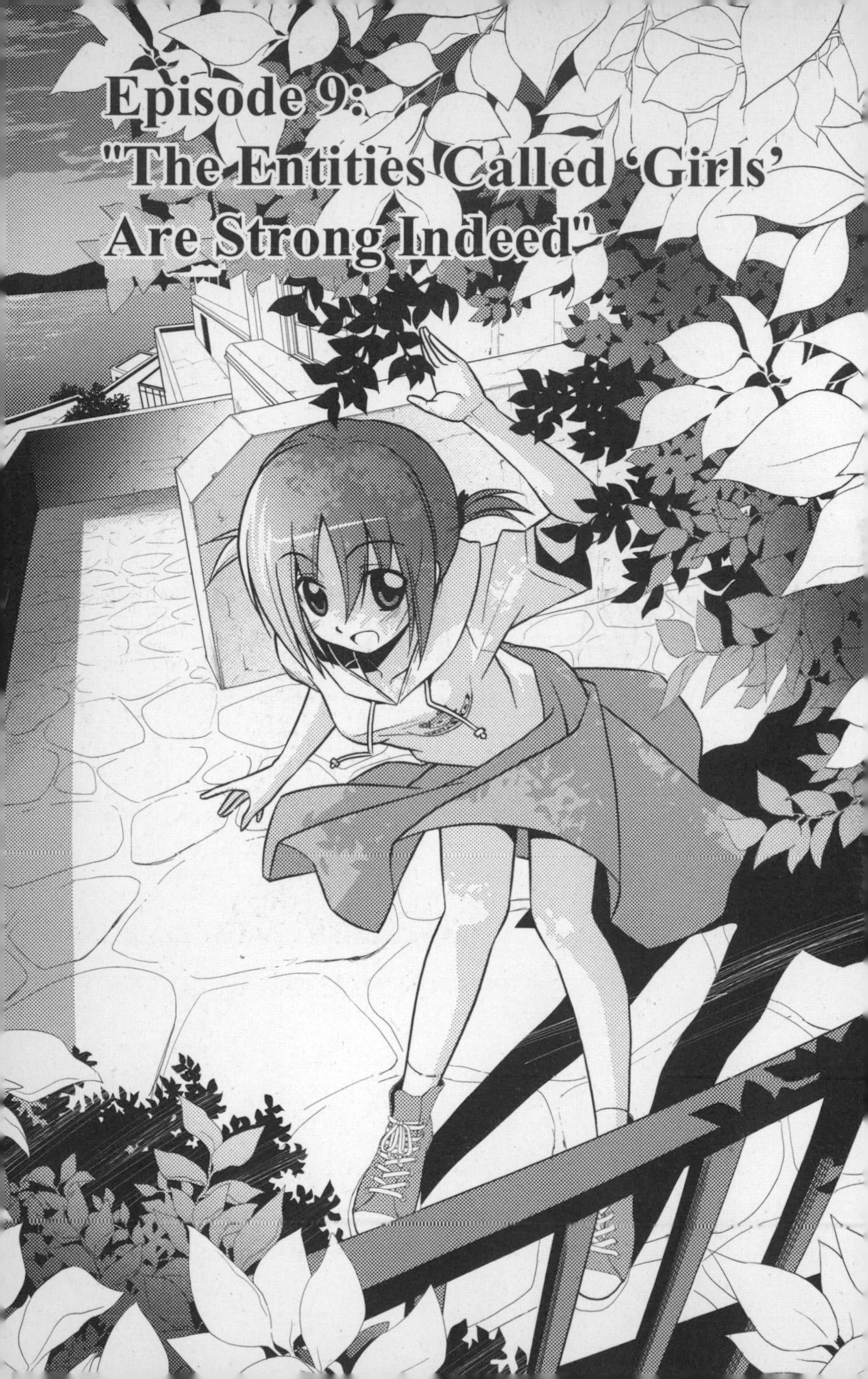
Episode 9:
"The Entities Called 'Girls' Are Strong Indeed"

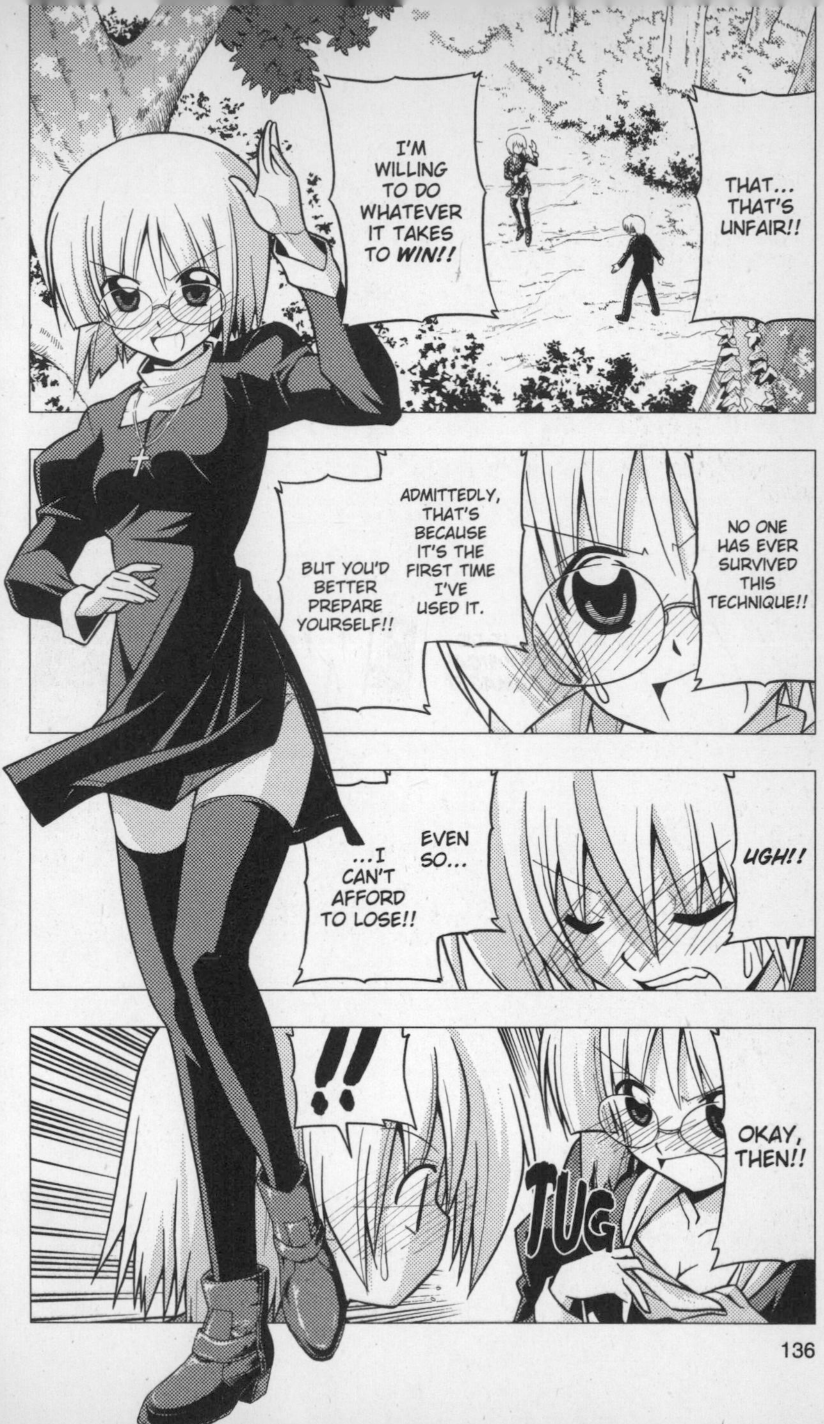
THAT... THAT'S UNFAIR!!
I'M WILLING TO DO WHATEVER IT TAKES TO WIN!!
NO ONE HAS EVER SURVIVED THIS TECHNIQUE!!
ADMITTEDLY, THAT'S BECAUSE IT'S THE FIRST TIME I'VE USED IT.
BUT YOU'D BETTER PREPARE YOURSELF!!
UGH!!
EVEN SO...
...I CAN'T AFFORD TO LOSE!!
OKAY, THEN!!
TUG
!!

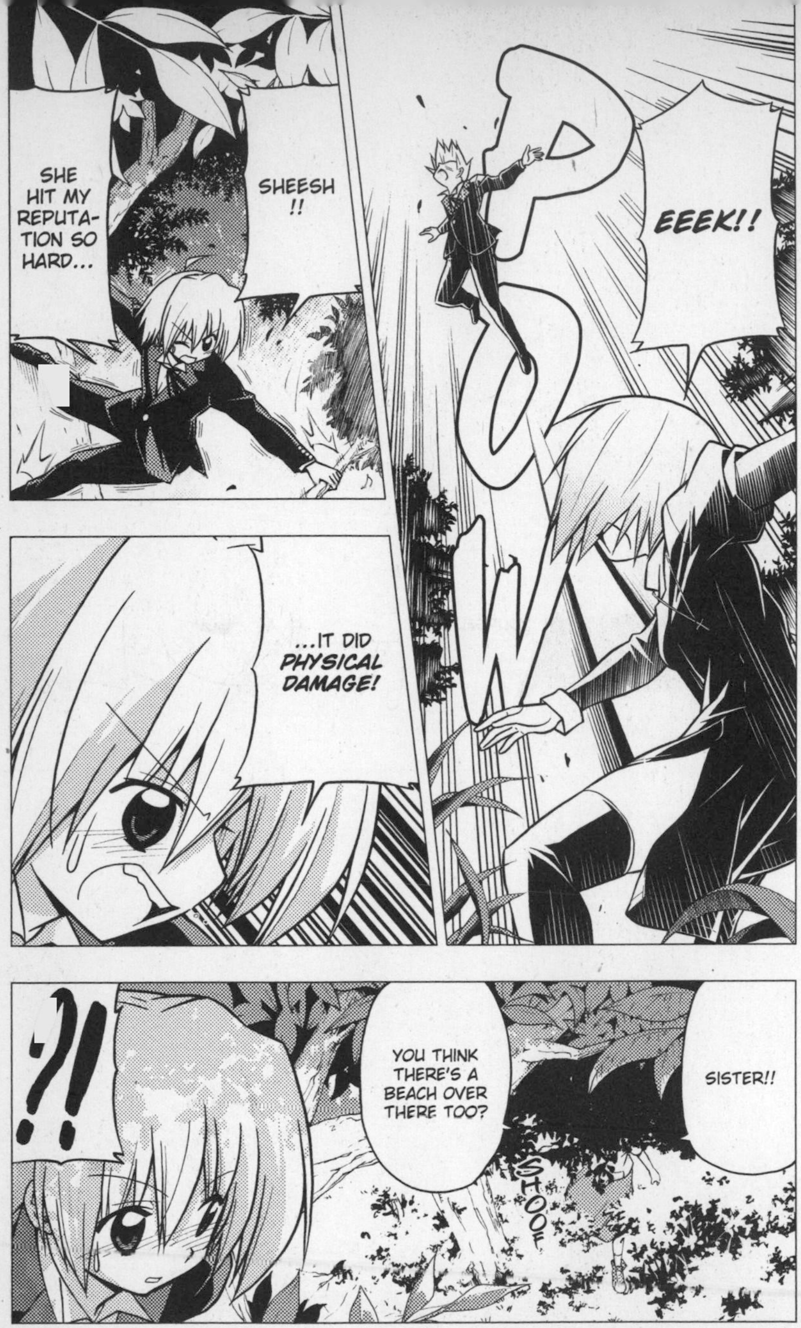
POW
EEEK!!
SHEESH!!
SHE HIT MY REPUTATION SO HARD...
...IT DID PHYSICAL DAMAGE!
SISTER!!
YOU THINK THERE'S A BEACH OVER THERE TOO?
SHOOF
?!!

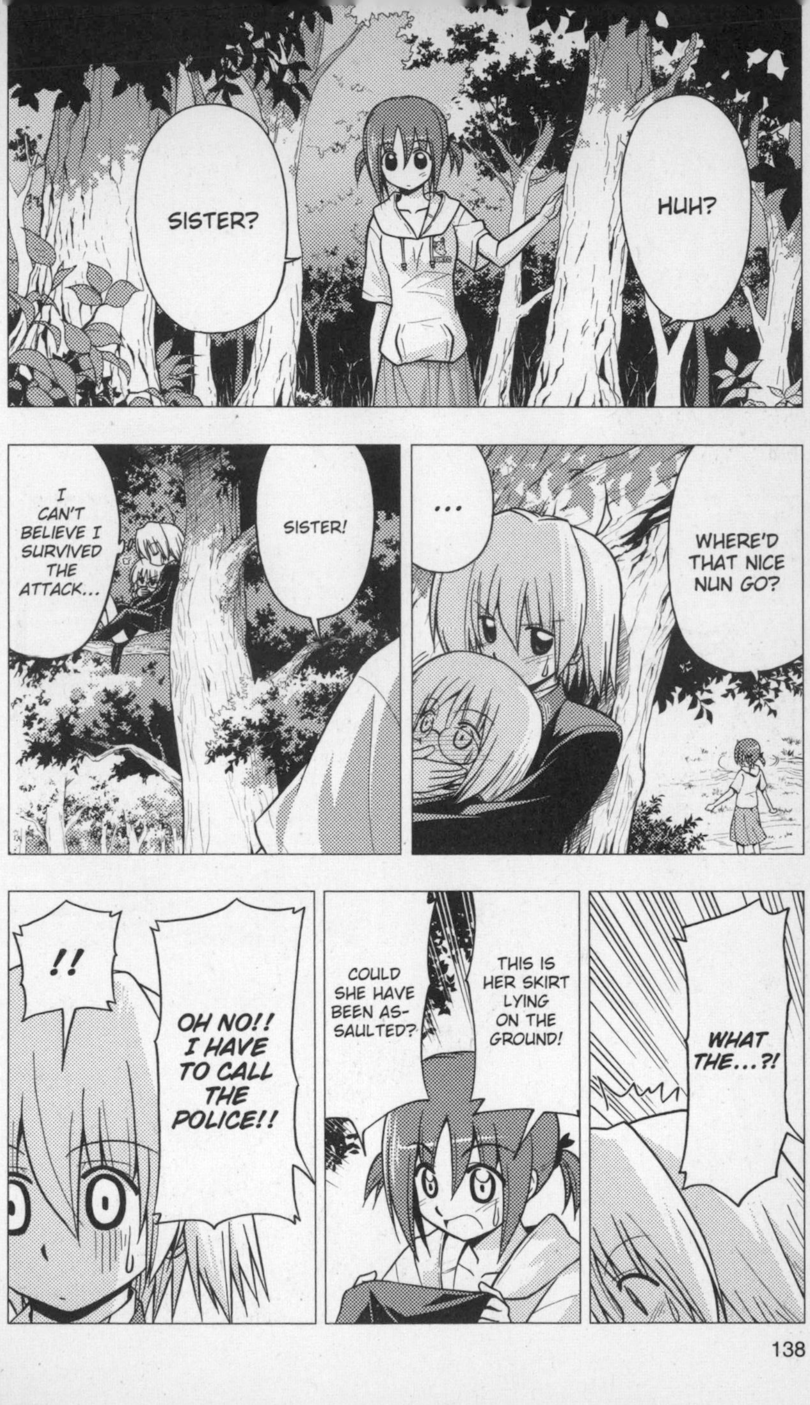
HUH?
SISTER?
WHERE'D THAT NICE NUN GO?
...
SISTER!
I CAN'T BELIEVE I SURVIVED THE ATTACK...
WHAT THE...?!
THIS IS HER SKIRT LYING ON THE GROUND!
COULD SHE HAVE BEEN AS-SAULTED?
OH NO!! I HAVE TO CALL THE POLICE!!
!!

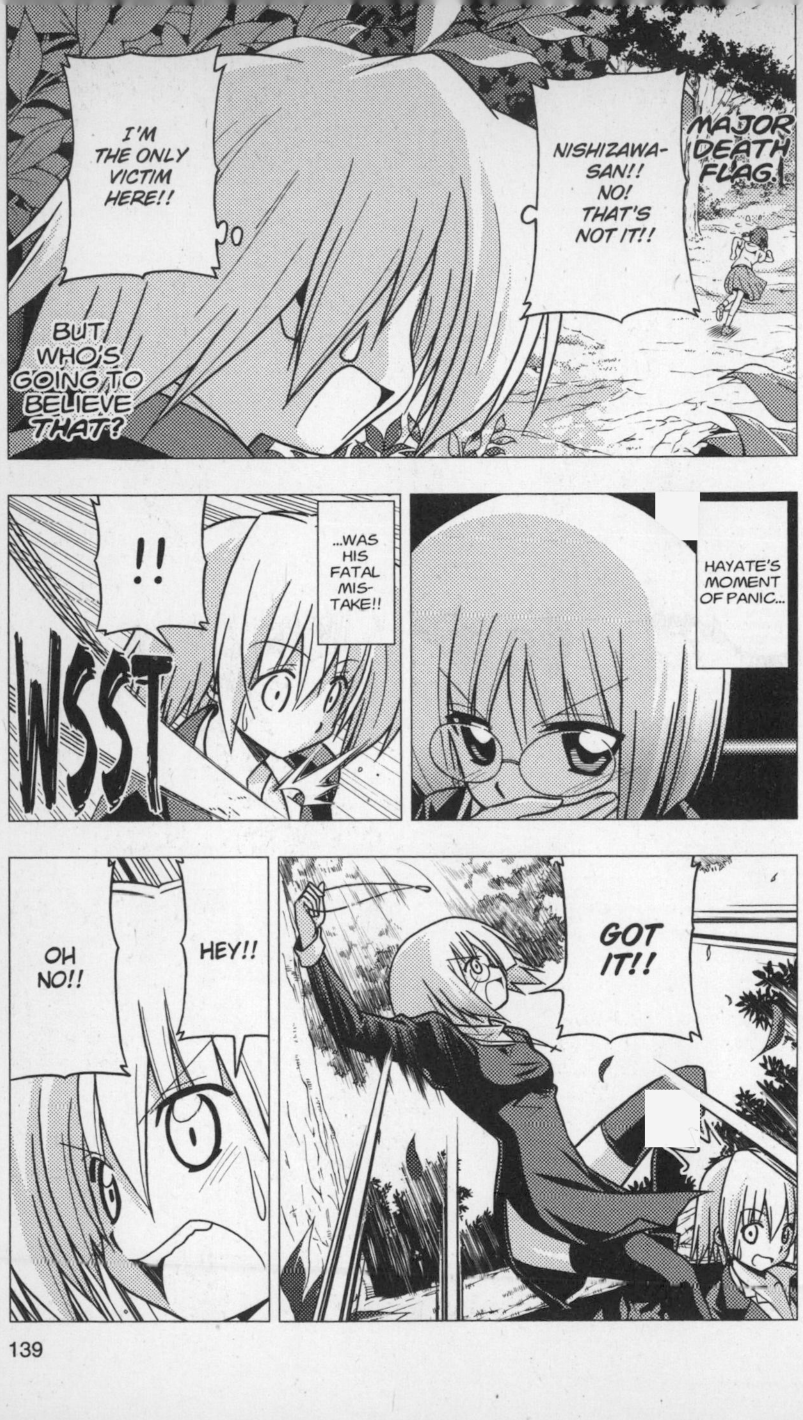
MAJOR DEATH FLAG.
NISHIZAWA-SAN!! NO! THAT'S NOT IT!!
I'M THE ONLY VICTIM HERE!!
BUT WHO'S GOING TO BELIEVE THAT?
HAYATE'S MOMENT OF PANIC...
...WAS HIS FATAL MIS-TAKE!!
!!
WSST
GOT IT!!
HEY!!
OH NO!!

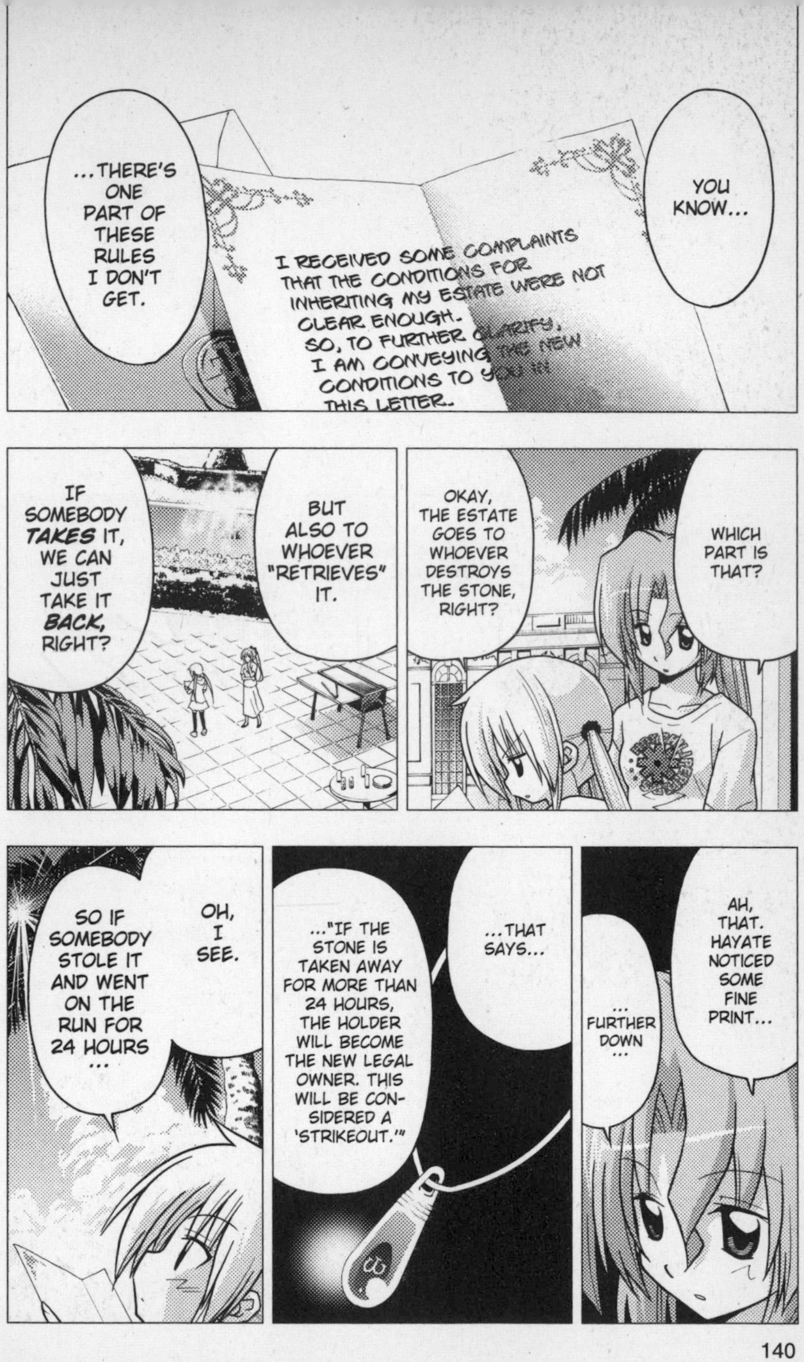
YOU KNOW...
I RECEIVED SOME COMPLAINTS THAT THE CONDITIONS FOR INHERITING MY ESTATE WERE NOT CLEAR ENOUGH. SO, TO FURTHER CLARIFY, I AM CONVEYING THE NEW CONDITIONS TO YOU IN THIS LETTER.
...THERE'S ONE PART OF THESE RULES I DON'T GET.
WHICH PART IS THAT?
OKAY, THE ESTATE GOES TO WHOEVER DESTROYS THE STONE, RIGHT?
BUT ALSO TO WHOEVER "RETRIEVES" IT.
IF SOMEBODY ***TAKES*** IT, WE CAN JUST TAKE IT ***BACK,*** RIGHT?
AH, THAT. HAYATE NOTICED SOME FINE PRINT...
... FURTHER DOWN ...
...THAT SAYS...
..."IF THE STONE IS TAKEN AWAY FOR MORE THAN 24 HOURS, THE HOLDER WILL BECOME THE NEW LEGAL OWNER. THIS WILL BE CON- SIDERED A 'STRIKEOUT.'"
OH, I SEE.
SO IF SOMEBODY STOLE IT AND WENT ON THE RUN FOR 24 HOURS ...

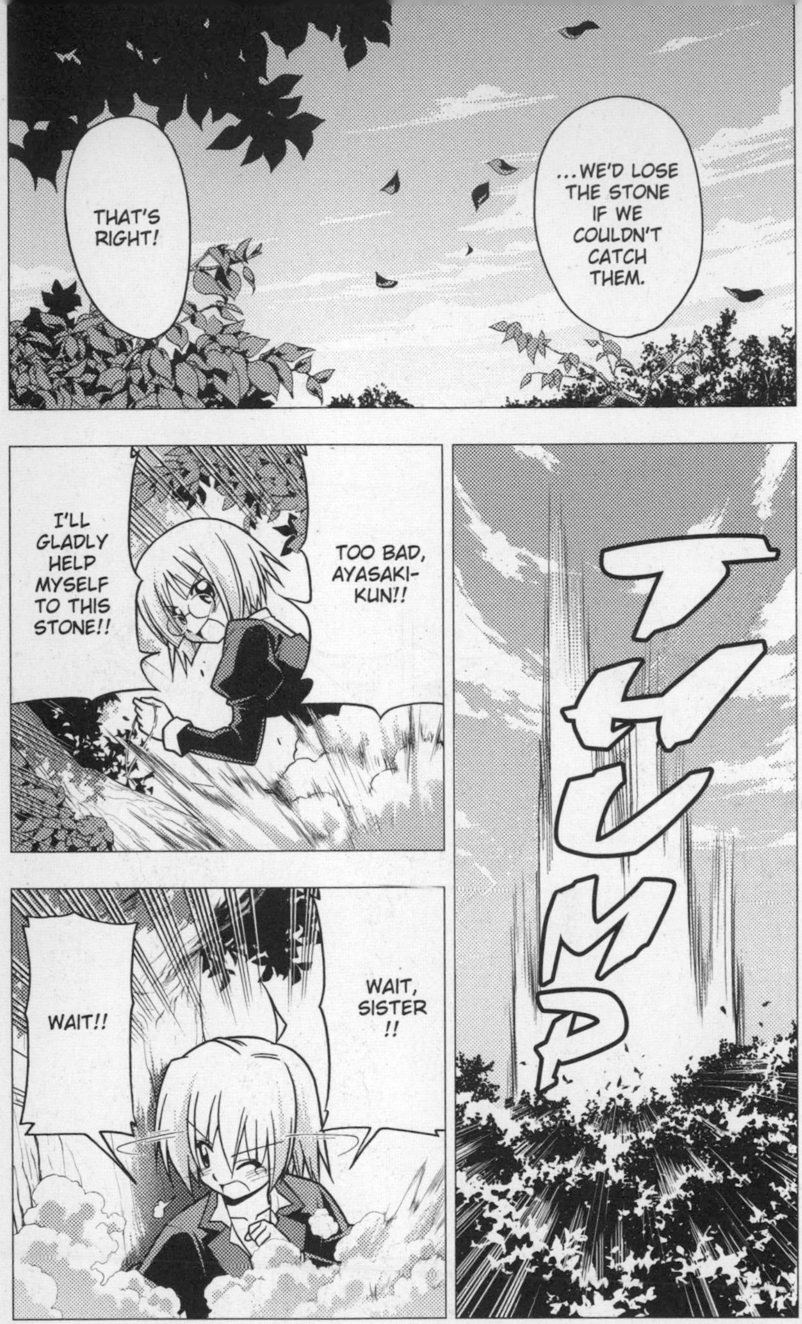
...WE'D LOSE THE STONE IF WE COULDN'T CATCH THEM.
THAT'S RIGHT!
JUMP
TOO BAD, AYASAKI-KUN!!
I'LL GLADLY HELP MYSELF TO THIS STONE!!
WAIT, SISTER!!
WAIT!!

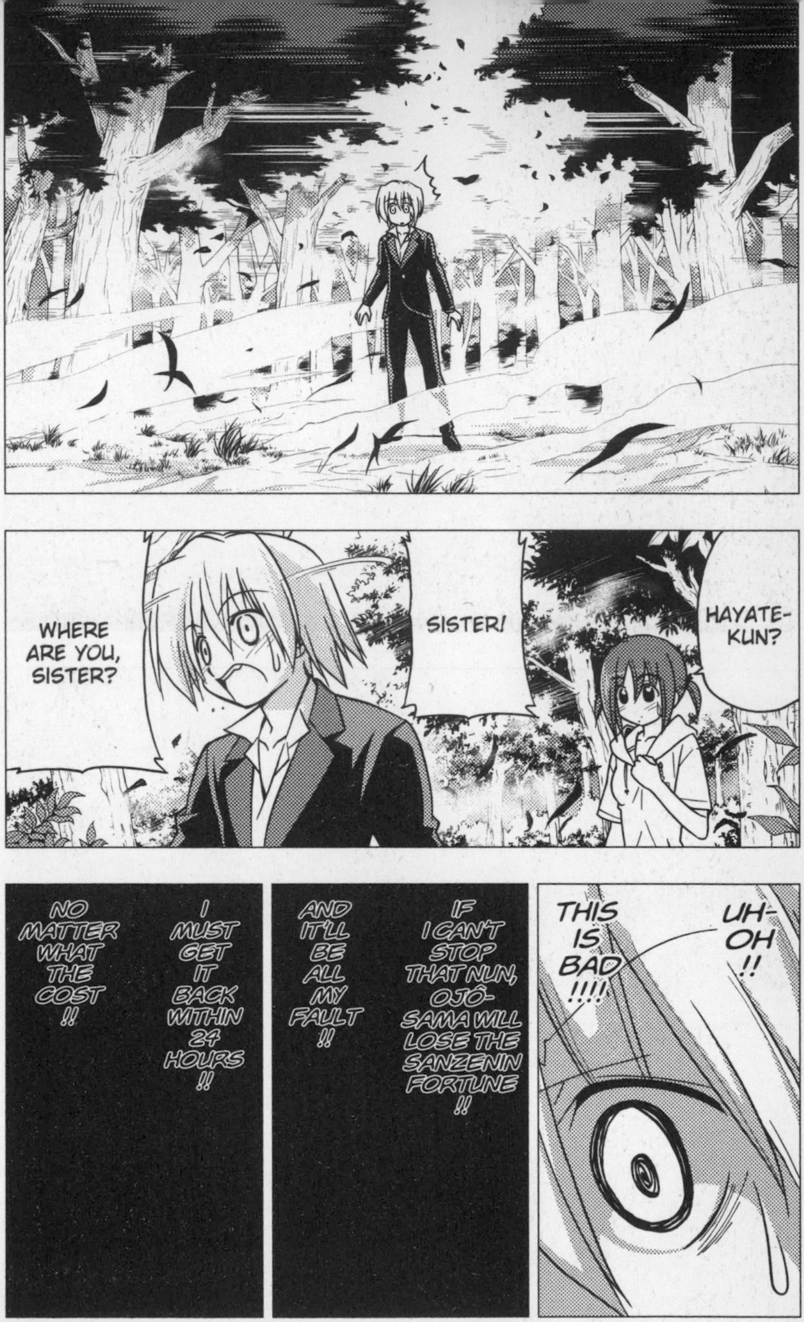
HAYATE-KUN?
SISTER!
WHERE ARE YOU, SISTER?
UH-OH!!
THIS IS BAD!!!!
IF I CAN'T STOP THAT NUN, OJÔ-SAMA WILL LOSE THE SANZENIN FORTUNE!!
AND IT'LL BE ALL MY FAULT!!
I MUST GET IT BACK WITHIN 24 HOURS!!
NO MATTER WHAT THE COST!!

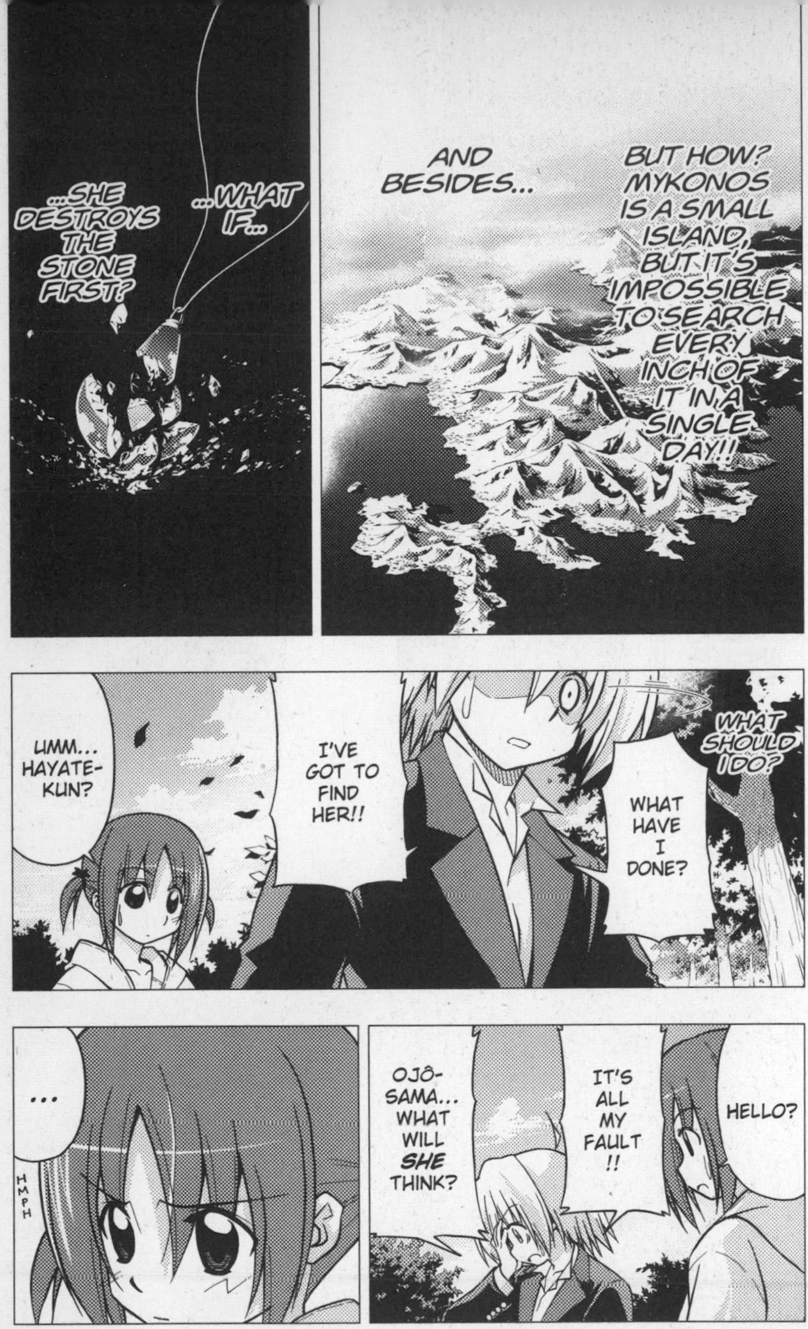
BUT HOW? MYKONOS IS A SMALL ISLAND, BUT IT'S IMPOSSIBLE TO SEARCH EVERY INCH OF IT IN A SINGLE DAY!!
AND BESIDES...
...WHAT IF...
...SHE DESTROYS THE STONE FIRST?
WHAT SHOULD I DO?
WHAT HAVE I DONE?
I'VE GOT TO FIND HER!!
UMM... HAYATE-KUN?
HELLO?
IT'S ALL MY FAULT!!
OJÔ-SAMA... WHAT WILL *SHE* THINK?
...
HMPH

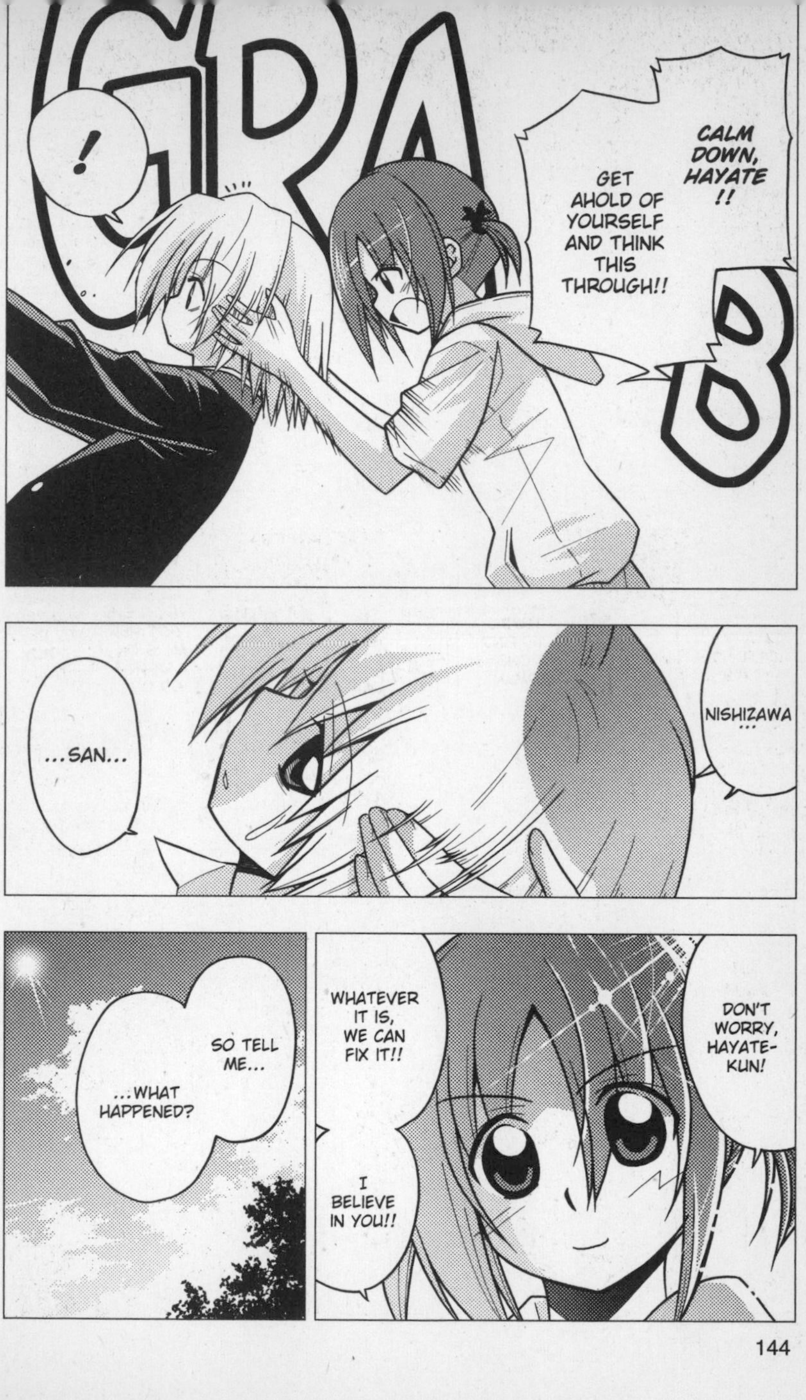
CALM DOWN, HAYATE!!
GET AHOLD OF YOURSELF AND THINK THIS THROUGH!!
GRAB
!
NISHIZAWA...
...SAN...
DON'T WORRY, HAYATE-KUN!
WHATEVER IT IS, WE CAN FIX IT!!
I BELIEVE IN YOU!!
SO TELL ME...
...WHAT HAPPENED?

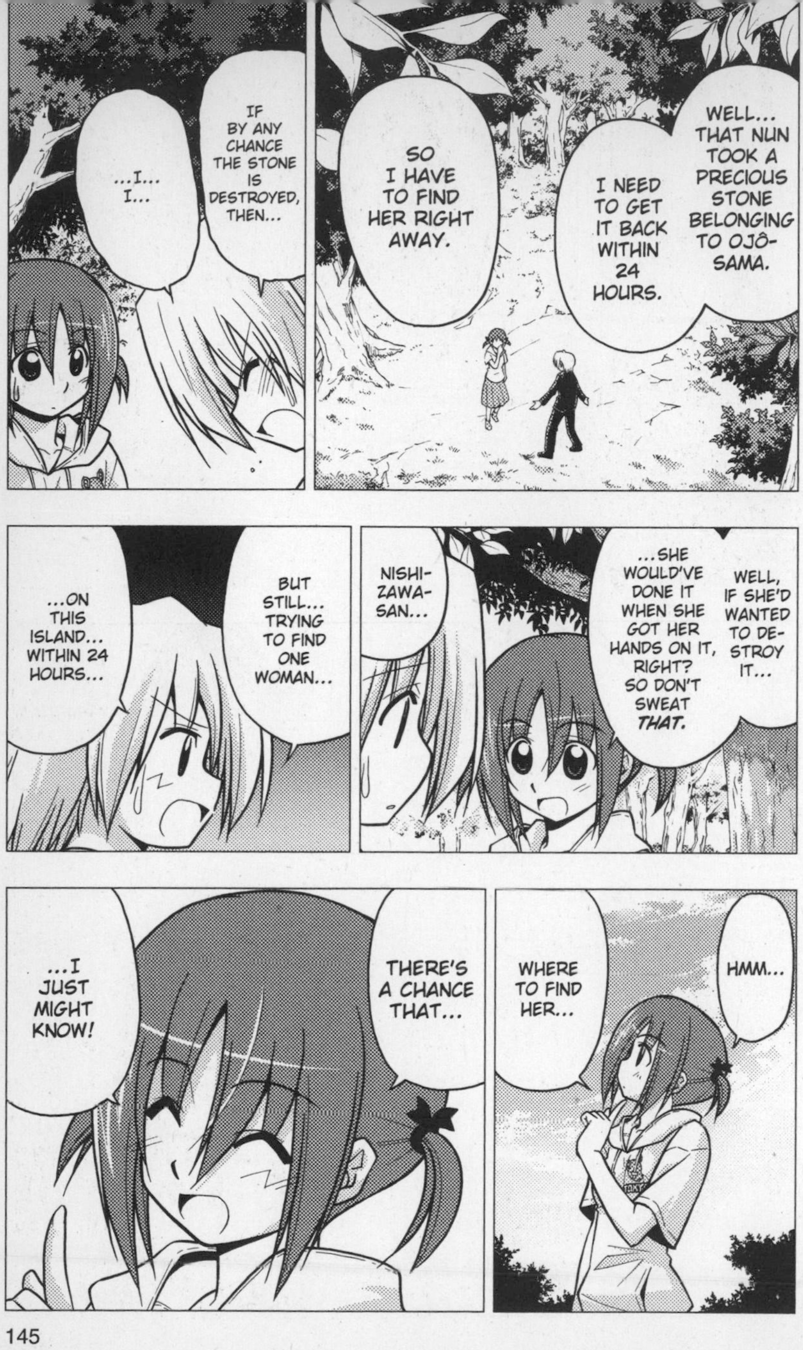
WELL... THAT NUN TOOK A PRECIOUS STONE BELONGING TO OJÔ-SAMA.
I NEED TO GET IT BACK WITHIN 24 HOURS.
SO I HAVE TO FIND HER RIGHT AWAY.
IF BY ANY CHANCE THE STONE IS DESTROYED, THEN...
...I... I...
WELL, IF SHE'D WANTED TO DE-STROY IT...
...SHE WOULD'VE DONE IT WHEN SHE GOT HER HANDS ON IT, RIGHT? SO DON'T SWEAT *THAT.*
NISHI-ZAWA-SAN...
BUT STILL... TRYING TO FIND ONE WOMAN...
...ON THIS ISLAND... WITHIN 24 HOURS...
HMM...
WHERE TO FIND HER...
THERE'S A CHANCE THAT...
...I JUST MIGHT KNOW!

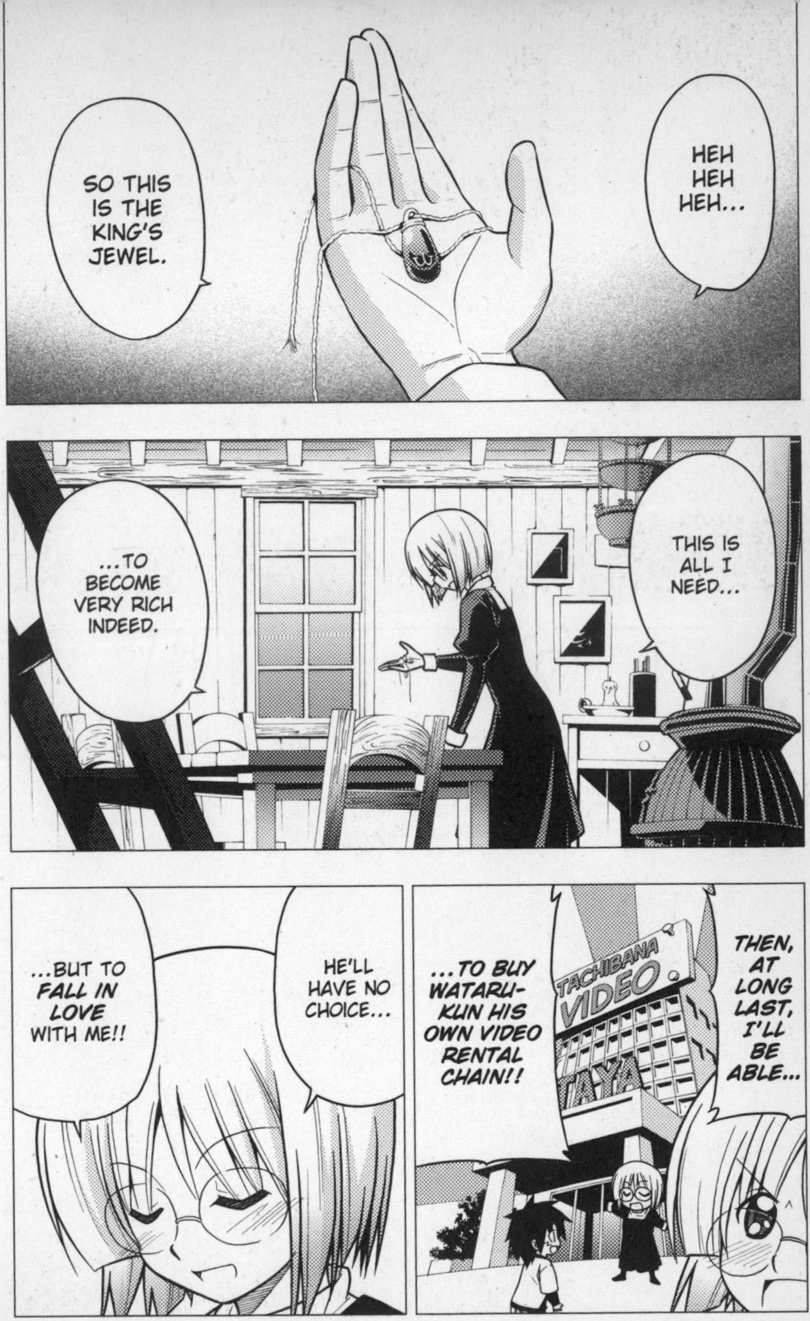
HEH HEH HEH...
SO THIS IS THE KING'S JEWEL.
THIS IS ALL I NEED...
...TO BECOME VERY RICH INDEED.
THEN, AT LONG LAST, I'LL BE ABLE...
...TO BUY WATARU-KUN HIS OWN VIDEO RENTAL CHAIN!!
TACHIBANA VIDEO
TAYA
HE'LL HAVE NO CHOICE...
...BUT TO FALL IN LOVE WITH ME!!

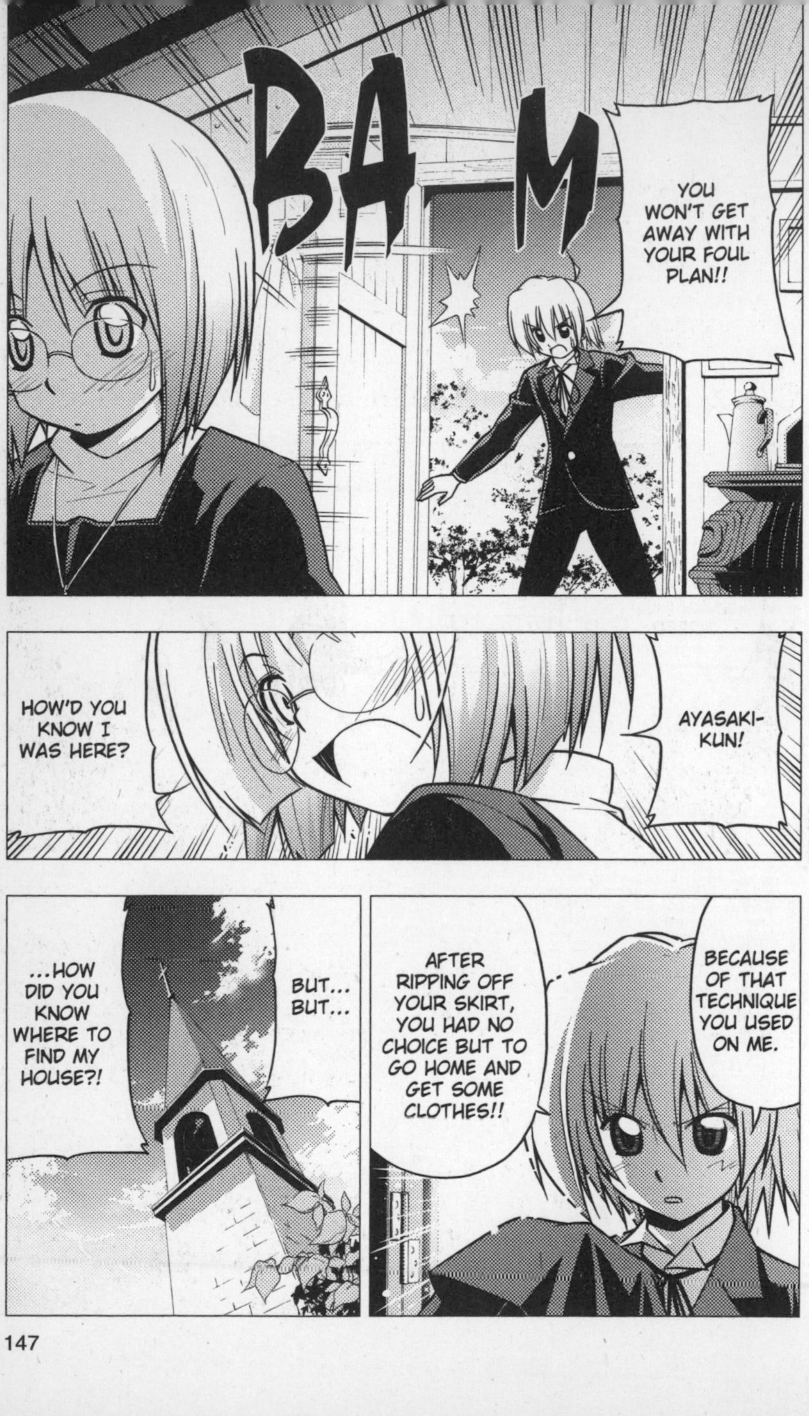
YOU WON'T GET AWAY WITH YOUR FOUL PLAN!!
BAM
AYASAKI-KUN!
HOW'D YOU KNOW I WAS HERE?
BECAUSE OF THAT TECHNIQUE YOU USED ON ME.
AFTER RIPPING OFF YOUR SKIRT, YOU HAD NO CHOICE BUT TO GO HOME AND GET SOME CLOTHES!!
BUT... BUT...
...HOW DID YOU KNOW WHERE TO FIND MY HOUSE?!

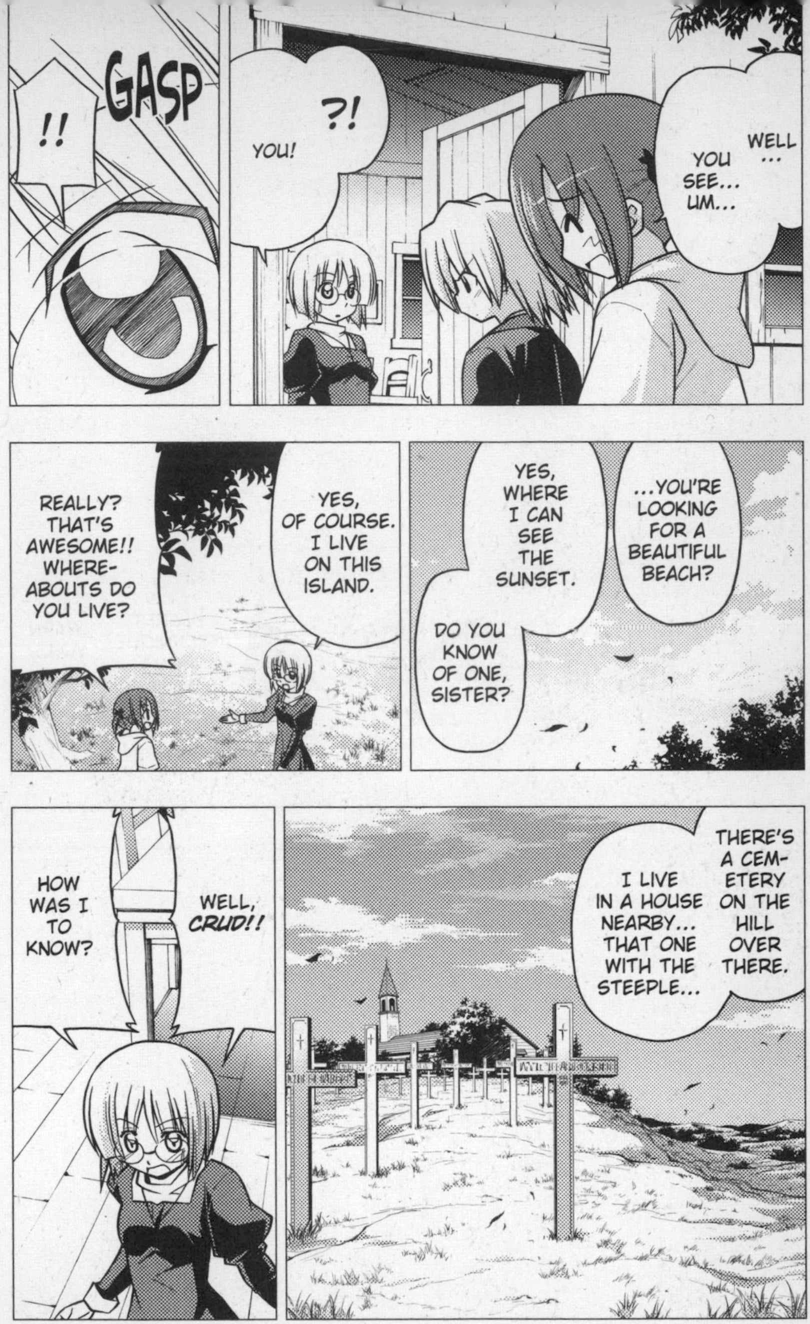
WELL... YOU SEE... UM...
?!
YOU!
GASP
!!
...YOU'RE LOOKING FOR A BEAUTIFUL BEACH?
YES, WHERE I CAN SEE THE SUNSET.
DO YOU KNOW OF ONE, SISTER?
YES, OF COURSE. I LIVE ON THIS ISLAND.
REALLY? THAT'S AWESOME!! WHERE-ABOUTS DO YOU LIVE?
THERE'S A CEM-ETERY ON THE HILL OVER THERE.
I LIVE IN A HOUSE NEARBY... THAT ONE WITH THE STEEPLE...
WELL, *CRUD!!*
HOW WAS I TO KNOW?

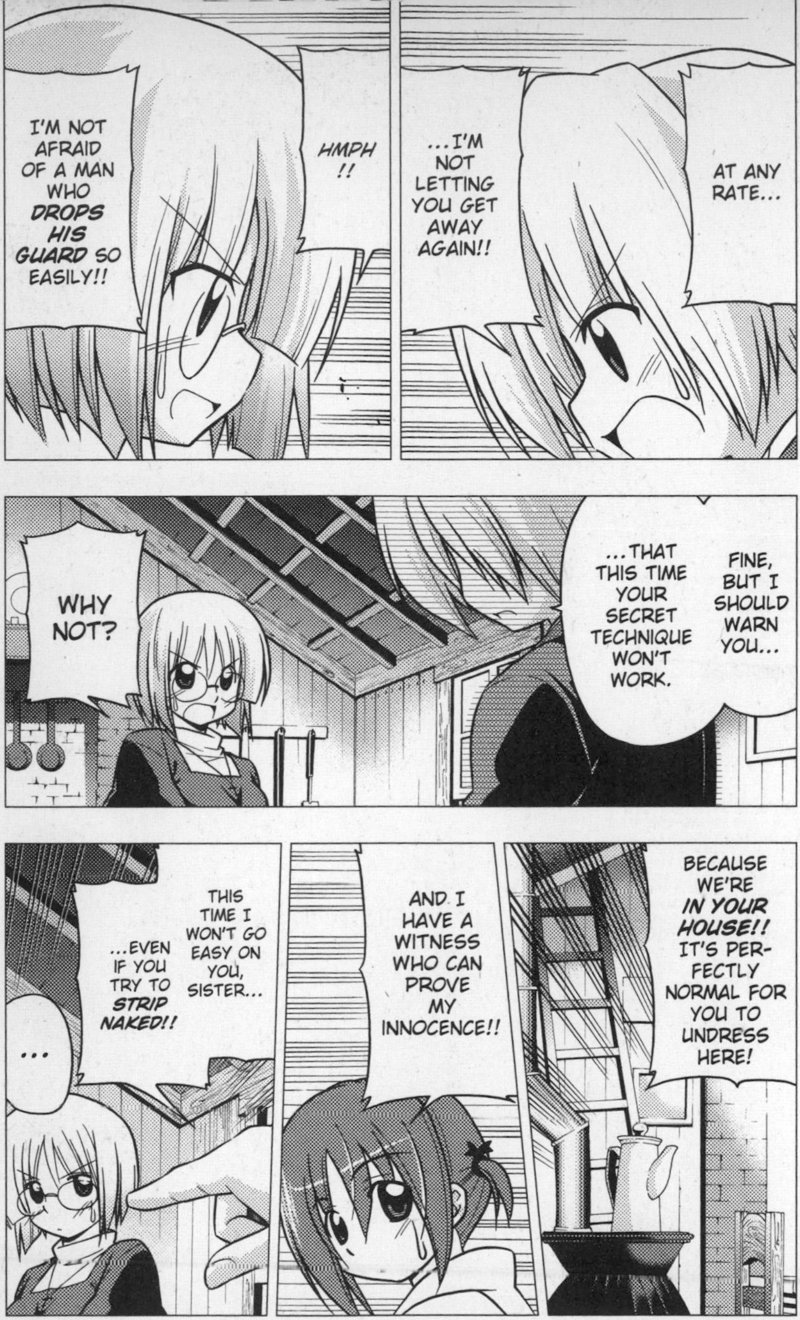
AT ANY RATE...
...I'M NOT LETTING YOU GET AWAY AGAIN!!
HMPH!!
I'M NOT AFRAID OF A MAN WHO **DROPS HIS GUARD** SO EASILY!!
FINE, BUT I SHOULD WARN YOU...
...THAT THIS TIME YOUR SECRET TECHNIQUE WON'T WORK.
WHY NOT?
BECAUSE WE'RE ***IN YOUR HOUSE!!*** IT'S PER-FECTLY NORMAL FOR YOU TO UNDRESS HERE!
AND I HAVE A WITNESS WHO CAN PROVE MY INNOCENCE!!
THIS TIME I WON'T GO EASY ON YOU, SISTER...
...EVEN IF YOU TRY TO ***STRIP NAKED!!***
...

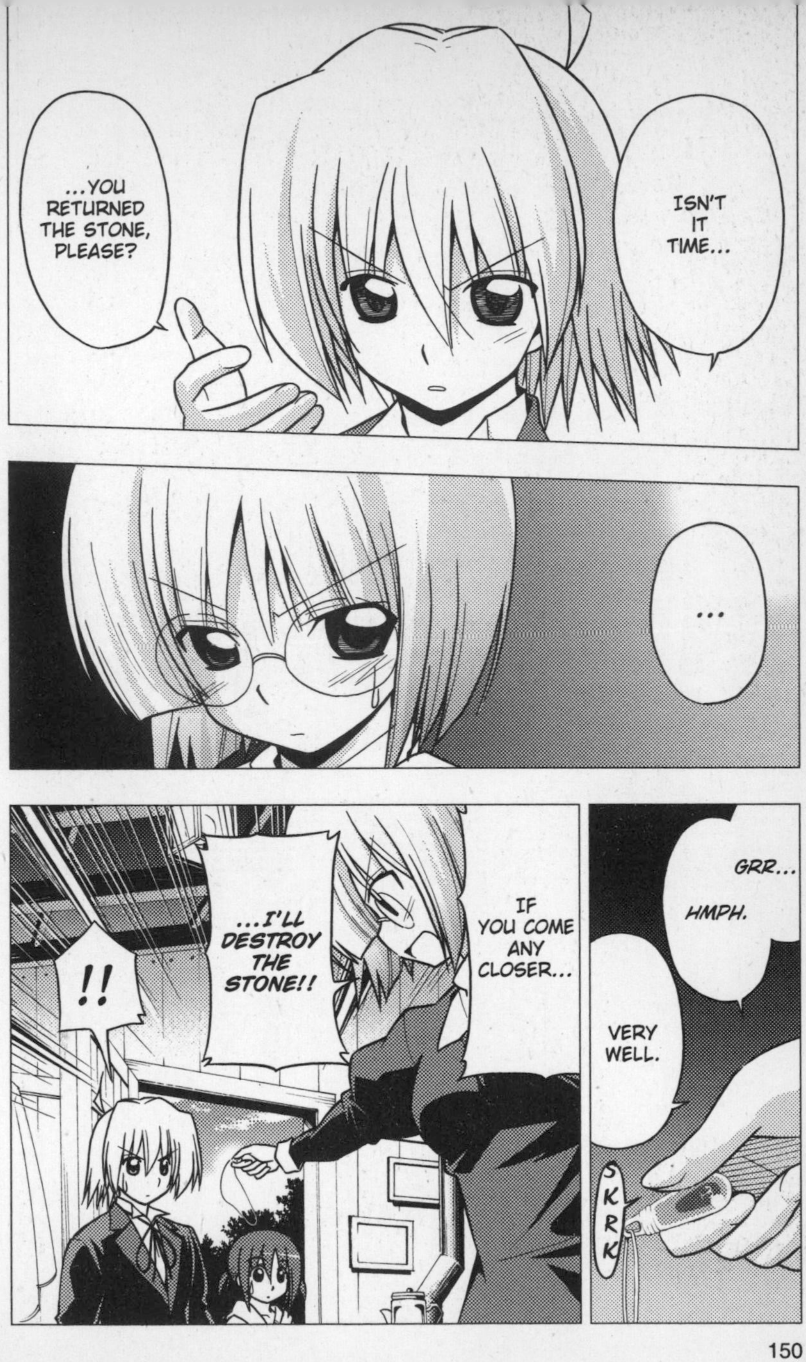
ISN'T IT TIME...
...YOU RETURNED THE STONE, PLEASE?
...
GRR...
HMPH.
VERY WELL.
SKRK
IF YOU COME ANY CLOSER...
...I'LL DESTROY THE STONE!!
!!

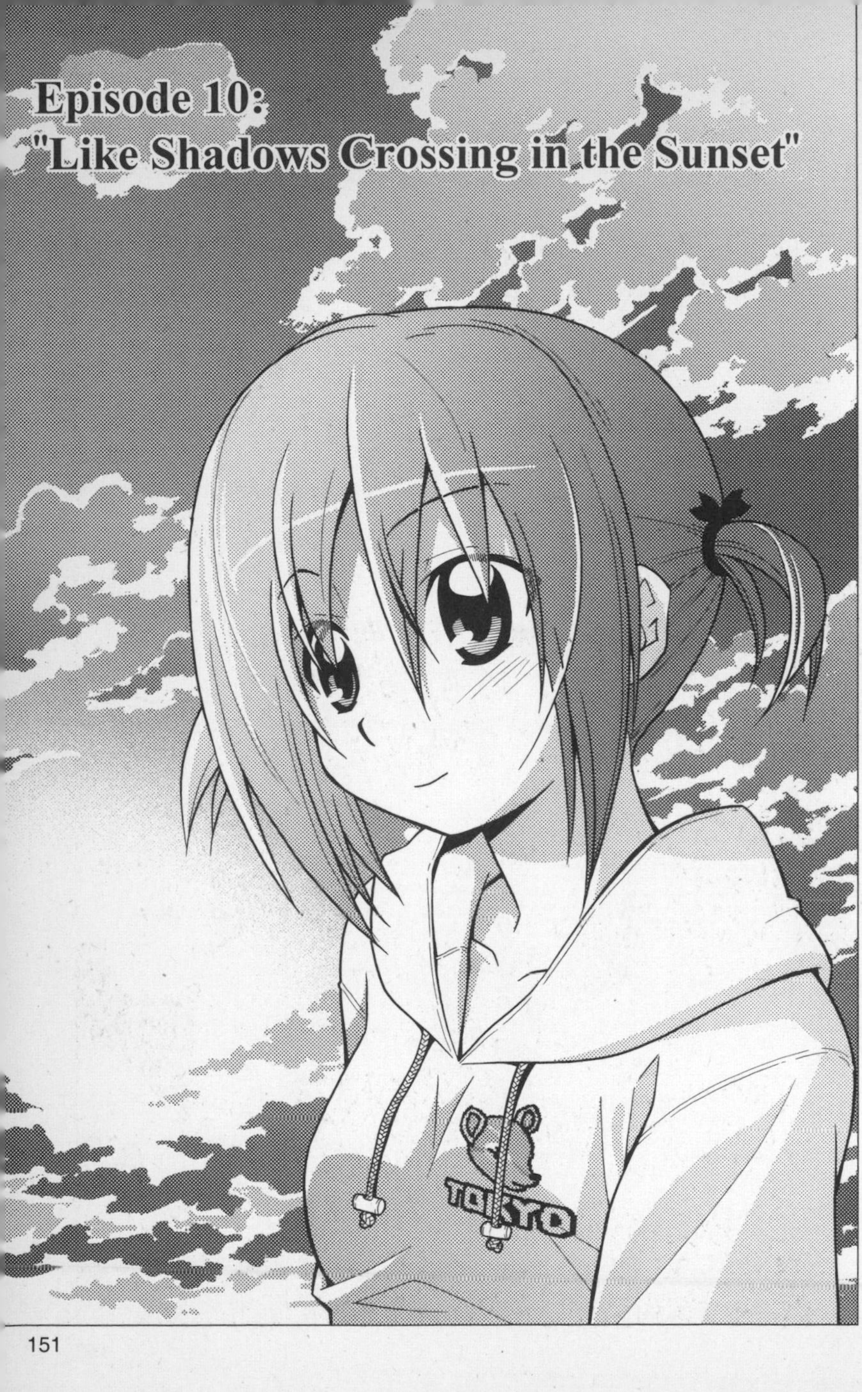
Episode 10:
"Like Shadows Crossing in the Sunset"
TOKYO

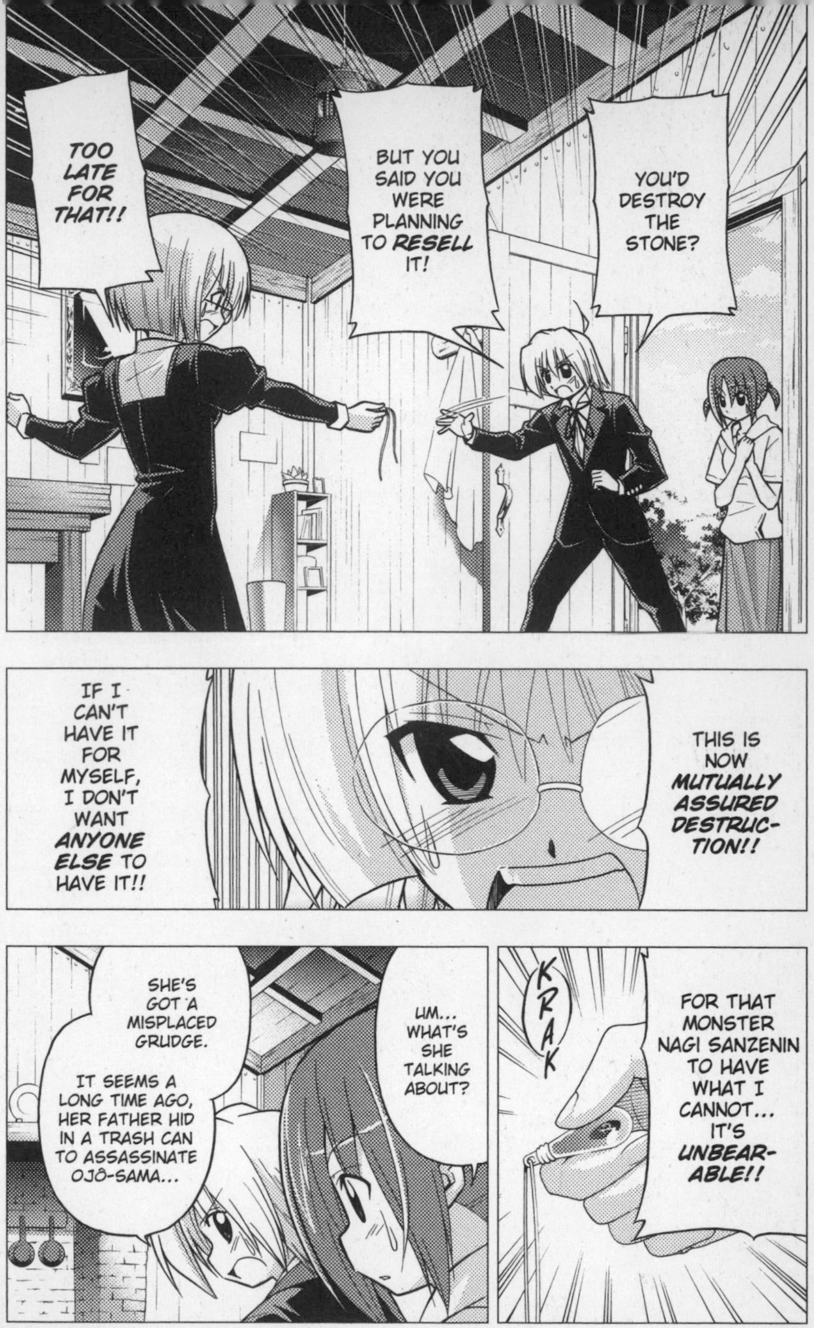
YOU'D DESTROY THE STONE?
BUT YOU SAID YOU WERE PLANNING TO **RESELL** IT!
TOO LATE FOR THAT!!
THIS IS NOW **MUTUALLY ASSURED DESTRUC-TION!!**
IF I CAN'T HAVE IT FOR MYSELF, I DON'T WANT **ANYONE ELSE** TO HAVE IT!!
KRAK
FOR THAT MONSTER NAGI SANZENIN TO HAVE WHAT I CANNOT... IT'S **UNBEAR-ABLE!!**
UM... WHAT'S SHE TALKING ABOUT?
SHE'S GOT A MISPLACED GRUDGE.
IT SEEMS A LONG TIME AGO, HER FATHER HID IN A TRASH CAN TO ASSASSINATE OJÔ-SAMA...

POP!!

NOT SO FAST!! (in Italian)

COULD THAT MAN HAVE BEEN HER FATHER?

WAIT!!

FSSST

!

GASP

...BUT THEN A BOY...

...LEAVING ME TO GROW UP POOR!!

...MY GRANDPA WAS MY ONLY LIVING RELATIVE! BUT HE SPENT YEARS BEHIND BARS...

AFTER MY FATHER DIED...

...WILL BUY ME LOVE!!

THAT MONEY...

...WON'T YOU FORGIVE HIM? HE IS STILL MY FATHER, AFTER ALL.

YEAH, YOU SAID SOMETHING ABOUT REVENGE, BUT...

POP! YOU REALLY STOLE HOW I FEEL.

...SINCE YOU'RE JUST A KID...

WELL... YOU MIGHT HAVE FORGOTTEN LUCA PAGANINI.

WHAT DO YOU THINK?

REC MEM THIS ONE.

BIG SMILE

AND WHEN I AM, MY TRUE LOVE WILL FINALLY NOTICE ME!!

OBSCENELY RICH!!

THAT'S WHY I WANT TO BE *RICH!!*

153

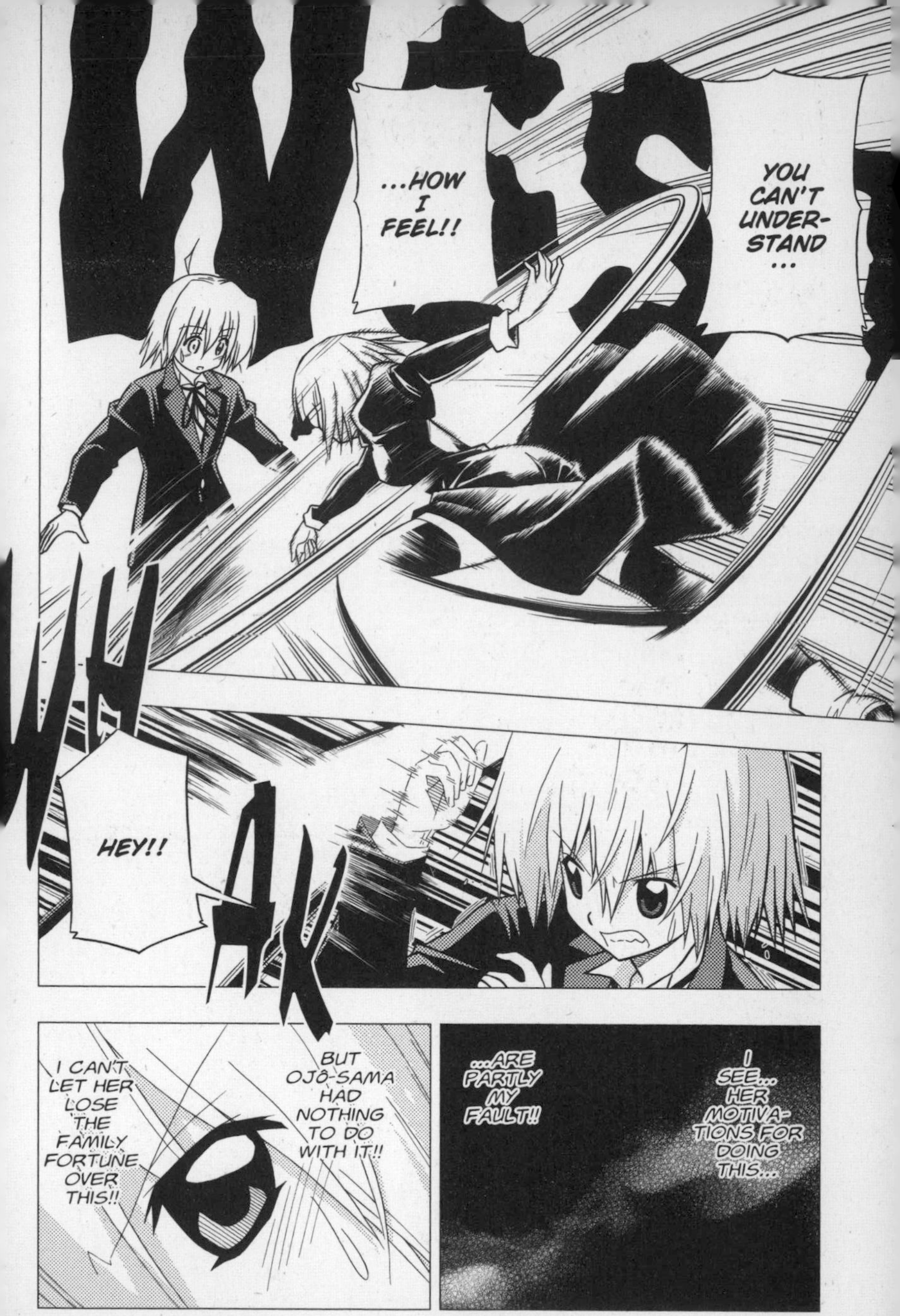
YOU CAN'T UNDER-STAND...
...HOW I FEEL!!
HEY!!
I SEE... HER MOTIVA-TIONS FOR DOING THIS...
...ARE PARTLY MY FAULT!!
BUT OJÔ-SAMA HAD NOTHING TO DO WITH IT!!
I CAN'T LET HER LOSE THE FAMILY FORTUNE OVER THIS!!

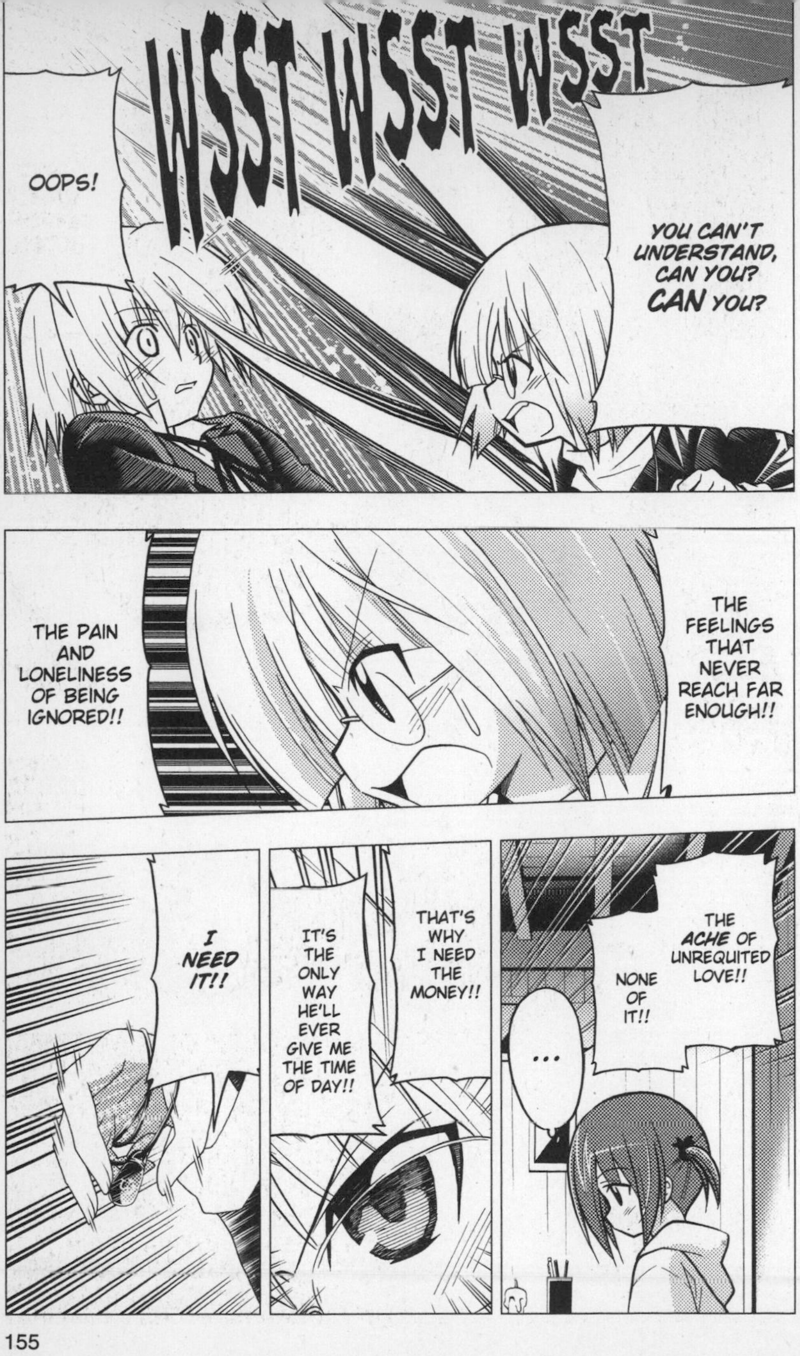
WSST WSST WSST
YOU CAN'T UNDERSTAND, CAN YOU? CAN YOU?
OOPS!
THE FEELINGS THAT NEVER REACH FAR ENOUGH!!
THE PAIN AND LONELINESS OF BEING IGNORED!!
THE ACHE OF UNREQUITED LOVE!!
NONE OF IT!!
...
THAT'S WHY I NEED THE MONEY!!
IT'S THE ONLY WAY HE'LL EVER GIVE ME THE TIME OF DAY!!
I NEED IT!!

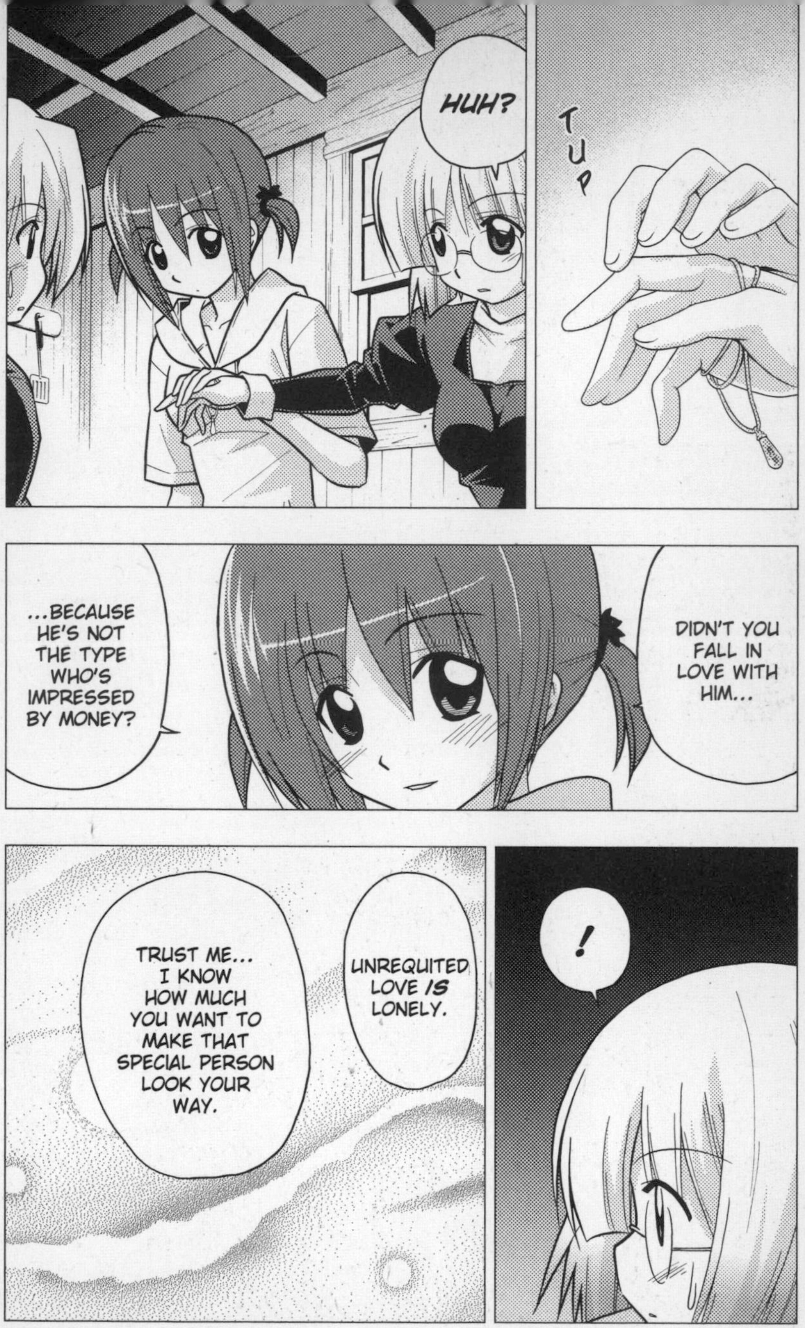
TUP
HUH?
DIDN'T YOU FALL IN LOVE WITH HIM...
...BECAUSE HE'S NOT THE TYPE WHO'S IMPRESSED BY MONEY?
!
UNREQUITED LOVE *IS* LONELY.
TRUST ME... I KNOW HOW MUCH YOU WANT TO MAKE THAT SPECIAL PERSON LOOK YOUR WAY.

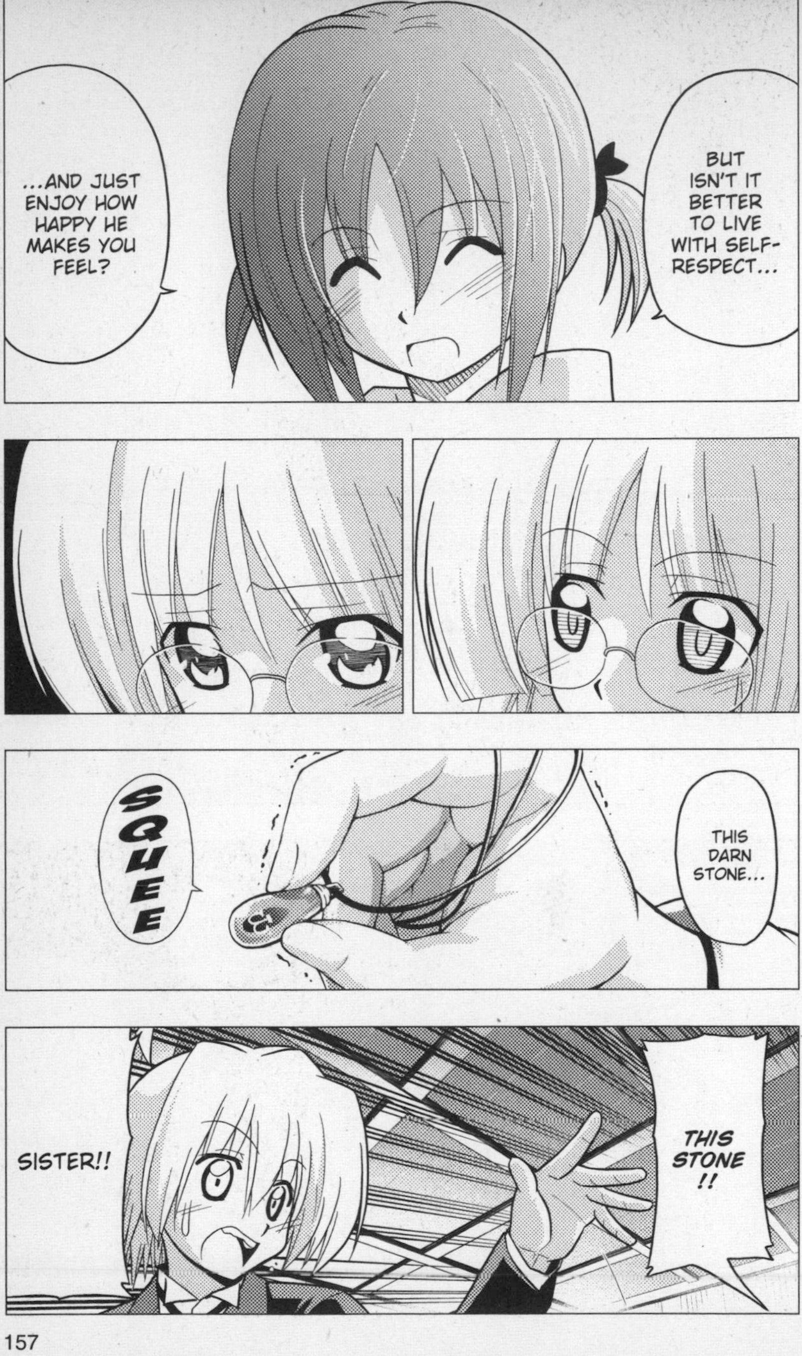
BUT ISN'T IT BETTER TO LIVE WITH SELF-RESPECT...
...AND JUST ENJOY HOW HAPPY HE MAKES YOU FEEL?
THIS DARN STONE...
SQUEE
THIS STONE !!
SISTER!!

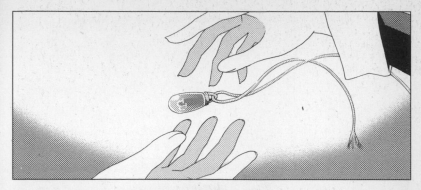

DARN YOU!!

THERE! YOU'VE GOT IT BACK!!

SHAA

SISTER...

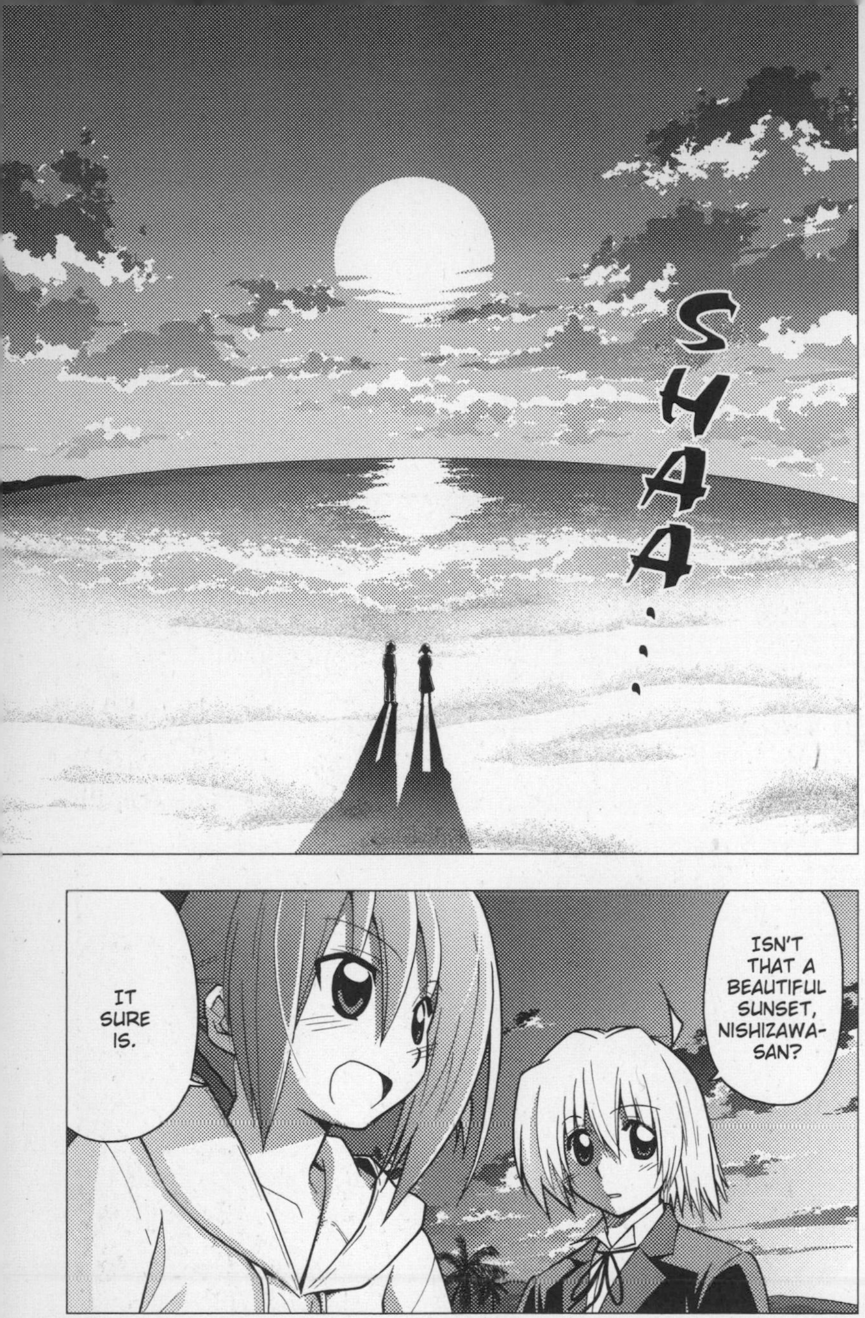
SHAA...
ISN'T THAT A BEAUTIFUL SUNSET, NISHIZAWA-SAN?
IT SURE IS.

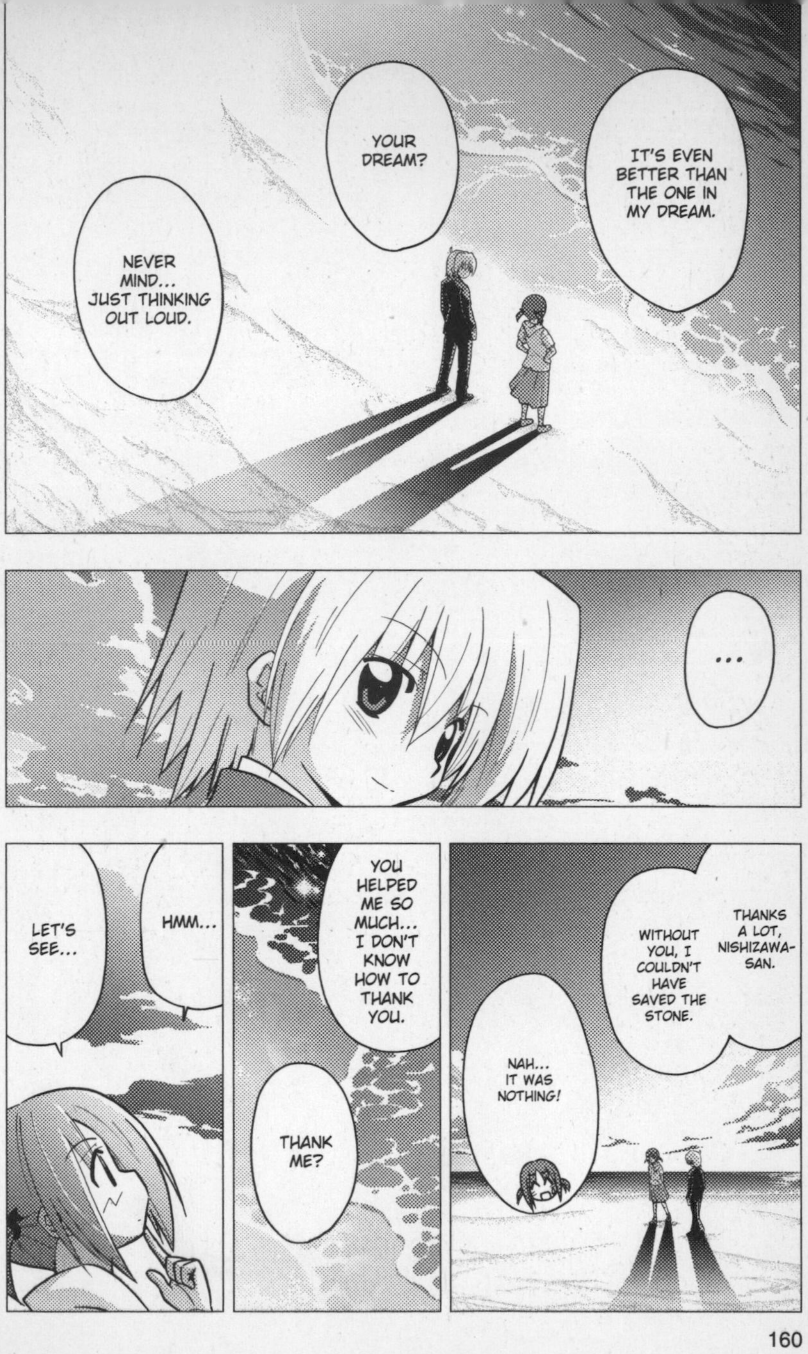
IT'S EVEN BETTER THAN THE ONE IN MY DREAM.
YOUR DREAM?
NEVER MIND... JUST THINKING OUT LOUD.
...
THANKS A LOT, NISHIZAWA-SAN.
WITHOUT YOU, I COULDN'T HAVE SAVED THE STONE.
NAH... IT WAS NOTHING!
YOU HELPED ME SO MUCH... I DON'T KNOW HOW TO THANK YOU.
THANK ME?
HMM...
LET'S SEE...

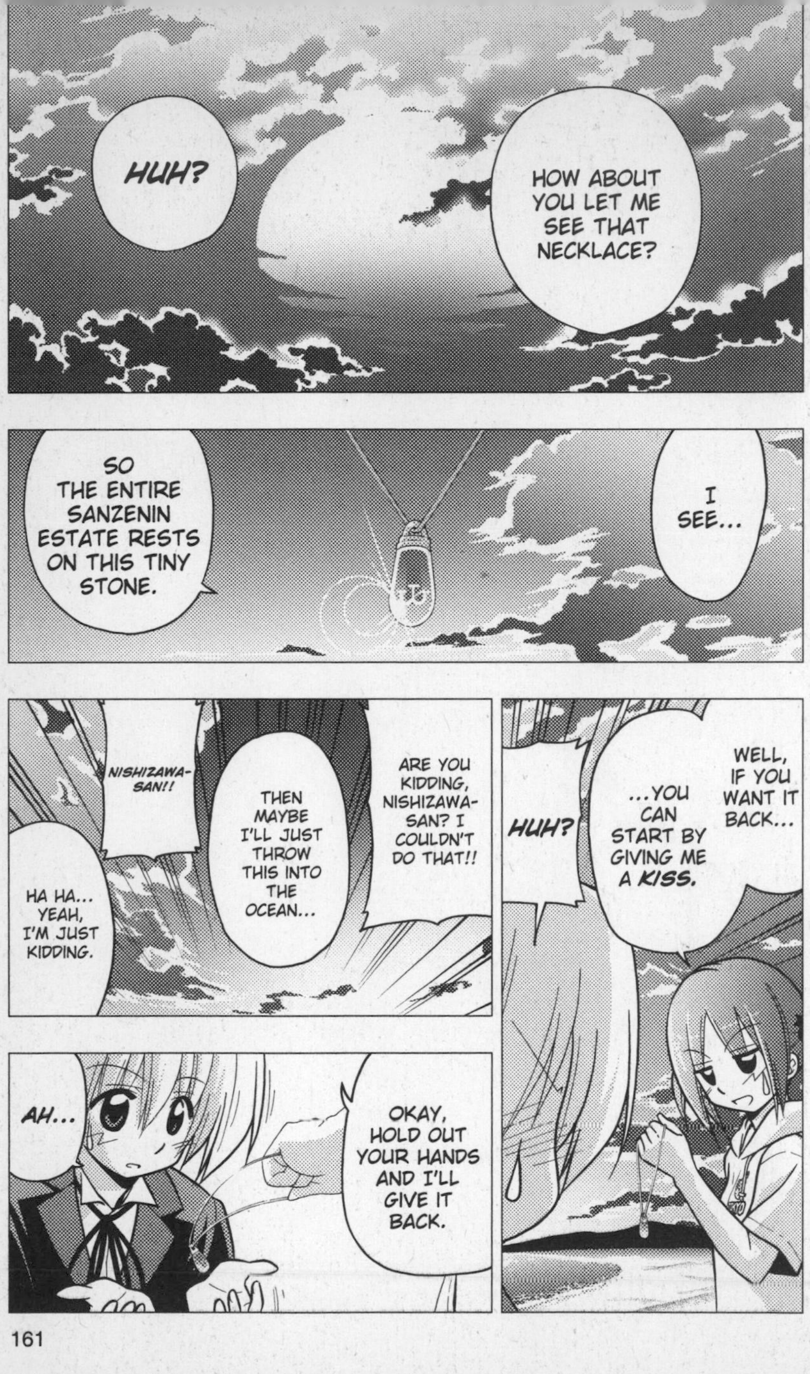
HOW ABOUT YOU LET ME SEE THAT NECKLACE?
HUH?
I SEE...
SO THE ENTIRE SANZENIN ESTATE RESTS ON THIS TINY STONE.
WELL, IF YOU WANT IT BACK...
...YOU CAN START BY GIVING ME A *KISS*.
HUH?
ARE YOU KIDDING, NISHIZAWA-SAN? I COULDN'T DO THAT!!
THEN MAYBE I'LL JUST THROW THIS INTO THE OCEAN...
NISHIZAWA-SAN!!
HA HA... YEAH, I'M JUST KIDDING.
OKAY, HOLD OUT YOUR HANDS AND I'LL GIVE IT BACK.
AH...

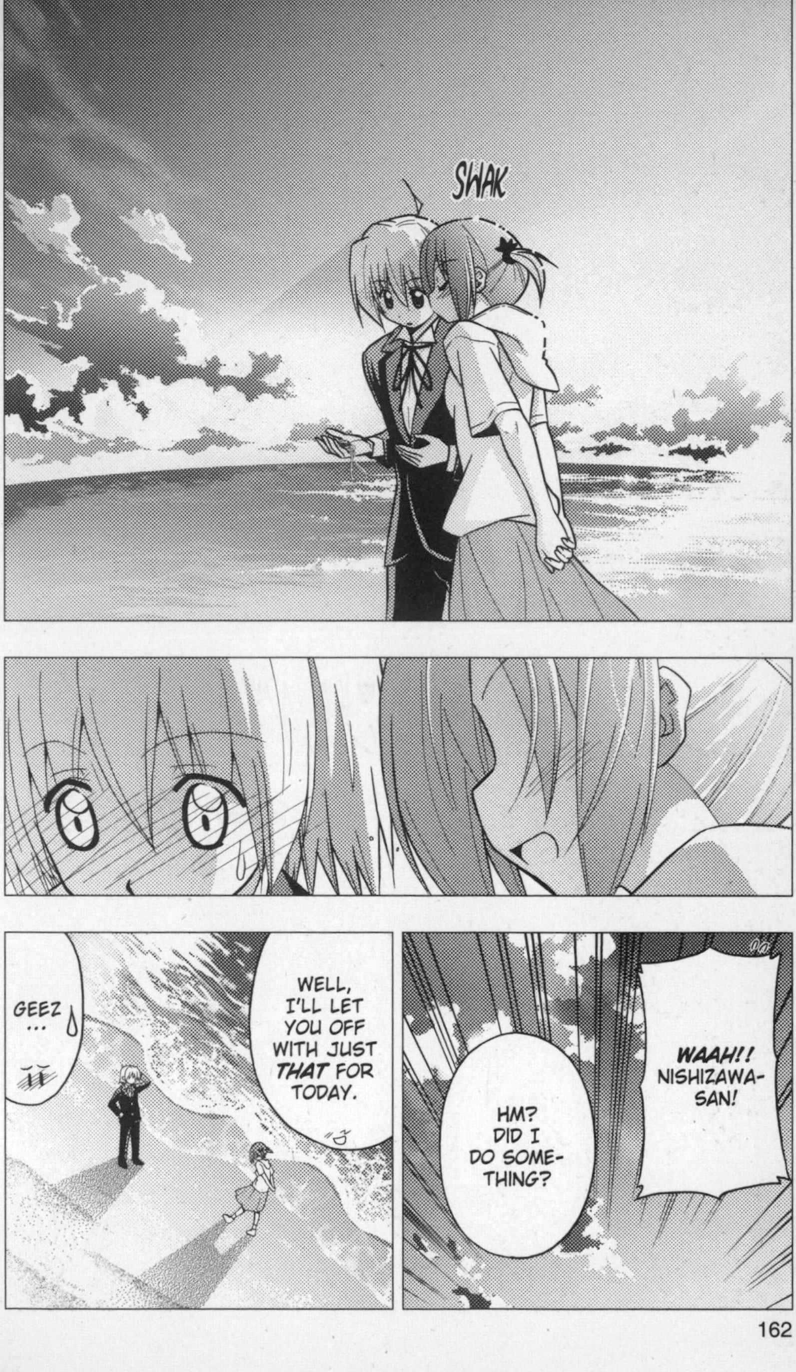
SWAK
WAAH!! NISHIZAWA-SAN!
HM? DID I DO SOME-THING?
WELL, I'LL LET YOU OFF WITH JUST THAT FOR TODAY.
GEEZ ...

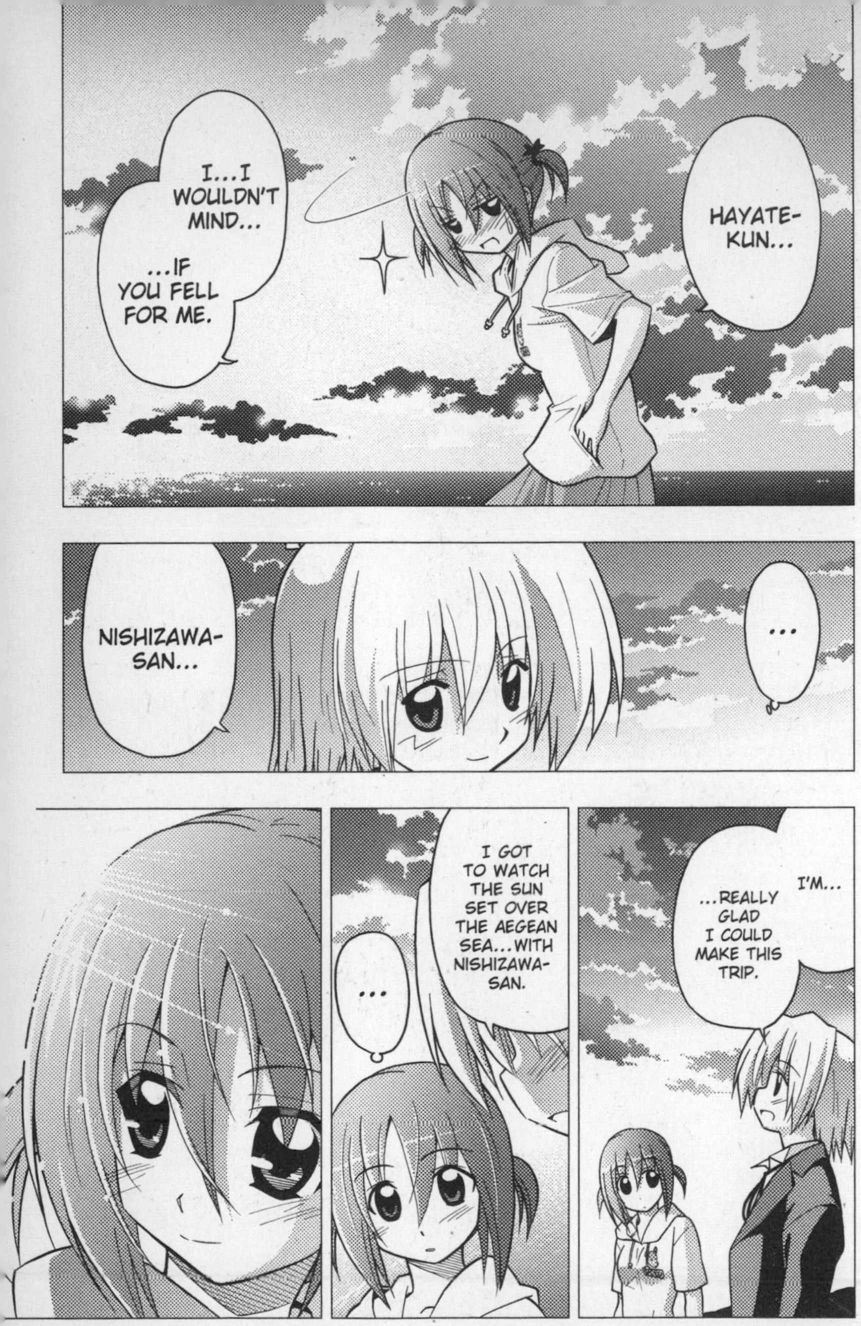
HAYATE-KUN...
I...I WOULDN'T MIND...
...IF YOU FELL FOR ME.
...
NISHIZAWA-SAN...
I'M...
...REALLY GLAD I COULD MAKE THIS TRIP.
I GOT TO WATCH THE SUN SET OVER THE AEGEAN SEA...WITH NISHIZAWA-SAN.
...

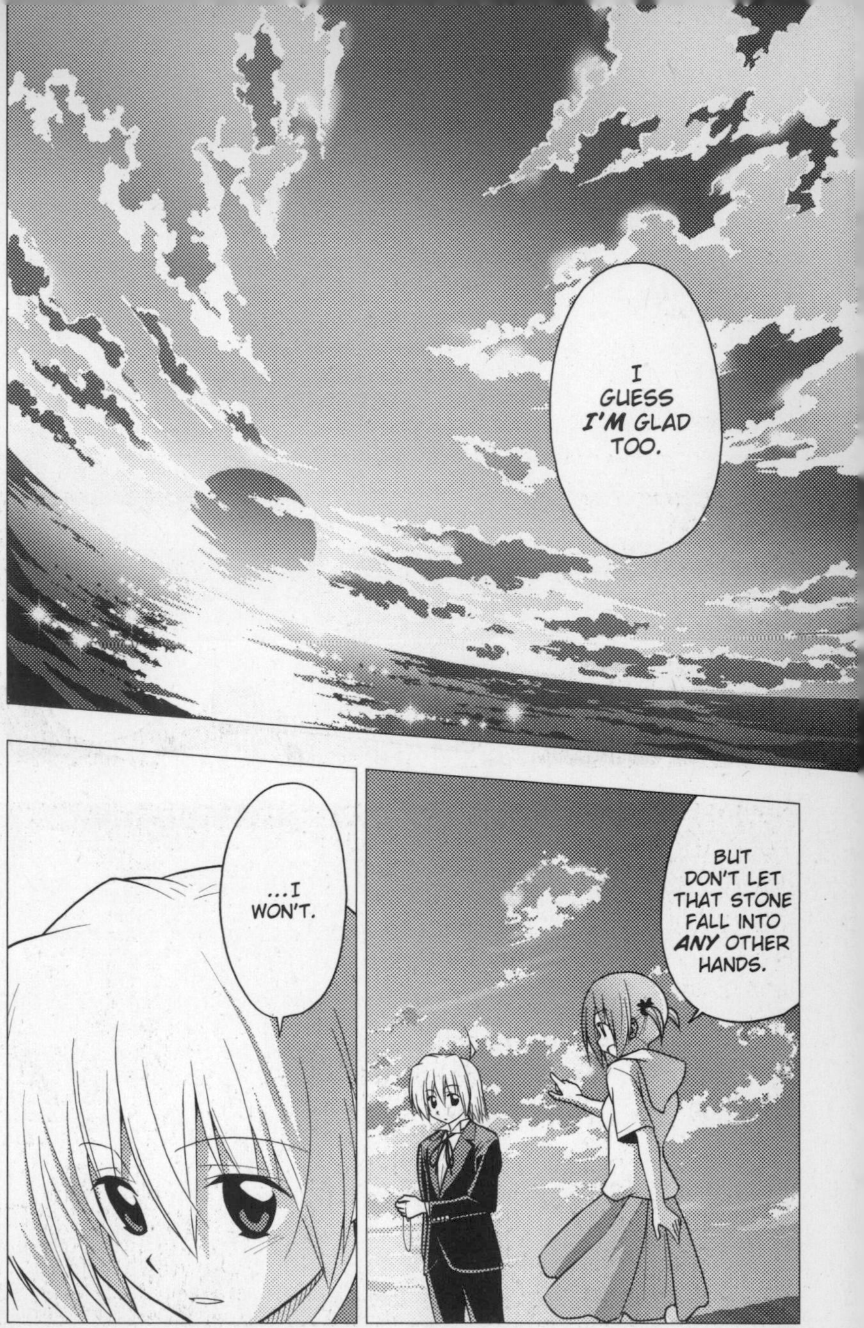
I GUESS I'M GLAD TOO.
BUT DON'T LET THAT STONE FALL INTO ANY OTHER HANDS.
...I WON'T.

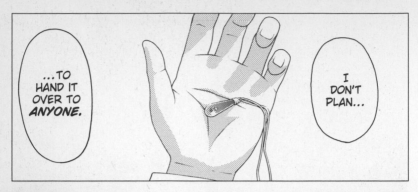

...TO HAND IT OVER TO *ANYONE*.

I DON'T PLAN...

NO MATTER HOW THEY CHALLENGE ME...

...AND...

...NO MATTER HOW STRONG THEY ARE...

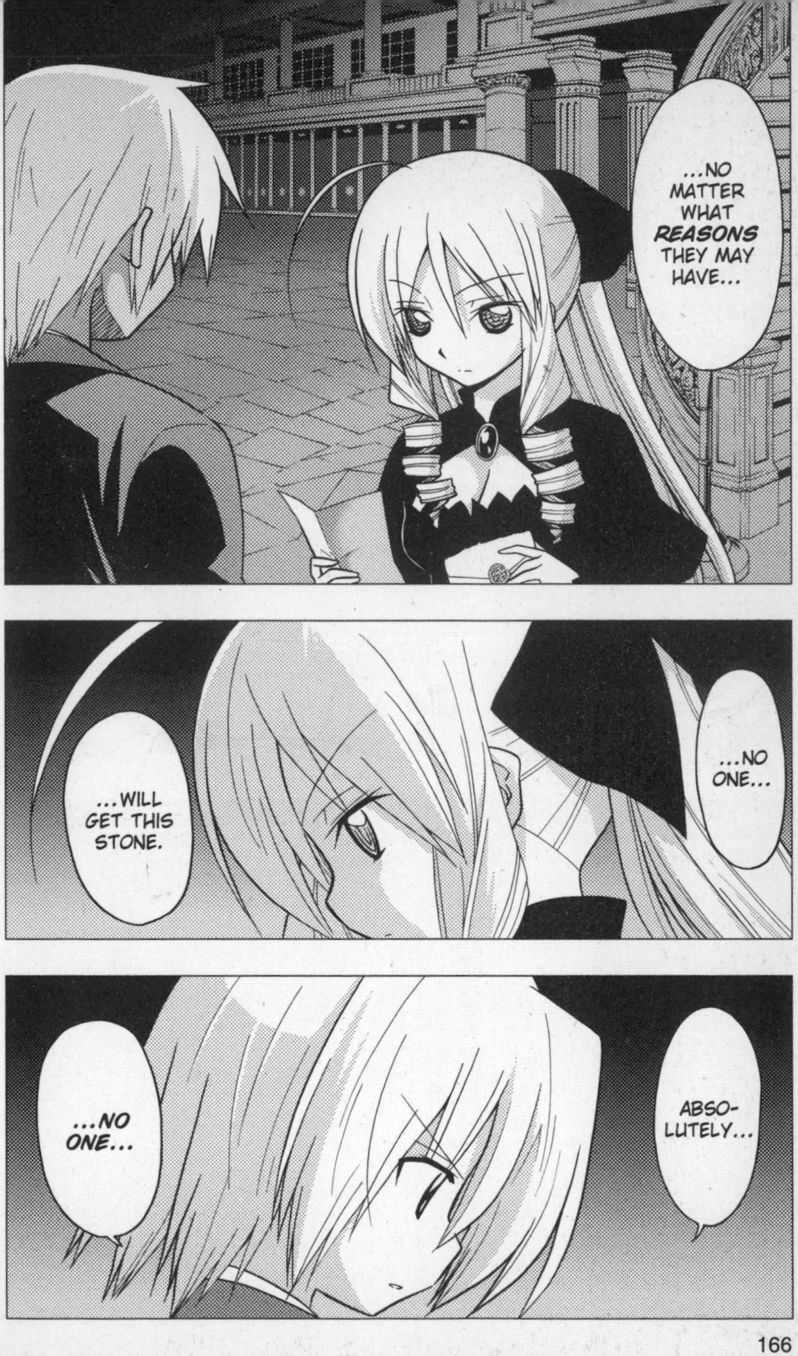
...NO MATTER WHAT **REASONS** THEY MAY HAVE...
...NO ONE...
...WILL GET THIS STONE.
ABSO-LUTELY...
...NO ONE...

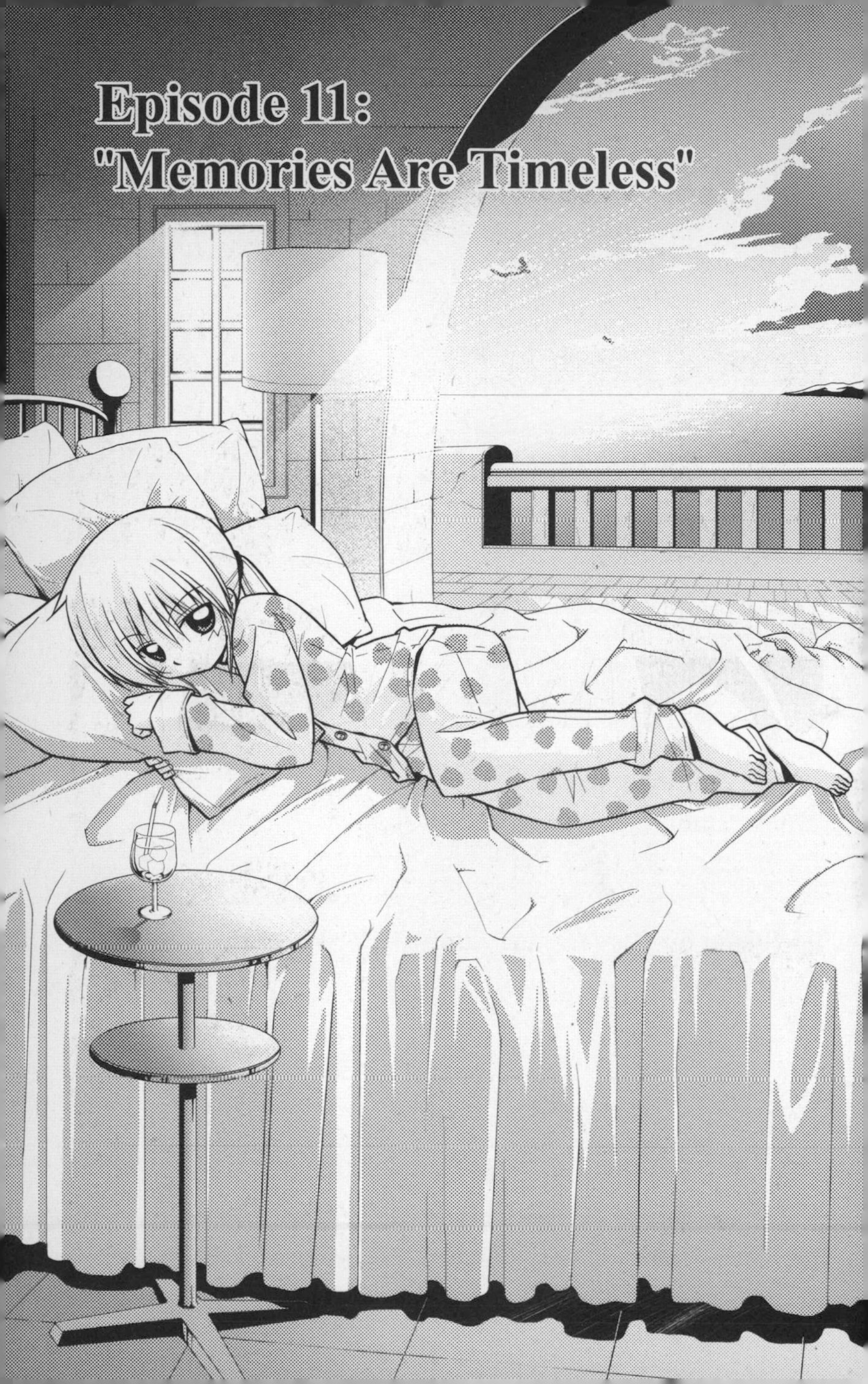
Episode 11:
"Memories Are Timeless"

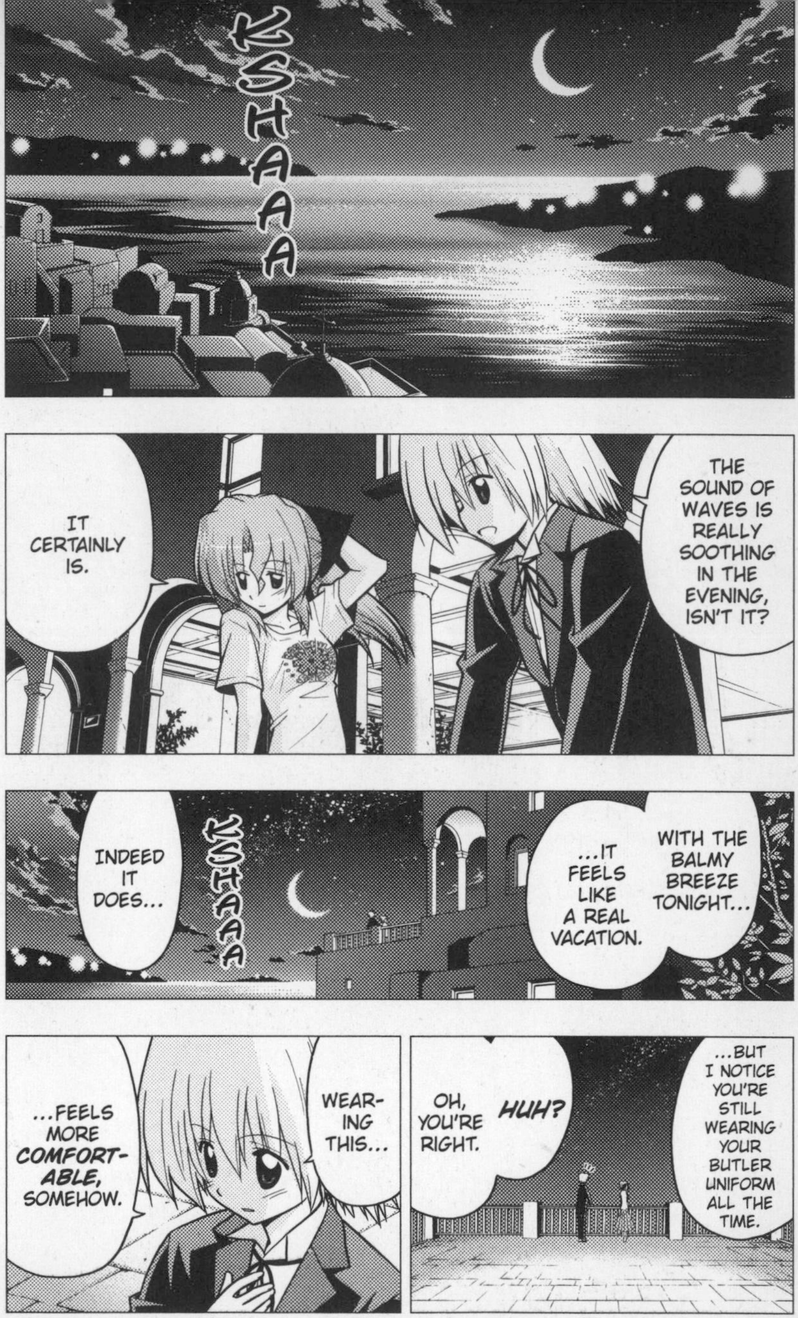
KSHAAAA
THE SOUND OF WAVES IS REALLY SOOTHING IN THE EVENING, ISN'T IT?
IT CERTAINLY IS.
WITH THE BALMY BREEZE TONIGHT...
...IT FEELS LIKE A REAL VACATION.
KSHAAA
INDEED IT DOES...
...BUT I NOTICE YOU'RE STILL WEARING YOUR BUTLER UNIFORM ALL THE TIME.
HUH?
OH, YOU'RE RIGHT.
WEAR-ING THIS...
...FEELS MORE COMFORT-ABLE, SOMEHOW.

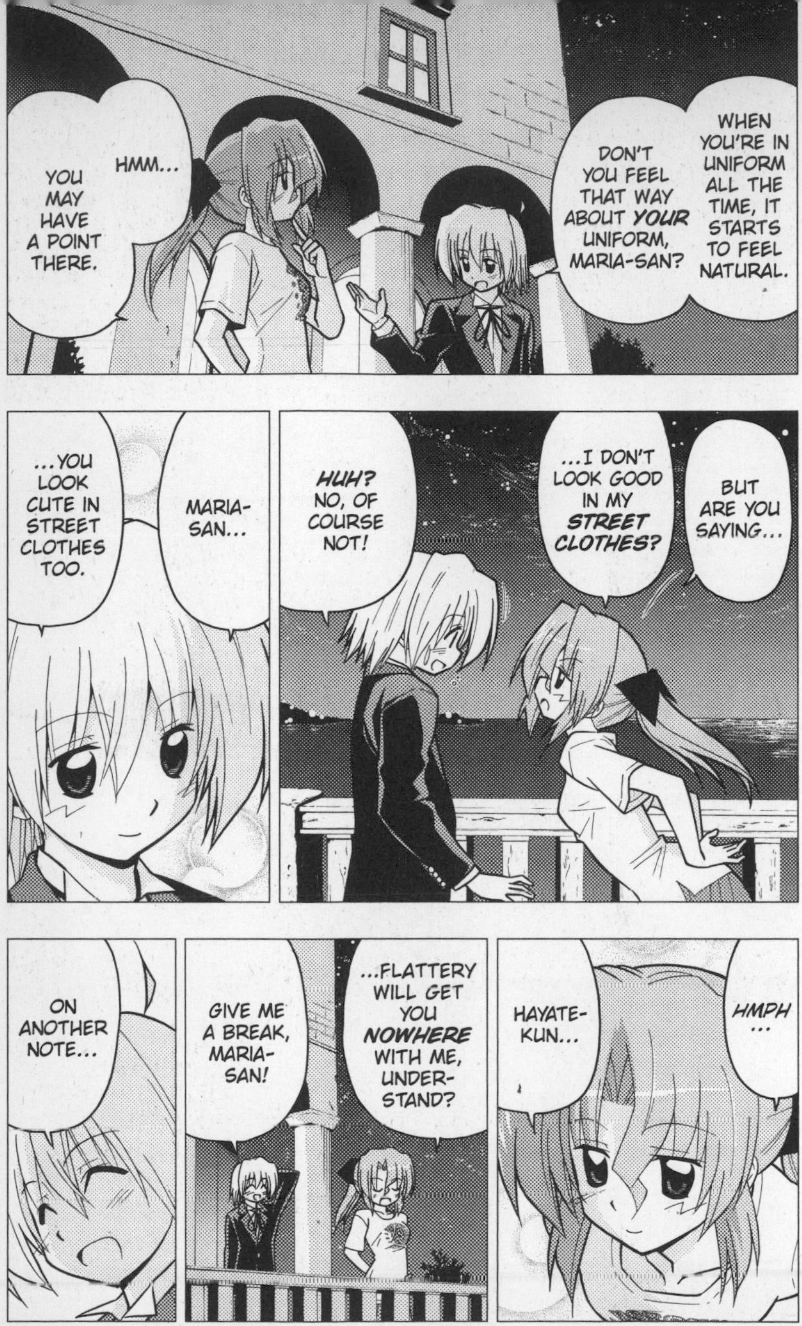
WHEN YOU'RE IN UNIFORM ALL THE TIME, IT STARTS TO FEEL NATURAL.
DON'T YOU FEEL THAT WAY ABOUT *YOUR* UNIFORM, MARIA-SAN?
HMM...
YOU MAY HAVE A POINT THERE.
BUT ARE YOU SAYING...
...I DON'T LOOK GOOD IN MY *STREET CLOTHES?*
HUH? NO, OF COURSE NOT!
MARIA-SAN...
...YOU LOOK CUTE IN STREET CLOTHES TOO.
HMPH...
HAYATE-KUN...
...FLATTERY WILL GET YOU *NOWHERE* WITH ME, UNDERSTAND?
GIVE ME A BREAK, MARIA-SAN!
ON ANOTHER NOTE...

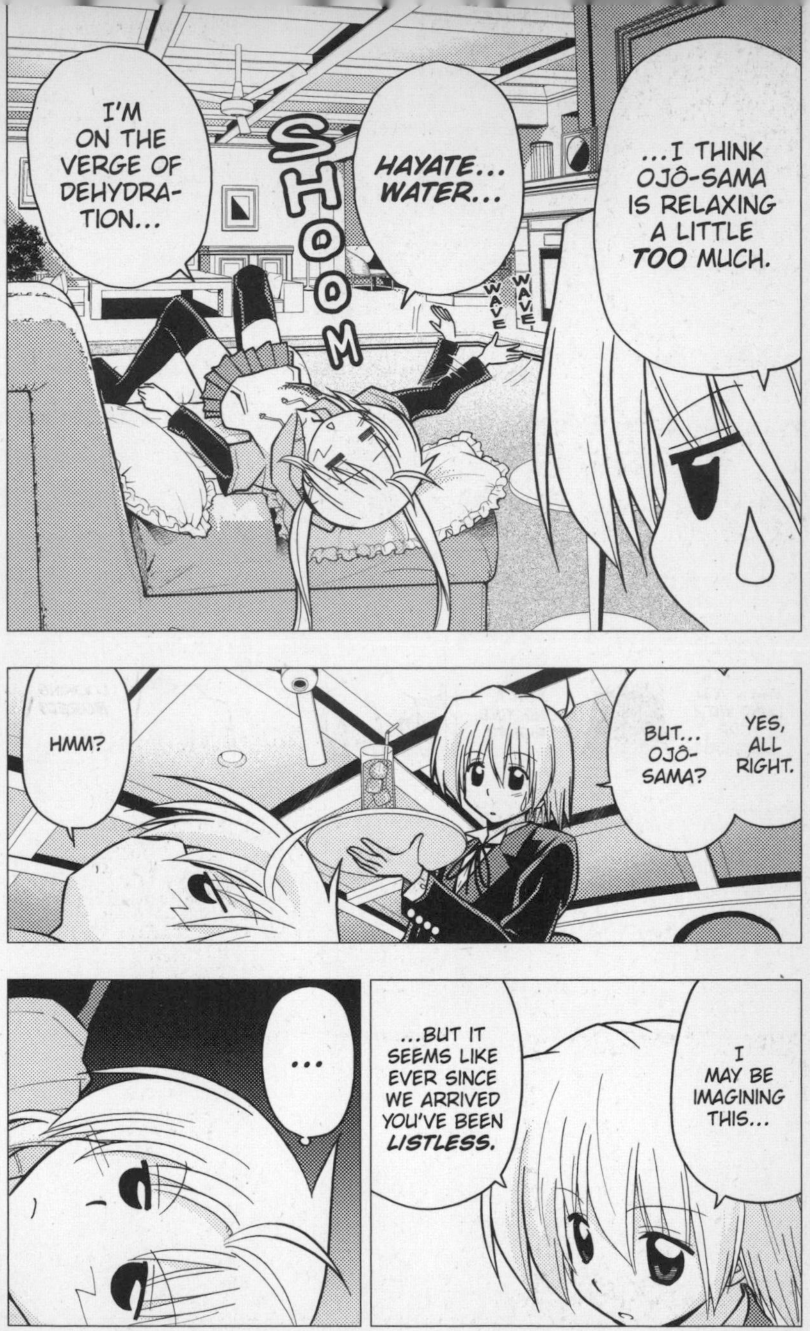
...I THINK OJÔ-SAMA IS RELAXING A LITTLE TOO MUCH.
HAYATE... WATER...
WAVE WAVE
SHOOM
I'M ON THE VERGE OF DEHYDRATION...
YES, ALL RIGHT.
BUT... OJÔ-SAMA?
HMM?
I MAY BE IMAGINING THIS...
...BUT IT SEEMS LIKE EVER SINCE WE ARRIVED YOU'VE BEEN LISTLESS.
...

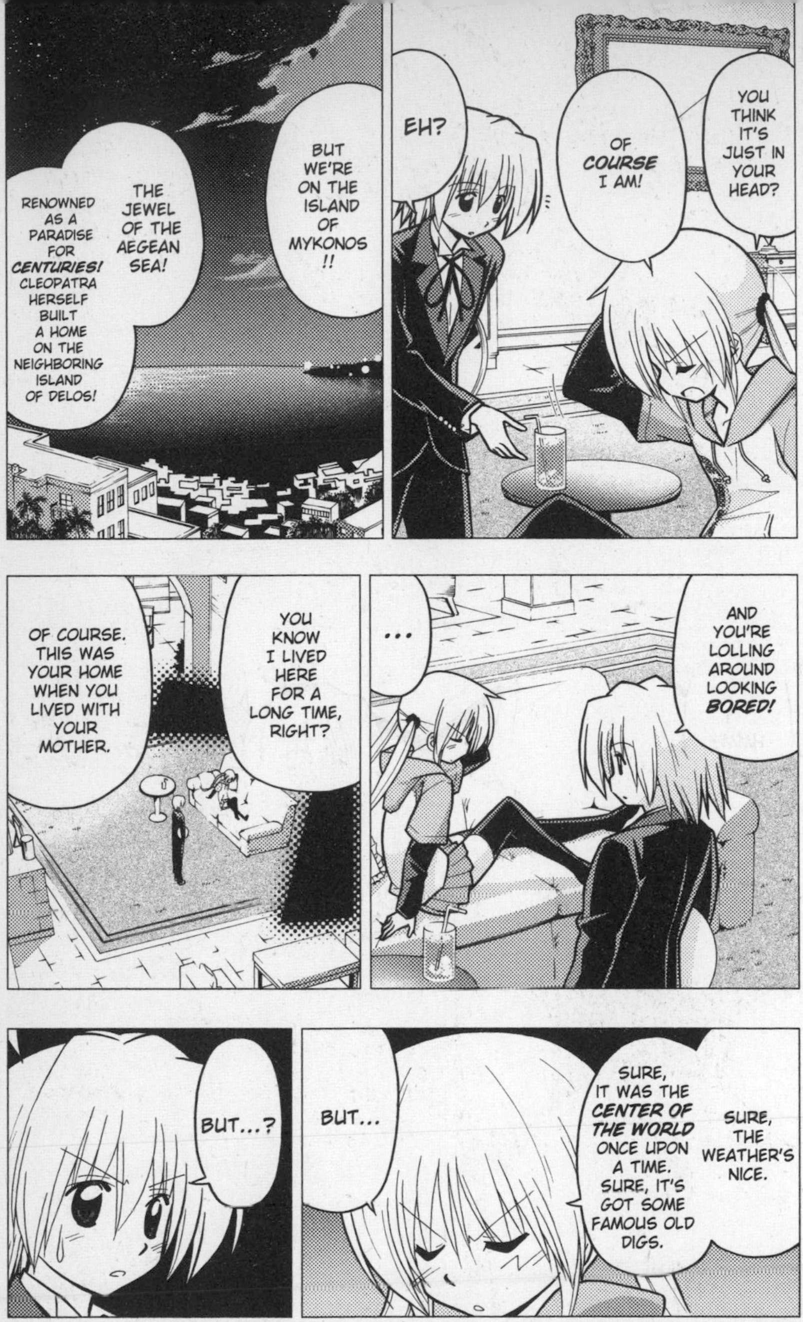
YOU THINK IT'S JUST IN YOUR HEAD?
OF COURSE I AM!
EH?
BUT WE'RE ON THE ISLAND OF MYKONOS !!
THE JEWEL OF THE AEGEAN SEA!
RENOWNED AS A PARADISE FOR CENTURIES! CLEOPATRA HERSELF BUILT A HOME ON THE NEIGHBORING ISLAND OF DELOS!
AND YOU'RE LOLLING AROUND LOOKING BORED!
...
YOU KNOW I LIVED HERE FOR A LONG TIME, RIGHT?
OF COURSE. THIS WAS YOUR HOME WHEN YOU LIVED WITH YOUR MOTHER.
SURE, THE WEATHER'S NICE.
SURE, IT WAS THE CENTER OF THE WORLD ONCE UPON A TIME. SURE, IT'S GOT SOME FAMOUS OLD DIGS.
BUT...
BUT...?

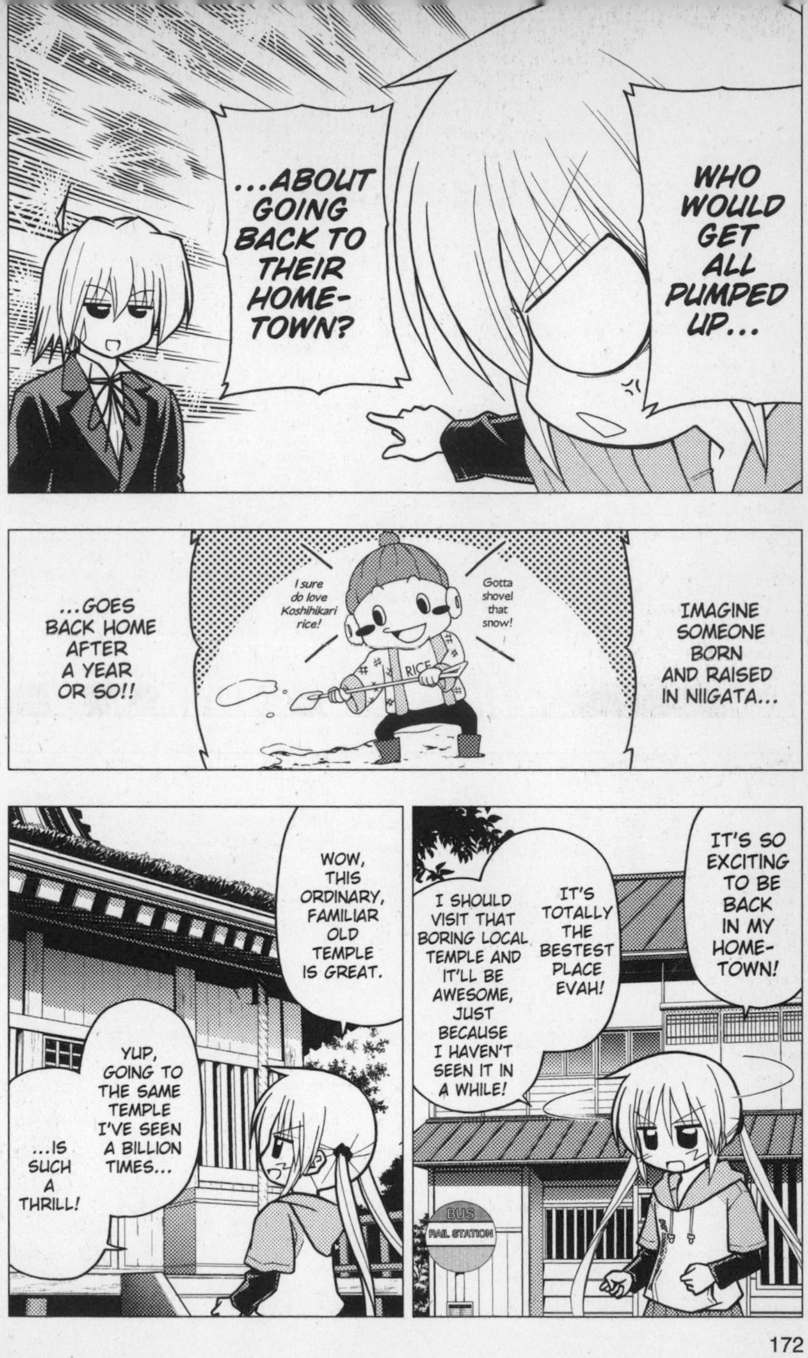
WHO WOULD GET ALL PUMPED UP...
...ABOUT GOING BACK TO THEIR HOME-TOWN?
IMAGINE SOMEONE BORN AND RAISED IN NIIGATA...
Gotta shovel that snow!
I sure do love Koshihikari rice!
RICE
...GOES BACK HOME AFTER A YEAR OR SO!!
IT'S SO EXCITING TO BE BACK IN MY HOME-TOWN!
IT'S TOTALLY THE BESTEST PLACE EVAH!
I SHOULD VISIT THAT BORING LOCAL TEMPLE AND IT'LL BE AWESOME, JUST BECAUSE I HAVEN'T SEEN IT IN A WHILE!
BUS
RAIL STATION
WOW, THIS ORDINARY, FAMILIAR OLD TEMPLE IS GREAT.
YUP, GOING TO THE SAME TEMPLE I'VE SEEN A BILLION TIMES...
...IS SUCH A THRILL!

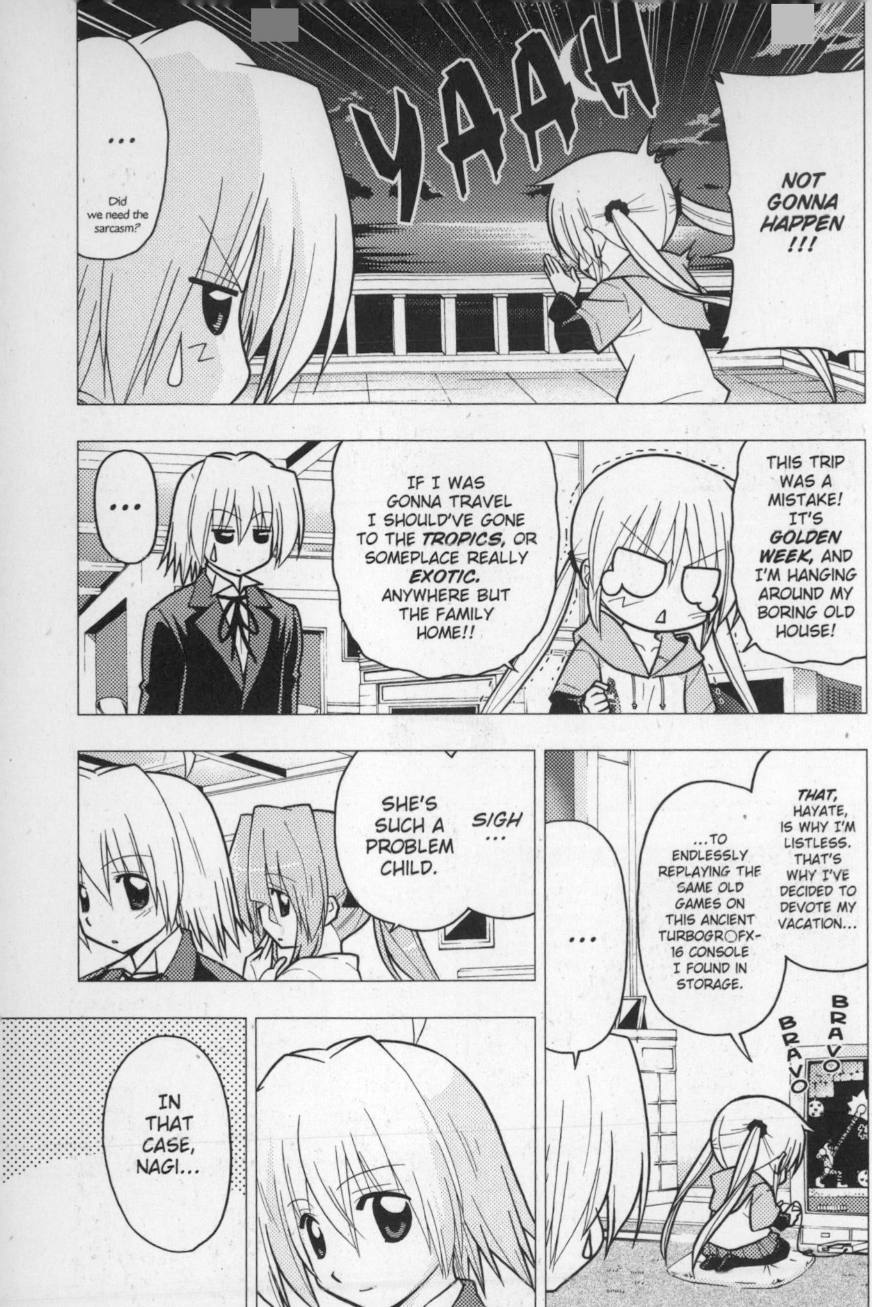
NOT GONNA HAPPEN !!!
YAAAH
...
Did we need the sarcasm?
THIS TRIP WAS A MISTAKE! IT'S GOLDEN WEEK, AND I'M HANGING AROUND MY BORING OLD HOUSE!
IF I WAS GONNA TRAVEL I SHOULD'VE GONE TO THE TROPICS, OR SOMEPLACE REALLY EXOTIC. ANYWHERE BUT THE FAMILY HOME!!
...
THAT, HAYATE, IS WHY I'M LISTLESS. THAT'S WHY I'VE DECIDED TO DEVOTE MY VACATION...
...TO ENDLESSLY REPLAYING THE SAME OLD GAMES ON THIS ANCIENT TURBOGR○FX-16 CONSOLE I FOUND IN STORAGE.
...
BRAVO
BRAVO
SIGH ...
SHE'S SUCH A PROBLEM CHILD.
IN THAT CASE, NAGI...

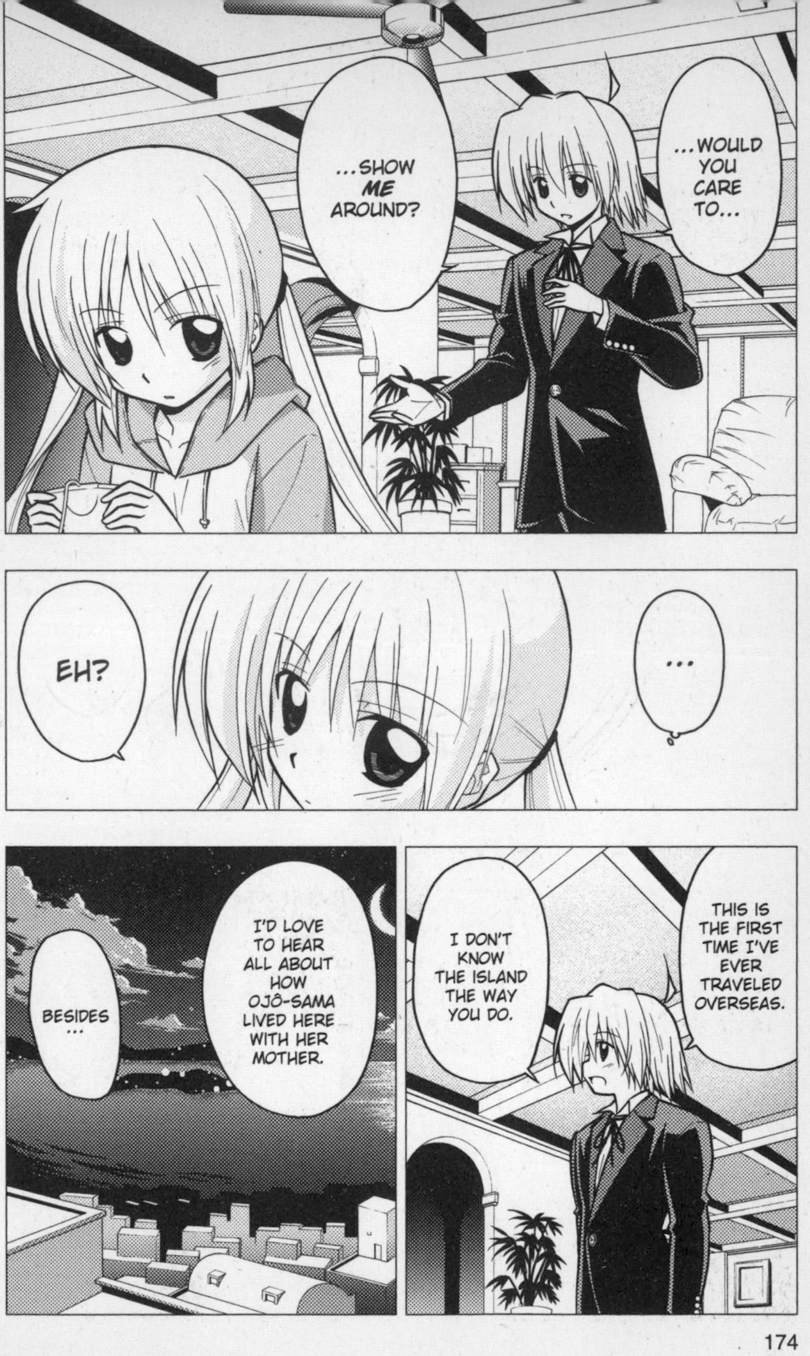
...WOULD YOU CARE TO...
...SHOW *ME* AROUND?
...
EH?
THIS IS THE FIRST TIME I'VE EVER TRAVELED OVERSEAS.
I DON'T KNOW THE ISLAND THE WAY YOU DO.
I'D LOVE TO HEAR ALL ABOUT HOW OJÔ-SAMA LIVED HERE WITH HER MOTHER.
BESIDES...

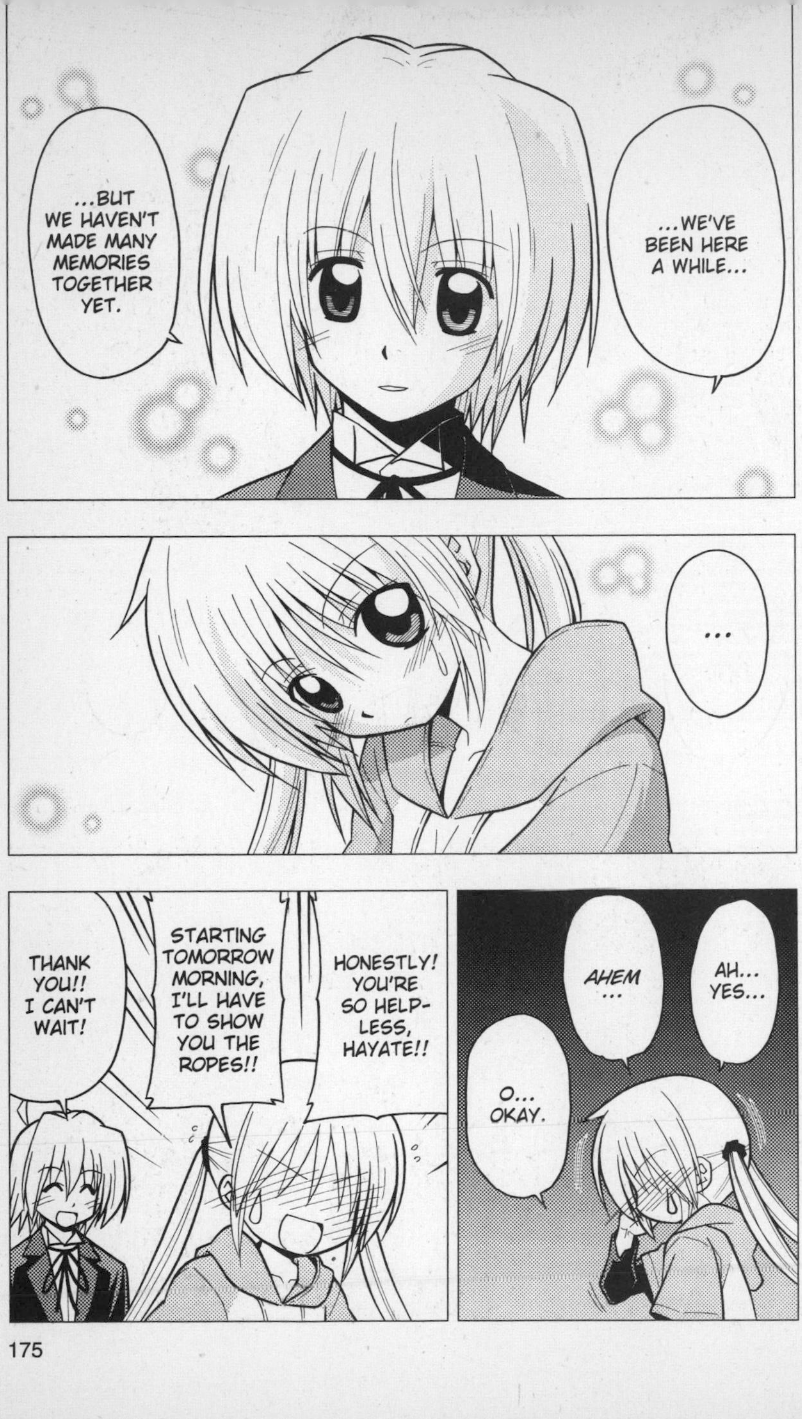
...WE'VE BEEN HERE A WHILE...
...BUT WE HAVEN'T MADE MANY MEMORIES TOGETHER YET.
...
AH... YES...
AHEM ...
O... OKAY.
HONESTLY! YOU'RE SO HELP-LESS, HAYATE!!
STARTING TOMORROW MORNING, I'LL HAVE TO SHOW YOU THE ROPES!!
THANK YOU!! I CAN'T WAIT!

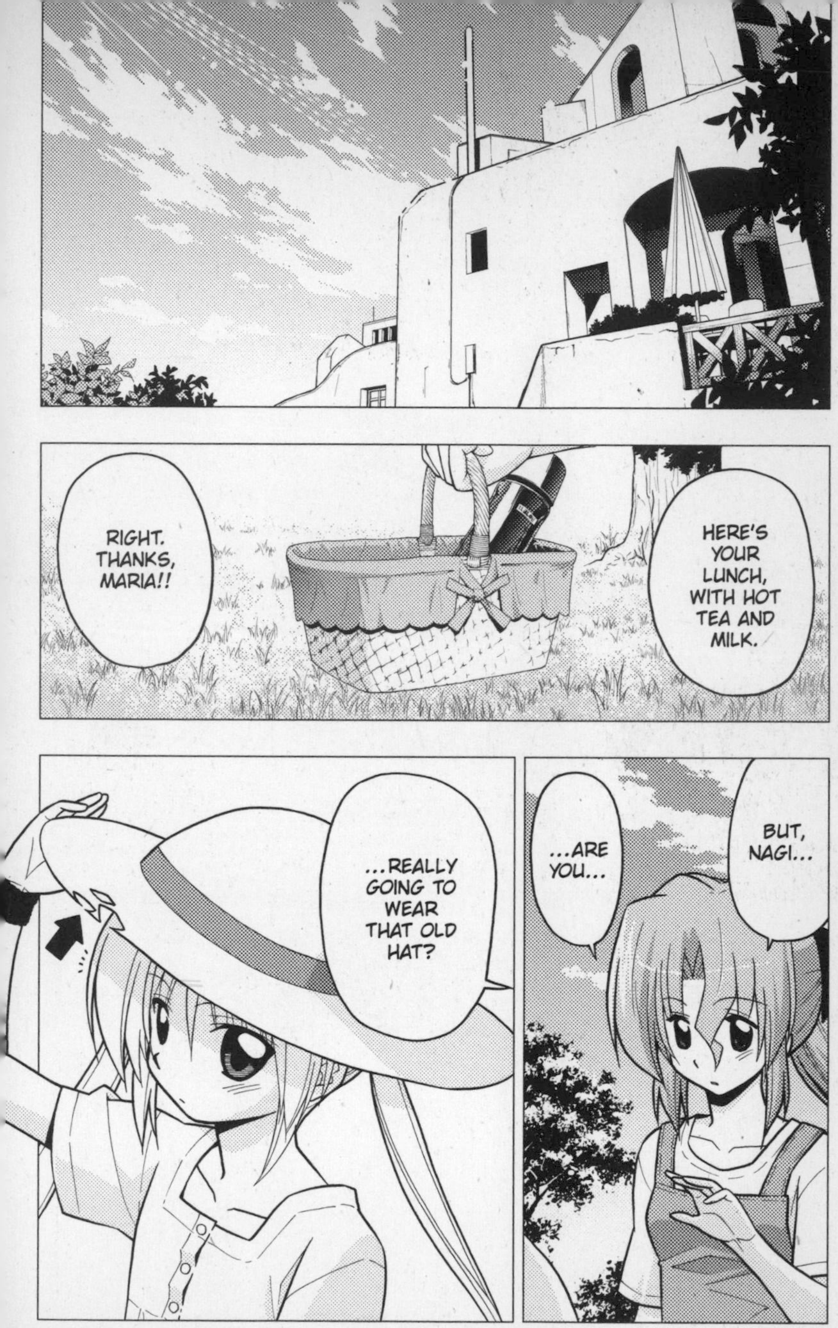
HERE'S YOUR LUNCH, WITH HOT TEA AND MILK.
RIGHT. THANKS, MARIA!!
BUT, NAGI...
...ARE YOU...
...REALLY GOING TO WEAR THAT OLD HAT?

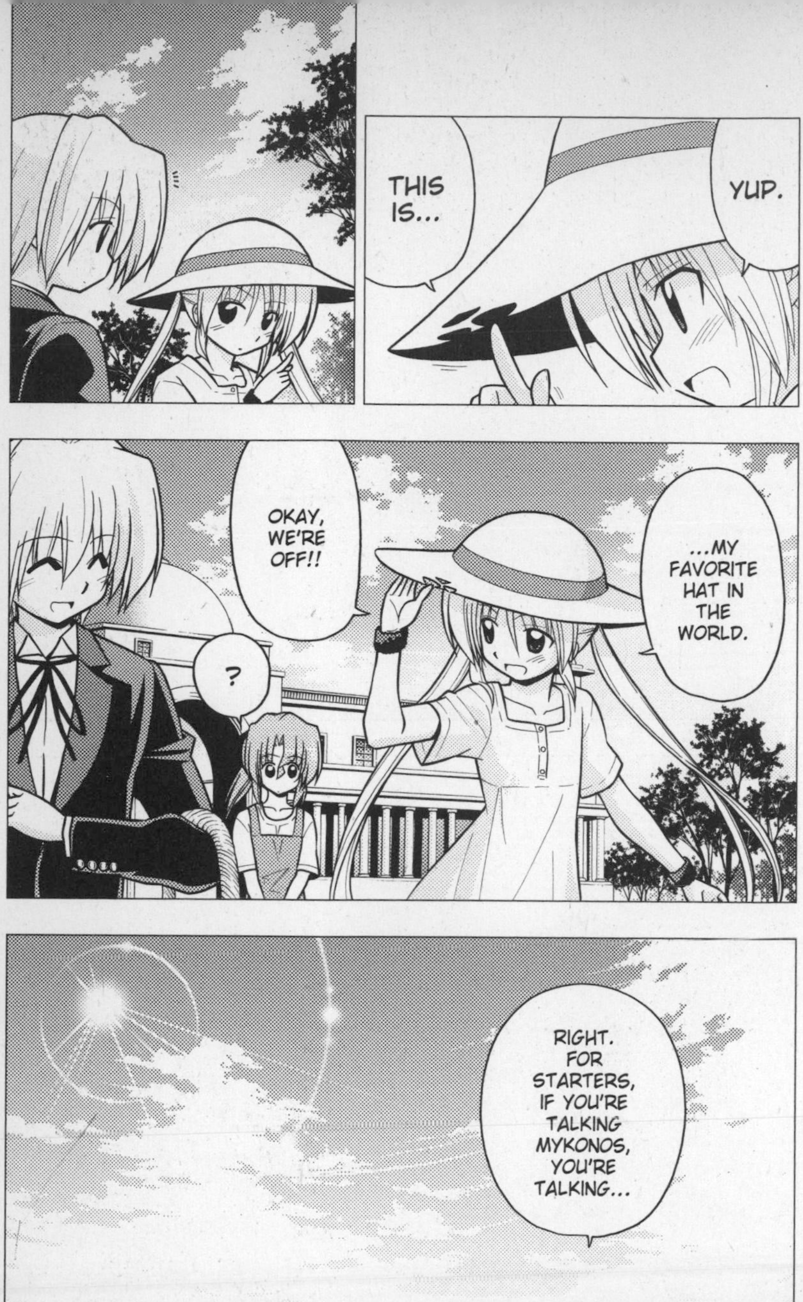
YUP.
THIS IS...
...MY FAVORITE HAT IN THE WORLD.
OKAY, WE'RE OFF!!
?
RIGHT. FOR STARTERS, IF YOU'RE TALKING MYKONOS, YOU'RE TALKING...

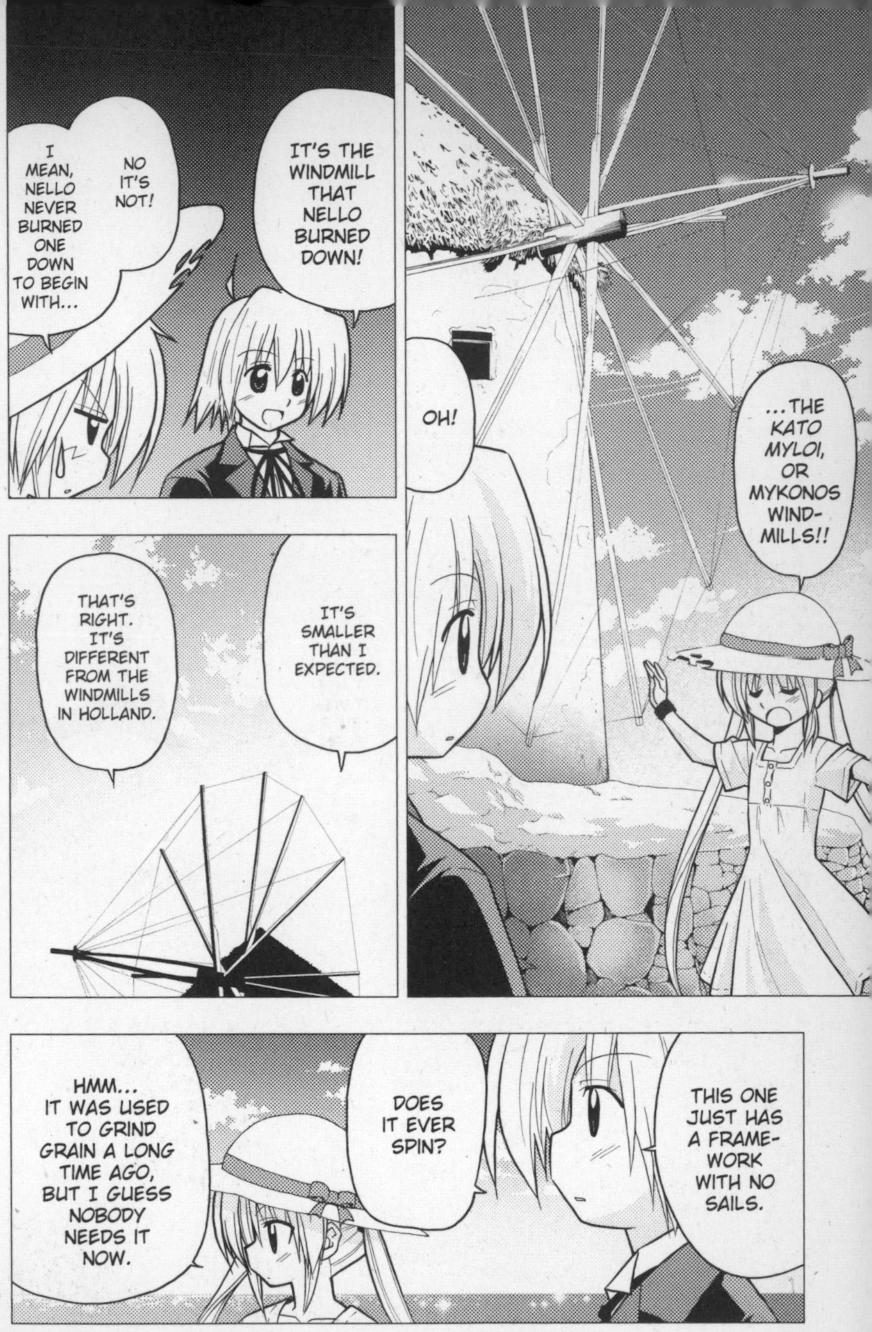
...THE KATO MYLOI, OR MYKONOS WIND-MILLS!!
OH!
IT'S THE WINDMILL THAT NELLO BURNED DOWN!
NO IT'S NOT!
I MEAN, NELLO NEVER BURNED ONE DOWN TO BEGIN WITH...
IT'S SMALLER THAN I EXPECTED.
THAT'S RIGHT. IT'S DIFFERENT FROM THE WINDMILLS IN HOLLAND.
THIS ONE JUST HAS A FRAME-WORK WITH NO SAILS.
DOES IT EVER SPIN?
HMM... IT WAS USED TO GRIND GRAIN A LONG TIME AGO, BUT I GUESS NOBODY NEEDS IT NOW.

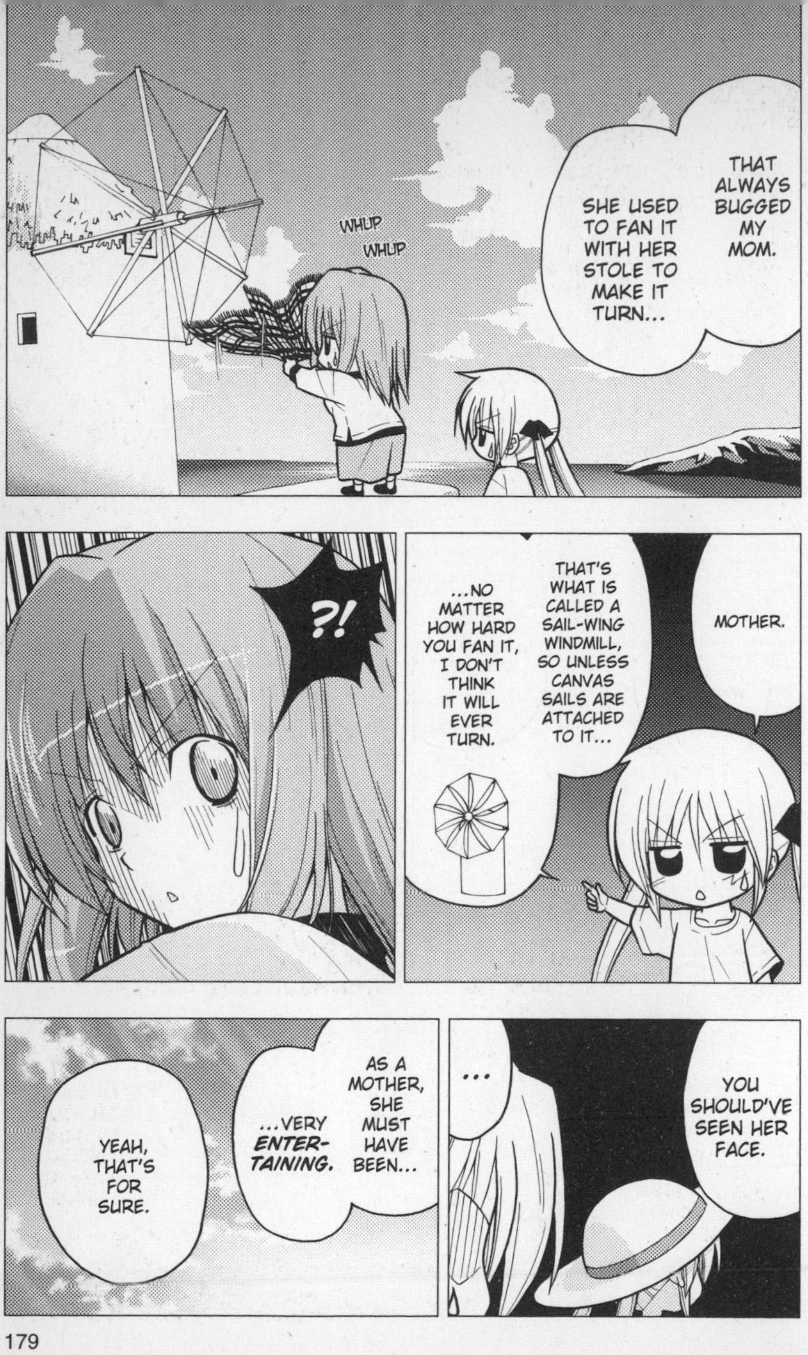
WHUP
WHUP
SHE USED TO FAN IT WITH HER STOLE TO MAKE IT TURN...
THAT ALWAYS BUGGED MY MOM.
MOTHER.
THAT'S WHAT IS CALLED A SAIL-WING WINDMILL, SO UNLESS CANVAS SAILS ARE ATTACHED TO IT...
...NO MATTER HOW HARD YOU FAN IT, I DON'T THINK IT WILL EVER TURN.
?!
YOU SHOULD'VE SEEN HER FACE.
...
AS A MOTHER, SHE MUST HAVE BEEN...
...VERY ENTERTAINING.
YEAH, THAT'S FOR SURE.

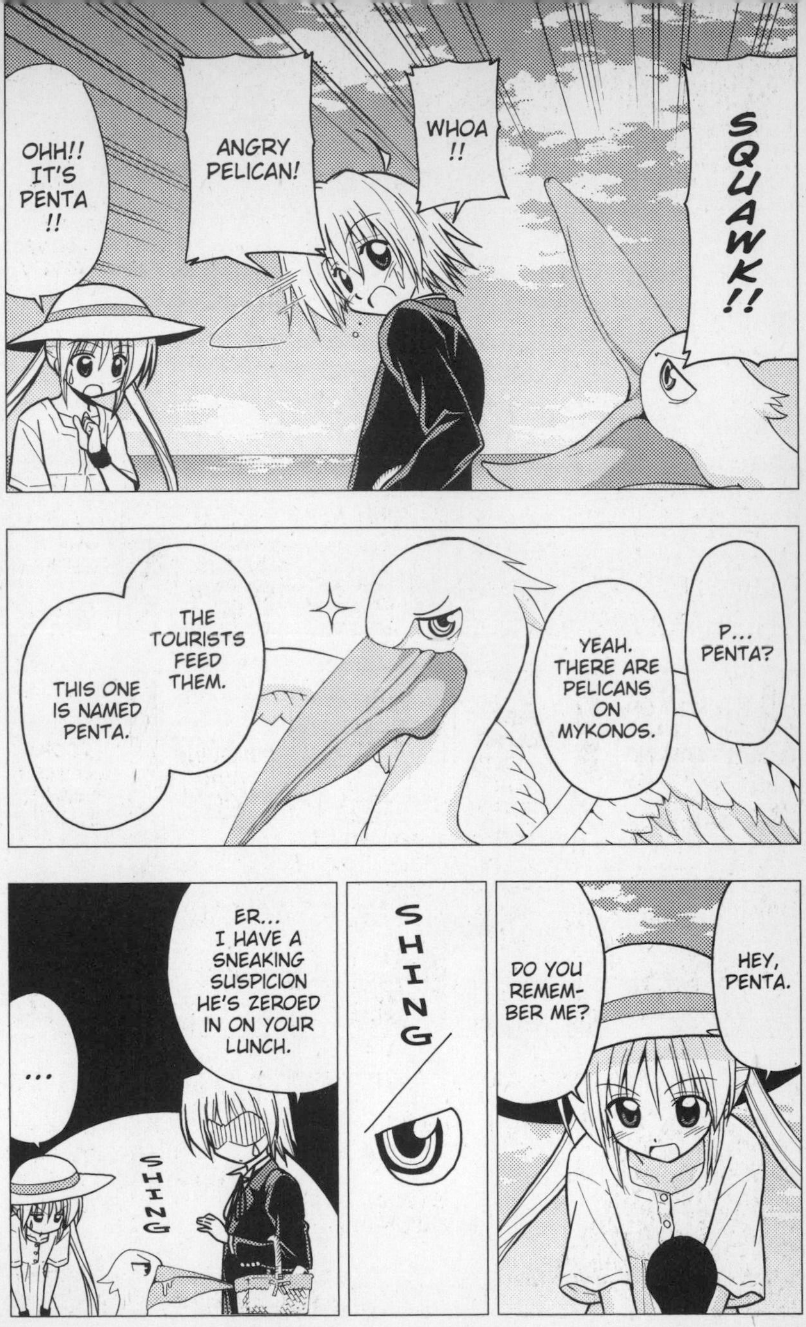
SQUAWK!!
WHOA!!
ANGRY PELICAN!
OHH!! IT'S PENTA!!
P... PENTA?
YEAH. THERE ARE PELICANS ON MYKONOS.
THE TOURISTS FEED THEM.
THIS ONE IS NAMED PENTA.
HEY, PENTA.
DO YOU REMEM-BER ME?
SHING
ER... I HAVE A SNEAKING SUSPICION HE'S ZEROED IN ON YOUR LUNCH.
...
SHING

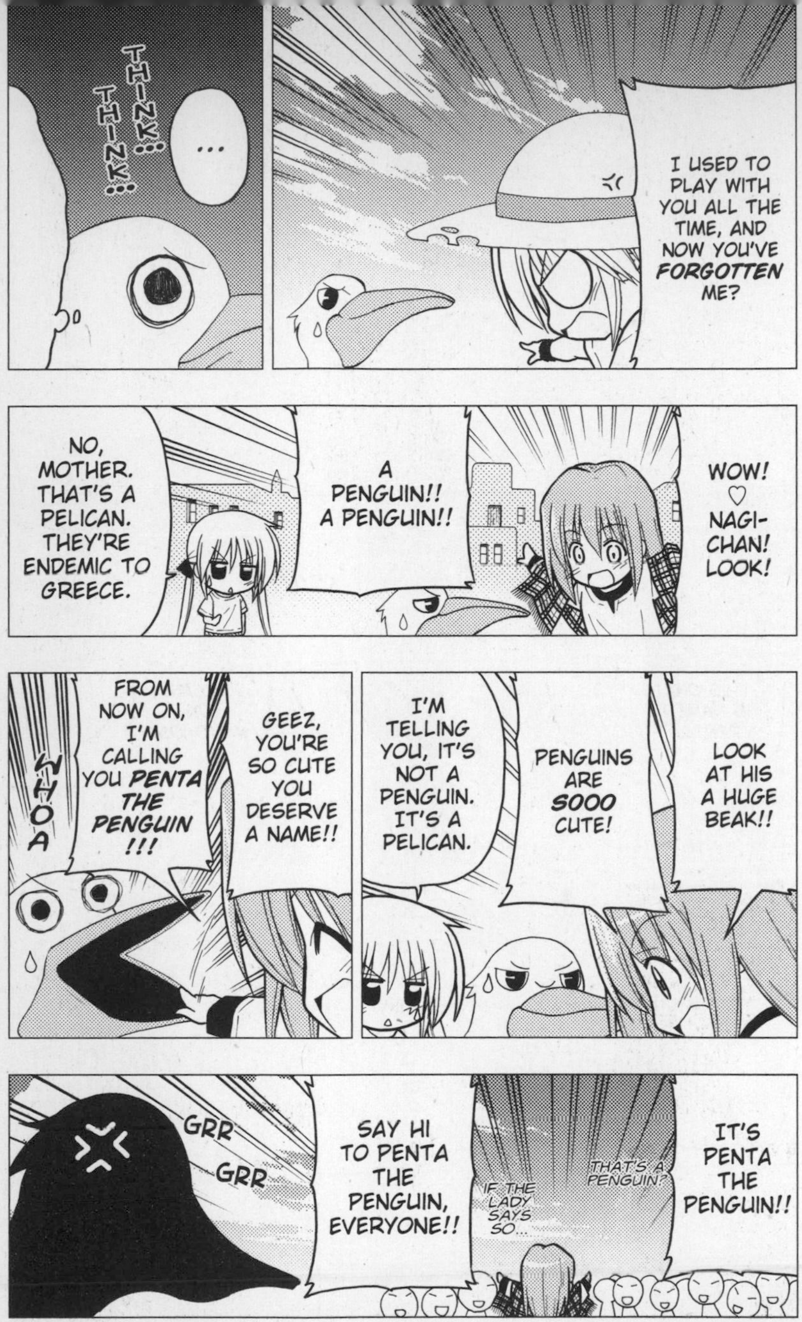
I USED TO PLAY WITH YOU ALL THE TIME, AND NOW YOU'VE FORGOTTEN ME?
THINK... THINK...
...
WOW! ♡ NAGI-CHAN! LOOK!
A PENGUIN!! A PENGUIN!!
NO, MOTHER. THAT'S A PELICAN. THEY'RE ENDEMIC TO GREECE.
LOOK AT HIS A HUGE BEAK!!
PENGUINS ARE SOOO CUTE!
I'M TELLING YOU, IT'S NOT A PENGUIN. IT'S A PELICAN.
GEEZ, YOU'RE SO CUTE YOU DESERVE A NAME!!
FROM NOW ON, I'M CALLING YOU PENTA THE PENGUIN!!!
WHOA
IT'S PENTA THE PENGUIN!!
THAT'S A PENGUIN?
IF THE LADY SAYS SO...
SAY HI TO PENTA THE PENGUIN, EVERYONE!!
GRR
GRR

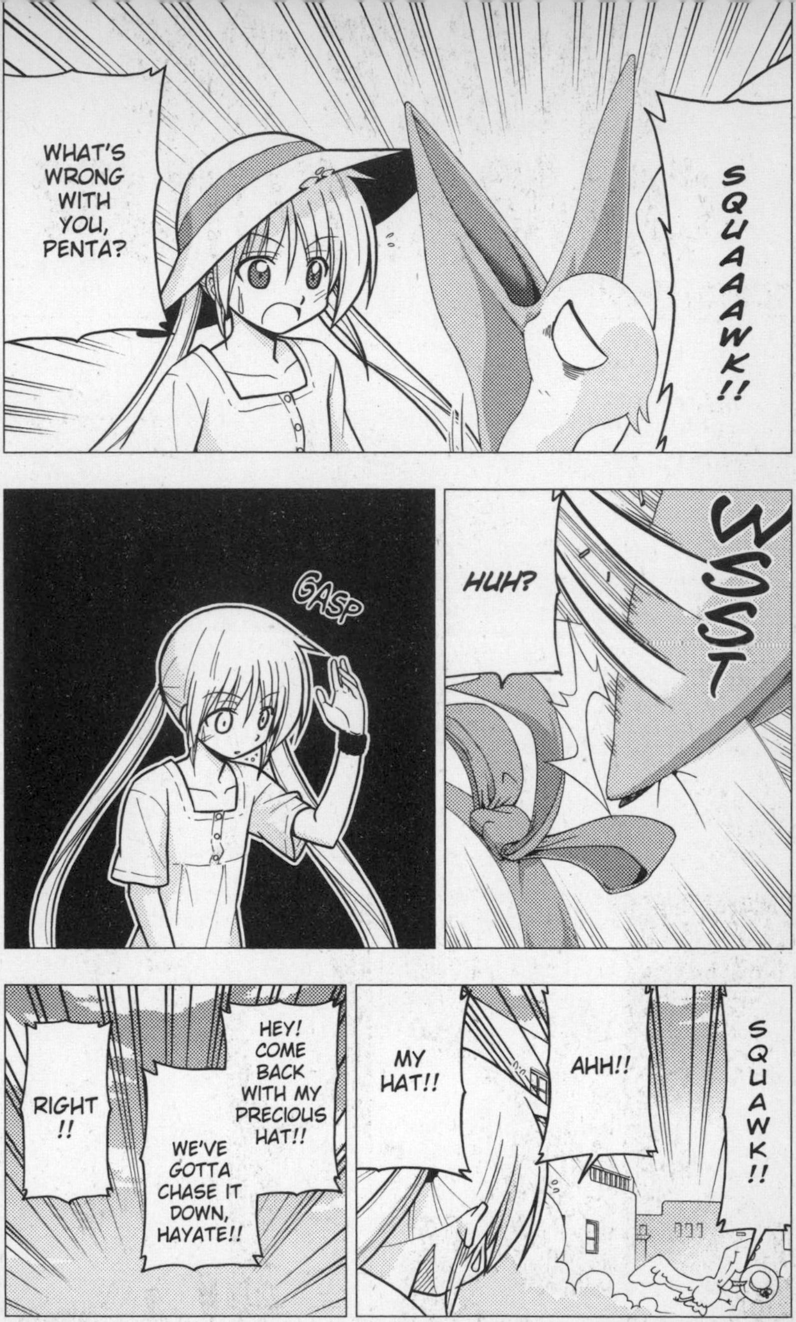
SQUAAAAWK!!
WHAT'S WRONG WITH YOU, PENTA?
WSSST
HUH?
GASP
SQUAWK!!
AHH!!
MY HAT!!
HEY! COME BACK WITH MY PRECIOUS HAT!!
WE'VE GOTTA CHASE IT DOWN, HAYATE!!
RIGHT!!

TO BE CONTINUED

HAYATE THE COMBAT BUTLER

BONUS PAGE

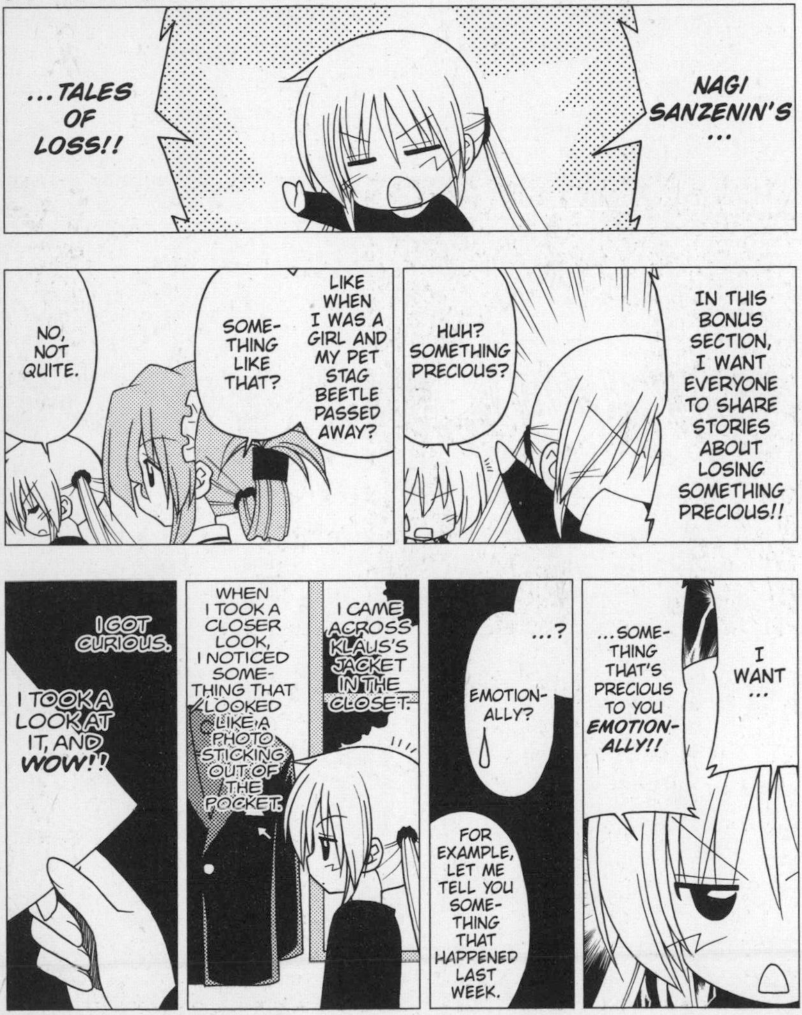

NAGI SANZENIN'S ...
...TALES OF LOSS!!
IN THIS BONUS SECTION, I WANT EVERYONE TO SHARE STORIES ABOUT LOSING SOMETHING PRECIOUS!!
HUH? SOMETHING PRECIOUS?
LIKE WHEN I WAS A GIRL AND MY PET STAG BEETLE PASSED AWAY?
SOMETHING LIKE THAT?
NO, NOT QUITE.
I WANT ...
...SOMETHING THAT'S PRECIOUS TO YOU *EMOTIONALLY!!*
...?
EMOTIONALLY?
FOR EXAMPLE, LET ME TELL YOU SOMETHING THAT HAPPENED LAST WEEK.
I CAME ACROSS KLAUS'S JACKET IN THE CLOSET.
WHEN I TOOK A CLOSER LOOK, I NOTICED SOMETHING THAT LOOKED LIKE A PHOTO STICKING OUT OF THE POCKET.
I GOT CURIOUS.
I TOOK A LOOK AT IT, AND *WOW!!*

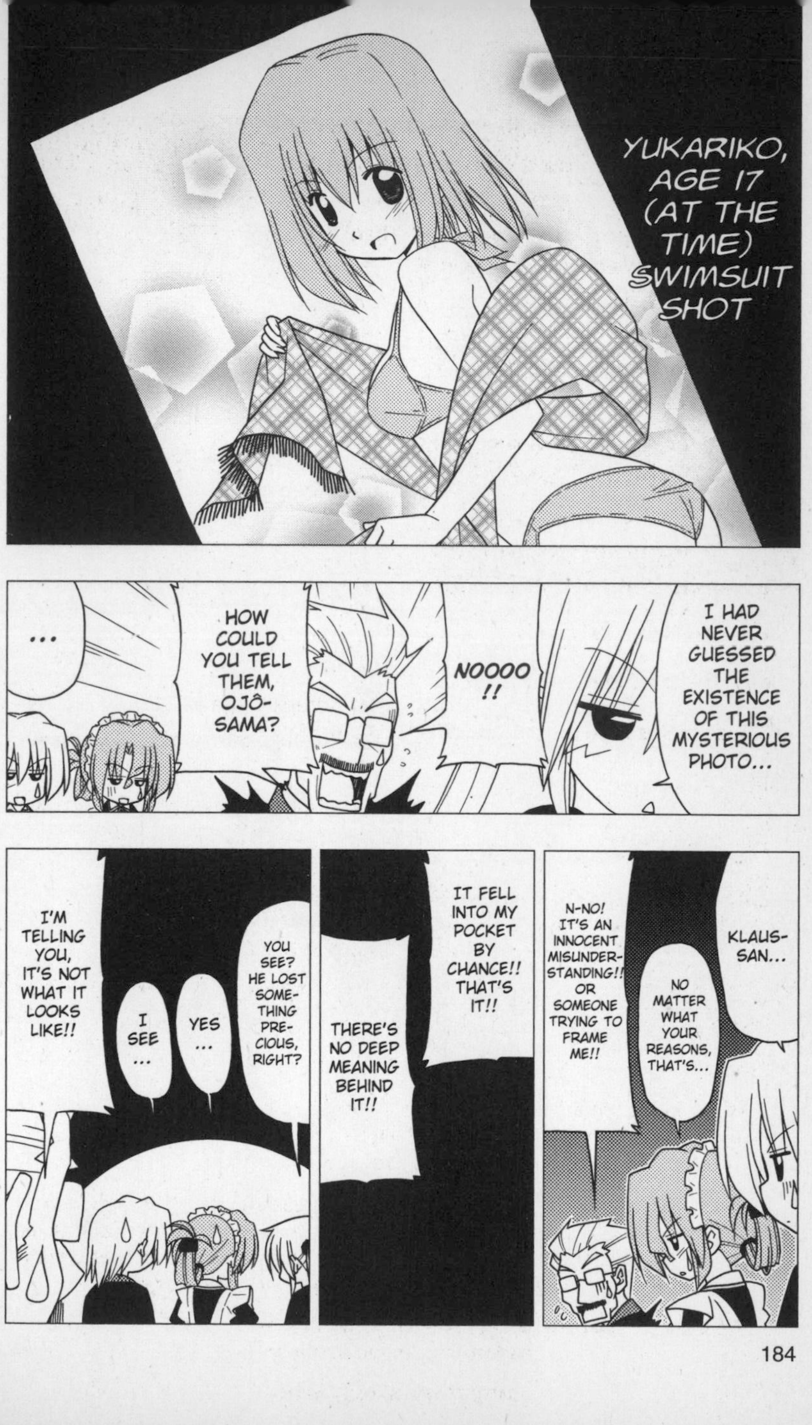
YUKARIKO, AGE 17 (AT THE TIME) SWIMSUIT SHOT
I HAD NEVER GUESSED THE EXISTENCE OF THIS MYSTERIOUS PHOTO...
NOOOO!!
HOW COULD YOU TELL THEM, OJÔ-SAMA?
...
KLAUS-SAN...
NO MATTER WHAT YOUR REASONS, THAT'S...
N-NO! IT'S AN INNOCENT MISUNDERSTANDING!! OR SOMEONE TRYING TO FRAME ME!!
IT FELL INTO MY POCKET BY CHANCE!! THAT'S IT!!
THERE'S NO DEEP MEANING BEHIND IT!!
YOU SEE? HE LOST SOMETHING PRECIOUS, RIGHT?
YES...
I SEE...
I'M TELLING YOU, IT'S NOT WHAT IT LOOKS LIKE!!

Special Bonus! Results of the Second Character Popularity Poll!

Here are the popularity poll results that appeared in *Shonen Sunday* #18 in 2009.
The total number of votes was 16,133! Thank you so much for responding!!

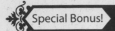

1. Hinagiku Katsura — 4,185
2. Maria — 1,814
3. Nagi Sanzenin — 1,776
4. Hayate Ayasaki.......................1,366
5. Athena Tennos.......................1,008
6. Izumi Segawa...........................905
7. Ayumu Nishizawa....................888
8. Sakuya Aizawa..........................881
9. Chiharu Harukaze....................705
10. Isumi Saginomiya....................437
11. Fumi Hibino..............................369
12. Aika Kasumi..............................187
13. Tama..149
14. Wataru Tachibana 148
15. Saki Kishima.............................146
16. Yukiji Katsura...........................118
17. Shiranui.......................................93
18. Miki Hanabishi............................76
19. Koji Kumeta sensei.....................75
20. Father (Linn Regiostar)................72
21. Risa Asakaze................................70
22. Klaus...56
23. Kotetsu Segawa...........................49
24. Yukariko Sanzeni.........................49
25. Kenjiro Hata sensei.....................48
26. Koutaro Azumamiya.....................39
27. The Goddess (Orumuzuto Nadja)...30
28. Sharna..28
29. Kyonosuke Kaoru..........................26
30. Taiga Okouchi...............................18

At last this manga has reached its fifth anniversary. It's now entering its sixth year! I've only been able to make it this far thanks to all of you. I really appreciate your support.

In the next volume, set in Athens, *Hayate* will reach a major turning point. This story is tough for me to write, but I intend to pull no punches and give it my all. I hope you enjoy finding out what awaits our heroes, although it's just the tip of the iceberg as far as the overall story arc goes…

Well, see you in the next volume! Oh, and please check out the *Hayate* webcomic I'm working on!

http://websunday.net/

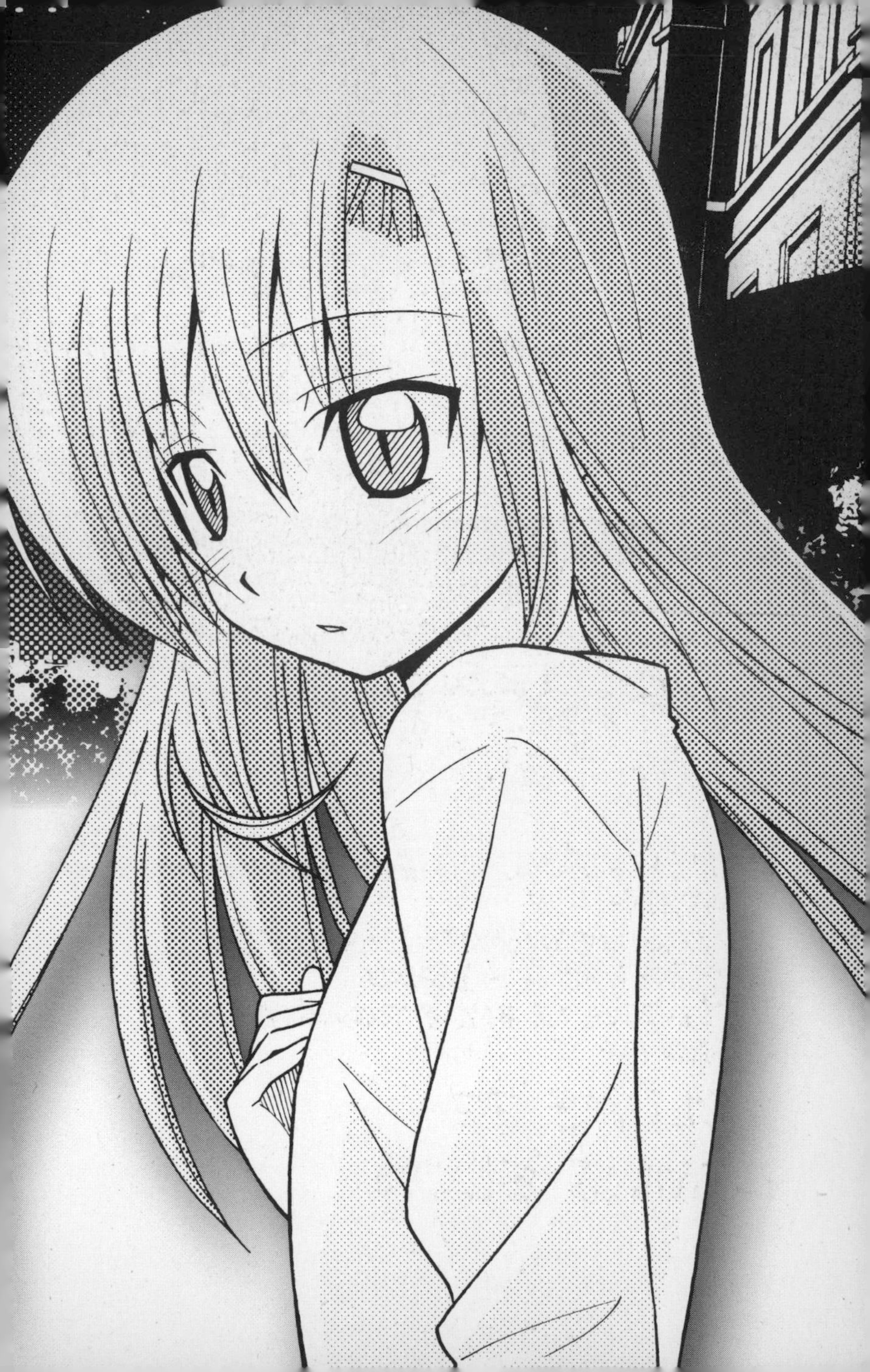

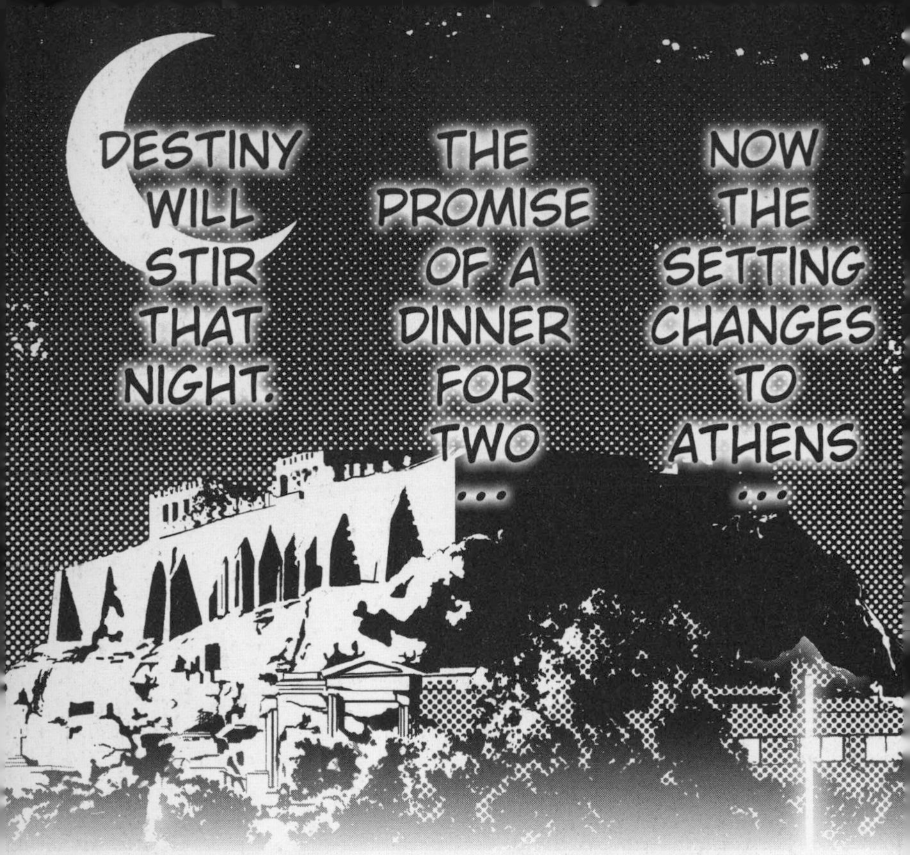
NOW THE SETTING CHANGES TO ATHENS...
THE PROMISE OF A DINNER FOR TWO...
DESTINY WILL STIR THAT NIGHT.

AFTER MYKONOS, THE GANG TRAVELS TO ATHENS.
AT LONG LAST, HAYATE IS GOING OUT TO DINNER WITH HINAGIKU.
LITTLE DOES HE KNOW THAT ATHENA IS BACK!

VOLUME 22 COMING SOON

When She Changes into a Swimsuit

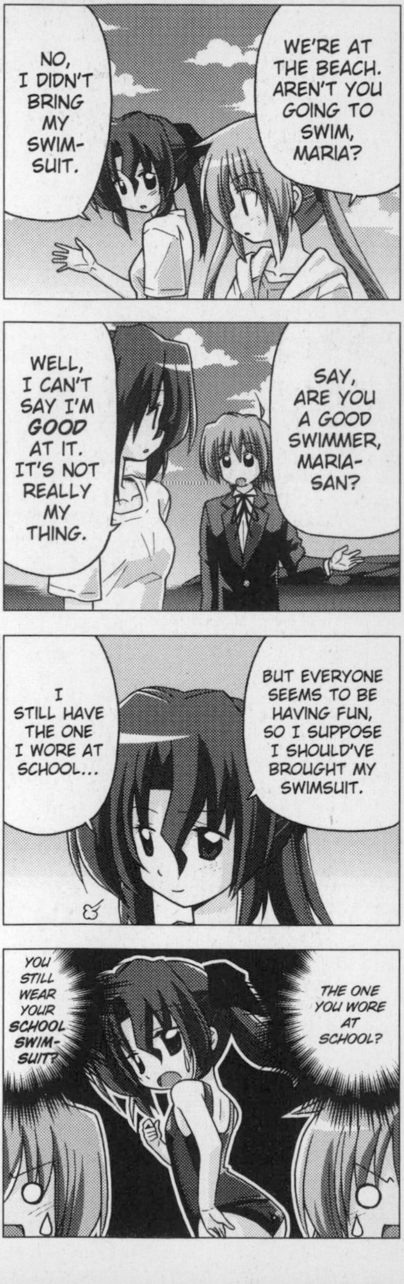
WE'RE AT THE BEACH. AREN'T YOU GOING TO SWIM, MARIA?
NO, I DIDN'T BRING MY SWIMSUIT.
SAY, ARE YOU A GOOD SWIMMER, MARIA-SAN?
WELL, I CAN'T SAY I'M *GOOD* AT IT. IT'S NOT REALLY MY THING.
BUT EVERYONE SEEMS TO BE HAVING FUN, SO I SUPPOSE I SHOULD'VE BROUGHT MY SWIMSUIT.
I STILL HAVE THE ONE I WORE AT SCHOOL...
THE ONE YOU WORE AT SCHOOL?
YOU STILL WEAR YOUR SCHOOL SWIMSUIT?

On the Banks of the Holy River

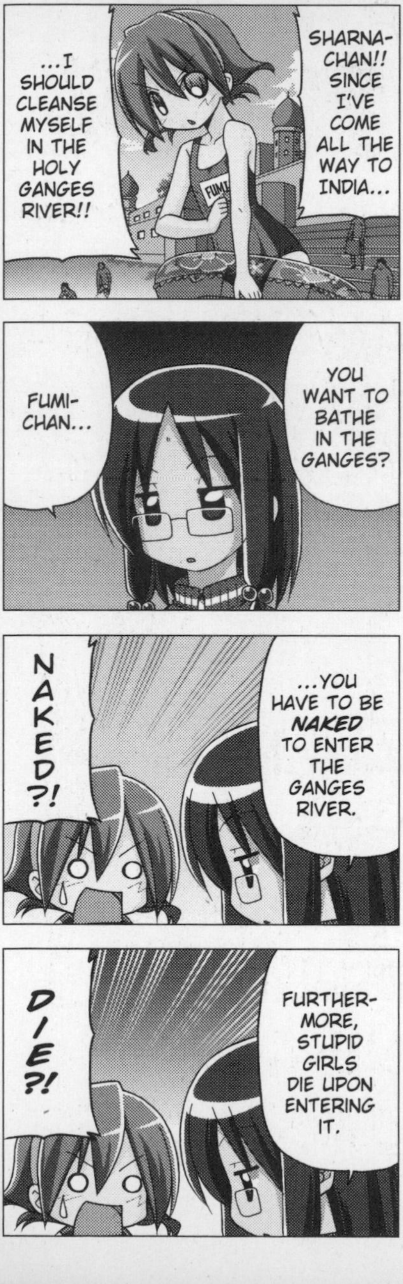
SHARNA-CHAN!! SINCE I'VE COME ALL THE WAY TO INDIA...
...I SHOULD CLEANSE MYSELF IN THE HOLY GANGES RIVER!!
FUMI
YOU WANT TO BATHE IN THE GANGES?
FUMI-CHAN...
...YOU HAVE TO BE *NAKED* TO ENTER THE GANGES RIVER.
NAKED?!
FURTHERMORE, STUPID GIRLS DIE UPON ENTERING IT.
DIE?!

HAYATE THE COMBAT BUTLER

⟨GAME OVER SCREEN SPECIFICATIONS⟩

WHEN THE GAME IS OVER, MARIA-SAN WILL GIVE YOU SOME FRIENDLY ADVICE!

YOU EXIST ONLY TO TRIP FLAGS.

CONTINUE AND TRY AGAIN!!

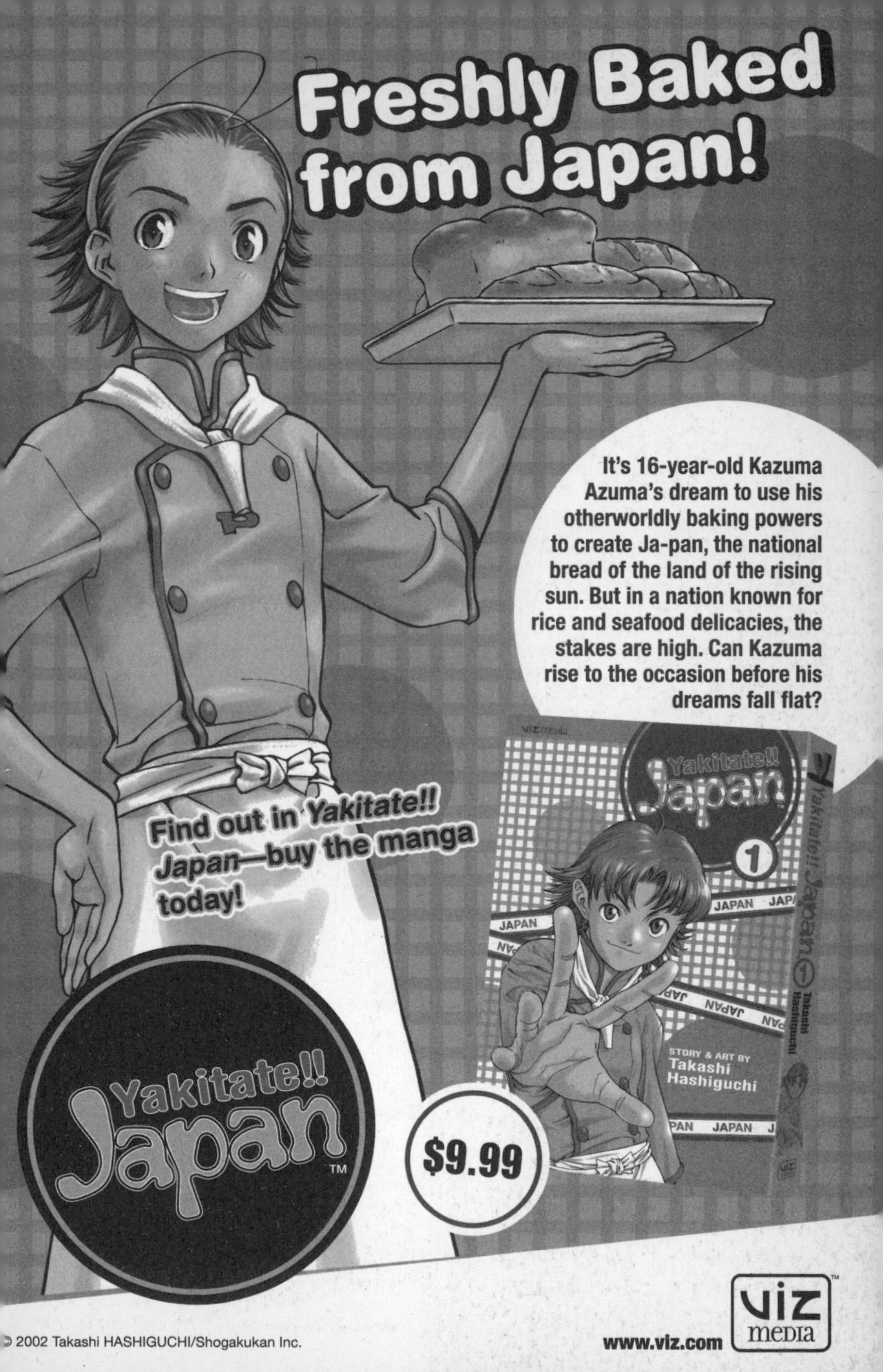
Freshly Baked from Japan!
It's 16-year-old Kazuma Azuma's dream to use his otherworldly baking powers to create Ja-pan, the national bread of the land of the rising sun. But in a nation known for rice and seafood delicacies, the stakes are high. Can Kazuma rise to the occasion before his dreams fall flat?
Find out in Yakitate!! Japan—buy the manga today!
Yakitate!! Japan™
$9.99
viz media
Yakitate!! Japan 1
STORY & ART BY Takashi Hashiguchi
www.viz.com
VIZ MEDIA™

Hey! You're Reading in the Wrong Direction!

This is the *end* of this graphic novel!

To properly enjoy this VIZ graphic novel, please turn it around and begin reading from *right to left.* Unlike English, Japanese is read right to left, so Japanese comics are read in reverse order from the way English comics are typically read.

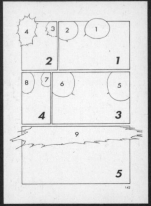

Follow the action this way

This book has been printed in the original Japanese format in order to preserve the orientation of the original artwork. Have fun with it!